THE POLITICS OF FAITH DURING
THE CIVIL WAR

THE POLITICS OF FAITH DURING
THE CIVIL WAR

TIMOTHY L. WESLEY

LOUISIANA STATE UNIVERSITY PRESS

BATON ROUGE

Published by Louisiana State University Press
Copyright © 2013 by Louisiana State University Press
All rights reserved
Manufactured in the United States of America
FIRST PRINTING

DESIGNER: *Mandy McDonald Scallan*
TYPEFACE: *Whitman*
PRINTER: *McNaughton & Gunn, Inc.*
BINDER: *Dekker Bookbinding*

Library of Congress Cataloging-in-Publication Data

Wesley, Timothy L., 1966–
  The politics of faith during the Civil War / Timothy L. Wesley.
    p. cm.
  Includes bibliographical references and index.
  ISBN 978-0-8071-5000-9 (cloth : alk. paper) — ISBN 978-0-8071-5001-6 (pdf) — ISBN 978-0-8071-5002-3
(epub) — ISBN 978-0-8071-5003-0 (mobi) 1. Religion and politics—United States—History—19th cen-
tury. 2. United States—History—Civil War, 1861–1865—Religious aspects. I. Title.
  E468.9.W474 2013
  322'.10973—dc23

                                                                                    2012027903

For Linda

CONTENTS

ACKNOWLEDGMENTS

Many wonderful people have helped me as I have worked on this project. First, I must thank my friend Bill Blair. To all who know and admire Bill, there is no better model of a professional historian. His reputation within the academy is exceeded only by his kindness and generosity as a scholar. The times he has helped me through the various hills and valleys of the writing process are too many to count, and yet he has never once begrudged the task. Tempering every suggested change with loads of encouragement, he has provided me with a model of mentorship that I will always strive to follow. And Mary Ann Blair, Bill's wonderful wife, has become a great friend to me and my wife, Linda, as well. Of all the great good fortune I have encountered in my career, without doubt my luckiest stroke has been meeting Bill and Mary Ann.

The George and Ann Richards Civil War Era Center at Penn State, directed by Bill Blair, is blessed to have in its affiliation some of the best historians to be found anywhere, and I have had the privilege of working with many of them. With both her words and her example, Nan Woodruff reminds me time and time again why historians matter. Amy Greenberg is one of America's leading historians of the antebellum period, but she nevertheless finds time in her outrageously busy schedule to help anyone who asks for it. Alas, few have asked her for more help than I have while working on this book. I am in awe of Mark Neely Jr., a truth I'm sure he has picked up on, and thus the numerous tidbits of constructive and occasionally down-home advice he has offered me on numerous occasions have meant the world to me. With both her friendship and professional guidance, Sally McMurry has lifted my spirits and illuminated my path on several cloudy days. And Tony Kaye, Bill Pencak, and Carol Reardon have each supported and encouraged me in numerous ways over the past years. All three are testaments to the fact that genuinely nice people can also be genuinely amazing scholars.

Barby Singer—who we all know really keeps the Richards Center going—is as kind and encouraging as she can possibly be. Without Barby, I doubt very much if I or any of my peers at the center would have ever finished any of our manuscripts. My colleagues and occasional office mates Anne Brinton, Will

Bryan, David Greenspoon, Antwain Hunter, Matt Isham, Kelly Knight, James Lewis, Tim Orr, Andrew Prymak, and Karen Fisher-Younger have each made my experience with the Richards Center and Penn State more fulfilling, each heartening me in their own way at various stages of this book's development.

This project has been funded by a number of donors to the George and Ann Richards Civil War Era Center. I have been the beneficiary of grants and research endowments funded by Lewis and Karen Gold, Lawrence and Gretchen McCabe, Mark and Ann Persun, George Middlemas and Sherry Petska, and, now deceased, Robert and Mary Brueilly Hayes. Like so many other scholars affiliated with Penn State and the Richards Center, I owe each of these generous souls a heartfelt thank-you.

I likewise extend thanks to a number of historians and other folks outside of Penn State. Randall Miller carefully read the entire manuscript and made important suggestions about how I might improve it. His generosity is humbling, and there is no scholar I respect more. A number of anonymous historians, moreover, read parts of the work and offered ideas about how I might strengthen particular elements. I don't know their names, but if they are now encountering some part of this book for the second time and thus know who they are, I thank them. Rand Dotson and Catherine Kadair, my editors at LSU Press, have been nothing but helpful and supportive, and I appreciate them immensely. After working with Stan Ivester, I can gratefully attest that his legendary status as a copyeditor is more than merited. Elizabeth Leonard's kindness to junior scholars is known throughout the academy, and like so many others, I owe her thanks. And the brilliant Susan Myers-Shirk at Middle Tennessee State University started me down the road of academia in earnest. I will be forever in her debt.

As do most who have ever authored a work in our field, I owe the professionals at numerous libraries and archives much gratitude. In addition to one- and two-day jaunts to local church repositories and county historical societies and special trips to find a particular document at a given library, I spent long days and sometimes weeks at such locales as the American Catholic Historical Society of Philadelphia, the Evangelical and Lutheran Reformed Historical Society at Lancaster, the Moorland-Spingarn Research Center at Howard University, the Presbyterian Historical Society in Philadelphia, the Southern Baptist Historical Library and Archives in Nashville, and the United Methodist Archives and History Center at Drew University in New Jersey. And of course, our own Penn State Special Collections Library has an incredible store of Civil

War–era diaries and letters, and I looked at most of them. To the folks at all of these places, I offer my warmest acknowledgments.

On a personal level, I owe so much to my sisters, Sue, Tammy, and Joyce, and to my brother-in-law, Mark, that I hardly know where or how to begin. Each of them has been a constant in my life, always helpful and encouraging. And even more importantly in terms of the peace of mind needed to immerse oneself in the past for days on end, I have always known that each of them was there for my parents, no matter what. My own career has carried me farther and farther away from the Volunteer State and from my parents, but thanks to my sisters and brother-in-law and their families, I have never doubted that all was as well as could be back home.

My appreciation of education and my interest in the past are both gifts from my parents. I have one of the best mothers in the world, as any of my boyhood friends can attest, and even as a child it was never lost on me what a real blessing she is. She celebrated every victory and soothed each defeat, but no matter which, she always believed in me. After working for more than thirty years in a sewing factory (while simultaneously running a household and raising four children), in her early sixties my mother hit the books and earned her high-school diploma. Simply stated, she is my hero. I am likewise fortunate to have had a great father. My Pop, Leon Wesley, never made it out of the eighth grade, forced by the exigencies of poverty into the workforce when just a boy. But he never failed to show me the many different ways in which a person can be intelligent and even a genius, can be altruistic even when struggling to make ends meet, and can always, if one chooses to, laugh. He was the best man I ever knew, and I miss him every day. So too do I miss my mother-in-law, Joan. A long time ago, when I had the idea of going to graduate school and thus moving seven hundred miles away with her only daughter, she thought only of Linda and of me and of what the opportunity could mean to us, and she never once complained. She was as good as gold. My father-in-law, Don, is fortunately hearty and hale and always a source of reason and calm. I am glad to call him my friend.

Lastly, I must thank my wife, Linda, the love and light of my life. This book, this career, this life really, is a fifty-fifty endeavor. She has made my life complete and my scholarship grammatically sound, and for both I thank her more than she will ever know.

THE POLITICS OF FAITH DURING
THE CIVIL WAR

INTRODUCTION

We find many clergymen again taking to politics, vainly imagining they can sway the public mind. Henry Ward Beecher has made a noise in the world, and others are at work to imitate him. These clergymen are made of and flattered. The women say soft things to them, and they are petted to death, and their heads cannot stand the fire. The result is, that all the labor of disinterested parties, who work and build a church edifice and society, and their labor lost and unproductive because the minister refuses to conform to the enlightened age in which we live, but must needs become a sensationist or political preacher.

—*Boston Investigator,* December 4, 1861

Can the church be rightfully indifferent to the question of loyalty or disloyalty? If it can—on what grounds? [New York Presbyterian] Dr. [N. L.] Rice's answer is: "That ministers and churches, as such, cannot settle those moral questions, which depend upon secular, civil, and political questions." And as they cannot "settle" them, he implies that they have nothing to do with them. But the principle is false, and the conclusion pernicious. . . . It was just so in the time of the Revolution. Ought ministers and churches to have kept silent then? If not, why now?

—*American Theological Review,* January 1862

POLITICAL PREACHERS were at the heart of the debate over the separation of church and state during the American Civil War.[1] American ministers and laypeople alike held various opinions about clerics who preached on political topics. The war brought to the forefront a controversy that had grown up in the prewar North over whether ministers had the right to exhort congregations to adopt political positions. While the antebellum question revolved around the issue of slavery, in the wartime context questions of loyalty and disloyalty became more important. Northern ministers did not constitute a monolithic group of cheerleaders for the nation, a position still dominant in historical scholarship. Nor did ministers abandon en masse their long-held religious ideas about the need to keep the pulpit separate from secular affairs. While numerous preachers saw the war in religious terms and as a result imagined for themselves a pronounced political role in its successful execution, other patriotic men of faith struggled to meet the demands of a people at war while honoring the apolitical dictates of their creed. And plainly, some northern preachers were patently disloyal. No matter their motives, scores of ministers drew the punitive attention of national, state, and local authorities through their perceived unpatriotic declarations in sermons and other forms of worship. And the story doesn't end with government intervention. Disloyal or otherwise politically discordant ministers also found themselves squarely in the sights of denominational leaders and members of their own congregations.

Of course, the story changes when looking at the Confederate South. There, slavery's clerical champions never came under fire—although most southern clerics inveighed against political preaching even as they engaged in the act. But over the course of decades southern preachers effectively rendered the South's central political concern, slavery, a domestic affair. The enslavement of four million people became a way of life, a "peculiar" but familial institution that ministers during the Civil War were obliged to defend from northern assault. Consequently, members of the Confederate clergy became wartime agents of southern nationalism, monitoring southern allegiance and often overseeing the proper wartime participation of their denominational memberships. And as their churches became targets for Union soldiers who occupied enemy territory, Confederate ministers actively fomented various kinds of political defiance.

The historical record supports three primary conclusions. First, America's largest denominations were not somehow co-opted by the state during the Civil War. Many church members and religious leaders were ardent flag wavers, but in most cases their zeal did not represent the compromise of their religious principles. To the contrary, Christians imagined themselves patriots because of—and not in defiance of—their religious beliefs. The recognition of such self-determination within America's churches requires an acknowledgment that the same kind of devout sincerity prompted other loyal Americans to nevertheless resist the politicization of their church, including many in mainstream traditions and not just those in peace churches and pacifist sects.

Second, by the time of the Civil War the separation of church and state was less pronounced than we imagine today. The death of established churches in the Early Republic had not resulted in the construction of a permanent and impregnable barrier between the sacred and the secular worlds. Mid-nineteenth-century Americans lived in a society in which the religious and the political overlapped almost to the point of amalgamation. When war came, it exposed that fact. At the same time that millions of church members looked to their preachers for political as well as spiritual guidance, therefore, numerous forms of worship were identified by authorities as manifestations of disloyalty and therefore threats to national security.

And third, studies of the infringement of civil liberties during the Civil War have underappreciated one of the pervasive forms of repression—that which occurred voluntarily within civil society. If we look only to the government and the Lincoln administration, we miss the activity of denominational authorities, congregations, and even local citizens in policing disloyalty in the pulpit. In straightforward terms, Civil War ministers were removed from their pulpits, excommunicated from their churches, and treated roughly by local members and nonmembers alike for what they said. And sometimes, they were punished for what they did not say as well. Preachers faced denominational scrutiny and governmental repression even when they remained silent, for that silence often entailed behaviors like refusing to pray for the president and ignoring the material support of soldiers in the field.

The rise of evangelical Christianity during the antebellum era brought ministers to the forefront of various political reform movements. Nevertheless, various scholars have suggested that preachers were relatively unimportant during the Civil War years. In fact, preachers had an *enormous* influence on American life and political affairs by the end of the antebellum age. In both the North and the South, the clergy was the de facto intelligentsia, by anyone's standards among the most educated and respected public thinkers in their respective societies. Preachers were clearly among the revered elite, for at a time when the average free white adult male in the United States possessed an average wealth of $2,580, Protestant clerics were worth (on average) $10,177 in the Old South and $4,376 in the antebellum North.[2] But most importantly, preachers were influential because they were the acknowledged point men of organized religion, and in both the North and the South by 1860 religious sensibilities and beliefs exerted a greater influence on American public and political life, historian Mark Noll reminds us, "than at any previous time in American history."[3] By the time of the Civil War, Americans imagined their political nation as being intertwined with the divine realm. Most northerners thought that democracy, and especially their nation dedicated to democracy, were sacred entities entrusted to them by the Founding Fathers. Others in the South believed that God had ordained the establishment of a new nation dedicated to their own "holy" ideas about the exaltedness of whiteness. Whichever the case, an extremely religious people in an equally traumatic age conceded to their spiritual captains a leading role in the affairs of the day, even if many disagreed on how—or if—that role should entail more than the cleric's constant prayers and religious edification of the masses.

In assessing the *political* aspects of *religious* men, I have looked at two broad categories of resources: material pertaining to the political value of what a preacher said *or* providing insight into the patently religious considerations that prompted the utterance (a sometimes difficult task given the conflated political/religious speechifying that was so common to the period). It is vital to know how the would-be "political" words of preachers were received. After all, the *result* of a sermon is just as important as the *intent* of its preacher. Ministerial motivations and behaviors would matter little in the larger sense if the greater society during the Civil War did not really care either way. Therefore I have used secular and governmental sources aplenty, notably the Federal government's *Official Records of the War of the Rebellion* and the remembrances of political and military leaders.[4] I have privileged the secular press in the understanding that partisanship often colored the opinions of columnists. Thus only when an espoused viewpoint or excerpt characterizes a whole category of quotations have I assumed its value as something more than just a partisan harangue. While quotes are used primarily when they are representative of an identified theme or multiply mentioned event, sentiment, or belief, as a social historian I have also utilized the extensive citation as an explanatory tool for the individual historical actor, a means of giving voice to those who lived the history I relate.

This work makes more use of denominational records than secular sources, including the denominational/religious press, published sermons, and numerous minister's letters and diaries. Such founts allow me to anchor this project in what ministers themselves thought about both their own political obligations to their country (or lack thereof) and the behavior of their fellow clerics. I have not included Jewish Americans in this study of the clergy. Although Judaism was certainly a part of America's religious make-up during the Civil War years and Judaism was and is likewise denominational, as a part of the larger American population between 1860 and 1865 practitioners of Judaism were collectively and contextually a minor force. And although this work's examination of Catholic clerics is a bit more abbreviated than that of Protestants, that is because the "official" Catholic position during the war, at least relative to the clergy, was essentially one of silence. When and where Catholic priests were an important part of the story, every effort has been made to include their voices in the narrative.

Because ministers interacted with the public, their church members, their denominational hierarchies of authority, and their local, state, and national governments over political issues, one must be ever mindful of how Christian churchgoers defined politics and political participation during the tumultuous years of the Civil War. No single contemporary approach encompasses the whole of American political life during the era. For white churchmen and women in the North and South, I have eschewed a purely national and presidential perspective that ignores the primacy of local influences in their lives in favor of an approach championed by practitioners of the once "new political history." In examining white politics immediately before and during the Civil War, in other words, I have emphasized social forces like fear, anger, and especially loyalty, have paid close attention to local and regional patterns of political affiliation and the political behavior such affiliations shaped (as with my treatment of Upper Southern Unionism), and have at all times assumed the representativeness of political parties as quantifiable links between popular political opinion and local, state, and national policy.[5]

But because the now-old "new political" approach focuses upon the ways in which social and cultural forces shaped individual and collective behavior in the established political arena, it is not adequate when examining African American politics during the Civil War. The white men who led America's prominent wartime denominations and who controlled the bulk of its local assemblies as both clergymen and gender-defined voting members did not need to construct an alternative political world with novel means of political expression. Most essentially, they had access to the vote, understood by historians as the quintessential political behavior. White "politics" of the nineteenth century essentially referenced all things related to the ballot box, including referendums, campaigns, the mechanics of elections, the products of those elected (legislation, statute, amendment), and the leadership and character of elected officials. But African Americans were most often denied such participation. Left little recourse, black people sought therefore to shape their own public lives and express their own political impulses in novel and often unperceivable ways. In considering the political efforts of African American clerics, therefore, I borrow from the expansive outline of the political realm that has been deftly staked out by Steven Hahn and others.[6]

Each chapter in my study is organized around a question or set of questions born in the contested participation of the denominational clergy in politics during the mid-nineteenth century. Setting the stage for a look at political preachers during the Civil War, chapter 1 tracks the increase in both number and importance of political preachers in the late-antebellum North and the related rhetorical attack against them that emanated from the Old South. Chapter 2 examines the augmented cultural and political authority that the Civil War produced for ministers in the Union, while chapter 3 surveys the many reasons northerners, and especially northern preachers, customarily considered "disloyal" political preachers a threat to the nation's very existence. Chapter 4 shows how and why the Civil War stands as the nation's first concerted campaign to check the ministry's freedom of religious expression, a campaign spawned by the political influence of disloyal ministers and joined in by a wide array of players. Chapter 5 sketches out and then fills in the three broad ideological categories into which wartime ministers themselves fell concerning the mixing of politics and the pulpit. Chapter 6 traces the southern clergy's development as an arbiter of Confederate loyalty and source of political opposition to Federal occupation. The degree to which political allegiances and loyalties compelled ministers to assume dissentious, indeed dangerous, positions during their region's wartime occupation is the focus of chapter 7. And finally, chapter 8 evaluates the African American clergy's formal and informal political leadership during the Civil War.

Historian Mitchell Snay asserted in 2003 that, when compared with other Civil War topics, "there are relatively few studies of religion" and that "the recovery of Civil War religious history has yet to occur."[7] That recovery effort can be aided by identifying and analyzing the political and apolitical behaviors and ideas of homefront preachers—not only the collective wartime clergy, moreover, but the individual minister as well. Considerations of northern ministers of the Civil War years as autonomous entities and rational actors capable of reaching their own conclusions and arriving at their own allegiances are rare and promise to reveal, in time, a different wartime church than has been posited.[8] But whether examining preachers in the wartime North *or* South, future researchers must guard against focusing exclusively on nationalized identities and hegemonic agents of culturalization, lest they fail to account for regional and even local influences on religion like the economic viability of an area, local ethnicity, immigration, and a locale's proximity to slavery. With that in mind, I pay close attention to the diversity of wartime denominationalism in the conviction that such accentuation best recreates the pluralistic realities of the time. In the end, I am not interested in presenting an ecclesiological or "high church" history; nor do I argue that rigid theological creeds were delivered to denominational preachers and then interpreted by those preachers in political terms. Instead, this book chronicles and assesses the efforts of civil and church authorities to control and/or censor the political behavior of wartime ministers and the ways in which those efforts were received or resisted by Americans in the pews and, even more importantly, the pulpit.

1

PREACHERS, SLAVERY,
AND ANTEBELLUM POLITICS

T HE GENERATION OF Americans that fought the Civil War inherited a
political tradition that celebrated the separation of church and state.
During the tumultuous years immediately preceding the war, certainly
the largest part of American church leaders kept politics and religion distinct.
And yet, between the end of the U.S.-Mexican War and the start of the Civil
War, political preachers became more numerous and controversial than ever
before. Three historical turns—the U.S.-Mexican War, the Fugitive Slave Act
of 1850, and the Kansas-Nebraska Act of 1854—collectively ushered in a new
but contested age of political preachers and thus paved the way for wartime
disputes over clerical partisanship. Historians have correctly identified the
role that slavery played in dividing antebellum denominations along sectional
lines and how those divisions in turn predicted the breakup of the nation.[1]
The events featured in this chapter were each unquestionably brought
about by slavery, and scholars have customarily treated them as episodes
in the disintegration of national unity. But if these events confirm that the
intersectional debate over slavery was bitterly discordant, they also reveal
that on an intrasectional level (at least within the North) the very notion
that preachers should join in that *or any* political debate was often equally
controversial.

The actions of northern and southern clerics respectively during these
three historical moments reveal the different attitudes toward political
preachers that developed in each section during the antebellum years. In the
North the appropriateness of so-called "political" preachers was subject to
constant consideration and review. Driven by the perceived unrighteousness
of the U.S.-Mexican War, the insults to conscience threatened by the Fugitive
Slave Act, and the proslavery effrontery of the Kansas-Nebraska Act, more
and more preachers within established denominational traditions took to
their pulpits and their writing parlors to indict the evils of slavery. Not every
cleric above Mason and Dixon's Line, however, welcomed the commingling of
preaching and politics. Northern critics of political preachers were compelled

by any number of motivations, including partisanship, a reverence for denominational tradition, a fear of the over-secularization of the ministry, and an earnest belief that the gospel of Christ deserved no less than 100 percent of a minister's efforts. Whatever their reasons, many northerners disparaged partisan preachers with scalding orations and acerbic prose, not at all ready to concede the growing political predilections of the clergy.

Meanwhile, Old Southern ministers conflated religion and politics as a matter of course. By the mid-1850s, the culturally unifying southern gospel proffered by clergymen was essentially a proslavery campaign—complete with what historian Mitchell Snay has called an elaborate and systematic "scriptural defense of human bondage"—and ministerial attacks on northern secular and political leaders were standard fare on southern Sunday mornings.[2] But those same southern preachers habitually harangued against mixing politics and religion. With impressive rhetorical acumen, discoursers in Dixie simultaneously defended slavery and attacked partisan preachers by assigning southern slavery to the domestic sphere, rendering it apolitical even as they repeatedly sounded its praises and indicted its foes.[3] Especially reprobate, in the estimation of southern proslavery proselytizers, were northern clerical adversaries of slavery. According to the Old South gospel, antislavery preachers in the North both violated their sacred charge (by introducing debauched politics into their sermonic considerations) and wrongfully attacked the venerated southern "way of life." On the peripheries of southern slavery, where the hegemonic authority of the planter was less pronounced, preachers sometimes found room to challenge slavery's power. Even there, however, the prescriptive and unifying influence of the southern proslavery gospel proved determinative as the antebellum age waned.

The rise of political preachers and the controversy they engendered during the prewar years sets the stage for everything that follows in my study. By chronicling the debate over slavery and the closely related but separate debate over political preachers, I seek to assess the divisiveness of the late 1840s and especially the 1850s, a period scholars already refer to as the "Decade of Disunion."[4] Of course Christians in the North continued to argue over slavery long after America's leading Protestant denominations split along sectional lines (Presbyterians in 1837 and both Methodists and Baptists in 1845). But in the late 1840s and 1850s, heated disputes over the propriety of political clergymen were added to that volatile mix. Political historian Michael Holt has examined the ways in which debates over slavery polarized the memberships of antebellum political parties, a polarization that brought about the ruination of the Second Party system. Similarly, religious historians must begin to assess the degree to which arguments among churchpeople over both slavery and the political nature of preachers—for preachers were sometimes political about other issues as well as slavery—divided Christians and thus hastened the great theological crisis that was the American Civil War.[5]

I

Throughout much of the first half of the nineteenth century, churchpeople in the North thought of political preachers in absolute terms. The majority of them agreed that abolitionist and proslavery sermons, no matter how restrained, were alike political exercises. Their consensus on the meaning of political preachers did not denote, however, agreement on the properness of partisan parsons. Some believed that the church and state must complement each other but not intermingle. Politics was the "counterpart in the corporeal of what religion is in the spiritual," a Christian communitarian offered in 1844, and the distinctive yet "universal harmony of Religion and Politics, is the anchor of hope for humanity, because it secures the enthronement of wisdom and love."[6] Other northern churchpeople, conversely, welcomed a politically integrated clergy. Hadn't there always been political preachers of a kind in New England, for instance, where so-called "occasional sermons" on topics of political interest to the community emanated even from colonial and Revolutionary War–era pulpits?[7] Certainly George Washington, esteemed by most antebellum Americans as the greatest of all the presidents, routinely called upon the clergy to oversee days of fasting and prayer, and preachers, in response, had expressed few qualms about incorporating the nation's political well-being into their efforts.[8] While differences of opinion over political preachers existed throughout the first half of the nineteenth century, the comparative pluralism of northern Christianity ensured those of all camps a fairly civil coexistence prior to the U.S.-Mexican War.

For a number of reasons, in fact, before the transformative events of the late 1840s and 1850s the northern debate over political preachers merited little notice. Denominational sameness did not characterize northern political groups during the 1830s and 1840s; nor were the members of the North's ascendant Protestant denominations characteristically likely to belong to one political tradition or another.[9] Thus as a rule neither pro- nor anti-political preacher pundits were vilified by northern political figures. And although church-affiliated voluntarism flourished in the North during the 1820s, 1830s, and 1840s like never before (spurred by millennialism, revivalism, or some combination of both), a minister's participation in public movements aimed at enhancing civic morality was considered appropriately apolitical by mainstream denominationalists.[10] Scholars have chronicled the largely uncontroversial role that preachers played in the early American temperance movement, for instance, and the same can be said of the clerical leaders of the Sabbatarian crusade.[11] The Protestant clergy reacted to the challenges of urbanization, industrialization, and immigration by launching or participating in dozens of reform movements. Aimed at ridding America of everything from poverty to prostitution, several such campaigns—like those against the supposed evils of drinking, gambling, and Roman Catholicism, to name but a few—necessarily pitched ministers into the secular fray.[12] Some parishioners were more pleased than others about the clergy's engagement with the temporal world, but as a rule the faithful accepted, and some even grew to expect, reform-focused clerical participation.

All of this lent itself to the fairly harmonious coexistence of differing opinions about political preachers within both the northern church and the public prior to the mid-1840s. However, with the strident opposition of scores of northern denominational preachers to the U.S.-Mexican War and subsequent Fugitive Slave and Kansas-Nebraska acts, a new age of political preaching was instigated. In essence, slavery and political issues related to slavery became so morally pressing in the late 1840s and 1850s that it became impossible, many clerics believed, to keep the churches and thus themselves as church leaders above them. The ranks of identifiably "political" preachers swelled. And as political preachers became more plentiful in the North, other churchmen and women believed they also became more problematic.

Countless parishioners and parsons alike were not ready for the newly aggressive ilk of ministerial activism that was unleashed upon the North during the national debate over the U.S.-Mexican War. Wary church members knew too well the painful denominational schisms that slavery—in the opinion of most northerners, the matter at the heart of the war with Mexico—had lately produced in the country. Presbyterians, for example, recognized the issue's divisiveness. The feud that ultimately resulted in the Presbyterian Church's division in 1837 began in the 1810s and 1820s with internal disagreements over not just slavery, but over theology and doctrine, church organization, and the best ways to organize, govern, and finance missionary efforts as well.[13] These concerns gave rise to conflicting camps of "Old School" and "New School" Presbyterians.[14] By the middle of the 1830s, however, Old Schoolers and New Schoolers were bound together chiefly, and identified almost exclusively, by their views on slavery. Little wonder then that, as their national church crumbled around them in 1837, most Presbyterians recognized, along with a commentator in Cincinnati's *Journal and Luminary*, that "the question is not between the new and the old school—is not in relation to doctrinal errors; but it is *slavery and anti-slavery*. It is not the [doctrinal] *standards* which were to be protected, but the system of *slavery*."[15]

Slavery was likewise at the root of the national Methodist Episcopal Church's breakup in 1845. It is true that ostensibly ecclesiastical questions over the power and scope of the church's hierarchical government plagued Methodism throughout the 1830s. Equally true, however, is that such differences were almost entirely sectional. Just as southerners in the broader nation called for a strict interpretation of the U.S. Constitution, so too did Southern Methodists demand a stiflingly narrow reading of the Methodist Episcopal Church's charter, a reading that prohibited the church from indicting slavery or censuring slave owners.[16] Certainly by the time the denomination collapsed formally on May 1, 1845—precipitated by the national governing body's ruling that Georgia's Bishop James O. Andrew must give up either his slaves or his church office—slavery's primary role in the denomination's dissolution was understood by members in both the North and South.[17] And when another Georgian, Baptist Reverend James E. Reeves, was banned from the missionary field by the Baptist Home Mission Society in 1844 because he owned slaves, it set in motion a chain of events that culminated in the dissolution of the Triennial Convention (the national Baptist conference of churches) and the formation of the Southern Baptist Convention on May 7, 1845.[18]

The church schisms of the 1830s and 1840s had calamitous consequences. Mainstream American denominationalism became entirely regional, and as such, entirely biased. Sectionalism within American Christianity robbed the tortured country of the ameliorating effects of nationwide fellowship, an especially dire loss when the political realm grew too inharmonious to accommodate such amity.[19] As Allan Nevins noted long ago, the breakup of the churches emboldened the Democratic Party, dampening the spirit of national cooperation among members of the last remaining national organization of real importance.[20] In the end, America's preeminent Protestant churches effectively forged a template for disunion, a model the broader nation would emulate a scant decade and a half later. And it must be said that, during these national denominational splits, at least some offended members were taken aback by their clergy's *ecclesiastical* partisanship—that is to say, their highly sectionalist and hostile participation in church politics.[21] In a sense then, a kind of "political" clergy no doubt played a significant role in the denominational divisions of the 1830s and 1840s.

But for the most part in 1837 and again in 1845, few denominationalists questioned the essentially religious nature of their respective clergies' involvement in these debates. The pre-split squabbles that beset American Presbyterianism, Methodism, and Baptistism were never *just* about the morality of slavery, after all, but about such issues as antislavery sentiment in church doctrine, resolutions, and policies, missionary efforts to the enslaved, and the participation of slave owners in their respective churches' hierarchy of authority.[22] In other words, no matter how belligerent on doctrine or defiantly for or against slavery a preacher might have revealed himself during these periods of church rupture, his behavior was theoretically contained within the religious sphere.[23] It was therefore not the memory of a secularly political clergy that many church members took from these years as much as a wariness of the disruptive dangers of preachers who carried the slavery question into their pulpits and church offices. The overwhelming majority of those same chary church members, moreover, were personally insensitive to the slaves' plight, as preachers knew well. For these reasons, more than a few northern ministers who were privately sympathetic to the slaves refused to broach the subject publicly during the tumult over the war with Mexico, lest they alienate their congregations.[24]

Other northern clerics of the day hated slavery and worked openly for its demise, but did so expressly through the church, eschewing politics. Historian Lawrence Friedman has noted the many clerics who parted ways with Garrisonianism in the 1840s, convinced that as William Lloyd Garrison waxed evermore "anti-church" and "anti-institutional" he likewise grew, in the words of Lewis Tappan, "lukewarm on the anti-slavery subject," having "loaded the cause with their no-government-woman's rights-non-resistant & c. until we have got among [the] breakers."[25] Tappan and a number of his closest acquaintances were not about to be deterred in their conviction that, "since churches and church-linked missionary societies were the agencies that promoted morality on earth," slavery's downfall would come not by ballot but *only* by bended knee once earnest "parishioners and clergy recognized the sins of bondage."[26] Nevertheless, most of the antebellum preachers who joined Tappan in his loathing of slavery were sedulously wary of the perils of practicing "politicized" preaching, even against such an evil as slavery. Thus when an antiwar preacher, quoted in Boston's *Emancipator and Republican* in 1847, wondered how any "minster of Christ" could *not* indict such a murderous war brought about by the "desire to extend the area of slavery," could *not* "plead the cause of nearly three million of his own countrymen," and could *not* indict the hundreds of cold-blooded murders that had been committed "under the sanction of a Government calling itself Christian," the largest part of his fellow countrymen—both in and certainly outside of the clergy and no matter their private sentiments on such issues—did not join him in his bewilderment.[27]

True enough, with each passing day the unnamed Bostonian became a bit less exceptional in his position. An editor for the *Advocate of Peace* noted in 1847 that, while in "the past year we have seldom found a preacher who had not in some way discussed the subject in the pulpit," he trusted yet "that the day is not far distant . . . when the pulpit will everywhere open the full strength of its moral batteries upon this most sinful sin" in a "fearless Christian rebuke of war."[28] The few but fervent members of the Liberty Party certainly hoped as much, and the role that their highly moralistic oratory played in acquainting more and more Americans with political preaching in the 1840s cannot be ignored. Numerous Liberty Party leaders were lay church members or ministers who nevertheless wanted to move beyond the churches and into a kind of abolitionism that emphasized sacralized political parties and the electoral process.[29] Eric Foner has written that "the Bible was the political textbook of the party and its organizers said they intended to bring Christian ethics into government." Not surprisingly, the Liberty Party's slogan was "vote as you pray and pray as you vote."[30] But while preachers played an important role in articulating the biblical imperative of antislavery and thus spreading the Liberty Party faith in the years prior to America's war with Mexico, in the opinion of most northerners they could no more legitimize partisan sermonizing than they could save the Liberty Party from the debilitating consequences of its own extremism.[31]

Indeed most American churchmen and women noted the trend toward a politicized clergy with chagrin, and many clerics were rewarded for their political sermonizing with the enmity of the public and the rebuke of their members. "From a worldly point of view," the biographer of Massachusetts Unitarian Congregationalist Reverend R. C. Waterston posited, Waterston's career would have been much more successful had he steered clear of "political preaching." But with such iniquities as the U.S.-Mexican War to vex him, Waterston could not abstain. "He declared from the pulpit that the Mexican War was a 'savage and bloody work,'" his chronicler penned, and no matter the response his proclamations engendered, Waterston "affirmed the 'weighty responsibility' of the Christian Church, so long as slavery darkened any portion of our land."[32] As the matter of political preaching became increasingly moralistic in the 1840s, both the number of clerics like Waterston who practiced such sermonic behavior and the level and tone of the rejoinders they elicited changed dramatically. Representative of both truths, so many New England parsons attacked the U.S.-Mexican War that a number of state executives mandated their silence. The governor of Maine, for example, reminded preachers in a Thanksgiving proclamation that "the day should be kept free from all political harangues or exhibitions of sectarian zeal."[33]

Antiwar preaching was not limited to New England. A group of Philadelphia Presbyterians indicted the war as an effort dedicated to "the extension of the slaveholders' power." Its object, they continued, was to bring about "peace at the expense of an ocean of blood, shed for the express purpose of extending the area of slavery."[34] And a number of ministers in Ohio lamented that, at the bidding of a "slave holding war making President," men were driven to "butcher innocent Mexicans, and with very few exceptions the ministry" remained silent about the whole godless affair.[35] Just as antiwar preaching was not geographically contained, moreover, neither was the often cold response it elicited from congregants. Reverend Samuel J. May was for instance accosted by members of his own Unitarian Universalist Church as he walked the streets of Syracuse, New York, in 1847. "Some of us do not like what you have said of public affairs," one parishioner proclaimed, and "we are very much displeased with you."[36]

Despite such pronouncements, clerical opponents of the war with Mexico did not back down. Reverend May for instance rebuffed his mini-mob of members flatly, proclaiming, "It is not the business of the minister to please the people, but to tell them what he thinks they ought to hear, whether it please them or not. I must preach to gratify my conscience, not to gratify your tastes."[37] Others had little patience for any denominationalist minister who refused to indict from the pulpit both slavery and the war then being fought to extend it. The most extreme of these clerical critics of the war in Mexico campaigned for Christians to abandon weak-kneed denominationalism and organized religion, as it then existed, altogether.[38] Like early Quakers in England, these "Come-outer" offshoots of prominent Protestant traditions delighted in disrupting church services through various measures.[39] A favorite tactic involved protestors attending a service anonymously and then standing mid-sermon en masse to recite Revelations 18:4, "Come out of here, my people, that ye receive not of her plagues."[40]

As a group in the North, only the Catholic Church saw few of its clergymen engage in anti–Mexican War oratory. Catholic leaders steered clear of pronouncements on the war for numerous reasons. As a hedge against Whig and then Know-Nothing oppression, many northern Catholics were Democrats. Some Catholic divines thus sympathized, no doubt, with their southern party mates and kept their tongues in check lest they prove unduly offensive to their brethren. Many more were sensitive to the common argument of Protestants that the war was one to rid North America of a usurpatious Catholic kingdom. "Mexico is a base, priest ridden nation," the editor of the *Presbyterian Covenanter* offered in July 1846, "and needs a scourging . . . and will probably get it."[41] The number of American Catholics in the area adjacent to Mexico (the American Central Southwest) was ten times greater than that of the Catholic Church's strongest denominational competitor in the region, the Southern Methodists.[42] The American army in Mexico would in short order win the war, it was thought; what might then happen if Catholic leaders alienated the American government by railing against its policies? Fresh off the defeat of one Catholic enemy, might American forces not be sent on another anti-Catholic crusade in the Southwest?[43] Moreover, the Catholic Church was by now under constant nativist scrutiny on the Eastern Seaboard, where the Roman Catholic population approached 1.5 million.[44] If an American public already convinced of Catholic venality and drunkenness added treason to its stock image of Catholics, what brutalities might be visited upon those northeastern Catholics by xenophobic extremists?

What's more, Catholic clerics of the day were dogmatically disinclined to speak on specific political issues, historian Mark Noll has observed, and were "deeply troubled" by those who advocated upsetting society in pursuit of their particular political goals.[45] Although the lion's share of Catholic divines in the prewar North were less obediently submissive to the dictates of Rome than their nativist foes could have ever imagined, American Catholic leaders in the 1840s nevertheless participated in a global revival in devotional piety within the Catholic Church that "looked upon human suffering . . . as a condition to be embraced for spiritual good."[46] In the estimation of many Catholic clerics, political efforts from the pulpit to ameliorate such tempering elements of American life as slavery and war ultimately contributed more to the ruination of society than to its salvation. For all of these reasons, virtually no Catholic priests offered any public declaration on the country's war with Mexico.

In the North's denominationally Protestant churches, however, the U.S.-Mexican War sparked a heated argument over both slavery and the related but separate issue of political preachers. And the Compromise of 1850, with its malodorous Fugitive Slave laws, only made matters worse.[47] Led by Henry Ward Beecher, mid-century northern ministers routinely referenced scriptural passages against slavery, offered diatribes against the immorality of slave owners, referenced the moral imperatives of the believer's "Higher Law" of conscience, and exhorted church members to defy the Fugitives Slave Act. The back-and-forth between Boston's Moses Stuart, Nathaniel Taylor, and other northern clerical critics of political preaching on the one hand and unabashedly political preachers like Beecher on the other quickly became a pulpit war for the hearts and minds of northerners over the scriptural status of—and Christian obligation to—fugitive slaves.[48] In that war, traditionalists from across the North lined up to indict political preachers. In 1850, Moses Stuart authored a pamphlet titled *Conscience and the Constitution,* soon to become known (erroneously) as a forceful biblical defense of slavery. Stuart believed the political manipulation of congregants by the church and its leaders was a "perversion of the right of private judgment."[49] Another common charge was leveled by an editor of New York's by-then conservative *Journal of Commerce.* The newspaperman indicted Beecher and others for "prostituting their professions and their pulpits and the Sabbath day to the preaching of Free-Soilism."[50] Even centrists in the North's rhetorical war over political preaching and the Fugitive Slave Act—or, clergymen who preached compliance to the Fugitive Slave Act *and* denounced the political evils of slavery—were not spared the wrath of denominationalism's anti-political preaching faction.[51] All who even broached the subject were damned, for as one religious commentator in a secular newspaper inquired, "What clergyman ever solemnized, and purified, and elevated the thoughts of his hearers by preaching about politics?" The answer, as he saw it, was of course "none." Instead, the political preacher—no matter his particular argument—"spreads his arms, and rolls up his eyes, and supplicates that the peace of God . . . may fill the hearts of his people, a portion of whom are ready for three cheers, while the remainder are ready to fight."[52]

The turmoil of 1850–51 was great. Prior to the secession winter of 1860–61, however, no political development troubled northern denominationalists more than the Kansas-Nebraska Act of 1854. To a greater extent even than the U.S.-Mexican War or the later response to the Fugitive Slave Act, the passage of the Kansas-Nebraska Act and its indignant reception by many northern people of faith was a transformative episode in the story of American political preachers.

In 1854 and 1855, churchpeople throughout the North responded in unprecedented numbers to the Kansas-Nebraska Act, convinced that it was a great moral and political wrong. Numerous denominations were represented in the host of incensed individual congregations, presbyteries, Methodist conferences, Society of Friends groups, and hundreds of ministers from the northwestern states, New York region, and those as far south as Indiana who inundated Congress with petitions, resolutions, and remonstrances.[53] These all paled, however, compared to the petition signed and sent to Congress by 3,050 New England clergymen of various denominations. The Kansas-Nebraska bill was, in the estimation of these clerics, "a measure full of danger to the peace and even existence of our beloved union, and exposing us to the righteous judgments of the Almighty."[54]

Many of America's premier preachers now joined Connecticut Congregationalist Reverend Leonard Bacon in deeming slavery "a question for the pulpit, unless the pulpit itself is to be dishonored and enslaved," and in labeling the ownership of a slave "prima facie evidence of wrong-doing." Little wonder then that Bacon and many ministers of his ilk led their congregations in opposition to the Kansas-Nebraska Act even as some within their churches called for moderation.[55] Evangelical Congregationalist Horace James of Worcester, Massachusetts, believed that preachers in the North became more important than politicians in the aftermath of the Kansas-Nebraska Act. "I am more convinced," James opined, "that this great crime of our country . . . must be expiated mainly through the pulpit and the church. This agency, chiefly, must destroy slavery, if it is ever destroyed and establish liberty, if it ever be established."[56] And for supporting the Kansas-Nebraska Act, Congregationalist Reverend S. L. Rockwood of Hanson, Massachusetts, predicted doughface

President Franklin Pierce's fate. "If hell were already full to overflowing," the vehement Rockwood fumed, "the Almighty would turn the very devil out to make room for such a recreant."[57]

The Kansas-Nebraska Act was thought so egregious by so many that it led important church leaders in the North to speak out politically for the first time. Rhode Island Baptist Francis Wayland, long an opponent of secularly opinionated preachers, was driven by the bill to abandon his traditional reluctance to apply moral attitudes and convictions to contemporary political concerns.[58] And he was not the only cleric to venture for the first time into the political realm after the Kansas-Nebraska Act. Ohio Methodist Edward Thomson, then president of Ohio Wesleyan University, deserted his customary position against affected preaching in a sermon titled "The Pulpit and Politics." According to one account, Thomson at long last argued "very conclusively, in the course of the discourse, that there are times and occasions when preachers should speak in regard to political as well as religious matters."[59]

Such political stands by ministers occurred before 1854, but hardly any then alive in America could remember a religiously rooted campaign of such scope. Survivors of the Revolutionary Age were few. Although denominationalists played an important role in the anti-Masonic politics of the Jacksonian era and the presidential victory of Thomas Jefferson was achieved in spite of the mobilization of Christians convinced either of Jefferson's anti-Trinitarian beliefs or his outright atheism, the denominational response to the Kansas-Nebraska Act easily trumped these episodes. In the North, political preachers became common—and they elicited a common backlash from conservative members, ministers, and political leaders alike.

The Bangor, Maine, parishioner who inveighed against (his pastor) Unitarian Reverend Joseph Henry Allen's leadership in the protest movement against the Kansas-Nebraska Act was representative of countless northern Christians who reckoned that the political activism of the denominational clergy had at last gone too far.[60] For instance a member of a Congregationalist church in New Hampshire listened quietly as his preacher railed against the Kansas-Nebraska Act, but would never do so again. "I am willing that the minister should have his own political opinions, and enjoy them undisturbed," he conceded. But he "did not subscribe my money [fifty dollars a year for the support of the church] to pay for preaching party politics and denouncing the rulers of our country and its institutions, nor will I go to meeting to be insulted by my minister instead of being instructed by the gospel." No doubt distressed that he would no longer frequent the church he had faithfully attended for thirty years, the disgruntled Christian nevertheless concluded, "I shall go no more."[61] And Presbyterian Reverend Edward Kirk of Albany, New York, predicted that partisan clerics would ruin the country. Lest the tide of political preachers was turned back, he predicted, "America, happy America" would become "the prey of angry passions, bloody strife, rapine, carnage and violence!!! Oh! My country, my beloved country," he wailed, "must thy glory set in such a night?"[62]

Secular voices were heard as well. An essayist in the Democratic *Republican Compiler* (Gettysburg, Pennsylvania) observed that, when the New England clergymen submitted their petition, "every sensible man regarded them as intermeddling fools. A similar estimate is put upon every one who attempts to preach politics from the pulpit." According to this critic, the reason for such contempt was not complicated. "No clergyman was ever sent to preach politics," he surmised, "and whenever he does it he is perverting his sacred mission to a purpose from which unmitigated evil alone can flow."[63] A writer in the *West Chester* [Ohio] *Republican* offered, "We take the broad ground, that no clergyman having the one great idea of his profession truly at heart, will ever be found anxious to mingle in the strife of politics." Those clergymen who chose politics, the commentator concluded, "not only lose their own influence, but they palsy the energies of those whose hearts are absorbed in the great work of directing men to their true and substantial happiness."[64] And such offended public responses to the political actions of northern clergymen in 1854 and 1855 were not limited to newspapers. Political luminaries as prominent as Stephen Douglas believed the petitions were "presented by a denomination of men calling themselves preachers of the Gospel, who have come forward with an atrocious falsehood." These were men, Douglas charged, in the act of "committing an atrocious calumny against the Senate," men who had "desecrated the pulpit, and prostrated the sacred desk to the miserable and corrupting influence of party politics."[65]

As evidenced by the heated response of many churchpeople to the Kansas-Nebraska Act and, in turn, the abhorrence with which that response was met, by the middle of the 1850s political preaching had polarized much of Christian America. The slavery issue had been at the heart of the U.S.-Mexican War and the Compromise of 1850 and was now central to the Kansas-Nebraska Act. That the rise in prevalence and controversy of political preachers in the North was inextricably linked to the slavery question, therefore, cannot be denied.

Other politicized issues, however, were occasionally taken up by ministers of the day. Both Protestants and Catholics argued over the appropriate role the clergy should play in the education of the nation's youth. Northern preachers who advocated an expanded role for women in society courted controversy, moreover, as did those who believed the church should assume a greater degree of financial responsibility for public institutions and programs dedicated to social welfare. Some Christians quarreled over the appropriate degree of subservience that ministers of the gospel, and really all who adhered to the teachings of Christ, owed the government when governmental policy violated their beliefs (as was the case, they held, when the Fugitive Slave laws mandated compliance and even assistance in the capture of escaped slaves).[66] Perhaps surprisingly, a number of antebellum laymen and clerics alike bickered over a proposed amendment to the Constitution that would have declared the United States a Christian nation.[67] But without question, the most significant "other" cause sometimes championed by ministers of the era was nativism and its political embodiment, the American or "Know-Nothing" Party.[68]

Although firmly rooted in Protestant xenophobia, political nativism in truth encompassed a number of contentious topics. Reminiscent of Lyman Beecher's sensational attacks on Catholics in the 1830s, Know-Nothing ministers in the 1850s for instance routinely associated Irish and German immigrants with intemperance. In widely circulated teetotalist oratories, unforgiving northern divines vilified the economic and political power wielded by the purveyors of liquor in America *and* the thickly brogued drunkards such traffickers purportedly left in their wake.[69] Other clergymen, still influenced by the shocking and manifestly false accounts of abuses within Catholic schools and Ursuline convents that scandal mongers like the *Boston Mercantile Journal* propagated throughout the 1830s and 1840s, equated Catholicism with the neglect and outright sexual abuse of children.[70] Among other things, they called for reforms that would eradicate the imagined surreptitious Catholic influence in American education.[71] And finally, scores of nativist ministers were convinced that the sorry state of America's political system—a system plagued, in their estimation, by corruption and graft—was the result of a vast Catholic conspiracy, perpetrated by the worldwide Catholic Church, and under the supervision of the Pope in Rome.[72] The Know-Nothing tactic of addressing emotionally charged issues like temperance, civic benevolence, education, and political reform *within the context of anti-Catholicism* (to say nothing of the indignation Know-Nothings provoked in their incessant talk of Catholic pedophilia) proved especially appealing to northern evangelicals. Hence Pennsylvania politician and newspaper editor Alexander McClure remembered long after its demise that Know-Nothingism "brought an unusual number of ministers into politics, largely from the Methodist and Baptist Churches, whose people were rather more aggressive than other Protestant denominations in their hostility to Catholics."[73]

But, as was also true of the national debate over political preaching itself, the slavery issue was Know-Nothingism's real sine qua non. No matter how much of an amalgamation of provincial concerns the Know-Nothings might have represented, political nativism would have stalled as a national movement well before it did if not for the antislavery sentiment fomented by the Kansas-Nebraska Act.[74] Although that act was not passed until May 30, 1854, the contest over how to organize the Kansas-Nebraska Territory began in Congress in early 1853, immediately ending the brief period of calm over slavery in the territories that the Compromise of 1850 had produced.[75] During 1853 and the early months of 1854 and then in the Kansas-Nebraska Act's aftermath, more and more exasperated northerners reasoned that their political captains had finally gone too far in placating the beneficiaries of southern slavery. Assuming that any political party complicit in such a damnable compromise with the enemies of northern free labor was beyond repair, they fled the Democratic Party by the hundreds of thousands and joined the fledgling Know-Nothings.[76] There were fewer than fifty official members of the Know-Nothing Party in early 1852; by the close of 1854, there were more than one million.[77] Many new members, including countless ministers, found their way into the movement chiefly because a more explicitly antislavery party had yet to be formed. As they awaited the Republican Party's emergence, they swelled the Know-Nothing ranks, but they were motivated first and foremost by their attitudes about slavery.[78]

Most furious of all the watch fires that burned within the nativists' circling camps, the slavery issue soon grew out of control, consuming the Know-Nothing Party in the flames. Although antislavery opinion stimulated northern membership in 1853 and 1854, the party's southern-dominated national council never wavered in its defense of the peculiar institution. By the end of 1854, therefore, Know-Nothing leaders in the mid-Atlantic states recognized the mounting disgruntlement of "thousands in the new [Know Nothing] party," in the words of a Pennsylvania newspaper editor, "with whom the anti-slavery sentiment is stronger than all other political purposes." Another Know-Nothing commentator in New England predicted that, in his neck of the woods, "the American [P]arty cannot stand an instant . . . after its anti-slavery principles are gone."[79] At the same time, southern party members grew incensed at northern Know-Nothing preachers who persistently conflated "Roman Catholicism and slavery" by casting both as "natural allies in every warfare against liberty and enlightenment."[80] All of this enmity came to a head at the party's national convention in June 1855. When southerners secured the party's endorsement of the Kansas-Nebraska Act and its extension of slavery into the western territories over the passionate opposition of northern members, it was the beginning of the movement's staggeringly rapid end.[81] Just as they had left the Democratic Party a few years earlier, northerners abandoned the Know-Nothings in droves and made their way into the newly established Republican Party. After Millard Fillmore's feeble showing in the 1856 presidential election, the Know-Nothings were all but dead, brought down by the politics of slavery.[82] But for a time, antislavery sentiment allowed the Know-Nothings to succeed in a way that no nativist group had before.

Undeniably, a number of Know-Nothing preachers entered the understood political arena for the first time in the 1850s because of their feelings about Catholicism, temperance, or some other issue of public morality unrelated—at least in their minds—to slavery.[83] In their seemingly novel behavior, however, Know-Nothing clerics exemplified a fundamental truth about political preaching in the antebellum age. The collective northern clergy's presence in movements of particular northern concern was in fact not new; it was simply deemed newly political, given the tenor of the age. Throughout the long antebellum era, the largest part of individual ministers in established Protestant churches apparently changed little in their attitudes about, or their levels of participation in, campaigns to change or preserve the existing social and religious order in the North.[84] Most preachers who championed causes like temperance in the late 1840s and nativism in the 1850s, in other words, held the same opinions and practiced much the same behaviors as ever, and no intellectual transformation on the issue of mixing preaching and politics was needed on their part. Anti-Catholicism and reform-related issues elicited emotional and religious responses among Americans throughout the late 1840s and 1850s, but such concerns were only occasionally so morally and politically determinative as to cause preachers to abandon long-held ideological aversions to political activism. Among clergymen of every religious persuasion, it was undoubtedly slavery and the political imbroglios that slavery expressly anchored—chiefly the U.S.-Mexican War, the Fugitive Slave Act, and the Kansas-Nebraska Act—that animated the lion's share of *truly new* political ministers after 1846, and no other issue did more to harm denominational unity.

No matter how much slavery acted as a catalyst, however, in the end slavery and political preaching were different issues. Numerous northern clerics always hated slavery and yet always eschewed political preaching in its entirety, no matter the political topic at hand, including slavery. The denominational and public argument over political preachers, an ever-present fact of life in the North by the 1850s, must therefore be considered on its own merits. Indeed, the quarrel over the proper political role of preachers added to the polarization of members within perhaps already inharmonious church congregations and pushed parishioners evermore away from their increasingly activist pastors.

II

Throughout the antebellum era, northern clerics routinely differed over political preaching. The same cannot be said of ministers in the Old South. Thinking themselves the ideological heirs of Thomas Jefferson, the South's political *beau ideal* who famously argued for a separation of church and state, southern denominational leaders rebuked the perceived partisanship of any minister who sermonically strayed beyond biblical expositions and/ or proslavery jeremiads.[85] But the southern clergy of the antebellum age was Janus-faced. Beginning in earnest in the early 1830s, the defense of slavery and the primacy of its role in southern ideas of republicanism and independence linked the southern clergy inextricably to the political world no matter how its members ranted against the amalgamation of politics and religion.[86] The same evangelicals who shied away from participation in political hullabaloos over tariffs, civil statutes, and state constitutions, for instance, habitually preached sermons insistent upon what one cleric called the divine approval of "our way of life."[87] In so doing, ostensibly apolitical southern ministers celebrated the political independence that slavery ensured, directly engaged anti-slavery and abolitionist politicians, and evaluated relevant Federal policy. All the while, they portrayed slavery (in its entirety, including all of its satellite endeavors) as a domestic institution of a kind with marriage and the paternalistic household, social customs thought likewise vital to southern religion and the southern worldview. In essence, southern preachers after the 1830s created for themselves an uneven rhetorical battlefield. Vehemently *attacking* northern preachers who maligned slavery, they simultaneously cast their own proslavery agitation as part of their duty-bound *defense* of a venerated southern domestic tradition.

It was an easy case to make to southern churchpeople. Certainly by the time of the U.S.-Mexican War, most in the South recognized that their economy revolved around the commercial agricultural products that slave labor made possible. The acquisition of slaves as property, moreover, was the primary indicator of individual economic success and cultural progress. Paternalistic and patriarchal to the hilt, southern society's every relationship was patterned after or informed by the master/slave dynamic. And lastly, if he was unwilling to consciously admit his own subjection, the southern everyman knew at least subconsciously that slavery's conflation of race and servitude (codified by legal statute and orchestrated by the planter elite) exalted whiteness and thus bred a comparative sense of self-worth in non-slaveholding whites that made their fealty to the slaveocracy palatable. As Drew Gilpin Faust asserts, in the antebellum South slavery became for white men the means of assessing and reassessing "the profoundest assumptions on which their world was built."[88] In such an environment, the quickened tempo of the southern clergy's drumbeat against political preaching in the 1850s was both predictable and well received.

The U.S.-Mexican War, the Fugitive Slave Act, and the Kansas-Nebraska Act each reinforced the dissimulative relationship between the southern clergy and politics. Southern ministers of every denomination, seemingly no matter where they were in the South, supported the war with Mexico even as they continued to deny their own extra-ecumenical motivations.[89] Charges that the war was unjust sprang chiefly from northern (chiefly Whig) politicians and abolitionists, including numerous ministers like Congregationalist Henry Ward Beecher and Unitarians Samuel J. May and Theodore Parker. True to form therefore, southern ministers who refuted the war's naysayers claimed both their own apolitical motivations and the God-vexing partisanship of their ministerial opposites. Kentucky Methodist Reverend Henry Bascom, for instance, celebrated the U.S.-Mexican War (and thus indicted its critics) not as a means of expanding slavery as his northern brethren claimed but as "part of a system of providential arrangements by which the Deity carried forward His purposes of mercy toward mankind."[90] Other southern Protestant leaders presented the war as a Christian struggle to free the oppressed people of Mexico from the grasps of European monarchs and Catholic overlords.[91] Surely such ostensibly non-political commentary on political issues was highly advisable on the part of southern preachers, for church members were increasingly vociferous in their certainty that spirituality and politics made strange bedfellows. As one nineteenth-century Texas churchman offered to renowned Baptist leader B. H. Carroll, southerners en masse anticipated that "Hell will be so full of political preachers that their arms and legs will be sticking out of the windows."[92]

The collective South's opinion of northern clergymen grew more negative as the prewar years wound down. Southern preachers were quick to remind anyone who would listen that northern clergymen assumed leading roles in resisting first the Fugitive Slave Acts and then the Kansas-Nebraska Act. According to historian Edward R. Crowther, during both of these affairs the "actions and attitudes of a highly visible minority of northern clergymen . . . provided southern apologists with easy targets for criticism."[93] Antislavery and abolitionist preachers and the religious newspapers they edited seemingly counseled open resistance to the laws of Congress and the Constitution. According to a southern minister writing during the uproar over the passage of the Fugitive Slave Act in 1850, the northern clergy and religious press routinely aligned themselves "against what they regard as . . . [Congressional] measures favorable . . . to the South."[94] A writer in Charleston's *Southern Christian Advocate* agreed, offering that "every Southern man knows" that the northern campaign against the Fugitive Slave Act was "a pseudo-religious movement, with its plan of conscience overriding the Constitution, exulting in its avowed determination to sweep from the nation what it considers the deep disgrace of Southern institutions."[95] Most southerners, it seems, were of a mind with a worried Tennessean. "If these 'despisers of dominion' speak the real sentiments of the Northern people," the southerner warned, "we have fallen upon evil times."[96]

The "abhorrent" political activism of northern preachers continued with the Kansas-Nebraska Act. Southern preachers of course indicted northern clerics for their eagerness to engage in political preaching. "Sermon texts," a New Orleans Methodist wrote, "should not be twisted. . . . Our commandments must be free from political taint."[97] Such Yankee text "twisters" made the issues at hand worse than they needed to be, an editor of a southern religious newspaper implied, by overstating the antislavery sentiments of the northern Christian church's rank-and-file members—some of whom were themselves slaveholders.[98] In addition to wrongfully divining the Bible and discounting the opinions of many under their charge, moreover, northern clerics seemingly advised violence and bloodshed. The likes of Henry Ward Beecher famously sent arms to Kansas in 1854–55, hoping—or so southern preachers claimed—that settlers there might "settle" the question of slavery in the territories by murdering proslavery families. Southern church leaders hoped the issue would be resolved instead through superior numbers of southern pioneers in the territories, whereby the "Western nomenclature of Squatter Sovereignty" would once and for all end the northern clergy's offensive "ecclesiastical interference in the matter."[99] After the northern clergy's supposedly profane response to the Kansas-Nebraska Act, the editors of the *Southern Baptist* could only deduce that the leaders of the northern "church, which acts in the squabbles of party platforms . . . is greedy for spoils." Noting that the contemporary Yankee clergy "can only excite pity or disgust," the writer left little doubt that, in his consideration, it was surely the latter.[100]

Thus southern preachers during the 1850s assumed for themselves the role of wise counselors or judicious sages. They privileged an oratorical style heavily infused with stories, parables, and proverbs, often illustrating the wrongfulness of their politicized northern foes in the church through calm but directed comparisons while avoiding the most patently partisan forms of rhetoric themselves. Northern churchpeople were portrayed as impetuous and worldly, especially when held up against both the heroes of scripture and the evidently long-suffering and restrained Christians who filled southern pews. Impugning political parsons in particular, southern preachers equated Christian ethics with the mannerly avoidance of contemptuous political arguments and emphasized the reasonableness and consolation of Christianity. Northern clerics, conversely, were accused of proffering a Christianity of liberalism and even radicalism.[101] And in the last decade of the antebellum age, southern clerics increasingly conflated their bucolic society with the Christian way of life itself. Thus northern ministers who led resistance to the Fugitive Slave and Kansas-Nebraska acts were doubly damned by southern preachers, for not only were they antislavery and thus anti-southern, but even worse, they were anti-Christian as well.[102]

Of course, the antebellum South was no monolith. Although the entire

South was a slave society—indeed scholars have convincingly argued of late that the entire United States was a slave society—much of the Upper South's history was in ways different from that of the greater South.[103] Before the 1830s, for instance, the vast majority of American antislavery societies (1,106 of 1,130) took root in the South's Appalachian hill country.[104] And, denominationally distinctive antislavery movements took shape in numerous locations throughout the region during the antebellum years. Some were waged aggressively, as was the campaign led by abolitionist Presbyterian John G. Fee in Kentucky in the 1850s, while others were more long-suffering, as with the opposition to slavery offered throughout the age by Brethren and Mennonites in Virginia's Shenandoah Valley.[105] Historian Carl Degler has surmised that throughout the prewar period it was "possible, at least in the Upper South, to discuss the disadvantages, if not the outright evil, of slavery, as long as two conditions were met. One was that the person making the criticism be a native Southerner—not an outlander or, worse, a Northerner." The other stipulation was that criticisms could not be made when slavery seemed particularly under duress, as was the case during the weeks and months after John Brown's attack on Harpers Ferry. When preachers grew accustomed to the limits of tolerance among upper southern Christians, they could preach with a startling degree of liberty. Thus a North Carolinian noted in the 1850s that he felt free in preaching "as strong and direct against slavery as you ever heard me in the north."[106]

But if Tennessee's Methodist Parson Brownlow and other native critics of the southern slave power for a time enjoyed a degree of ministerial freedom of speech in places like East Tennessee and western North Carolina, it did not last.[107] As James McPherson argues regarding denizens of the less productive regions of the Southern Piedmont and Tidewater regions, but as was true everywhere in the South, southerners "were linked to the plantation regime by numerous ties of self-interest and sentiment" even when and where slavery was not an observable part of their daily lives.[108] The U.S.-Mexican War, resulting as it did in the accumulation of territorial lands that in the 1850s would either facilitate slavery's expansion or seal its doom, raised the stakes in the estimation of antislavery and proslavery pundits alike. Certainly Old South denominational leaders like South Carolina Presbyterian James Henley Thornwell and Mississippi Presbyterian Benjamin Palmer grew more fervent in their rhetorical assaults upon political preachers. Sympathetic to their brethren in the Deep South, proslavery evangelicals in the Upper South like Baptist James R. Graves and Presbyterian Frederick A. Ross in turn assumed an aggressively proscriptive position regarding denominational ministers and slavery as well as the rights of southerners.[109] As the U.S.-Mexican War gave way to the politically disruptive events of the 1850s, the parameters of appropriate ministerial speech in the South—everywhere in the South, and especially when such speech included indictments of slavery—contracted even more.

The southern crackdown on "political preachers" increased throughout the 1850s as northern antislavery and abolitionist agitators—and for our purposes, particularly activist northern clerics—received more and more attention in southern newspapers, political oratories, and denominational pulpits.[110] That crackdown demonstrated the culturally unifying power of slavery over southern Christians of every distinction. When Washington, D.C., Unitarian Reverend M. Daniel Conway, an opponent of slavery, informed his father in Falmouth, Virginia, of his plans to visit in September 1854, his father begged him to stay away. "It is my sincere advice not to come here," the elder Conway pleaded, for even "If you are willing to expose your own person recklessly, I am not willing to subject myself and family to the hazards of such a visit. Those opinions [of local ruffians] give me more uneasiness just now than your horrible views on the subject of religion, bad as these last are."[111] Conway perhaps underestimated the ever-increasing malice that southerners bore toward alleged clerical quislings. Convinced that his hometown and his own people would tolerate him, in January 1855 Conway traveled to Falmouth anyway—only to find his father's words prophetic.

As Conway walked the streets of his youth, a group of men including "former schoolmates hailed me and surrounded me" and demanded he depart Falmouth at once. Those within the crowd reminded Conway that, in addition to his title of minister, he was also politically "an abolitionist. There is danger to have that kind of man among our servants, and you must leave." Soon "a number of the rougher sort" in the mob grew more belligerent, and "crowded up, and there were threats." Reverend Conway scurried out of Falmouth, glad that he had met no real harm.[112] But when he made his way back to his own church in Washington, even the supposed liberality of Unitarianism afforded him no protection. After an 1856 sermon against slavery and the many laws and statues that propped it up, Conway's congregation was so distressed that it could not sing the traditional sermon-closing hymns. A church committee was formed to determine "whether he who thus persists in the desecration of his pulpit shall continue in the exercise of pastor." The committee and the church's membership thought not, and M. Daniel Conway was dismissed as pastor, whereupon he immediately left for Ohio.[113]

Not only did denominationally liberal southern Christians participate in the post–U.S.-Mexican War backlash against political preachers, but non-slaveholding churchmen did as well. For much of the later part of the 1850s, Wesleyan Methodist Reverend Daniel Worth boldly encouraged his antislavery church members to flee for "more congenial climes." At his prompting, by 1858 most who could afford it—nearly half of his church's total membership in all—had done just that.[114] Thus the citizens of Guilford, North Carolina, who convicted Worth of circulating copies of Hinton Rowan Helper's antislavery tome *The Impending Crisis of the South* and of preaching in a manner "to make slaves and free negroes dissatisfied with their condition" were likely unsurprised at the preacher's antics. But according to the Fayetteville, North Carolina, *Presbyterian*, the condemning jury was made up almost entirely of non-slaveholders.[115] Neither Worth's clerical collar nor the jury's mostly secondary relationship with slavery trumped the southern belief that preachers should steer clear of politics, and especially antislavery politics. The aged Worth was allowed to retire to New York, never to see his native North Carolina again.

There are instances of ministers who defied popular southern attitudes against political preaching in the 1850s and fared much worse. Methodist Reverend Solomon McKinney of Texas was given seventy lashes for his antislavery effrontery before being driven from his home and church in Dallas in 1859, while Fort Worth Methodist minister Anthony Bewley was hanged in 1860 for allegedly fomenting a would-be slave insurrection, a charge the moderate Methodist denied until his death.[116] As all of this suggests, by the close of the 1850s, southerners had rendered ministerial opposition to slavery—or as they called such behavior, political preaching—a truly dangerous endeavor. They joined in what one historian has called a broader campaign of "political, rhetorical, and social" censorship and punishment against northerners and northern sympathizers, an effort to eliminate any and all northern-born ideas that posed a threat to their way of life and beloved institutions.[117] Such measures worked to near perfection, especially within the clerical ranks.[118] As the events of the post–U.S.-Mexican War years unfolded, southern church leaders became more and more convinced that northern preachers had all but abandoned the gospel standard in favor of the political stump. They were not about to allow such a degradation to beset the South, especially when it threatened an internal attack upon slavery.

2

THE POWER AND PLACE OF THE WARTIME
NORTHERN MINISTRY

I N SHORT ORDER after Fort Sumter, Americans recognized the magnitude of the war and the unprecedented peril in which their beloved Union now stood. As they looked to the clergy for guidance, more and more of them abandoned their concerns over political preaching and grew critical of all but the most expressly patriotic preachers. By their fellow ministers, important members of the laity, and select leaders of the secular and religious presses, preachers were increasingly expected to play a key role in securing the Union's ultimate victory, and they were closely watched. Although patriotic expressions were exalted in whatever form they took and treacherous pronouncements were conversely subject to the public's disapprobation no matter from whom they came, there was no comparable public interest in the behavior of any other professional class of citizens on the homefront.[1]

Such widespread and collective attention to ministerial positions on loyalty and politics suggests the real importance of denominational ministers in mid-nineteenth-century American life. By the time of the Civil War the denominational clergy in the North was more influential in American society than ever before, a status that the Civil War only amplified. An appreciation of this clerical primacy, itself the result of the incredible expansion of denominational Christianity during the first half of the nineteenth century, allows for fresh insight into how the war blurred the lines between piety and politics, or at least explains why northern Americans of the day might have increasingly seen the two as intertwined.

I

The scope of Civil War–era ministerial prominence can best—perhaps only— be understood within the context of denominationalism.[2] Denominationalism shaped mid-century spirituality and church life in the North far more than did voluntarism, transcendentalism, and spiritualism *combined*.[3] Secularly speaking, denominationally influenced beliefs informed northern literary and intellectual thought, civic culture, and politics in fundamental ways.[4] "As a promoter of values, as a generator of print, as a source of popular music and popular artistic endeavor, and as a comforter (and agitator) of internal life," Mark Noll writes, "organized religion was rivaled in its impact only by the workings of the market, and those workings were everywhere interwoven with religious concerns."[5] Denominationalism and denominationalists were everywhere in America by the middle of the century.[6] According to the 1860 Federal census, for example, only the Nevada Territory reported no Catholic houses of worship; in the rest of the catalogued states and territories, the Catholic population was striking. There were more than 1,000 Catholic churches in just four northern states, for instance (360 in New York, 271 in Pennsylvania, 222 in Ohio, and 205 in Wisconsin).[7] Out of roughly 31 million free and enslaved Americans in 1860, 4.5 million of them were Catholics.[8]

More numerous even than American Catholics were American Protestants. In the estimation of the Federal government, there were twenty-eight distinct Protestant denominations in the United States by the end of the 1850s.[9] The names of well over four million free Americans appeared on the membership rolls of churches within these traditions (to say nothing of enslaved but nevertheless formally enrolled Protestants), but that number tells only part of the story. Historians of antebellum and Civil War–era religion use a one-for-three ratio as a rule of thumb.[10] For each recorded member of a Protestant tradition, three more Americans adhered (in a general sense) to the tenets of that denomination and attended its churches from time to time. In other words, if on some Sunday morning during the weeks leading up to the war every available seat in an American Protestant church were occupied by a free American of one Protestant persuasion or another, two-thirds of the nation's free population would have been in attendance.[11]

The denominational clergy's influence was not confined by the broad walls and heavy doors of America's Catholic and Protestant churches, however. With their oft-repeated public utterances and widely published sermons, prominent ministers informed the opinions and attitudes of the speech-listening and newspaper-reading unchurched as well.[12] After the spring of 1861, those same preachers provided men and women both inside and outside of the church a language and providential explanation with which they could make moral and spiritual sense of the unimaginable and personally overwhelming experiences of war. As Randall Miller and his fellow authors of *Unto a Good Land* remind us, most people of that era, even the unchurched, "sought or accepted generally religious explanations for the events of the time."[13] Plagued by questions about the nature of suffering and sacrifice, church and country, and even life and death, virtually *all* within the collective wartime public looked to ministers for answers.

Of course, Americans who never darkened the doors of any denominational church—be they unchurched believers, religious cultists, or outright atheists—were comparatively rare by the beginning of the Civil War, and had been for a while. Although estimates vary, it is likely that as many as 80 percent of Americans attended organized church services (some much more often than others) during the last few prewar years.[14] There remained secular scoffers, and church leaders still labored to craft an appropriate denominational response to the skepticism voiced by Charles Lyell and other late-antebellum men of science.[15] Small groups of adherents to largely mystical systems of belief like Swedenborgianism, moreover, could be found throughout the North.[16] But even those who rejected the strictures of any single tradition often joined together in groups that became de facto denominations, as with Universalists. What's more, Christian theologies that insisted on local autonomy and eschewed hierarchical fealty—as was the case with many Baptist groups, for instance—nevertheless privileged conferences that became outlets for the discussion of religious and political issues and assured among ostensibly individualistic churches a palpable degree of sameness. In an era commonly characterized as one of the most religious periods in America's national past, denominationalism clearly served as both the model for and the central arbiter of that religiousness. Between 1830 and 1860, Christian denominations effectively institutionalized religious impulses and in so doing became, as C. C. Goen puts it, the "visible framework of the social bonds created by such impulses," an association that yielded ministers an extraordinary degree of authority.[17]

Consider, for example, the Methodists. Between 1840 and 1860, Methodists of one kind or another founded at least thirty-five colleges and universities.[18] In 1850 there were 2,024 weekly papers, both secular and denominational, published in America, but only 100 of them had a circulation of more than 5,000 subscribers. The circulation of all 5 of the official weeklies published in the North by Methodist Episcopals exceeded that figure, and the church's *Christian Advocate and Journal* (New York) was 1 of but 8 weeklies in the entire country in 1850 with a circulation of more than 30,000.[19] Such denominational publications were as important as secular offerings in the lives of Christian readers because of the reader's appreciation of the publication's supposed moral virtues. As an editor of a denominational newspaper wrote in 1854, religious newspapers were returned to again and again by Christians as a sort of lens through which they viewed the world at large, often "referred to in the conversations of friends and neighbors; its opinions and statements are quoted; in fact, it comes at last to be regarded as a sort of living companion, and as an old and reliable friend."[20]

On the electoral front, Methodists dominated the congressional delegations of numerous northern states in the decade leading up to the war. In Indiana, for instance, eleven of the state's thirteen congressmen, its governor, and one of its senators were practicing Methodists in 1852.[21] And northern Methodists were not alone in their late antebellum material and political prosperity. Referencing a trend that started well before the war, historian Michael Hamilton observes that by the war's close northern "denominations enjoyed unprecedented wealth, social standing, and respectability. Episcopalians, Congregationalists, Presbyterians, Christians (Disciples), and especially the Methodists all had growing central bureaucracies, fine new church buildings, networks of colleges and seminaries, and better-educated clergy than ever before." Hamilton finds it particularly ironic that, as a result of their late antebellum and Civil War ascendency, northern "Baptists, who in their early years were a 'poor and illiterate sect' composed of a 'contemptible class of the people,' would soon count the wealthiest man on earth—John D. Rockefeller—as one of their Sunday-school teachers."[22]

Two key factors brought about denominationalism's unparalleled growth in the North in the prewar years. First, European immigration to the United States exploded. In the nine-year period encompassing the Great Irish Potato Famine and the German Revolutions of 1848 (1845 to 1854), almost three million immigrants arrived in the United States, more than had come in the previous *seven* decades combined.[23] The overwhelming majority of these post-1845 immigrants were Catholics from Ireland or one of the German states, and although a few ultimately settled in comparatively Catholic-friendly southern cities like Baltimore, Louisville, and New Orleans, most stayed in the North.[24] Northern Catholicism's immigrant-fueled expansion ruffled many Protestant and nativist feathers, but vehement anti-Catholic and anti-immigrant antagonism hardly thwarted the ascendant Catholic Church's social and political influence in the 1850s. To the contrary, nativist attacks prompted northern

Catholic leaders not only to disparage their would-be Whig, then Know-Nothing, and finally Republican oppressors, but to increasingly declare the correctness of Catholic participation in local Democratic politics as well, their aversion to political preaching not withstanding.[25] Orestes Brownson, the most influential American Catholic publisher of the age, expressed an opinion held by many fellow churchmen and women when he declared, "Catholics are better fitted by their religion to comprehend the real character of the American constitution than any other class of Americans, the moment they study it in the light of their own theology."[26]

The second reason for organized Christianity's late-antebellum surge in the North was the democratic nature of the ascendant Protestant denominations themselves. After the Revolutionary War, America fell into a pronounced religious stupor. Church historian William Warren Sweet labeled the period the most religiously dormant "in the history of American Christianity," while Sydney Ahlstrom has offered that the churches "reached a lower ebb of vitality during the two decades after" the Revolution "than at any other time in the country's religious history."[27] Once-dominant traditions like Congregationalism and Anglicanism suffered in the post–Revolutionary War decades because of their inflexible power structures and non-participatory orders of worship. In a young nation that both celebrated its own rough-hewn potency and rhetorically privileged equality, moreover, everyday Americans grew tired of predestinarian (or, strict Calvinist) doctrines that limited their individual religious potential and negated their right of spiritual self-determination. By the dawn of the nineteenth century, the nation's religious heartbeat had grown faint indeed.

But a national re-quickening of religious sentiment that scholars have coined the Second Great Awakening began in the early 1800s and started the self-styled "people's" religions on their slow but precipitous rise. Originating with emotional and extended camp meetings on the frontiers of Kentucky and Tennessee, by the 1830s the flame of evangelical revivalism had swept through much of Ohio, New York, and New England. Ministers like Charles Grandison Finney carried northern evangelicalism's banner forward, rejecting Protestantism's most Calvinistic overtones and, in their post-millennialist belief in the perfectibility of mankind, fueling the reformist ethos that in time characterized the antebellum North.[28] By roughly the late 1840s the now-dominant faith traditions in the North, Baptistism and Methodism, provided a structure of authority that allowed for advancement and accomplishment without sacrificing the sense of individualism so central to the Arminianist, "whosoever will" doctrine that post–Second Great Awakening Protestantism privileged.[29] Arminianist doctrine, in turn, jibed neatly with the prevailing northern political themes of the day. All of the successful Protestant groups of the antebellum years incorporated attractive elements of democracy into their church's hierarchical structure and daily congregational existence, elements such as church constitutions or charters, member-elected lay leaders and church counsels, and care for indigent members.

The nature of its clergy reiterated antebellum denominationalism's egalitarian sensibilities. Northern clerics in antiformalist traditions that privileged uneducated or lay ministers drawn from the people "served as a powerful symbol," as Nathan Hatch has offered of Methodist preachers, "that the wall between gentleman and commoner had been shattered," and thus they "had a great appeal for upstarts who hungered for respect and opportunity."[30] Newly dominant Baptists and Methodists therefore believed that their clergy, made up of tough-minded and principled everymen, was the antithesis of the planter-serving southern clergy. Even preachers in formalist church traditions predicated on educated clergymen, as was true of Presbyterianism, continued to educe great respect from the democracy-loving faithful throughout the late prewar years. Such reform-minded clerics exalted free labor and helped set the minds of their listeners against the perceived exploitive tendencies of the southern slaveocracy. Enjoying an ever-expanding cultural importance as its chief spokesman, preachers benefited mightily from denominationalism's flowering in the late 1840s and 1850s. But they also facilitated such growth as well.

II

The arrival of the Civil War, with its conflated political/religious meaning and its introduction of death and suffering to the American people on a new and grand scale, only increased the church's relevance in the nation's troubled affairs. To quote Abraham Lincoln, "blessed be God, who, in this our great trial giveth us the churches."[31] As America's wartime identity as a churchgoing nation broadened, so too did the already pronounced role that affiliated preachers played in the Union's spiritual and political discourse. Preachers, after all, were the indispensible point men of American denominationalism.[32] Secular figures like Wendell Phillips and others who quickly recognized that denominationalism's power must be brought to bear in the war effort believed it incumbent upon ministers, in the name of the Union, to endorse what many of them had once maligned as political preaching. "Wherever men's thoughts influence their hearts, it is the duty of the pulpit to preach politics," Phillips offered in early 1861. Loyalty and country were now the watchwords that even ministers must bear upon their lips, and those northern Christians who still valued doctrinal propriety above patriotism threatened their own nation's future in ways that southerners, presented by Phillips as being in agreement on their first principles, did not.[33]

Many prominent northern preachers urged their brother ministers to serve their countrymen and women in spiritual *and* secular ways. Henry Ward Beecher advised ministers to take the lead in forging national policy, declaring, "In a country where every citizen is called to make magistrates and laws, where he must shape policies or leave wicked men to do it, if one is bound more than another to be acquainted with public affairs, and to enlighten men concerning them, it is the religious teacher."[34] Beecher and many like him deemed support for the Union a holy effort and imagined themselves obliged to shepherd others toward this recognition. "When the question to be decided turns on moral principles, when reason, conscience, and the religious sentiments are to be addressed," a group of Presbyterian ministers offered early in the war, "*it is the privilege and duty of all . . . to bring truth to bear* on the minds of fellow citizens.[35] In the estimation of many reverends, such patriotic clerical endorsements were downright essential to victory. Writing in the war's last year, Methodist Reverend Joseph Horner of Ohio wondered if Christian principles compelled men to shun the war's violence. "We [ministers] may not teach thus," Horner asserted. "The necessities of our national existence to-day forbid such teaching. Patriotism demands that the sanctions of our holy religion be given to its [the country's] combat for humanity, unity, and stable peace."[36] The power of the pulpit, most preachers thought, was not minimized by war but made exponentially more important.[37]

The public largely conceded such eminence to ministers. Although Republican Orville Hickman Browning of Illinois made a distinction between what he deemed appropriate gospel and inappropriate partisan sermonizing, he recognized that his ideas about the minister's limited function were no longer in vogue among his beleaguered fellow Americans.[38] The majority of northern laypeople expected the preacher to offer political insight, Browning concluded, and "were disappointed" when they left services without "hearing a stump speech."[39] Throughout the Union, Christians by the millions clamored for political sermons that reminded them what the war was about. David Edwards, for instance, praised a Methodist minister, Dr. Thompson, who "preached . . . a good lecture on Slavery as the cause of our national danger," while United Brethren Cyrus Mortimer Hanby inveighed in 1862 against those "who have so become so regardless of the Constitution and laws of that country which has given them all power and position they possess."[40] Parishioners similarly looked for reassurance that their cause was too righteous to be forsaken by a just God, and therefore all with the war, despite appearances, was well. Sarah Preston Everett Hale wrote approvingly for example of Unitarian minister Samuel K. Lothrop and his sermon titled "Fight the Good Fight of Faith," in which Lothrop detailed the causes of the Union defeat at Bull Run, compared the fight to the "moral battle of life," and illuminated how the embarrassing rout prepared the way both for future Union triumph and personal spiritual victory.[41] Churchpeople found such messages appealing, for when preachers like Lothrop linked God's retribution in the present to the accomplishments of a glorified future, they tapped into the powerful millennialist beliefs that provided solace and hope to so many of their parishioners.[42]

The steadfast Reverend Lothrop was far from unique in recognizing that patriotic messages were especially resonant after great battles, be they won or lost. In the wake of Bull Run, Caroline Barrett White reported that Brookline, Massachusetts, Congregationalist minister Jeremiah Diman offered a "rousing" and "cheering sermon this morning for the times. He has the true spirit—is not to be discouraged by one defeat."[43] Waves of similar post-battle lectures followed every major turn of the war. Chambersburg, Pennsylvania, New School Presbyterian preacher Samuel J. Niccolls channeled the incensed sentiments of his denominational kinsmen in noting the repulsion of the invading southern horde after the Battle of Gettysburg. Niccolls proclaimed that "the free-soil sent forth unwonted foliage to cover their trail, and hide the wounds they had made, so that now we have scarce a sign that they were here, save where the grass grows ranker over their graves." All was as God had ordained and they as Christians, Niccolls believed, must not harbor doubt. "Nor must we, today, forget to record our gratitude for a good and stable government," Niccolls continued, "securing prosperity and protection to all alike. This is God's ordaining among us. Law has maintained its just supremacy."[44]

Like Sarah Everett Hale and Caroline Barrett White, the majority of wartime northerners desperately wanted to hear their ministers promote the cause of the United States and damn those aligned against her. As year passed into awful year, in fact, increasingly war-weary congregants on the homefront not only *wanted* but *needed* such encouragement. It was no accident that a majority of the innumerable Fast Day, Thanksgiving Day, and Sabbath Day expositions offered throughout the wartime Union dealt with loyalty.[45] In such oratories, preachers equated patriotism with true Christianity, as was true of Brooklyn's Catholic Father Joseph Fransioli and Philadelphia's Presbyterian Reverend Thomas Brainerd, both in 1863.[46] Presbyterian Reverend Samuel Spear surely spoke for most of his fellow loyal clerics in proclaiming: "The people are bound by their allegiance to the King of Kings to rise in their majesty, and swear upon the altars of their country that this rebellion shall be suppressed. They would be traitors to God, as well as man, if they did otherwise. I have hence felt it a solemn duty to speak freely and frequently upon this subject, to rebuke treason, and do all in my power to strengthen the public heart in this good work. It has seemed to me that the duties of the patriot and the Christian are in this case so identified, that in order to be the Christian consistently, one must be the patriot."[47] According to Presbyterian Reverend Samuel Dunham of New York, such patriotic ministerial influence "was made to tell mightily on the side of the Union" during the war's darkest days. "It is doubtful what might have been the fate of our government," Dunham remembered long after the fact, "had not the patriot heart of the country been continually fired by the eloquent pleas of the pulpit."[48] Without doubt, Dunham was right. The clergy's pulpit offerings mattered a great deal in the embattled Union.

Wartime ministerial importance was conveniently portable, and the words of loyal sermonizers sometimes helped maintain homefront harmony even when they strayed from their own familiar lecterns. Near the front lines, devoted clerics lent a degree of calm to chaotic conditions brought on by the unprecedented realities of war. United Brethren minister-in-training George A. Funkhouser, for instance, preached at revivals open to soldiers and civilians near his camp in southern Pennsylvania in 1862. Funkhouser wrote of the tumult that news of the impending draft had stirred. "I never saw such a time among the people—Many a mother's heart trembles for fear her son and husband will be drafted. I preached several times at this to the best of my abilities." Funkhouser's efforts proved effective, for he reported in the same journal entry, "I never attended church meetings in this district [in which] we had better order."[49]

In New York City, Catholic Archbishop John J. Hughes traveled some of Gotham's grimiest streets promoting Irish-American military enlistments. Because of his anti–Emancipation Proclamation opinions and his delay and then diffidence in speaking against the 1863 draft riots, Hughes's importance to the Union war effort (as both a recruiter at home and an emissary abroad) is occasionally overlooked. The sometimes controversial Archbishop Hughes was an unequivocal patriot, however, and was no doubt personally responsible for the presence of tens of thousands of men in the Federal ranks.[50] Others helped defuse incendiary situations. In October 1862, when Irish coal miners in Cass Township in Schuylkill County, Pennsylvania, gathered in protest of the Federal draft, Catholic Bishop Father James Frederic Wood of Philadelphia arrived in time to address the would-be rioters and diffuse the situation. After the danger of an armed uprising had passed, Pennsylvania Governor Andrew Curtin asserted, "the decision and promptness, but more the presence of Bishop Wood, who kindly went up when requested, has relieved us all."[51] In nineteenth-century America and especially during the Civil War, the clout of the cloth was not confined by the four walls of the local church. Preachers were interpreters who outlined the righteous causes of the war and made sense of the unimaginable carnage it had produced, counselors who encouraged personal devoutness while demanding unwavering political allegiance, and mollifiers who brought calm to panic and reassurance to the troubled minds of their own parishioners and strangers alike. And in all of these homefront roles, parsons enhanced their significance in northern society.

President Lincoln understood that preachers became, with war, the bellwethers of American popular opinion. According to Richard Carwardine, Lincoln therefore "worked hard to keep open two-way channels with the leaders of this influential constituency, and to deal sensitively and respectfully with them, aware not only of their power but also of the deep reservoir of goodwill on which he could draw." Lincoln was unwilling to see the Union's future victory endangered by concerns over religious freedom. That said, the president accommodated preachers whenever practical, recognizing that his relationship with clergymen "provided him with a way of both reading and reaching potent opinion-formers."[52] Thus when President Lincoln struggled with the implications and justifications of a presidential declaration on emancipation, he met with several ministers in the spring and summer of 1862. Lincoln earnestly sought both spiritual insight and an understanding of the political attitudes of Christians, by far the Union's largest identifiable constituency. His approach worked. By the time the attentive Lincoln issued the preliminary Emancipation Proclamation in September 1862, he knew full well that the measure's best chance of success stemmed from its "fusing Christian emancipationist sentiment with loyalty to republican free will."[53] Moreover, by entertaining the supplications of ministers—who in some cases informed the opinions of thousands of congregants each Sunday—and factoring their concerns into his actions, Lincoln all but ensured the proclamation's widespread endorsement by the Protestant mainstream which, in turn, shaped the broader political reaction of the nation as a whole.[54]

Clearly, President Lincoln grasped a key truth. Preachers on the homefront were collectively the most politically determinative force within affiliated American Christianity, the only members of the greater church family who exercised significant *yet immediate* authority over others. True enough, national church bodies often crafted their denomination's published political rhetoric. But national bodies could not match the cleric's direct impact upon the populace because churchwide edicts and dictates were almost always delivered—and thus interpreted—by occupants of the local pulpit. And while lay members carried their church's tenets into the streets, their homes, and onto faraway battlefields, the laity's understanding of those tenets was largely shaped by the instructive offerings of more accomplished denominational figures. True enough, national religious figures routinely made their way into the denominational press and thus shaped church members' opinions. They did not do so half as much, however, as did local ministers under whose voices millions of Americans sat each Sunday. In the world of wartime denominationalism, only preachers on the homefront could both defy their superiors and directly preach the elements of that defiance to their followers, and only they could argue in earnest (if in error, perhaps) that the nature and tradition of their priestly office afforded them the right.

3

PARTISANSHIP AND POTENTIAL DAMAGE
Why Americans Feared "Disloyal" Preachers

I N MOST CASES, northern ministers supported the Union war effort and the Lincoln administration and worked doggedly to sustain the resolve of both citizens at home and soldiers in the field. Some clerics, however, spoke ill of the president and other political leaders or highlighted northern societal inequities in positing that the Union's shortcomings might very well bring about its own defeat. And still other clergymen, at least in sentiment if less often in deed, were openly disloyal to the Union. Much can be learned about the margins of loyalty in the wartime Union by examining how such politically wayward preachers were identified in public discourse. The behavior that provoked condemnation depended upon a loose interpretation of what made for treasonous behavior. In one very broad respect, however, that interpretation was unambiguous. Christian patriots expressly linked speech from the pulpit with the preservation of the Union. Religious worship and political speech were not free when they conflicted with the security of the country.

Northerners believed that the exigencies of war made an already influential clergy even more vital to the nation's health and well-being. Of whom much is given, however, much is expected. Northern preachers were not granted societal primacy with impunity but were instead expected to meet the Unionist demands of their political chiefs, church hierarchies, local members, and fellow citizens. Toward that end and from the war's outset, loyal Christians and secular leaders in the Union kept a keen ear out for ministerial treachery. Be they anti-administration partisans, antiwar conciliationists, or blatant pro-Confederates, all sorts of clerical nonconformists were scrutinized.[1] Such vigilance was considered well founded, for as Episcopal Bishop William Jay observed in the 1850s, even in the North the churches were filled with "fallible and sinful men," and thus perfidious pastors had been with them always and would ever be.[2] The attention paid to ministers was often not meant to exonerate those under suspicion but instead to confirm, at least in the minds of their accusers, their disloyalty. And many ministers were weighed in the balance and found wanting. As Ohio Presbyterian Reverend R. L. Stanton noted in 1864, "The great body of the clergy of all denominations in the loyal states, have unquestionably been loyal to the General Government. But not a few, and among them men of ability and influence, have shown decided sympathy with the rebellion."[3]

Many in the Union looked to clergymen for hope and sustenance it is true, but they also recognized that ministerial influence could prove as malevolent as it was mollifying. There was a society-wide campaign to check such negative influences by proscribing supposed disloyal preachers in the North. But before a cleric could be reviled, he had to be revealed. If Reverend Stanton was correct and more than a few homefront preachers were disloyal, how did he and other Americans find out about them? What kind of rhetoric did Americans listen for when they eavesdropped on homefront churches and oratory halls in the effort to identify clerical sedition, and what potential acts of clerical disloyalty did they most fear? In short, why did loyal Americans fear disloyal clergymen to begin with? Both ministerial behavior and what that behavior meant to northerners who pored over such words and deeds situate preachers squarely in the middle of wartime concerns over internal security, a positioning long overdue.[4] Americans in the Union acted out of both political partisanship and reasonable fears of the impact disloyal preachers might have on critical wartime variables like recruitment, troop and homefront commitment, and enemy morale. They were aided in their identification efforts by the leaders of their political parties, the editors of the newspapers that they read, and by their own determinative ideas about citizenship.

I

A dominant theme of this study is the religious sincerity of the positions often taken by believers before and during the Civil War. And yet, clergymen accused of disloyalty were routinely Democrats, and those doing the accusing were just as routinely Republicans. As with most aspects of mid-nineteenth-century American life, partisanship played a role in what preachers said and how their words were received. Because of their political beliefs and attachments, Civil War–era clergymen were maligned by critics who sometimes found it unnecessary to separate a minister's political affiliation from his assumed disloyal opinions on the monumental issues of the day. Many Republican Christians thus surely offered a heartfelt amen to the unidentified preacher who wrote in the widely read *Harper's Weekly* in 1864, "In a civil war men must be judged and treated according to the colors they show. If they choose the enemy's colors they must expect . . . the treatment of an enemy." Such colors were apparently donned exclusively by Democrats, for "Clearly, when political differences have ended in civil war, no earnest, devoted man . . . will wish to associate familiarly either with those who are so shallow as not to feel the terrible reality of the condition, or [with] those whose sympathies belong to the party which he opposes with arms."[5] And while true for all politically dissenting churchmen, Democratic ministers were especially targeted for their political proclivities by Republican members who believed such penchants indicated treachery.

Northern churchmen and women increasingly conflated support of President Lincoln and his administration's war policies with church loyalty and Christian righteousness. As adherents of America's dominant faith traditions conferred upon the Republican Party the mantle of true religion, then, the Democratic minority—both within and outside of their church and especially in the ministry—came under increased religious scrutiny. Bryon C. Andreasen offers that "during the war, a kind of super-patriotism became the standard fare of evangelical sermons, as ministers and laymen alike championed a 'Holy War' interpretation of the struggle." In such a climate, clerics who engaged in ostensibly *political* acts like criticizing President Lincoln or critiquing Republican war policies were considered *religiously* blasphemous. In fact, the very Christianity of divines who offered such utterances, or conversely, refused to offer countervailing endorsements of Abraham Lincoln and the war from behind their pulpit, was routinely assumed specious.[6]

Be they as large as the *New York Tribune* and *Philadelphia Press* or as small as the *Beaver Argus* (Beaver Falls, Pennsylvania), prowar newspapers proved instrumental in campaigns to identify and indict such Democratic clergy.[7] Routinely observed by the editors of such publications was the hypocrisy of those Democrats and southern sympathizers who railed against political preachers most stridently. A writer in the *Philadelphia Press*, for instance, voiced a commonly heard charge during the war when he noted that Democratic ministers abhorred political preaching when "politics means Union, and loyalty, and devotion to the sacred cause of Government," but when the preacher's own traitorous leanings are being proffered, "his idea does not prevent him from polluting the sacred desk with diatribes against the Government, and sneers at its rulers."[8] Later in the war a writer in the

Republican *Franklin Repository* of Chambersburg, Pennsylvania, identified the same trend. "Wherever you find a man sincerely and unequivocally loyal," the unidentified pundit wrote, "there you find one who receives 'aid and comfort' from the religious sentiment of the people, thus expressed through the churches." Such uplifting manifestations of Christian sustenance were however disdained by traitors, or so the essayist believed. "On the other hand," he continued, "when you meet with a man openly and avowedly disloyal, there will you find one who accuses the church and her ministers of 'fanaticism' and of 'mixing up politics with religion' in passing such resolutions as she has done on the state of the country."[9]

Arguably the best, and certainly the most biting, accusation of Democratic hypocrisy on the subject of political preaching was offered by an anonymous South Dakotan, who listed the founding principles of the New Church, described by the acerbic westerner as the "Copperhead Church," as:

1. No political preaching tolerated—except for "Peace Democracy."
2. No agitation of the slavery question—except in favor of it.
3. No church action in favor of the war—except against the Government.
4. No politicians admitted to the church—except peace Democrats.
5. "The Gospel" only to be preached—that is, the divinity of slavery, the innocence of rebels, and the exceeding wickedness of abolitionists.
6. The "salvation of the world," through faith in Christ,—except "niggers."
7. Christ came into the world to save sinners—except "niggers and abolitionists."
8. "Peace and good will to men," especially rebels and traitors, but slavery for "niggers" and damnation here, and hereafter, to Black Republicans and War Democrats.[10]

Not only did most within the secular Republican press question the objectivity of a given Democrat's particular charge against political preachers, many editors impugned the religious sincerity of their foes. "It is a little singular," a secular Republican columnist offered in 1864, "that many of those persons who seem to care so greatly for the godly reputation of the ministry are seldom in church, but may often be found at the drinking saloon and the theatre, while others of them [who] are church members are not generally . . . the most pious of all professious [*sic*] of religion."[11] A writer in *Harper's Weekly* noted that accusations "about political preaching proceeds from people whose party discipline requires the support of slavery, and who therefore insist that because politics have touched the subject it has ceased to be a moral question." Did such apparently indulgent Democrats, the writer wondered, object to "preaching against swearing, or lying, or thieving, or profaning the Sabbath day by reading novels?" He answered his own query snidely, "Oh no; that is legitimate preaching. But if old Rum Puncheon hears a clergyman denounce drunkenness and the makers of drunkards he rises, and thumps down the aisle, and bangs out at the door, and wishes the parson wouldn't preach those d——d political sermons. . . . It is remarked that horses always spring if you touch them on the raw."[12]

In the estimation of undeniably biased Republican editors, hypocrisy on the part of Democratic preachers rendered their ostensibly peace-loving piety questionable and their concern for the integrity of the clergy little more than sounding brass and tinkling cymbals. Republican commentators charged that Janus-faced Democrats hurt the cause of righteousness by failing to recognize the evils of secession and disunion. As the Republican editors of *The Agitator* (Wellsboro, Pennsylvania) put it early in the war, the Union cause was sacred, and patriotism and Christianity were inseparably linked; therefore "at such a time, my brethren, the King of peace Himself calls 'to arms,' and war becomes a part of religion, and 'cursed is he that keepeth back his sword from blood.'"[13] Even moderate Republican newspapers like the *Philadelphia Press* (whose editors admitted that the general "objection in the minds of the people against ministerial interference with politics" was not unjust when sincere) linked the appropriateness of ministerial political consciousness to the godliness of the cause. "We, therefore," a *Press* writer offered in late 1861, "read of the exertions of the ministry with peculiar pleasure. Let these gentlemen go on in their good work. A man will fight better who prays to God and keeps his powder dry." Such men of conviction knew their duty as Christians and citizens and soldiers because they understood what the war meant. "Above all," the anonymous columnist observed of the politically aware preacher, "he has the conscience of this fight, and in the rebellion we want men who feel the principles at stake, and appreciate the holy cause for which they fight."[14]

It is worth remembering that the Civil War was not, after all, simply a political event but also a religious crisis, especially perhaps for those denominationalists on the northern homefront who were constantly forced to defend their very Christianity because of their politics. Certainly Democratic ministers in the North, the majority of whom supported the Union if not always the Lincoln administration's prosecution of the war, recognized that they were under siege and responded accordingly. Fortunately for them, they did not have to craft that defense out of whole cloth but could instead recycle many of the elements of their campaigns against political preaching of the antebellum years. Wartime Democrats in the church deflected Republican criticisms, according again to Bryon Andreasen, by "attacking the moral pretensions of the religious majority; by attacking the behavior of the politicized clergy; by contesting the moral high ground through proclaiming Christian peace initiatives; by declaiming a general social declension in the North they attributed to an illicit merger of church and state perpetrated by the religious majority."[15] This ploy by Democrats imitated the conflating tendencies of their Republican antagonists. Just as Republicans commonly asserted that Democrats, traitors, and slave owners were one and the same, Democrats equated Republicans with abolitionists, warmongers, and race-betrayers.

Democratic newspapers throughout the North played a key role in the *defense* of the Democratic ministry by going *on the offensive* against Republican ministers who were overtly political. Two themes, the destruction of first the country and then the church, were most common in their rhetoric. Democratic newspapermen constantly pointed out how prevalent political preachers were and linked their rise in number to the coming of the war and the general ruination of the country. As was true of the editors of scores of other partisan papers in the North, the publishers of a wartime New Jersey newspaper stated their conviction "that the distraction of our country has been produced by introducing politics in the pulpit, and ministers of the Gospel ignoring the teachings of Christ and becoming political haranguers, both in the meeting on the Lord's Day and at other times."[16] Another columnist in Pennsylvania observed that "the power of politicians wearing clerical robes to do mischief within the domain of republican institutions, has already been felt among us, and has pretty generally aroused a feeling against them." Given as much, he continued, "it becomes our highest duty to destroy their influence . . . and let them make their living as best they can, outside the church and pulpit."[17] Further representative of this mentality was a reporter in Cincinnati's conservative *Inquirer*. Characterizing antislavery Archbishop John Baptist

Purcell and his underlings as "bloodthirsty incendiaries," the angry chronicler asserted that history would note among "the darkest features of this period the cruelty of an inexorable priesthood, which, when the war lagged, howled on the fainting champions to their bloody work" and "cried out, in the name of God, for more and more revolting sacrifices."[18]

Conservative secular editors habitually linked Republican clergymen to all of the evils in the country that had presumably brought on the war. Although the purveyors of such evils—particularly abolitionists but also parsons who had for instance decried the U.S.-Mexican War and vociferously opposed the Fugitive Slave and Kansas-Nebraska acts—were considered dastardly alike, and the politicized preacher was cast in a darker light than all others. "These impertinent clerical babblers are destroying religion," one editor wrote, "and doing more to destroy the country than all the other causes combined."[19] Secular Democratic newspaper publishers, editors, and contributors took upon themselves the role of defender of the Christian faith against what one called the "leaven of infidelity which is sapping the foundations of Christianity, and with it law and order and all respect for authority."[20]

Secular newspaper writers in the wartime North noted the debilitating impact political preaching had not only on the nation's harmony but on the gospel charter of the churches as well. "The Sabbath was made for religion," an editor reminded his readers midway through the war, but Republican preachers had "degraded it to a day of political conventions."[21] Most Democrats accused radicals of such degradations. They claimed, in the words of a Pennsylvania redactor, that "the attack of the infidel forces was directed as fiercely against the church as against the Union, and it is to be feared that they have succeeded in doing almost as great injury to one as to the other."[22] A commentator in an Ohio Democratic paper observed, moreover, "It is surprising that preachers cannot see and understand that they are doing irreparable mischief wherever they attempt to dictate to their hearers and congregations on the subject of politics. They are breaking up and disorganizing churches all over the country."[23]

Especially as the 1864 presidential election neared, purveyors of Democratic papers cautioned that the true church was being destroyed by radical Republican political actors. Representative of such views, a New York editor in 1864 warned, "In the eyes of those who have the one fanatical idea which lies at the basis of the Republican party . . . the interests of the Church of Christ, its purity and peace, and its onward progress in the salvation of men and the renovation of the world are of no account." Christians were, the indignant layman continued, the pawns of Republican politicians "who are using them as a stalking horse on which to ride into power."[24] Another Democratic editor echoed such notions by relating a November 1864 incident in which a vile Republican minister had "[u]ndertook to instruct his listeners *how to vote!* He in effect stated that all who did not vote for Abraham Lincoln would be eternally damned! Did mortal man ever hear of such a bold and shameless assumption? . . . Where does he find his authority for making the political opinions of a man the ground of his damnation? . . . We are astonished that Christian professors can countenance such a mockery of religion—such a prostitution of the sacred office of the ministry—such a violation of the holy Sabbath day—such a desecration of the pulpit and sanctuary of the most High God!"[25]

Sometimes exaggerated no doubt, these stories reflected simple but likely sincere beliefs. Many in the wartime North feared that politicized ministers were leading men into the political arena instead of into the light of salvation. As one editor accused, "in place of preaching 'peace and good will among men,'" politicized preachers "take every occasion, in and out of the pulpit, to excite their hearers to deeds of hate and carnage . . . if they are not of the class denounced in the Scriptures as 'Wolves in Sheep's Clothing' then we know of nothing to which these terms can be applied with appropriateness."[26] Expanding the analogy, a Centre County (Pennsylvania) Democrat accused political preachers of being "no longer true pastors and preachers, trying to save souls by instilling righteous precepts and desires—but human tigers howling for blood—'wolves in sheep's clothing,' 'roaring lions, seeking whom they may devour.'"[27] Political preachers jeopardized souls, Democrats believed, for in addition to replacing the saving gospel with vile politics in their offerings to the wayward, their actions divided the brethren, bringing "estrangement of the members of the church, and often, final outbreaks."[28] In all this, secular Democratic editors essentially charged Republican clergymen with both breaking holy bonds between men and destining the unchurched to ignorance and condemnation.

II

Republicans maligned Democratic ministers from the pulpit, pew, and printed page during the Civil War. And the democracy often gave as well as it received. Given partisanship's hold on Civil War–era denominationalists and the influential secular press of the day, it is difficult to know when an accused preacher's political affiliations alone were at the heart of the charges against him. Because the terms "disloyalty" and "treason" were used almost interchangeably in documents from the period and because treason is narrowly defined in the Constitution as an act of levying war against the United States, some scholars have assumed that most public accusations of disloyalty or treason on the northern homefront were for political effect only.[29] But the proscription and harassment of disloyal ministers was more than an outgrowth of political biases *in its entirety,* as is suggested by two important qualifications.

First, there were acknowledged patriots and Christians within the Democratic Party, men whose national and religious fidelity were equally unassailable. Staunch Episcopalian and Secretary of War Edwin M. Stanton, for instance, was not just any Democrat but was the single most visible prosecutor of disloyalists in all of the Union. Stanton was joined in the Christian and prowar Democratic ranks by dozens of notable figures, including military leaders like Benjamin Butler and John Logan and politicians like Governors John Brough of Ohio and Joel Parker of New Jersey.[30] Republican churchpeople who lumped generic Democrats and traitors together in their public and religious rhetoric must have therefore recognized—at least when dealing with individual ministers or churchpeople—that all Democrats were not *by definition* traitors.

Secondly, mid-nineteenth-century churchpeople and really all Americans used terms like "traitor" and "treason" in earnest. Antebellum Americans in the main believed they had both a right and the ability to interpret the Constitution for themselves, a legacy of Jacksonian democracy.[31] According to constitutional scholar James Viator, the antebellum everyman was a "teleological or telic" interpretivist who "read the Constitution in light of the great goals and ends of government enshrined in the Declaration of Independence" and "looked to the overarching goals and purposes for which the Constitution was devised and the boundaries it set against not only the judicial will but the wills of all citizens."[32] This big-picture approach spared antebellum Americans from the need to be familiar with the Constitution's finer points and was largely independent of education or even literacy, to say nothing of facilitating broad constitutional interpretations that could prop up virtually any viewpoint. In short, antebellum Americans invoked the

Constitution with a feeling of ownership that Americans today can scarcely imagine. Among those affiliated with the North's ascendant denominational churches, a special sense of constitutional familiarity developed as a result of the judiciary's tendency to let laws and statutes privileging Christianity go unchecked. According to legal expert Donald Drakeman, in fact, "The most noteworthy aspect of church-state litigation in the first half of the nineteenth-century was that there really was none to speak of." Aside from a few verdicts in support of anti-blasphemy laws and other seemingly pro-religious statutes, the antebellum courts were remarkably silent on church-related issues.[33]

And so, mid-century Americans who maligned a minister as a traitor meant no hyperbole; when it came to the Constitution, they believed they knew what they were talking about. The Constitution states that "Treason against the United States, shall consist only in levying War against them, or in adhering to their Enemies, giving them Aid and Comfort. No Person shall be convicted of Treason unless on the Testimony of two Witnesses to the same overt Act, or on Confession in open Court."[34] In America only those who confess to or are caught in a treasonous act—an act moreover that is both overt and verifiable by two or more witnesses—can be reasonably tried for treason. During the Civil War, the act of "levying war" against the United States was easily discernible; the Supreme Court had ruled in 1807's *Ex Parte Bollman* that "there must be an actual assembling of men, for the treasonable purpose, to constitute a levying of war."[35]

But what of giving "Aid and Comfort" to the enemy, in this case, the Rebels? And, what constituted an overt act? Americans had always privileged these more nebulous aspects of treason's legal definition.[36] The vagaries of the Constitution's "aid and comfort" passage had for instance facilitated the enactment of the Alien and Sedition Acts and added to the uproar over the Hartford Convention, two events that Unionists knew well and referenced often in indicting disloyalists. Most believed that unfaithful northern preachers buoyed flagging Confederate spirits and emboldened internal quislings through their treasonous language. The large audiences that preachers often addressed assured that there was nothing covert about their treasonous sermons, moreover, a truth further established by the wide-scale press coverage such oratories elicited.

The public's notion that rhetoric fell within the wartime definition of treason was seconded in the nation's courts. In his instructions to a grand jury in 1863, for example, Massachusetts District Judge Peleg Sprague noted that "for more than seventy years" the national government had afforded potential traitors too much leeway in response to the people's fears of an overly intrusive Federal authority. As a result, Americans had "seen incitements to rebellion by every air that that could mislead the mind, or inflame the passions."[37] Indeed the prewar "Criminal Code," Sprague pointed out, "touched no measure that had not ripened into an overt act of levying war, or actual interference with the administration of the law." But the "breaking out of this rebellion" changed things, Sprague declared, and since the war's outset Congress had passed numerous laws and statutes—loyalty oaths, for instance—that were not *just* reactionary, but also preventative.[38] Proscribing what was said as well as what was done, such "statutes reach the incipient steps," Sprague pointed out, "which lead to resistance and rebellion."[39]

Both in and out of church and no matter how partisan, northerners who spoke of ministerial treason did so based on what they imagined were actionable offenses and identifiable behaviors. Peleg Sprague's conceptualization of treason held sway in the Union, reproving preachers and politicians who spoke to the assembled masses in unambiguous terms against the United States. But significantly, Sprague's fellow northerners recognized that his theorized "incipient steps" toward rebellion could be made in both obvious and obscure ways. Consider another quote from the Reverend R. L. Stanton. Northern ministers, Stanton wrote, displayed their disloyal colors "sometimes in overt acts, often in speech and in their writings . . . and sometimes by a reticence which has been quite as significant as any open line of conduct."[40] The Ohio Presbyterian's words give testament to two types of disloyal speech in the wartime North: the expressed and the implied. Northerners who referenced these categories in their indictments of ministers were universally understood, for the concepts of expressed and implied disloyalty were known and used during the Civil War by church leaders, politicians, and members of the secular public alike.[41] Weighed within the balance of expressed and implied ministerial disloyalty, some pronouncements were too bluntly treasonous to be misconstrued while other determinations depended on the opinion of the person making the assessment.

Disloyalty was of course assumed when ministers called for the Union's military defeat, the establishment of an independent Confederacy, or after the Emancipation Proclamation, the preservation and expansion of southern slavery. However, some preachers were castigated for advocating a conciliatory policy toward what they believed was a mistreated South even as they insisted that their loyalties were with the Union. Walking such a rhetorical razor's edge was the unnamed Catholic clergyman who "advocated the rights of the South against the fanaticism of the North unflinchingly" and in that advocacy pledged, "What the South wants the Government to do, in reason, we will urge the Government to do." Nevertheless, he was quick to add that the current state of affairs left him no recourse but hoping for Confederate defeat, declaring that he could not "endorse the caprice that would pull down the building which shelters us all. . . . WE MUST HAVE GOVERNMENT."[42] Most northerners ignored the nuances of southern-centric viewpoints and instead assumed that such lukewarm patriotism was no patriotism at all.

Other preachers spoke ill of the president (and, less often, members of the administration and Union military command) or otherwise highlighted northern iniquities to show how wrongheaded leaders and societal shortcomings might bring about Union defeat. These sermonic observations, their pronouncers held, were not disloyal as much as they were instructive. In one such case in Newark, New Jersey, Unionist churchgoers insisted that Episcopal Reverend Edward Josiah Stearns, a visiting cleric from Maryland, had, "in his discourse pointedly justified the course of the South, and denounced the North." The response of those in attendance on that early fall morning in 1861 varied. Some hissed, others got up and left, and the church's vestrymen "demanded and procured the manuscript, which has been laid before the United States District Attorney."[43] Reverend Stearns claimed his sermon contained no justification of the South, "the whole question of the right or the wrong of that course having been purposely left untouched," and was instead a primer on the North's sins.[44] Criticisms of the United States from the pulpit were not uncommon during the war. Truly, given the Jeremiad tradition that had always existed in American Christianity, they were to be expected. American ministers had bemoaned the immoral state of American society and predicted its related downfall since long before the Revolutionary War. But war constricted the limits of acceptable clerical criticism. It mattered little to most Americans how blatantly or subtly political a sermon was if and when the assumed sentiment behind it was infidelity to the Union. The war was to be won and the Union preserved. Civil liberties and religious freedoms were to be honored when convenient, but the Union was not to be sacrificed on its own principled sword.

Conciliatory tones and Jeremiads were not all that could cause a preacher's loyalty to be questioned. Many ministers retained their prewar aversions to discussing politics. Some were sincerely motivated by religious principles, but others no doubt believed that silence was their only tenable means of opposing the Union effort. Most avid patriots in the pews suspected as much of mainstream denominational preachers when they refused, in their sermons, to damn the South and extol the virtues of the Union. As famed editor of the *Philadelphia Press* John W. Forney offered in 1864, "I repeat what I have so frequently said, and always believed, that there is no creature more infamous, no wretch more debased, than he who, appointed to administer and to illustrate the work of God, ascends the pulpit and refuses to denounce this war against the only really Christian Government on the face of the earth. The crime of such a man is a greater crime and a greater scandal when he remains in a loyal State."[45] Offended church members did not care if a preacher's silence or vagueness was rooted in his ideas about the absolute separation of the church and the state or in his conceptualization of a Christian's separate duties. Because of the exaggerated clerical importance that the war had brought about, most northerners now believed that ministerial endorsements of their country and damning of its foes were not just appropriate but were in truth crucial acts, be they political or otherwise.

The same wartime clerical importance that prompted northerners to demand patriotic pronouncements from their preachers likewise caused them to fear that disloyal ministers would prove especially detrimental to the maintenance of the Union war effort. Although historians have acknowledged a meaningful degree of Unionist clerical opposition in the Upper Confederacy, none has adequately considered the role that ministers played in fomenting wartime dissent in the Union. Northerners, however, knew better. Again to quote the prominent John W. Forney, "What sort of loyalty can be expected of a congregation that sits under the teaching and preaching of a clergyman, calling himself a divine, who refuses to condemn this sacrilegious warfare against freedom and against God, or who openly sustains it? With a dishonest shepherd you cannot expect a pious and faithful flock."[46] As this quote intimates, two characteristics of the clergy compelled the administration, church hierarchies, and public to take seriously the threat posed by disloyal preachers, even those who hailed from non–border states. First, ministers had the public's ear. Exceeded only by politicians in their ability to address the masses, pastors of even small congregations were often heard by thousands over the course of a year. Secondly, their words carried the weight of religious propriety. Men and women who would not abide disloyal talk in the streets were more likely to listen to such counsel from the pews given the respect enjoyed by the local parson. Unionists believed that disloyal clergymen, like water against the rock, wore down their more persuadable congregants.

The sheer number and broad geographic scope of suspected disloyal ministers was startling to most. Clerics like Hartford, Illinois, Methodist Oliver H. McCuen; New Jersey Presbyterian Samuel Jones; Philadelphia Protestant Episcopal J. W. Cracraft; and Washington, D.C., Presbyterian John H. Bocock and Episcopalian William Norwood were a few of the numerous suspected disloyal ministers whose stories were featured in northern secular and denominational newspapers, public lecture halls, and pulpits.[47] These anti-Union men were believed to cause damage even when they failed to convert the whole of their flock to their political beliefs. Within a common body of churchmen and women, it was feared, divided ministerial allegiances routinely bred heated strife and eventually split even devout groups of believers, eventually jeopardizing both the parent denomination's national or regional scope of influence and the spirituality of individuals as well.

Common were complaints like the one voiced in New York by German Methodist Bishop W. W. Orwig in 1863. Orwig had "reason to lament the fact that . . . individual members, and, in some cases, larger portions of the congregations, have suffered themselves to be led astray . . . into unbecoming censures of our Federal Government" and in so doing had "themselves suffered injury to their souls, and some have made a shipwreck of their faith, and have fallen prey to Satan and the world."[48] Clearly, church leaders like Orwig understood that, if weak-minded individual members and larger portions of local congregations were being "led astray" into disloyalty, perfidious local ministers did the leading. Echoing the Bishop's lamentation, a group of Methodists who met later that same year in Buffalo voiced deep regret that some ministers had allowed themselves to be carried away by party strife and indulged in sermonizing characterized by "contemptuous epithets" that "ferment discord, and alienate brotherly feeling to such a degree that the interests of religion and the country become secondary maters." The Methodists avowed that treacherous behavior of this ilk was particularly "culpable and unworthy a Christian and especially a minister."[49]

Concerns about the impact of disloyal preachers went beyond the belief that they splintered congregations and contributed to apathy on the northern homefront. Civil and church authorities feared that rebellious ministers boosted the morale of the southern enemy. Surely, their reasoning went,

Confederates read of the disloyalty that plagued northern Christianity and interpreted this as proof of the divine sanctification of their own cause. Especially in the border Union, moreover, traitorous preachers were thought not only to facilitate, but also to incite, the treasonous acts of their members. By preaching against the Federal draft, unfaithful clerics caused able-bodied men to avoid service as soldiers. In a popular 1864 poetic indictment, an unnamed patriot provided a litany of these and other sins most often ascribed to (literally) Rebel-rousing rectors:

Copperhead Sneaks

You that incited rebellion and treason;
You that have aided it all that you can;
You that have fought against conscience and reason,
And all of the rights that are sacred to man. . . .
    . . .
You that have aided this carnage and plunder;
You that have urged a resistance to draft;
Open your eyes with abhorrence and wonder!
Can you see who so long have been daft?
Mobbing and riots will bring retribution;
Stand by the laws and the old Constitution,
Cowardly Copperheads crawl to your holes!
    Holes! holes! holes! h-o-l-e-s![50]

As "Copperhead Sneaks" confirms, loyal northerners believed a day of retribution for politically treacherous ministers was on its way. Soldiers in the field, privy to the dealings of suspect sermonizers back home, especially hoped that day was fast approaching. Church-based disputes over ministerial loyalty gave men in the ranks reason to question the homefront clergy's level of commitment to the war effort. Pennsylvanian Colonel Daniel Leasure of the 100th Pennsylvania wrote, "We know what we are fighting for, and we know that Copperheads are the most dangerous enemies our country has. May the curse of our country's God pursue them to dishonourable graves and the black and begrimed grandfather of all traitors sit cross legged on their tombstones and snigger over them."[51] Similarly scornful of disloyalists in the church, Private James Stewart of the Pennsylvania Light Artillery encouraged his mother to change her church of record, writing, "I despise rebels of any kind, and I think the church in Pittsburgh is a little on the Rebel principle of the Confederate States."[52] A Philadelphian identified only as "J.H." wrote the editors of the *Philadelphia Press* to praise the ban imposed in Alexandria, Virginia, upon a disloyal Baptist preacher by Colonel Edgar Gregory of Philadelphia's own 91st Pennsylvania. J.H. noted, however, that homefront clerics just as guilty of treason were too often left unmolested for doing the same. Accusing Allegheny City Presbyterian Reverend William Swan Plumer of treachery, J.H. wondered, "Does not equal justice require that he too should be silenced? Shall he be permitted, even in this indirect way, to give aid and comfort to the enemy? Is a traitor in Allegheny town entitled to greater lenity than a traitor in Alexandria?"[53]

In rare instances, something other than a preacher's words or silences sealed his fate. In addition to the discord disloyal preachers fomented, clergymen even in the Upper North could be dangerous as potential fifth columnists. By definition itinerant preachers were mobile, certainly more so than most within the general population, and carried information from point to point. When Swedenborgian clergyman Sabin Hough ran afoul of authorities in Ohio in 1861, for instance, letters of supposedly treasonous content from the likes of Clement Vallandigham were found on his person.[54] Undeterred, upon his release Hough continued his dubious ministry throughout the Ohio Valley. His seditious career culminated in his participation as courier in a complex conspiracy to rescue Confederate prisoners from Camp Chase in Columbus, Ohio. According to a writer in *Harper's Weekly,* "prisoners once out with their axes were to be provided with arms, and then they were to storm the penitentiary, release John Morgan and other Confederate officers, and the whole party was then to start for the Ohio River and cross near Maysville." C. W. H. Cathcart, the would-be leader of the raid, was to receive a commission in the Confederate States Army as reward for his services. Cathcart and other principles of the plan were arrested at Hough's house.[55] "If such clergymen do not wear hemp," quipped a New York columnist in reference to Hough, "there is no use cultivating the crop."[56]

Patriots knew what to listen for in their efforts to locate ministers who were cut from the wrong kind of cloth. And they knew why such disloyal preachers were to be feared. Treacherous congregational pastors who sapped their congregants' commitment to the war effort were threats to the Union. Even without church members to corrupt, moreover, disaffected clerics like the minister-spy Sabin Hough lessened the nation's chance of victory. In the estimation of Union-loving denominationalists who now believed that both their church *and* their nation were consecrated entities, disloyal ministers everywhere and of every ilk compromised the health of the church and the life of the country and were thus doubly damnable for their betrayal. They would in time, it was hoped by loyal northerners, be justly rewarded.

4

THE ASSAULT ON DISLOYALTY IN
THE NORTHERN MINISTRY

MINISTERS UNDERSTOOD BETTER than most that the eyes and ears of the people were upon them. The bulk of preachers welcomed the public's increased attention, thinking it necessary if the clergy was to lead the patriotic vanguard on the homefront. At times, however, popular and church inquiry revealed parsons who were unable or unwilling to meet their nationalistic obligations. When that happened, all kinds of forces arrayed themselves against perceived treacherous clerics. Americans in the Union, aware of the cultural and political influence exerted by preachers and thus of the threat posed by unfaithful clerics, during the Civil War challenged the clergy's freedom of ministerial expression in sustained and meaningful ways for the first time in the nation's history. And unlike what transpired in the Confederacy, the northern story of clerical conflict suggests a decided rupture with the past.

Believing perhaps that the Union clergy was of limited cultural and political importance or that its members were unanimously loyal and of pro-administration sentiment, scholars have pushed preachers to the margins of their accounts of political arrests during the Civil War.[1] And while a few historians have considered the harrying of northern ministers for their controversial political speech, most within that small number have focused almost exclusively on the actions of government agents and the policies of the Lincoln administration.[2] However, northern preachers accused of disserving their country faced not only the chastising intervention of Federal and state authorities but the censure of their fellow ministers and denominational officers, the estrangement of their local congregants, and the disparagement of the secular public as well. Alike interested in checking ministerial influence when that influence was applied disloyally, the leaders of all of these seats of authority—the nation/state, the church, and the people—deemed it their place and in their interests to act in unprecedented ways. Their shared Civil War effort to delineate in the name of the Union the acceptable parameters of sermonic speech represents the first real challenge to the authority and autonomy of America's denominational preachers. Highlighting this dynamic undercuts the impression that the members of the northern clergy were effectively "cheerleaders all" for the Union.[3]

I

From time to time before the Civil War, small groups of concerned citizens and elected officials worked to check the supposedly inappropriate sermonizing of some particular segment of the northern clergy. Without exception, however, those efforts had proven neither rigorous nor pervasive. Religious leaders played a role in the politics of the American Revolution, and patriotism was a subject of concern. However, the primary role of religion in the period was one that diffused authority throughout the citizenry rather than garnering it for church or state leaders. "The essence of colonial American religious development," Jon Butler writes, was "the evolution of a lively, multifaceted, multiracial, multiethnic religious world brought forth mainly by independent groups and individuals rather than by the state." In other words, the American Revolution was an incredibly destabilizing event that seriously discredited the old and often state-affiliated denominations that had dominated organized belief in the Colonial Era.[4] Indeed, a few institutional fragments (most notably the Congregational Church) and academic influences were all that was left of Colonial America's last church-centered regime, Puritan New England, its centralizing power destroyed by the secularization of the American Revolution.[5] Essentially, then, there was no campaign needed to limit the power of the clergy during and immediately after the Revolution because ministers, for the most part, enjoyed limited societal influence.

The Early National period witnessed the formal end of state-sponsored religion in America. Absent the sheltering hand of state authority, no doubt some of that day feared that the churches and their ministers were to become the victims of widespread and even government-endorsed oppression. But while church attendance—and relatedly church wealth and cultural influence—waned during the period, more than anyone else preachers *themselves* contributed to their own separation from the public and their political concerns.[6] The trend that Adam Smith noted in 1776 of American clergymen becoming "men of learning and elegance" who gathered at Harvard and Yale and scorned the "arts of gaining proselytes" became more pronounced in America during postwar decades of increasing religious apathy.[7] This gulf between clerics and the rest of America bothered few within the secular community, most of whom found it difficult to think of the greater clergy without recalling the Anglican roots (and related pro-British attitudes) of many leaders of America's still-dominant faith traditions. Throughout the remainder of the eighteenth century, there remained little need to check northern clerical clout or otherwise fear the influence that preachers might exert in nonreligious matters.

The story of religion and the War of 1812 is one of religiously rooted differences over the future of the nation more than one of controversial religious leaders and the responses they elicited.[8] True enough, newly forceful Baptist and Methodist preachers throughout America endorsed the war while members of older and established denominations often did not. Especially in New England, numerous clerics were of a mind with Congregationalist Reverend Elijah Parish, who maligned "the Jeffersons, the Burrs, the Madisons of the country . . . [who] will as soon give liberty to their African slaves as unembarrassed commerce to their New-England subjects."[9] But for several reasons, there was no bona fide crackdown on antiwar New England clergymen during the War of 1812. First, in numerous ways New England was an entity unto itself, a characteristic that led many to advocate, in the words of William Gribbin, "a functional secession from the Union, making full political separation unnecessary."[10] A small Federal government, taxed by war with the world's dominant military force and led by men hundreds of miles away from Boston or Hartford, could devote little of its energies to monitoring distant pulpits and curbing "virtual" secession sentiment.

And New England's antiwar clerics were highly circumspect in their criticisms. Until very late in the conflict, most avoided talk of secession or treasonous behavior and clung instead to the rhetoric of constitutionalism. Congregationalist Jeremiah Evarts, for instance, instructed his disgruntled fellow churchmen that they "must do nothing inconsistent with our constitutional obligations." Similarly, Congregationalist Unitarian minister Nathaniel Thayer concluded, "The only safe and sure remedy for present evils is a vigilant and Christian use of your elective rights."[11] Federalists ministers, aware of the dangers of anarchy, urged dissent only within carefully defined, constitutional limits.[12] Even after a radical minority of Federalists adopted secessionist views late in the war, the bulk of New England's dissenting ministers clung to the protective shield of American republicanism. In so doing, they channeled dissent "through institutions well founded in the legal and extralegal traditions of American constitutional and political theory" rather than risk the further deterioration of public virtue and the destruction of the political nation.[13] Although the Madison administration undeniably engaged in a degree of wartime political oppression, little suggests that government officials, at any level, or the churches took significant steps to silence ministers for their controversial opinions.

As both church rosters and attendance expanded in post–War of 1812 America, ministers became more prominent in society, but they also shared the same nationalistic inclinations that inspired most Americans.[14] Therefore, preachers who increasingly meddled in politics usually troubled few within the church and even fewer outside of the church proper. In the 1830s and 1840s, the opposition of Whiggish clergymen (chiefly Congregationalists) to the rabble-rousing tendencies of Jacksonian democracy, and the participation of clergymen in controversial reform movements like abolitionism, brought northern ministers into the public arena. However, because Congregationalism (along with every other old-guard denomination) declined in membership during the period and because of the sectional nature of the debate into which Congregationalist clerics (almost all of them in New England) entered, troublesome clerics of the 1830s and 1840s never threatened their northern neighbors enough to warrant a censuring response.[15]

The U.S.-Mexican War in essence created a new world, one in which the role of ministers in American politics was ever expanding. Clerics featured prominently in disputes over the war and then the war's legacy. Preachers for instance led opposition to the Fugitive Slave Act and then the Kansas-Nebraska Act. But the great age of church schisms had passed by then and ministers, despite the protestations of leading political figures like Stephen A. Douglas, were emboldened and protected by their broader membership's near unanimous support. Quite simply, all of the pieces of a sustained test of ministerial autonomy did not fall into place until the Civil War brought them into place.

The Civil War pushed dissent from the realm of acceptability and into the realm of sedition. Before the war an abolitionist minister might have alienated fellow denominationalists, but few would have considered the expression of such sentiment criminal. Although a pro-slavery minister who advocated treating southerners with sensitivity might have been maligned as a doughface in some quarters, he would not have been considered a quisling by definition. But the Civil War was regarded by many as a contest against those who threatened the nation's very existence. For the first time in America, the stakes were sufficiently high to justify proscribing preachers in their pulpits, even at the expense of religious freedom. Government officials were suspicious of ministerial clout because that influence, when wielded in the interests of secessionism or the Confederacy, harmed the greater war effort. Loyal denominational leaders feared that a few treacherous ministers could sully the image and limit the viability of their entire affiliated church. And on a still more basic level, congregants—convinced that any and all who took sides with sedition were traitors to their church and neighbors alike—wanted especially to punish reprobate preachers.

II

During the Civil War, disputes about ministerial loyalty and church speech routinely spilled over into the secular world. Owing both to northerners' sacralized image of their political nation and to the sheer number of denominationalists in the greater public, men and women carried news of what transpired behind church walls into their community's streets, schools, shops, and saloons. When that happened, state and especially Federal officials—the arbiters of the public sphere—proved ready to act. From common soldiers to military governors, from local magistrates to the president, enforcement agents and policy-makers tried to contain the damage done by perceived disloyal ministers during the Civil War. In the process, they established and then carried out some of the most restrictive measures toward ministers of the gospel that Americans had ever witnessed.

Government involvement in church affairs was distinctive in that it often involved the imprisonment of ministers. Even though the bulk of suspected disloyalists detained in the wartime North were released after relatively short periods of confinement (provided they were not implicated in specific instances of espionage or treason), arrests nevertheless deterred clerical disloyalty in two very effective ways.[16] First, a daunting aspect of a minister's detention was the society-wide perception that such an arrest, regardless of the outcome, served as an official declaration of treachery. Unless he was intent upon making his way to the Confederacy, a minister targeted by Federal and state authorities was virtually guaranteed a life of sorrow. Second, arrests of parsons served as clerical wake-up calls. Ministers who began the war convinced that their position and holy vestments protected them from the hard hand of civil authority learned, in case after very public case, that such was no longer true.

The Federal government's interdiction into clerical affairs was no longer predicated solely on what a clergyman did or said. What a wartime parson refused to say sometimes proved just as damning. The most obvious indication that a new age of government interest in the rhetoric of reverends had arrived was the implementation of numerous wartime loyalty oaths that included, and in a few cases were expressly aimed at, clergymen.[17] Most Federal oaths were narrow in scope and aimed at elected and appointed employees, jurors, and attorneys who argued in Federal courts.[18] However, in border states like Kentucky and Missouri, Federal authorities demanded ironclad loyalty oaths of citizens else they be arrested and banned from the receipt of pensions, the rights of commerce, the ownership of land and other property, and the exercise of the elective franchise.[19] In a scenario repeated in both occupied Confederate states like Louisiana and Tennessee and Union states like Maryland and Missouri, for instance, clergymen were mandated by military authorities to swear allegiance to the United States. When they refused, "while they may have committed no other kind of disloyal act," they were to be "dealt with as rebellious and disloyal men, and expelled from the State."[20]

Increasingly, in the estimation of Federal officials, clergymen were categorized in the class of public professionals that included lawyers and teachers.[21] Of course, preachers bemoaned that the government now compelled them to avow their loyalty along with everyone else, with no distinction made between the clergy and the masses. But the trend did not abate. And, following the Federal lead, state governments too in time demanded declarations of ministerial fidelity. The Kentucky state legislature, for instance, spelled out the oath it required of all its ministers:

The following is a copy of the law passed by the Legislature, and approved by the Governor of Kentucky, August 31, 1862: *Be it enacted by the General Assembly of the Commonwealth of Kentucky*: Sec. 1. That no person shall solemnize marriage until, in addition to the present requirements of law, he shall file in the office of the County Court of the county of his residence, a written affidavit, subscribed by him and sworn to before some person legally authorized to administer an oath, of the following purport and effect, namely: "I do solemnly swear (or affirm, as the case may be,) that I will support the Constitution of the

United States and the Constitution of this State, and be faithful and true to the Commonwealth of Kentucky and the laws and Government thereof, so long as I continue a citizen thereof; and I do further solemnly swear (or affirm) that I will not aid, assist, abet or comfort, directly or indirectly, the so-called Confederate States, or those now in rebellion against the United States or the State of Kentucky, so long as I continue a citizen of this State, so help me God."[22]

In addition to imprisonment for repeated offenses, the state of Kentucky imposed a fine of up to five hundred dollars for solemnizing a marriage without taking the oath.

Ministers officially accused of disloyalty came most often from the border states.[23] Because parts of the lower Union were either under martial law or in close proximity to the front, military authorities in the region were on hand to act. And act they did, for Federal agents and officers considered church-based resistance in northern border areas to be no different from similar church-based resistance in occupied parts of the Confederacy. The administration's "one nation" political rhetoric aside, acts of ministerial antagonism and other church-affiliated hostilities toward government agents in the border Union and rebellious South were thought of as belligerent acts of an enemy people. Typical was the report submitted by a Major Tompkins concerning the arrest of a Missouri minister and his entire congregation. "I told them that they have to prove by acts that they loved our Government," Tompkins stated. Surely his captive audience listened attentively, for it would not have proven wise to defy one who boasted, "I make the rebels I shoot tell me all."[24]

Authorities understood that a disloyal cleric's words could do harm even when offered far from the church. Pro-Confederate preachers in the border states were feared as conduits through which information flowed to the Confederacy. Dozens of cases transpired during the war similar to that of Methodist Samuel B. Leech, minister of a church in Sandy Springs, Maryland, who was arrested and confined in Fort McHenry for suspected disloyal acts that included participation in "clandestine correspondence with persons in Virginia."[25] Border-state clerics threatened to prod antagonistic local populations toward political and military opposition to the war. Thus the residents of Boston or New York never experienced a day like the one witnessed by border-state citizens on July 26, 1862, when for the vague charge of disloyalty officials arrested Presbyterian Reverend Thomas Hoyt of Louisville and James H. Brooks of St. Louis in Cincinnati; celebrated Baptist "revival preacher" Reverend Thomas J. Fisher in Campbell County, Kentucky; Reformed Christian Church Reverend W. H. Hopson of Lexington, and numerous other preachers "all over the state of Kentucky." Many of those arrests, one Kentuckian theorized on that memorable day, were motivated by "fears of the result of a free election, on Monday next."[26]

Some border-state ministers were destined for trouble because of the particular nature of church logistics in politically divided regions. Borderland denominational churches were occasionally shared by separate groups of ardent Unionists and equally dedicated disloyalists. A Methodist church in Missouri was, by agreement of its members, "used alternatively by the Methodists, North and South." On one Sunday morning, southern-sympathizing Methodists arrived to find an American flag tacked to the pulpit, a remnant of the last meeting held by the Unionists with whom they shared the building. Unfazed, the Rebel preacher delivered his sermon. When Unionists attempted to hold the same flag aloft over the door as the minister exited, forcing him to pass under the Stars and Stripes, it proved too much for the assembled disloyalists to bear. A female member of the church knocked the American flag to the ground, and others stomped on it with glee.[27] In northern Kentucky, the membership of the Covington First Presbyterian Church was equally divided between Union and Rebel sympathizers. An American flag hung in a local hall that was scheduled to host a church festival. "The loyal ladies of the Congregation wished the flag to remain, but the Secesh women demanded its removal" and insisted that if an American flag flew it would be matched by the Confederate flag. The church's Unionist pastor concurred (to the vexation of local Unionist authorities and in solid Kentucky-neutral fashion), and the event transpired under no flag at all.[28]

Shared buildings and other cooperative efforts between neighbors of contrasting political loyalties were realities of church life in parts of the Lower North. However, Americans elsewhere often considered border-state ministers who brokered compromise with Confederate sympathizers to be something other than mere peacemakers. Not lost on Federal authorities was that church-sharing pacts—no matter that they usually represented ministerial acts of negotiation and concession intended to deter violence within their local communities—accommodated American citizens who openly prayed for the failure of the Union and its war effort. Those who held counsel with the seditious were traitors of a kind themselves, it was thought, and the clashes that inevitably grew out of such arrangements were all rooted in disloyalty. As such, they were no longer simple church affairs. They fell under the charter of campaigns by Union officials to ensure the loyalty of suspect church members and particularly ministers. There were many such first-time campaigns in the border states during the war. Secretary of War Edwin Stanton, for instance, issued in 1863 an order that confiscated all Methodist churches in and around St. Louis "in which a loyal minister, appointed by a loyal bishop of said church, does not now officiate" and placed them under the authority of Methodist Bishop Edward Ames.[29] In January 1864, a War Department directive instructed Federal commanders to turn over to the American Baptist Home Mission Society (ABHMS) all Baptist churches "in which a loyal minister of said Church does not now officiate." In February of that year, missionaries of the United Presbyterian Church were given permission to seize Associate Reformed Presbyterian churches in rebellious southern states, and on March 10, 1864, a War Department dictate cleared the way for military officials to give other Southern Presbyterian churches to missionaries of the Board of Domestic Missions of the Presbyterian Church (Old School) and the Presbyterian Committee of Home Missions (New School).[30]

Federal intrusions into border-state church affairs and attempts to subjugate ministers there were not conducted entirely by broad decrees and wide-scale campaigns. Some proscriptive edicts were much more case-specific. When Reverend Libertus Van Bokkelen resigned the pastorate of Baltimore's Saint Timothy's Episcopal Church in 1864 because of conflicts with southern sympathizers within his congregation, Major General Lew Wallace ordered that no services would be held again at St. Timothy's "except by a successor of undoubted loyalty."[31] Likewise in Baltimore in 1863, after military commander Major General R. C. Schenck ordered that Methodist churches within the city hold services under the American flag, Reverend John H. Dashiell defied the order and was quickly arrested. Enraged, Dashiell's fellow ministers attempted to circumvent the mandate by convening meetings in different public buildings. Not to be outdone, Provost Marshal William Fish then issued an amendment to the original order that required the Methodists to fly the American flag no matter where they met.[32]

Governmental repression of suspect border-state clerics was an important, if historiographically underappreciated, part of the Union war effort. If such official efforts to hold preachers in places like Kentucky and Missouri in check have been overlooked by recent scholars, however, the ways in which allegedly perfidious preachers farther north of Mason and Dixon's Line were dealt with have been even more forgotten. This historical amnesia is understandable. Unlike much more common border-state interactions between clergymen and the Federal power that almost always involved military authorities and were thus diligently recorded, arrests of perceived disloyalists in the non-border Union were carried out by any number of local, state, and Federal authorities with varying degrees of documentation. Simply stated, such affairs are more difficult to track down in the historical record—provided they were formally recorded in the first place. In fact, Mark Neely Jr. argues that when the war ended nobody knew how many civilian arrests had been executed north of the border states. After almost a century and a half later, he added, "No one knows now."[33] But even in the absence of hard and fast numbers, some illuminating truths about the government's dealings with ministers in the Upper North are readily discernible.

Ministers suspected of disloyalty were repeatedly arrested in states such as New York, Pennsylvania, and Ohio. To a greater degree than was true in the border states, upper-northern clerics were often detained for behavior that was at best incidental to their church office.[34] For instance, numerous clergymen were seized as publishers of Copperhead newspapers, as was true of John Duffey, editor of Philadelphia's *Catholic Herald,* and James McMaster, the Catholic editor of New York's *Freeman's Journal.*[35] In cases like that of Ohioan Sabin Hough, moreover, a minister's clerical identity was all but irrelevant when he was involved in real acts of espionage and armed resistance to Federal or state authority. And in a way that border-state disloyalists would have never dared, some upper-northern ministers initiated contact with government agents themselves. After being ridden out of Wales, Massachusetts, on a rail, for example, suspected traitorous parson and one-time Justice of the Peace Cornelius Miller took his assailants to court, all sixteen of them.[36] But if not the norm, the detention of upper-northern preachers for nothing more than their words was far from exceptional. And even if the exact number of clerical seizures for expressed disloyalty in places like New York and Pennsylvania is difficult to guess, what is certain is that the arrests of perceived disloyal ministers were noticed by their ideological kinsmen and served as object lessons of what greeted similarly suspicious behavior.

The national government had a vested interest in perpetuating such deterrence, although President Lincoln was careful to neither alienate ministers nor engage in the arbitrary repression of religious thought that could erode internal support for the Union's cause. President Lincoln recognized that pronouncements like the one featured in a Maine newspaper in the middle of 1863 were far from anomalous. "The liberty of speech does not involve the liberty to preach treason. Nevertheless," the unnamed pragmatist wrote, "beyond the theatre of war the right to prohibit the preaching of treason does not involve the right to do so by the summary process of military authority. . . . [T]he law is open, and there are deputies; let them implead one another."[37] Accordingly, Lincoln and those under him used arrests to excise, like a cancer, the most disloyal clergymen, a means of checking the spread of churchly treachery without cutting too deeply into the body politic and risking a pervasive negative reaction. So, when Federal marshals for instance arrested Campbellite Reverend Judson D. Benedict in Buffalo for preaching resistance to the draft, provost marshals exiled Presbyterian Reverend Henry Paynter of Booneville, Missouri, for refusing to swear an oath of allegiance to the Union, or when Union soldiers apprehended Episcopal Reverend A. R. Rutan of Luzerne County, Pennsylvania, for preaching pacifism, they acted upon measured directives from Washington—be those instructions case-specific or entailed in standing orders—and in anticipation of the stifling impact their actions would have upon the local population.[38]

President Lincoln knew and approved of such arrests. True enough, in a famous early 1863 letter to General Samuel Curtis in St. Louis, Lincoln avowed that "the U.S. government must not . . . undertake to run the churches" and advised Curtis, "let the churches, as such take care of themselves." But more importantly, sandwiched between Lincoln's expressions of restraint was the simple but revealing statement, "When an individual, in a church or out of it, becomes dangerous to the public interest . . . he must be checked." When dealing with political dissenters in the ministry, Lincoln believed firmly in the nation's right to act in its own interests no matter what religious concerns existed contradictory to those interests. And in the same letter, Lincoln set the stage for a still greater abatement of ministerial freedom in the future. He did not condemn the detention of ministers who could "be charged with no . . . specific act or omission," but merely expressed an uncertainty whether such men could be permanently exiled "upon the suspicion of his secret sympathies" alone. His uncertainty notwithstanding, even then the president was willing to let local military authorities issue decrees of expulsion on such grounds.[39]

By June of 1863, Lincoln no longer equivocated. In a letter to Erastus

Corning and others, the president allowed for the policing of thought, writing that "arrests in cases of rebellion" were routinely made "not so much for what has been done, as for what probably would be done . . . more for the preventive, and less for the vindictive" in cases in which "the purposes of men are much more easily understood, than in cases of ordinary crime. The man who stands by and says nothing, when the peril of his government is discussed, can not be misunderstood. If not hindered, he is sure to help the enemy."[40] Such declarations ruffled more than a few Unionist feathers. After a spate of church-related edicts from the War Department in January and February, Charles P. McIlvaine, the country's most respected Episcopal bishop, for instance, chided the president: "For an officer of the Army to be vested with authority to say . . . 'I cannot indeed charge you with and disloyal teaching—but you do not preach as *I think* a loyal man should do, or as I think the congregation ought to be taught, and therefore *I bid* you vacate your pulpit . . . and I put in your place, a minister who will preach and pray *as I, a Provost Marshall or a Commanding General,* think a minister ought' . . . I say, such interference would in my mind be a most grievous trespass and abuse; equally injurious to our cause, and offensive to every rightly judging mind."[41] Lincoln was wary of the needless agitation of the denominational community and occasionally discomfited by the interventionism of his War Department, but he was not convinced by McIlvaine or anyone else to stop Stanton's interdictions into church affairs or arrests of preachers in the border states. That the church was important Lincoln knew well, but the nation was more important still.

Lincoln's attitude toward disloyal clerics in the North crystallized over time. Through it all, of course, the master politician never forgot that the support of America's churchpeople was essential to the prosecution of the war and stepped lightly when possible, lest he blur the line, as Richard Carwardine puts it, "separating governmental and ecclesiastical jurisdiction."[42] He consistently frowned upon oaths of allegiance for ministers in loyal states and amended Stanton's edict placing Bishop Edward Ames in authority over disloyal Methodist churches. Clearly, Abraham Lincoln was not the Constitution-killing tyrant suggested by the likes of novelist Gore Vidal and historian Edmund Wilson. As the work of Mark Neely especially suggests, Federal and state suppression of political opposition—and by extension the persecution of suspect preachers—in the Union could have been much, much worse.

But Lincoln grew increasingly transparent in his disdain for ministers who defended their treacherous diatribes with arguments about religious freedom. The president would have changed his temperate approach even more had he feared for a minute that the bulk of the clergy in the Union was disloyal. As long as ministers were not openly anti-Union, Lincoln was willing to allow them to arrive at tolerable political positions in their own good time. Secretary of War Stanton after all—and not President Lincoln—became synonymous with hard-line policies toward church leaders, and Lincoln was more than willing to allow Stanton that role. But Lincoln was in charge. He loomed large in the North's collective political consciousness and established the culture of command in the country. In his speeches and letters, Lincoln augmented the public gospel of nationhood and made it clear that the preservation of the Union (later coupled with the abolition of slavery) was both his and the people's holy mission.[43] In fulfillment of that mission, President Lincoln, along with various state governors and innumerable local magistrates, effected the greatest degree of Federal and state oversight of ministerial behavior that the country had ever witnessed. The days of clerical carte blanche had ended. Suspect ministers who found themselves in the crosshairs of Federal and state policy, therefore, became anathemas in their own land.

III

If governmental efforts to curtail the clergy's freedom of speech took ministers aback, such sacralists were no doubt doubly chagrinned by the actions of their fellow denominationalists. During the Civil War, leading elements of the North's churches proved willing to proscribe ministerial conduct in the name of the greater patriotic good. Not all of these efforts originated with general assemblies and national conferences. Most loyal Americans were wary of untrue clergymen, but few were as alarmed as their embarrassed brother ministers. In both the Union's border and non-border regions, preachers themselves led the effort to identify and ostracize disloyal fellow clerics.

The words of the moderator of an 1862 meeting of Presbyterian ministers in Ohio give testament to the fury that treacherous parsons provoked in Union-loving clergymen. Enraged to find suspected disloyalists among his charge, he proclaimed, "I expect to meet some of these men [his fellow ministers, but those of southern sympathies] in heaven; but before that, I expect to see them hanged upon earth; AND I SHALL REJOICE IN THAT HANGING."[44]

In this instance, even the reserved sense of propriety characteristic of Presbyterian ministers did nothing to dissipate the white-hot anger on display when ministerial patriotism was in question. It was all but unimaginable to many loyal ministers that someone else could be of the same denominational pedigree, subject to the same theological constricts, and willing endorsers of the same creeds, and yet believe that support for the Union and its war effort was negotiable. Disloyal preachers deserved ignominy if not the fires of hell, or so many patriotic parsons believed. As Catholic Father L. Washburn predicted in 1863 in reprimanding disloyal Catholic leaders, "the church is destined to live when croakers are dead and damned." "[S]o will our beloved country live, when complainers and faultfinders and copperheads are known," Washburn concluded, "only as we remember Benedict Arnold and the Tories of the past . . . as we remember Paine, Voltaire and others who lived to complain of the church, and died unlamented and forsaken of God and man."[45] Along similar lines, when a Marylander named Mason was arrested and charged with "preaching treason," one of his offended contemporaries quipped that "Mason could never die in a better time for his country than now. He could serve it more in five minutes on the gallows than he has in all the years of his life."[46]

At the root of betrayal, loyal religious leaders surmised, resided a fundamental un-Christianity. Unitarian Reverend Jasper L. Douthit accused disloyal clerics of preaching "for Satan instead of Christ" and believed them eager in that effort to "Modify the Ten Commandments and the Golden Rule" but careful not to "disturb the Evil One!"[47] All who were not ardent Lincolnites found themselves vulnerable to such aspersions. With each passing day of the war, loyal churchpeople more and more equated rhetorical dissent with treason and reprobation and slave mongering and virtually every other "detestable" incarnation evident in American life. In time, they applied the Copperhead label to the perceived evil lot of them; thus in the church world the term "Copperhead" carried a much less specific disapprobation than it did in the political arena. And as a Methodist Episcopal clergyman wrote in 1863, most loyal northern denominationalists were convinced that any preacher who was a "Copperhead cannot be a Christian; and he who is not a Christian is not a proper person to preach the Gospel."[48] Because the pronouncements of even marginally important denominational figures were heard and read by so many homefront citizens in the North, moreover, such patriotic harangues by Unionist clergymen provided powerful examples to all those invested in squashing clerical treason.

Historians have noted elsewhere the power of religious imagery in motivating spiritually minded Americans to take action. Denmark Vesey and Nat Turner, for example, incorporated scriptural prophecies into their politico-religious messages and presented themselves as Christian oracles.[49] The loyal minister's familiarity with scriptural parables and homilies and the dramatic language patterns of the Bible proved similarly advantageous in his efforts to construct memorable and resonating oratory against errant clerics. Referencing John of Patmos's Book of Revelations, for instance, Methodist Reverend Peter Cartwright of Pleasant Plains, Illinois, employed the most common tactic of wartime ministers in their verbal assaults on disloyal clergymen: combining the politician's highly literate use of metaphor and hyperbole with the scripture-based language of the evangelical sermon. "If God will have mercy on me, I would rather die than that this glorious government should be overthrown," said Cartwright. "If we must be destroyed," he went on, "I hope the Lord will do it, and not give us into the power of Tories. . . . Rivers of blood will flow, but this Union must stand though the heavens fall."[50] Newport, Kentucky, Methodist Reverend William Black preferred this approach. Peppering his prose with apocalyptic references to end-time prophesy, Black prayed in 1861 that the Union must be preserved "even though blood may come out of the wine press even unto the horses [sic] bridles, by the space of a thousand and six hundred furlongs." Eager to weigh in on both wartime politics and religion, the Kentuckian continued, "Let Davis and Beauregard be captured to meet the fate of Hamann. Hang them up on Masons and Dixon's Line, that traitors of both sections may be warned. Let them hang until the vultures shall eat their rotten flesh from their bones . . . hang until the rope rots, and then let their dismembered bones fall so deep into the earth that God Almighty can't find them in the day of Resurrection."[51]

Some loyal ministers sought to engage the metaphor of "Copperhead" to drive home their indictments of rebellious rectors, displaying their skills as wordsmiths. Methodist preacher and Wesleyan College of Connecticut President Joseph Cummings provided an example of this with his biting commencement speech in 1864. The speech was so replete with inventive indictments of traitors that one listener concluded, "if there was a copperhead present he heard enough to keep him on the writhe till another commencement."[52] Another unnamed Methodist Episcopal minister characterized secession as "a snake which, though cut in pieces, will not die until sundown," and warned that talk of peace and olive branches by ministers "who sympathize with the rebels, is the spotted skin that covers the Copperhead."[53] Lastly, some ministers played upon the "copper" component of the Copperhead moniker to question the mettle, as it were, of disloyal clergymen. Methodist Reverend G. W. Paddock of Kansas, speaking to church leaders in New York, asked: "Are there any copperheads amongst your ministers? If there are, get the Bishop to transfer them to Kansas, and we will let them look into the face of Quantrell [sic] and pick the flattened bullets from their parlor walls, the bullets which were aimed at them and their children: then the copper will all be rubbed off of them, and underneath will appear the pure gold of liberty, patriotism, and righteousness."[54] As these examples show, patriotic ministers embraced a no-nonsense approach to patriotism that demanded everyone be "with us or against us." Copperheads were traitors and traitors were Copperheads, men like the Reverend Paddock held, and arguing Democratic traditions or constitutional principles did nothing to lessen the wickedness of such turncoats.

When damning disloyal fellow ministers, preachers throughout the North privileged recognizable biblical excerpts in their efforts. Revelation's rivers of blood, Genesis's "by the sweat of thy brow," Exodus's Moses-led deliverance of the Israelites, Galatians' "there is neither bond nor free," and Christ the New Testament redeemer were but a few of the most common references that evangelical patriots wove into the sermons. In so doing, they added gravitas to their indictments and addressed the faithful in an allegorical language with which all of their congregants were familiar. Given the inarguably demoralizing and potentially materially destructive force that traitorous preachers exerted, a more valuable application of ministerial skill is difficult to imagine. With their heated invectives against perfidious parsons, loyal preachers provided Americans unaccustomed with criticizing clergymen with both the encouragement and model they needed. Concerned with the tangible impact of clerical infidelity on military recruitment, morale, civilian support, and internal security and convinced that treason was even more abominable when offered from behind the holy lectern, border- and non–border state preachers took the lead in policing the offense.

Of course local ministers were limited in their abilities to punish wayward parsons. They did not possess the power to order brother ministers how to preach, nor could they push out of the denominational family those clergymen who persisted in their disloyalty. Only national and regional governing bodies exercised such authority. The church leaders who met in annual bodies like general assemblies, conferences, synods, and presbyteries constituted representative ecclesiastical polities that addressed their denomination's concerns. They ruled on such doctrinal issues as the endorsement of creeds or new scriptural interpretations, on ecumenical efforts like missions, on organizational matters like clergy placement and the formation and maintenance of committees and boards, and on topics relative to specific members and ministers such as grants of ordination. They sometimes censured members, ministers, and entire congregations. Occasionally, they expelled errant members and clergymen from the church. There were exceptions to this form of governance. Some independent-minded evangelical traditions like the Baptists favored associational bodies that had no formal power. And Catholicism vested more authority in particular individuals—most notably the archbishops who led America's respective archdioceses—than was true of Protestant groups, although even archbishops met in conferences whose edicts had a degree of authority over all constituent members.

Regardless of the form these informal or formal founts of authority assumed, their collective will was expressed in the adjudication of disputes over ministerial behavior. Contingent upon the body's level of authority, these pronouncements became church law. The directors of almost every wartime northern Christian denomination used their power and influence to stipulate the loyal pulpit speech of their preachers and punish those who strayed. This is far from surprising, for when the leading lights of wartime denominationalism assembled in governing bodies, disloyalty was the most commented-upon ministerial behavior.

On an individual level, however, the fates of unabashedly disloyal ministers were almost always sealed before their cases reached the highest denominational governing bodies. Convening for a scant few days each year and pressed for time, national or regional governing groups dealing with incontestably treacherous individuals commonly did little more than confirm the disciplinary actions of a local church's administrative body or that of some other subordinate church group. The largest number of ministerial cases for which extended denominational trials were conducted therefore did not involve patently traitorous behavior. Reflecting the contentiousness that beset the wartime church, most deliberations were of nuanced ministerial rhetoric and behavior, words and deeds that in the prewar era would have been discussed in the context of religious and political conservatism but not treason. Illinois Methodist Episcopal Church Reverend Oliver H. McEuen, for instance, was tried before a fifteen-member district body and expelled from the church in 1863 for saying that the Methodist Church had become enamored with political preaching and offering that Democratic members should organize a more conservative church.[55] When the larger Illinois Annual Conference convened the following month in Springfield, more ministers were brought up on charges of disloyalty. One such reverend, William Blundell, was charged specifically with "disloyalty to the Government of the United States for failing to identify with any of the movements looking to support the government," with "failing to pray in public for the President or Armies of the United States," and with "Gross immorality for failing to observe a day of National Thanksgiving as proclaimed by the President."[56]

Between 1860 and 1865, 121 ministers at annual conference meetings in Illinois, Indiana, and Ohio were brought before church disciplinary bodies. That number, moreover, does not factor in charges adjudicated by local bodies that were not appealed to annual conferences. Most of these affairs involved charges of disloyalty. And at least 244 ministers in those same conferences retired during the period, while 197 ministers were relieved of circuit duties without event. It is likely that many who retired or were removed from the pulpit for unspecified reasons were likewise the target of scrutiny over their suspected seditious behavior.[57]

Disputes with and disciplinary measures against clergymen were not limited to Methodist bodies. The Episcopal Church in Maryland was beset by troubles owing to the numerous rectors who defied the Maryland Episcopacy's Prelate Bishop William Rollinson Whittingham's directive to pray for Lincoln and the Union and to observe presidential fast days. The rectors' insubordination revealed "their rebel proclivities," one clergyman deduced, indicating that "the clergy and the Bishop have been brought into open collision upon the issue."[58] In a single incident in 1864, seven United Brethren ministers in Ohio were called up before a conference panel and dismissed.[59] The Lutheran General Synod's endorsement of the Union and indictment of slavery in 1862 begat internecine conflict between the Synod and members of lesser bodies, as was true when many members of the Wittenberg Synod of Ohio acted against the national body's resolution.[60] Protestant Episcopal bodies, Baptist conferences, Catholic archbishops like New York's John J. Hughes, and governing authorities of virtually every kind of northern denomination punished suspected disloyal ministers. As the Reverend Robert Stanton noted in 1864, "there is disloyalty of the rankest kind among the ministers of the Gospel."[61]

Issues of individual clerical disloyalty presented knotty problems, but just as pressing to those who set church policy were concerns about their collective ministry's loyalty. Therefore, appropriately loyal ministerial behavior was often mandated in declarations of support for the United States government and its war effort. Commonly referred to as loyalty resolutions, these pronouncements were made by church leaders at annual meetings throughout the war. Famous for what has since been remembered as the Gardiner Spring Resolutions, the 1861 Old School Presbyterian General Conference in Philadelphia passed the nation's first important wartime pledge of denominational loyalty.[62] The resolutions articulated the General Assembly's majority opinion on political preaching and made clear the assembly's expectations of all of its ministers. "There are occasions," one resolution read, "when *political* questions *rise into the sphere of morals and religion;* when the rule of political action is to be sought, not in consideration of State policy, but in the law of God." And now, the assembled Presbyterian clerics declared, "When the question to be decided turns on moral principles, when reason, conscience, and the religious sentiments are to be addressed, *it is the privilege and duty of all who have access in any way to the public ear,* to endeavor to allay unholy feeling, and *to bring truth to bear* on the minds of fellow citizens.[63]

The Gardiner Spring Resolutions provided a model for the scores of denominational loyalty resolutions that followed during the war. Ministers were to preach unflinching loyalty to the Union as ordained not just by the laws of man but by the laws of God. Importantly, the political had grown so pressing as to become moral and religious; all had melded into one concern identified simply as the "truth." The 1863 incarnation of the General Assembly of the Presbyterian Church, Old School, certainly followed suit, admonishing its ministers "to stand by their Country; to pray for it; to discountenance all forms of complicity with treason" and "to sustain those who are placed in civil or military authority over them."[64] Similar concerns about the clergy's behavior pervaded much of American denominationalism's upper echelons. The leaders of northern Methodism (America's largest denomination when the Civil War began), for example, were embarrassed by the treasonous reputation of Methodist clergymen in southern Maryland and the Methodist clergy's perceived soft attitude toward slavery in the antebellum era. As a result, numerous Methodist conferences dictated ministerial partisanship of a pro-Union ilk. Besides dictating ministerial behavior concerning such ecclesiastical concerns as the order of worship, the singing of psalms, and the nature of prayers, the national General Conference of Evangelicals

(Methodist) in 1863 instructed ministers "as preachers of the gospel, to support the Government in every proper measure."[65] Ranging in scope from required prayer for the Union to the exhibition of proper reverence, fealty, and obedience to the government, the Evangelical Association's loyalty requirements practically mandated patriotic preaching.[66]

Similarly, northern New School leaders of the Presbyterian Church forbade ministers from remaining silent in the nation's moment of crisis. Reiterating the Unionist position it had championed in numerous prior resolutions, the New School General Assembly asserted in the war's final year that it was the obligation of ministers to indefatigably condemn the South and secession. "Let the religious sense of the Church," the General Assembly declared, "in her pulpit ministrations, and through the actions of her judiciaries, mark this sin [treason] as of the deepest dye."[67] The Lutheran General Synod that met in Lancaster, Pennsylvania, in 1862 issued its florid loyalty resolution as recognition of the ministerial "duty to give public expression to our convictions of truth on this [the war] subject, and in every proper way to cooperate with our fellow citizens in sustaining the great interests of law and authority, of liberty and righteousness."[68] Such modeling was apparently not without warrant, for the synod's resolution expressed "deep disapprobation of ministers" within the Lutheran convention who cooperated with treason and fomented insurrection.[69]

The authors of loyalty resolutions were calculating in their prescriptions, aware that any directive issued expressly to the ministers under their authority would be interpreted by the church's critics as an acknowledgment of disloyalty within the denomination. Thus most loyalty resolutions included general encouragements to bring about the appropriate patriotic behavior of all members. Given that ministers served as emissaries between church authorities and the laity, however, such Unionist proclamations required more of preachers than of others, thrusting reverends into the role of publicly advocating patriotism in a way not demanded of the general membership. The Lebanon Conference of the East Pennsylvania Synod of the Lutheran Church recorded early in the war that nearly "all the brethren represented the war question as being *the* question and that the interests heretofore manifested in spiritual matters had more or less abated."[70] Aware no doubt of the purported southern sympathies of a number of Lutheran preachers in the area, the conference declared, "Resolved, That in the opinion of this Conference, it is the duty of *all true patriots* to rally around the standard of their country and contend for the continuance of those principles of civil and religious liberty that were triumphantly established by our fathers."[71] Although this pronouncement offered instruction to all Lutherans, there is no doubt that members of the ministry were expected to pay it particular heed and likely elicited the emphasis.[72] A convention of Maine Unitarian ministers certainly considered it wise to encourage unambiguous clerical speech in the preamble of their loyalty pronouncement: "In the present momentous crisis . . . when not merely the precious legacy of liberty and self-government" were in peril but "even our national existence, the members of this Convention do not wish to leave their sentiments doubtful, nor their patriotism liable to be misunderstood."[73]

Denominational governing bodies issued hundreds of loyalty resolutions during the Civil War. Nearly all of them included patriotic inducements directed at clergymen.[74] Indeed, nationalistic declarations became so standard that any hesitancy to issue them raised suspicion among Unionists. Thomas Curtis wrote the *Boston Investigator* from Philadelphia early in the war, for instance, to question the value of the Presbyterians then assembled in his town who "Even while I write this . . . in their annual meeting are quarreling over the wording of a resolution of Loyalty to the United States Government, in their day of trial."[75] But not every pronouncement was the work of a group. Pope Pius IX sympathized with the Confederacy, a position numerous northern church prelates endorsed. Consequently, no institutional pronouncement of Catholic loyalty was issued during the war. According to one Catholic chronicler, although northern Catholics claimed "not to be behind any in loyalty" and scores of Catholics joined the Federal ranks, as a group the Catholic "clergy held their [collective] peace."[76] But *individual* Catholic newspapers and loyal church figures very often cultivated the loyalty of their fellow churchmen and women. Notable Unionists like Cincinnati's Archbishop Purcell and New York's Archbishop Hughes are best remembered for such efforts, but they were not alone. Baltimore's Father Constantine Pise, in a sermon reprinted in numerous (although mostly Democratic) newspapers, sincerely urged Catholics to "throw ourselves at the foot of our altars and pray for our country, the President, and all our fellow citizens."[77]

Regardless of their individual or collective authorships, loyalty edicts demanded ministerial compliance, and their authors were quick to punish those who refused to obey. The Methodist Reverend Phillip Germond of Connecticut refused to sign a number of loyalty resolutions passed by his church unless the words "unqualified loyalty" were struck from each document. Although a number of Methodists ministers pleaded Germond's supposedly principled case, his governing conference "emphatically" dismissed him, offering that "we suppose that gentleman will now quietly subside into that obscurity from which he never should have emerged."[78] A Universalist minister who identified himself only as "A.R.A." asserted in 1863 that anyone like Germond "who, in times of peril, refuses to extinguish the old partisan camp-fires, rally under the national banner, and put himself in patriotic relations with the national authorities" was an "idolater and no patriot." The bitter fruits of past ministerial hesitancy were then being reaped, A.R.A. offered. Fewer and fewer "Christian teachers who would have testified against this evil [slavery]" filled the clerical ranks as the war neared, A.R.A. recalled, "but God, who never leaves himself without a witness, speaks now from the cannon's mouth. . . . The testimony we would not hear from the pulpit, he compels us to hear from intrenchments, forts, ironclads, and monitors."[79]

Much can be deduced from the sheer number of wartime loyalty resolutions. If the fidelity of clergymen—who more than any other sector of denominationalism were the instructive focus of such resolutions—had not concerned the North's religious leaders, such resolutions would have been superfluous. As it was, church leaders felt compelled to repeatedly avow their devotion to the Union and that of their subordinate preachers at least in part as a means of deflecting criticisms born in the real disloyalty of some within the clerical fold. Most ministers were loyal just as most on the greater northern homefront were loyal. But some were not. Within the ministerial ranks of every religious tradition were those who were not patriots. For fear that the disloyalty of some should cause an entire denomination or diocese to be painted red with one broad brush, governing bodies and their individual equivalents (i.e., bishops and archbishops) declared the loyalty of all their members and acted to ensure the patriotic behavior of all affiliated ministers. Resolutions were sincere expressions of love and support for the United States, to be sure, but they served the additional purpose of establishing the boundaries of appropriate ministerial behavior.

Because historians have attributed the restriction of homefront freedoms almost exclusively to the Federal power, self-policing churches and church leaders seldom appear in the scholarly literature on wartime civil liberties. But individual ministers and governing bodies deemed it necessary during the

Civil War to restrict the freedom of ministerial expression. Clerics identified their disloyal opposite numbers and then empowered their parishioners and the public with the tools needed to join them in their ousting campaigns. On a larger scale, denominational bodies proved both reactionary and preventative, dealing sternly with disloyal individual member ministers while outlining the expectations of their entire clergy's future loyal behavior. They reminded their subjects that whole denominations had divided in previous decades because of arguments in which ministerial behavior—what ministers should and should not do and say—had featured prominently.

In another sense, however, American denominationalism's immediate past was illusory. The church schisms of the previous decades had been brought about by northern and southern camps willing to bid the other side goodbye. Thus the division of the national churches was accomplished with deceptive ease.[80] Americans a decade later erroneously assumed that the same neat and tidy separation might be accomplished between political sections of the nation. But because American Protestantism had long ago established a penchant for break-offs and splinter groups, the notion that the "true" church could not encompass multiple adherents to roughly the same church tradition was not present in 1837 or 1845. In essence, the schisms of the past had not caused denominationalists to believe that to be on the other side was to be un-Christian as much as it was to be deceived or misguided. Members could let other members leave their church because such a departure did not compromise their own religious legitimacy. But northern Christianity's relatively new conceptualization of a hallowed United States and the threat the war posed to her made things different now. Disloyal preachers could not simply be let go. They had to be punished, contained, and if possible, reformed. If, in both the nation's and their church's best interests, denominations acted in unprecedented ways to limit the power of their preachers during the Civil War, it is only because they were living in unprecedented times.

IV

Preachers in the Union found themselves caught in a denominational cross-fire. Their freedom of religious expression came under fire not only from above, but from below as well. Ministers might have expected as much. Like America itself, mid-nineteenth-century denominational Christianity was a burgeoning representative democracy. Members of the Civil War–era clergy were unquestionably authoritative, but they were also beholden to congregants who expected the opinions of their local pastor, at least on crucial issues like slavery and the war, to jibe with their own. In essence because local church bodies hired or at least paid ministers, church members felt empowered to challenge local clerics who strayed too far from majority opinion within their congregations. And since the local church did not exist in a vacuum and local church members were also community members, townspeople outside of the church were equally privy to the local pastor's views. When those views seemed disloyal, church membership or even attendance was not needed to enter the criticizing fray. Like the Federal and various state governments and the founts of denominational authority, local churchpeople and citizens felt compelled to act against clerical freedom of speech in the name of the Union and victory.

Preachers who defied their memberships could no longer lean upon the local church's sheltering arms. The implications of such severance were frightening. During the Civil War, congregants for instance effectively entreated draft boards for exemptions for beloved parsons, as was the case with the impressive letter-writing campaign undertaken by devotees of Methodist Episcopal Reverend Jacob MacMurray of Pennsylvania.[81] And after the Enrollment Act of 1863 allowed draftees to avoid service by paying a three-hundred-dollar commutation fee, money-raising drives for ministers became common. Both Democratic and Republican ministers offered such courses of action to their congregations as a means of ensuring the continued spiritual health of the church, but they could not have done so had their own station within the church been in doubt. As it was, commutation "love offerings" became the preferred draft-avoiding tactic of church leaders of every denominational distinction, including Peace Church leaders, and soon were widespread in northern cities and towns. In covering the exemption of Presbyterian Reverend Morris Sutphon, for example, the *Philadelphia Inquirer* reported that "in most cases" such collection-plate commutating was practiced by the churches of Philadelphia no matter the congregational or denominational affiliation.[82] But the many advantages of residing comfortably in the good graces of their memberships did not keep all preachers snugly in place. As is true in every age, clerics during the Civil War left their charges for any number of reasons, some surely noble and others not. And when the relationship between a homefront preacher and his local church and townspeople fractured along fissures of loyalty, his path became rock-strewn indeed.

Just as governmental intervention alone threatened preachers with incarceration and church proscription alone could lead to a preacher's excommunication and the loss of his professional identity, local affairs too were in ways unique. For instance, government representatives and religious authorities seldom dealt summarily and violently with disloyal ministers. However, local public officials and parsons sometimes censured the rabble-rousing efforts of disloyal churchpeople in immediate and forceful ways. Staunchly patriotic Indiana Methodist Reverend William Copp clearly believed in the quick and harsh punishment of disloyalists. When Copp, just months removed from his service as a captain in the United States Army, strolled to the podium before a crowd of over five hundred in Calumet, Indiana, in 1863, most imagined he would talk about religious life in the service. They were wrong. Instead, Copp "took the stand, opened the Bible before him; unbuttoned his coat; took from his side-pocket a navy revolver, which he deliberately placed by the side of the Sacred Book, and announced that his subject would be, 'The Bible and Bullets.'" What the Reverend Copp—whose recent pulpit harangues had targeted two local church leaders—meant soon became apparent. To a crowd comprised of both Republicans and Democrats, Copp announced his intention to "take a vote of the meeting to see how many of those present would 'assist in hanging the Copperheads of that county.'" Predictably, the Democrats in attendance withdrew to the street, to be followed immediately by some of their Republican countrymen. In the ensuing melee, two Democrats were wounded and one killed.[83]

Itinerancy also factored into the unique nature of local efforts to reign in disloyal clergymen. Clerics averse to maintaining a local base commonly delivered sermons as guest speakers. Referred to as evangelists, such men were almost always known and highly regarded for their gift of oratory. But a number of prominent northern evangelists espoused opinions that were prejudicial toward the Union if not patently treasonous. By mid-1862, for instance, the attitudes of roving Universalist Reverend Charles Chauncey Burr, former editor of *The Gavel* and *Universalist Palladium*, author of the noted religious work *A Discourse on Revivals* (1840), and one-time mesmerizer, were known well beyond his Hudson Valley home. Without doubt, most of Burr's most offensive (at least in the estimation of Unionists) deliberations were recorded in black and white. Burr had established the *Old Guard* in New York City in June 1862, a monthly paper that from its beginning was so consistently anti-Lincoln and sympathetic to the South that it can only be called a Copperhead vehicle.[84]

Reverend Burr's views were thus known to those who came to hear him offer a public message at a hall in Pascack, New Jersey, in August 1862. When Burr "vehemently counseled resistance to the collection of taxes for sustaining the Government," according to a correspondent with the *Paterson Guardian*, and "in various other ways displayed the cloven foot" of disloyalty, his rhetoric was more than his audience could abide.[85] In short order the "lecture was brought to an abrupt halt," and Burr became the target of a heavy volley "directed at the speaker," although Burr's ability to avoid being struck meant that it was an attack "evidently manned by volunteers who as yet had never had much practice at the business." Burr was lucky on two fronts. He emerged largely unscathed after making his way to a back passage of the building and then into a wagon that afforded him a retreat, albeit one conducted "in great disorder." Most fortunately for Burr, his attackers fired eggs and not bullets.

Ironically, Burr's reputation as a southern sympathizer probably saved his life. Had the people he addressed not known his allegiances and resultantly anticipated his diatribe, Burr might have encountered men and women who carried not eggs but, as a matter of daily habit, only clubs and guns. The melee he initiated ended without any real harm, but Burr's Copperheadism was no joke.[86] Although he superciliously avowed his innocence at Pascack and proclaimed at that time his hope for the "perpetuation of this Union," his *Old Guard* and oratorical efforts left no doubt about his true leanings. By the close of 1862, Burr had emerged as an unabashed supporter of Clement Vallandigham.[87] Evangelists like Burr tested the wartime limits of small-town forbearance. They seemingly assumed that an offensive but not otherwise dangerous or actionable utterance made in New York City or Boston retained such status when repeated in more rural settings like Pasack, New Jersey. They erred, owing both to the different degrees of tolerance existent among large and small populations respectively and to the reputation of the preachers themselves that drew attendees intent upon opposing a predictable message.[88] If disloyal itinerants often met with trouble when attempting to deliver their spurious gospel in strange environs, to a large extent they carried that danger there with them.

The role of traveling evangelists must be recognized when considering wartime ministerial disputes in the local setting, but itinerant preachers did not represent the norm. Just as the local pastor anchored Civil War–era denominationalism and most of mid-nineteenth-century church life was framed by the walls of the local church, most local efforts to limit ministerial authority grew out of disputes between religious shepherds and members of the local churches that they led. In numerous cases, years of warm relations between beloved ministers and congregants melted away when a pastor's loyalty to his country became questionable. For example, when war came to the doorsteps of Gettysburg's German Reformed Church, many of its members felt fortunate to have at their lead such a respected cleric as the Reverend Theodore Park Bucher, the church's pastor since 1859.[89] A Marshall College graduate and former faculty member of the Milton Academy, Bucher had witnessed the church's enlargement and improvement, leading to the church's rededication in 1862, and the popular implementation of the church's first pew rental system.[90] But Bucher's loyalty was called into question by some in the town from the war's earliest days. Indeed, owing to his seemingly ambiguous attitudes toward the conflict and the discord that ambiguity bred among some of the faithful, not all within Bucher's church were enamored with him by 1863. One account observed that of late "by some people of the town the Reformed Church was called 'The Rebel Church.'"[91] According to a twentieth-century chronicler of the affair, "Whispers over back fences around town" maligned the church and questioned "Bucher's loyalty to the Union and accus[ed] him of using the pulpit to preach political and social ideals."[92] Staunch Unionists within Bucher's congregation understandably cringed at such aspersions.

The Battle of Gettysburg brought things to a head. Bucher's behavior before, during, and after the battle ruffled the feathers of a number of church members, none more so than Church Trustee John Hoke. Hoke stated in a meeting of the church's leaders that "the Pastor was seen in the company of Rebel Officers during General Early's occupation of the town, fraternizing with them," that Bucher "prevented Reverend S. Phillips from preaching a Union sermon during the latter's visit here," and most damnably, that under Bucher's direction the church "appraised the damages done to the church by its occupation by the military at $1500" in an apparent "attempt to defraud the Government."[93] These kinds of allegations were not rare in Gettysburg. More than a few post-battle accounts were of a kind with that offered by *New York Times* reporter L. L. Crounse, who two weeks after the battle recorded the "shameful conduct" of many in Gettysburg toward Federal troops and bemoaned the fact that, although "the Army of the Potomac had a right to expect a more enthusiastic greeting in loyal Pennsylvania than in rebel Virginia," such was nowhere the case.[94] But even as the reputation of the town itself suffered, many in the Gettysburg German Reformed Church were unwilling to impugn the name of their minister.

The charges against Bucher were serious. He was accused, among other things, of preaching sympathetically for the Confederacy while failing to support the Union from the pulpit. Facing such accusations, Bucher resigned on September 12, 1863. However, the members of a Joint Consistory Panel—lay leaders and elders of the Gettysburg and nearby Flohrs and Marks German Reformed Churches—asked Bucher to rescind his accusation and instead found fault with Bucher's chief accuser, John Hoke.[95] Bucher had not compromised his pulpit with disloyal sermons, they claimed, but had brought glory to it in his course of "avoiding the introduction and discussion of politics in his ministrations, believing that politics are for politicians, and that Christ and Him Crucified are the proper themes for the pulpit and the Christian minister."[96] The Consistory Panel's efforts were fruitless, and Bucher soon left Gettysburg to accept a call from a Reformed Church in Ohio. Even in the wake of Bucher's departure, however, the panel contested Hoke's accusations and ultimately suspended him "from the privileges from the church for one year . . . in the hope that he may see the error of his course, and become improved."[97]

Bucher's true allegiances may never be known, but much suggests his patriotism. Under severe attack for his disloyalty to the Union, Bucher found support among the lay leaders of his church, a church that celebrated a "Roll of Honor" consisting of ten members who fought in the Federal army (no members fought for the Confederacy). Most convincingly, the church's recorder indicated that opposition had grown up against Bucher in Gettysburg owing to a "misapprehension of facts or willful perversion of them."[98] Townspeople's suspicions and the accusations they spawned did not convince those loyal to Bucher that his reticence to support the Union from the pulpit was de facto proof of his, or their, disloyalty. Even when abstract questions of principle became much less important than dealing with the immediate realities of war in their yards, streets, and buildings, the Consistory Panel ruled, a preacher need not prove his fidelity in discernable ways to warrant his congregation's "abiding confidence in [his] loyalty and patriotism" and to expect of them support that "never for a moment" wavered.[99] In the opinion of the church's elders and deacons, the office of reverend carried an assumption of appropriate, and appropriately loyal, ministerial sentiment. But as was true throughout the Union, the leadership of the German Reformed Church of Gettysburg could not mandate local public opinion. Even when church bodies saw no call to censure their clerical leaders, they found themselves powerless to sway community opinion and usually unsuccessful in convincing neighbors in other churches to tend to their own affairs.

Gettysburg's more fervently Unionist residents despised Bucher and his supporters. They believed that his supposed disloyal use of the pulpit merited more than intrachurch concern. That a northern town so near the Shenandoah Valley hosted multiple political viewpoints was to be expected. Prewar Christians, however, could have never predicted the exaggerated extent to which wartime citizens considered it their duty to police ministerial speech within the walls of local churches other than their own. Bucher was not the only preacher ostracized by the greater number of Gettysburg's townspeople. Although Lutheran Reverend J. K. Miller had sought service with the Union Army, for instance, he still earned criticism for "his steady and persistent adherence to the Democratic faith," which "incurred the displeasure of leading Abolitionists in his town, who by their heartless proscription . . . rendered his position not only an unpleasant one, but one which threatens the withdrawal of a livelihood for himself and family."[100] As townspeople in dozens of similarly divided northern communities peered figuratively and literally through church windows, worshippers in the pews grew weary of the attention. In time many could no longer abide knowing that their fellow townsmen and women believed them in alliance with traitors. As the Bucher and Miller cases reveal, pressure from non-member townsmen was often as great a factor in local ministerial disputes as the attitudes of careworn church members themselves.

The "local" in local disputes over ministerial speech did not mean small town or community automatically, as is illustrated in the case of Presbyterian Reverend William A. Scott. A friend of Andrew Jackson's, Scott once held the pastorate of the president's tiny Presbyterian church on the grounds of the Hermitage in Nashville. After decades of service, Scott became the first minister of the Calvary Presbyterian Church in San Francisco when it was formally organized on July 23, 1854. There he quickly assumed an important role in the burgeoning community. As had been his pattern wherever he labored, Scott helped found numerous schools and churches. Still, controversy followed Scott. He opposed the compulsory reading of Bible passages in the newly founded public schools and, even more unpopularly in the raucous frontier town of San Francisco, vehemently opposed vigilante justice.[101] Most importantly, Scott's prewar writings make it clear that he valued an independent pulpit and resented efforts to mandate clerical discourse. He asked in 1859, "Is it not true that if one pulpit has the courage to utter an honest opinion that does not happen to coincide with the rest of the pulpits, that then all the pulpits and the papers that have neither the capacity to understand nor the moral honesty to comprehend . . . open their batteries upon him?" While Scott believed that ministers were to be thinking men and labeled the efforts of local officials and church figures to censure opinionated parsons "the tyranny of fanaticism," he was convinced that the pulpit was no place for partisanship.[102] Wherever he went, Scott persistently kept his own political beliefs out of the pulpit proper as part of what one biographer labeled a "lifelong policy of never mixing politics with religion." Nevertheless, because of his non-pulpit utterances and non-clerical writings, few of Scott's day and place had to wonder what those beliefs were.[103]

William Scott was sympathetic to the South. Born in Tennessee, he had studied under the Reverend Charles Hodge when Hodge still considered slavery a natural and beneficial institution. Scott had owned slaves in Louisiana and had voiced strong support for the U.S.-Mexican War and the land gained in the Mexican Cession.[104] Most revealingly, William Scott blamed antislavery radicals for the country's woes. In response to the heated northern abolitionist reaction to the Fugitive Slave Acts, Scott wrote in 1850 that "the contest is for and will really result either in the abolition of slavery or the dissolution of the Union, and much as I love the Union, and much as I wish the negroes all to be free [if somewhere else], yet I am for dissolution rather than dishonor and shame to the South and a forced emancipation."[105] Scott, in all of these opinions, had courted trouble for much of his professional life. The two became much better acquainted, however, during the spring and summer of 1861.

The Civil War created great conflict within Scott, a personally opinionated clergyman ostensibly averse to addressing political issues in the pulpit.[106] Moreover Scott, a cleric with a known affinity for the South, found himself in a city and ministering to a local church comprised overwhelmingly of Unionists. When the members of his congregation predictably demanded overtly Unionist preaching, Scott did what seemed least offensive and most tenable to him in that instance. He assumed the garb of peaceful conservatism, declaring himself "positively opposed to civil war between the American States for any cause, or under any circumstances" but otherwise suggesting the war was none of his denomination's concern.[107] Most aggravatingly to his congregants, he prayed for all parties involved—not only Abraham Lincoln, but Jefferson Davis as well. His strategy proved inadequate. From both the pews of his church, one of the city's largest, and the street corners of the city came calls for Scott's resignation. Months passed filled with accusations and counter-accusations, critical newspaper coverage, and condemnation by the Presbytery of California. Through it all, including formal censure by his denomination, Scott held his position when, on the morning of Sunday, September 22, 1861, he set out for his church to preach.

A restless crowd of more than two thousand outside of Scott's Calvary Presbyterian Church placed Union flags at the top of the church and on the front lampposts. On the building opposite the church, they also strung up an effigy of the preacher, bearing the sign "Dr. Scott, the reverend traitor."[108] When Scott arrived, he pushed his way into the church, preached a non-controversial sermon, prayed generically for the head of the government (singular), and made his exit. However, his departure was achieved amid a shower of threats from the angry crowd, who shouted, "hang him" and "down with traitors." Scott's son, William, was recognized and accosted by some in the crowd. In an apparent act of self-defense, William struck a policeman. He was arrested and released the next day. Aware at last of the danger he and his family faced in San Francisco, Scott resigned the pastorate of Calvary Presbyterian Church on September 23, 1861. Scott, his family, and a number of friends totaling twenty in all then sailed for refuge in England. Scott had been censured by his denominational hierarchy, but clearly it was his local congregants and, more importantly, unaffiliated San Franciscans who ultimately forced his hand. As the Scott case makes clear, local efforts to curtail clerical freedom—predominantly the result of sometimes arguably disloyal clerics crossing paths with unarguably loyal church and secular communities—were often governed more by mob rule than by the rule of church law.

Occasionally, preachers successfully resisted local and congregant efforts to shape their rhetoric. Prominent New York Presbyterian Reverend Henry J. Van Dyke, for example, claimed that the charges of disloyalty leveled against him were specious and stemmed wholly from his unwillingness to preach politics as a proponent of the Doctrine of Spirituality of the Church; his clerical peers insisted that Van Dyke was vigorously pro-southern.[109] Ultimately exasperated, Van Dyke threatened a lawsuit against William Dunham, a recently resigned twenty-four-year member of his congregation who persisted in accusing Van Dyke of sedition. Wrote Van Dyke's attorney to the willful ex-congregant, "Rev. Henry J. Van Dyke has been given to understand from various sources that you have recently . . . stigmatized him as a traitor and a copperhead, and that you have declared that he should be driven from the city of Brooklyn." Van Dyke's advocate warned that only a prompt retraction and heartfelt apology would keep legal proceedings for slander from being initiated.[110]

No retraction came. Van Dyke then opted to forgive his accusing brother in Christ. Most found Van Dyke condescending in his feigned piety, however, given his persistently questionable exploits. Van Dyke, among other things, refused to enter his church after members attached an American flag to its spire in the wake of Fort Sumter and maintained his boycott until the church's membership took the flag down. And while he adamantly refused to make announcements from the pulpit of sewing circles to aid the city's sick and wounded soldiers or of the upcoming meetings of such groups as the Sanitary and Christian Commissions, Van Dyke catered to the "openly and notoriously disloyal and Secessionist" elements of his church. On at least one occasion Van Dyke welcomed into his pulpit a guest speaker so known for disloyalty that military authorities ran him out of Kentucky.[111] Clearly Van Dyke was disloyal. Equally clear is that he was bothered by the accusations leveled against him; those unconcerned with the disparaging things that others say rarely threaten litigation to bring such aspersions to an end, after all. But if Van Dyke was stung by the members' campaign to constrain his pulpit behavior, he was not about to cede any of his authority or oratorical freedom.

Van Dyke was exceptional in that he neither left his pulpit nor was forced to resign, both common outcomes when a preacher's loyalty came into question in the Union. Instead, he steered his local church toward a more southern-sympathizing position. "Before the rebellion was over," the *New York Times* reported, "nearly every family of northern origin and loyal sentiment had left the [Van Dyke's] church."[112] But in a broader sense, Van Dyke's story is not rare. Not just isolated to the Lower North, local efforts to curtail a suspected minister's freedom of pulpit speech occurred everywhere in the Union, from the border states to New York, Ohio, Pennsylvania, and even California. Such incidents reveal the degree to which all patriots, and not just church members, considered the sermons and public pronouncements of every minister their business. Preachers had always been important local figures, and Americans in such a religious age were not eager to call them to task. But in the end, local church and community members proved willing to do just that, perhaps ironically convinced that the war—and more specifically the consequences of defeat in the war—mandated in the name of Christianity the constriction of the Christian preacher's oratorical liberties.

Virtually every quarter of wartime northern society experienced assaults upon the freedom of ministerial expression and thus the power, authority, and influence of the denominational clergy. Federal and state leaders, agents, and soldiers, loyal preachers and denominational governing bodies, and local church and community members all believed that their labors furthered the cause of the Union. Given the new exigencies of war, moreover, they thought of their efforts as being little if any different from those carried out in the broader secular nation. Attacks upon suspect ministers took their place alongside campaigns against disloyal politicians that included arrests and the suspension of the writ of habeas corpus, against treasonous newspapers that resulted in the imprisonment of editors, and against unscrupulous businessmen that entailed boycotts, seizing assets, and cultivating societal embarrassment.[113] Thus the local citizens, church members, soldiers, politicians, and even ministers who proscribed preachers during the Civil War participated in a nationwide turning away from the effectively blind veneration of the clergy. Undeniably, religion played a prominent role in postwar America, as is evident in the spiritual overtones of the South's "Lost Cause" and the North's so-called "Social Gospel." True as well is that denominational preachers continued to play leading roles in the religious lives of local congregants and maintained at last a hand in local secular affairs. But by the end of the sustained and multi-participant attack upon ministerial autonomy that was the Civil War, the preacher was in many ways just another American professional, no longer cosseted in all things by the fealty of the masses and the shield of the pulpit.

5

WHAT THE PREACHERS THOUGHT
Political Preachers in the North

I T IS CLEAR THAT preachers who, for whatever reason, refused to figuratively wave the Union standard from behind their consecrated lecterns garnered widespread reproach. And yet, many ministers and their defenders persisted in avoiding partisan preaching. Clearly many intractable Union clerics resisted the politicization of their pulpit—and endured the individual proscription that such resistance provoked—because of their Confederate sympathies.[1] But while the treacherous motives and unalterably treasonous behaviors of *all* northern ministers who bemoaned the merging of politics and religion have long been assumed, there is more to the story. Many wartime preachers on the Union homefront possessed deep and apparently well-intended concerns over the proper role of the clergy and the denominational minister's personal autonomy, concerns historians since have left largely unexamined.

All preachers who believed themselves compelled to stick strictly to the preaching of the gospel and avoid the debauched world of politics were not disloyal. For many Christian leaders who spoke out against political preaching, their position was but an outgrowth of their innate religious conservatism, an expression of their belief in the separateness of spiritual life. And conversely, not every political preacher was a wild-eyed partisan who, in the throes of some patriotic frenzy, abandoned ages-old ideas about the distinctiveness of religious thought and sentiment. Instead, many preachers became wartime pragmatists, not devotees of political proselytizing per se but realists who amended their attitudes to fit the exigencies of the age. Scores of sacralists recognized that the dogmas of the quiet past were inadequate in the spiritual storm that was the Civil War. In their estimation the tenets of Christianity were unalterable and the saving and soothing of souls must always predominate, but the integrity of the church was not fundamentally compromised when ministers addressed their beleaguered country's political woes.

It is impossible to understand preachers during the Civil War without considering their efforts to reconcile their attitudes about political preaching with the necessities and constraints of war. In those reconciliation efforts, northern church figures and lay leaders fell into three different categories of thought on the issue of political preaching. This conceptual paradigm, with its acknowledgment of an ideological contested ground, bucks the long-dominant scholarly trend of presenting wartime ministers as all politically activist or all politically silent.[2] Political preaching in the Union was not *just* a matter of partisan churches or a manifestation of the supremacy of political—as opposed to religious—ideas in the minds of American Christians.[3] Simply stated, preachers in the Union participated in a real and principle-based debate over the degree to which the Christian church should, through its ministers, involve itself in the nation's greatest political crisis.

I

Americans before the Civil War largely exhibited an "all or nothing" attitude in defining political sermons. Antebellum sermons were not customarily analyzed in nuanced ways, nor were messages characterized in any but the broadest of terms. Antebellum northerners thought a sermon "political" when it addressed even the slightest non-biblical or ecumenical concern (so too did most Old Southerners, when slavery was removed from the equation). They did not debate particular definitions because most were either for or against political preaching in the whole and not in part. Essentially, prewar Americans understood political preaching much as Supreme Court Justice Potter Stewart would understand obscenity ("I know it when I see it") a century later. They did not need to define it, but they knew it when they heard it. Therefore, while late-antebellum northern preachers certainly argued over the legitimacy of partisan sermonizing and the clergy's proper place, if any, in the nation's political affairs, in general they did not bicker over the definition or meaning of political preaching.

But as the literal and figurative smoke from Fort Sumter wafted northward, it made hazy the lines of distinction between what was moral and religious and what was purely political. Most in the Union agreed that secession and the war it initiated were challenges to the sovereignty of their government, if not to the very existence of the United States. Still, many Unionist ministers insisted that the gospel was, and must forever remain, unchanged. It was their sacred obligation to keep their religion pure and undefiled, no matter how dire things became in the temporal world. But for other clerics, whose conceptualization of the United States no doubt included ideas about core human issues such as self-worth, individual autonomy, and religious freedom, the splintering of their political nation portended more than just political consequences. They avowed that, because their country was itself a religious entity, old characterizations of "political preaching" were useless. With war, in short, determining what was inappropriate political sermonizing and what was not became more subjective for ministers on the Union homefront, many of whom vilified the southern secessionist clergy while increasingly imbuing their own nation with holy meaning.

Among wartime clergymen, three broad categories of thought concerning the preaching of politics existed. Ministers as a rule imagined that religion and politics were divided altogether into *separate spheres*, were conditionally separated on the basis of their attendant *separate duties*, or were equally vital (at least here on Earth) constituent or *separate components* of an all-encompassing Christian ministry. The first and most conservative conceptualization of political preaching routinely espoused by northern ministers was predicated on the unconditional departmentalization of a Christian's life. Essentially, some northern clergymen not only embraced the idea of distinct religious and political spheres but sought the absolute separation of those spheres. Although used in a Confederate text, the language of the foundational document of the Presbyterian Church in the Confederate States of America represents such a viewpoint. The true church must "recognize nothing but the new creature in Jesus Christ. The moment it permits itself to know the Confederate or the United States," these advocates of what can accurately be called a *separate-spheres* doctrine charged, "the moment its members meet as citizens of these countries" it became unduly political and threatened to introduce the political difficulties of the world into the house of God.[4] Such ideological separatists in the North included members of mainstream denominations, German-descendant pietistic sects, nonconformist and quietistic "Peace" denominationalists, and the midwestern evangelicals who during the war led what became known as the "New Church" movement.[5]

Democrat and Methodist preacher John Van Buren Flack epitomized a separate-spheres minister. Flack hoped to exist in a local community of Republicans, he claimed, by "minding [his] own business and preaching the gospel, not party politics."[6] To his dismay however, Flack increasingly encountered congregants in rural Illinois who would not allow him to sermonically avoid politics and instead preach the gospel and nothing else.[7] Flack had company in his ostensibly apolitical impulses, including fellow Methodist and Illinois Democrat Rumsey Smithson, who was famously political as a private citizen but believed his political interests and his professional duties as a minister had no bearing upon each other whatsoever. Flack and Smithson, along with other ministers in Illinois, Missouri, and Ohio, formed the nucleus of the Protestant New Church movement during the war. Although many of its adherents were pro-southern, the New Church movement was fundamentally a collection of break-off groups from mostly Methodist and Baptist churches orchestrated by men who earnestly believed themselves engaged in a conservative campaign to save the true church from corruption through politics.[8] The most famous such group was the religious society called the Christian Union, an Ohio-based organization of evangelical denominationalists that formed in early 1864 and, by war's end, claimed adherents throughout the Midwest.

It is hard to imagine a more concrete expression of separate-spheres sentiment than that offered by an Ohio body of Christian Unionists in mid-1864. "Whereas," church leaders proclaimed, "We believe that political preaching . . . has been the cause of much evil; and, whereas, we are commanded in the Scriptures to abstain from every appearance of evil, therefore, we prohibit it and forbid all political preaching, or political discussion in our religious meetings; and ministers or members being guilty thereof, shall be dealt with for immoral conduct."[9] Separatism in the name of religious purity led Christian Union founders to refuse "to vote for resolutions of war" or "pray for the success of the war." Christian Unionists declared as founding principles that spiritual fruits were the only conditions of membership and that all should seek a "Christian union without controversy" in which partisan preaching was eschewed.[10] Lest one imagine that Christian Unionists and other advocates of separate spheres were simply abandoning their world to the devil, such denominationalists believed they need not dabble in politics to feel confident in the future. As their religiously separatist ancestors had preached in an earlier American age, "if the United States were in the right, 'God will maintain his own cause, whether the righteous nation pray for his interposition or not.'"[11]

Those who championed the notion of completely separate religious and secular spheres believed their attitude towards political preaching was supported by the lessons of history. Mainstream denominational leaders reminded their adherents that even America's most devout Christians—pacifists, pietists, and the like—now suffered the consequences of their past politicized piety. They referenced such proof as an often-reprinted essay from 1839 that bemoaned Quaker participation in the political struggles of the Revolutionary age, an essay characterized in 1864 by the editors of the *Friend's Intelligencer* as "singularly applicable to the age in which we live." In that cautionary missive intended for Friends and non-Friends alike, Quaker leader John Comly asked, "what real friend of Truth and peace, in the non-resisting spirit of the gospel, can believe that the maintenance of civil rights will sanction . . . violation of religious and pacific principles?" Had Quakers not dabbled in politics in years past, Comly offered, "there is with us no doubt the [S]ociety [of Friends] would have been less molested and many of its partners would have suffered less." The past, Comly concluded, and mainstream separate-spherists now concurred more than twenty years later, plainly taught Friends to "be separate from the mixtures and confusions of human policy and political expediency."[12] Similarly useful to separate-spherists was a Mennonite editor who believed compromises with the secular and political world had led past Christians toward warmongering. "Had the professors of Christianity continued in the purity and faithfulness of their forefathers, we should now have believed that war was forbidden; and Europe, many long centuries ago, would have reposed in peace," he wrote.[13]

If the separate-spherists had an archetype, it was Presbyterian Reverend Stuart Robinson of Kentucky. Robinson believed that Christ reigned supreme over the civil government of the United States as "the Lord Christ as King of Nations" and over the ecclesiastical government as the "Lord Christ King of Saints." These two jurisdictions, Stuart argued in classic separate-spheres style, were "ordained of Christ to be kept distinct." Therefore, it was wrong for the church "to pronounce upon the question of the duty of the National Government . . . in reference to civil and military policy, and declare 'loyalty' to be in common with orthodoxy and piety."[14] Although certainly pro-southern in much of his rhetoric, Robinson vehemently espoused separate-sphere beliefs for decades prior to the war. His wartime concerns were likely no more rooted in Copperheadism than were those expressed by a group of separate-spherists, many of them from the upper Midwest, at the 1862 Presbyterian Old School General Conference in Columbus, Ohio. Led by the Reverend A. P. Forman of Missouri, the group warned against the assembly making rulings based on points of "political dogma" and not principles gleaned form the Bible.

Moreover, they reminded their brethren, "citizens owe allegiance to the State, and are bound to uphold and maintain the civil government; but the Church, as such, owes allegiance only to the Lord Jesus Christ; his kingdom is the only kingdom she is bound to uphold—hence she can be loyal only to her King."[15]

Sometimes ministers espoused separatist opinions because they were the least offensive to their religious sensibilities. Struggling with the ideological question of political preaching, native New Jerseyean and Episcopal clergyman Noah Hunt Schenck observed, "it may be well to inquire for a moment, how far a commissioned preacher of the Gospel of Christ may go in the discussion of . . . questions of a political character as stand related to spiritual life in the individual or in the Church." Concerned with the nature of government from the religious perspective, Schenck did not find fault with those who believed it a "part of the Christian ministry to stand guard at the door of our municipal institutions" and to "counsel in the hour of political emergency." But even as Schenck declared that a preacher, "by reason of his vocation, loses not a whit of his citizenship," he also admitted that there were times when it was "inconsistent for him to vindicate it."

In Schenck's estimation, the time for restraint came when political matters tempted a preacher to speak out. Political sermonizing lay beyond the great charter of the ministry, the "limitation of our warrant" Schenck called it, which was to preach nothing more than justification through faith and the righteousness of Jesus Christ. Straying from that ministerial charter, Schenck believed, bred discord within the church and contributed to confusion in the world. "Whatever may be the preacher's rights as a man, and privileges as a citizen," the reverend offered a crowd of congregants in Baltimore in 1861, "he has no right as a minister of Jesus, as a curator of souls, he is not privileged in the pulpit or out of it to plunge into . . . such a partisan position upon these issues which heat the public mind as shall lose for him the sympathy and cordial regard of any portion of that congregation whose souls are committed to him for instruction and guidance."[16]

Schenck was far from disloyal, but his religious conservatism led him on principle to disparage political sermonizing, even pro-Union sermonizing. Echoing the same separate-spheres sentiment was a contributor to Boston's *The Liberator* identified only as Milton, who suggested that ministers, as citizens, had "rights as citizens, and therefore we may give our position so long as you give it as *citizens*." But when ministers made use of their priestly office "intending . . . that the influence of your ecclesiastical position shall be brought to bear in the support of a political measure, then I think I am safe in saying you have exceeded your rights."[17] "The great business of the Gospel ministry," another separate-spheres advocate declared, "is, unquestionably, not to take part, officially, in the political strifes of the day, nor to augment social agitation; but rather to pour oil upon the troubled waters, and, more especially, to hold up Christ crucified as the hope of a dying world."[18] To do anything less as a minster fanned the flames of dissonance. "It is not a subject for boasting, but for sorrow and shame, that so many of the clergy are meddling in politics," one New England commentator offered. "The safety of the country never can be secured" until preachers learn to remain in their proper sphere, he went on, "which is to take care of the eternal welfare of their flocks, and to preach peace and good-will to men."[19]

Separate-spherists believed that any other tack might steer the church into perilous waters. Concerned that the introduction of politics into ministerial discourse would prove fatal to his denomination, an Ohio Presbyterian clergyman admitted, "Much has been said, in certain quarters, about politics in the pulpit and the churches" and that "often the very thing complained of has been done by those making the complaint." Nevertheless, because other denominations had been rent asunder by the introduction of politics into church affairs, Presbyterians must take heed. "There is another danger," he cautioned, "against which a Christian people and churches should be guarded. There is a tendency in times of trouble and excitement to bring political differences into church action. If a minister has been . . . in sympathy with an opposite political party, he will scarcely be heard. Church members differ in politics, and bring their differences into the church." His warning went out not to "those who are evidently disloyal, but where there are merely conflicting views of State or National politics—let the churches be warned in time, and avoid a great danger."[20] Although this Ohioan's separatists views echoed those held by many non-slave-state religious conservatives, most Old School Presbyterian opposition to political preaching was heard in border areas where the war and its root cause, slavery, were experienced in more immediate ways than by denominationalists farther north.

Church members and preachers sometimes defied their own denominational traditions in arriving at separate-sphere positions, as was true of the leaders of a body of Connecticut Congregationalists midway through the war. No group was more antithetical to religious-political separatism than was the Congregationalist clergy. Most famously, Congregationalist Henry

Ward Beecher, prior to the 1864 presidential election and from his pulpit inside Brooklyn's Plymouth Church, gave "notice to his people that he shall preach a political sermon every Sunday evening till the presidential election." To those who might have taken offense to his brazenness, Beecher advised, "if they do not want to hear political preaching they may stay away."[21] Many did just that, for even Congregationalists sometimes longed for a church free from any and all political considerations. According to an admittedly gloating southerner's account of the event, the Old Congregational Society of New Boston, Connecticut, "where Dr. Lyman Beecher so long preached," grew so weary of political preaching that its lay leadership resolved: "The Pulpit Committee of this society are herby instructed that whenever they employ a minister of the Gospel to preach in their meeting house on the Sabbath, they shall first inform said minister that he is employed to preach the Gospel truth according to the Bible doctrine, Christ and him crucified, and that only. That he is strictly prohibited by a vote of this society from delivering any discourses of any description upon the present war, and that he shall not allude to the matter either in prayer or sermon."[22]

As a report that initially ran in the *Hartford Times* reveals, other northern Congregationalists felt the same. One such congregant, tired of his preacher's "constantly preaching, praying and exhorting upon political issues," was one day asked to lead the congregation in prayer. The old Democrat and lifelong Congregationalist asked of the Lord, "Let us hear something of thy word and mercy on the Sabbath. We have already been plied to fullness with political fanaticism. . . . If politics are to rule, I shall claim one-half of the time in behalf of the Democratic Party, so that there may be a fair discussion within these walls. Amen." According to the newspaper account, this was the first prayer ever publicly uttered within the church on behalf of the Democracy; after it was concluded, there was within the church "a silence of half an hour, and the meeting then adjourned." As of November 1862, when the account was reprinted in a Utah newspaper, "from that time forward, the minister attended to his gospel duties and left political questions to be settled by the people outside of the church."[23] Apparently, separate-spherism could sometimes be forced upon wayward church leaders.

The antebellum Catholic tradition featured both apolitical sermons and diocesan leaders who wielded much political and social authority. Thus Catholics were well schooled in a brand of separate-spheres religion that did not malign the political world as much as it simply stressed its distinctiveness.

Catholic leaders were routinely pro-southern and pro-slavery. And, they were by and large anti-Republican. But many were also sincere in their aversion to the introduction of political concerns into their priestly duties. Catholic prewar and wartime leaders were not expected by their parishioners to serve up anything like political preaching. The liturgically scripted Latin mass rendered political asides—and really any variation from the centuries-old order of worship—unlikely. All in all, this meant that a majority of northern wartime Catholic leaders ardently advocated the absolute separation of church and political-military concerns *in the church proper* even though several made known their opinions on the war and on the position their charges should assume in the conflict in other venues and written mediums.

Many such leaders were undoubtedly pro-Confederate. Pope Pius IX addressed Jefferson Davis in an 1863 letter as "the Illustrious and Honorable Jefferson Davis, President of the Confederate States of America." The Holy Father then celebrated the South's peaceful desires while offering, "Would to God that the other inhabitants in those regions (the Northern people), and their rulers, seriously reflecting upon the fearful and mournful nature of intestine warfare, might, in a dispassionate mood, adopt the counsels of peace." In so doing, Pius IX came nearer a formal recognition of the Confederacy than did any secular European leader.[24] Although the papal attitude provided American Catholics the leeway to be effectively pro-southern in their conservative outlook, many American Catholic leaders and lay people maintained their conservative religious sensibilities *and* remained loyal to the Federal government. Writing in 1864, Catholic writer and southern sympathizer Dr. Thomas Nichols correctly characterized New York Archbishop and staunch Unionist John J. Hughes, for instance, as someone who was once "opposed to abolitionism and to the war; and yet his influence was used, by adroit management, to fill the ranks of the Federal army."[25]

Catholic hierarchical pronouncements on political preaching from within the Church itself were not the norm during the war, although a number of important Catholic figures were certainly heard from during the conflict. When offered, such directives most often privileged separate-sphere attitudes. At the war's outset, for example, the Provincial Council of Cincinnati advised: "The spirit of the Catholic Church is eminently conservative, and while her ministers rightfully feel a deep and abiding interest in all that concerns the welfare of the country, they do not think it their province to enter into the political arena. They leave to the ministers of the very human sects to discuss from their pulpits and in their ecclesiastical assemblies the very exciting questions which lie at the basis of most of our present difficulties."[26]

Other important Catholic leaders concurred. In the months before the war, Baltimore Archbishop Francis Kenrick was aghast that a priest would presume to set forth, even away from the pulpit and in the press, "his own opinion as the norm of action; and that moreover on the most grave and difficult of questions [of allegiance to government]."[27] Likewise, Bishop Martin John Spalding of Louisville, Kentucky, believed priests were to steer clear of politics and that a number of American bishops were too willing to intervene in just such matters, as he expressed in a letter addressed to the Holy See in 1863. In a later dispatch, Spalding called out Archbishop Purcell of Cincinnati by name as one such errant clergyman, indicting him for unduly meddling in politics.[28] These and similar missives prompted Rome to establish and then reiterate the global Catholic leadership's position in letters to assumed partisan clerics, as when Pope Pius IX expressed to New York Archbishop John J. Hughes a confidence that parishioners "would comply with our paternal admonitions and hearken to our words the more willingly as of themselves they plainly and clearly understand that we are influenced by no political reasons, no earthly considerations, but impelled solely by paternal charity, to exhort them to charity and peace."[29]

Among Catholic notables in America, most vociferous in their separatism were the editors of a number of Catholic newspapers, publications that acted as mouthpieces for their locality's governing archdiocese. Such offerings were occasionally so conservative as to embarrass the admittedly traditionalist bishops and archbishops they featured. Philadelphia's *Catholic Herald,* for instance, recognized as the "official organ" of Bishop of Philadelphia James F. Wood, was forced to carry Bishop Wood's disavowal after the paper's editor, John Duffey, defended in print the South's secessionist actions as an appropriate defense of their constitutional liberties.[30] Even more infamous than Duffey were the editors of Baltimore's *Catholic Mirror,* Michael J. Kelly and John B. Piet, who were twice arrested during the war for their arguably treasonous writings.[31] Upon inspection, the *Mirror* seems clearly to have been ardently anti-black, antiwar, anti-abolitionist, and anti-Lincoln, but many "suspect" pronouncements were principally calls for peace and indictments of priests who worked against its arrival. "Unhappily many of these ordained peace-makers," an editor of the *Mirror* offered in early 1862, "take fire at the mention of the word [peace], and brand as a traitor the most ardent Unionist if he does not adhere to the bloody dogma of coercion."[32] Like Kelly and Piet, James McMaster, editor of the controversial Catholic New York periodical the *Freeman's Journal*, was arrested and his paper stopped for almost a year early in the war.[33] The *Freeman's Journal* too routinely carried scathing attacks on political priests and partisan preaching. That such pieces often featured essays by southern writers caused McMasters little grief, as was true of his decision to feature Natchez, Mississippi, Bishop William Elder. In a piece published in the *Freeman's Journal* late in the war, Elder offered (in perfect separate-sphere fashion) that to pray for a politician was to abide a "betrayal of my sacred trust and a deep injury to the church, in which alone are my hopes of eternal salvation."[34]

Catholic leaders and newspapers in the United States during the war were overwhelmingly Democratic and sometimes vehemently anti-black. Such was to be expected. Any other political response to the anti-immigrant, anti-Catholic nativism present in the burgeoning Republican Party would have seemed counterintuitive. So too did the employment competition between Irish immigrants and free blacks in northern cities, along with the shared Democratic identities of most Catholics and the southerners who oppressed African Americans in the slave-owning South, steel many northern Catholics in their distrust of so-called "black" Republicans. Historians have at times been too quick to assume, however, that their Democratic and anti-administration inclinations equated to Catholic disloyalty in every instance. As was true across the broad spectrum of northern Christianity's separate-sphere ranks, the truth is more nuanced. Philadelphia's *Catholic Herald*, for instance, was not a Copperhead rag along the lines of John Duffey's *Catholic Mirror* or, arguably, the *Freeman's Journal*, nor was Baltimore's Francis Kernick necessarily a traitor, despite the fact that both the *Catholic Herald* and the cleric were anything but supportive of the Federal government's every move.[35]

It warrants noting that a handful of important separate-spherists in the Union, men such as Stuart Robinson of Kentucky, actively endorsed the Doctrine of the Spirituality of the Church, a southern-originated Presbyterian campaign for an apolitical denomination. Lest *all* wartime separate-spherists be similarly categorized, however, three important points must be made. First, clerical endorsers of the Doctrine of the Spirituality of the Church were often (but not always, as with the Reverend Robinson) new in their embrace of such an overarching principle and highly inconsistent in its application. In other words, southern-sympathizing Presbyterians routinely embraced the Doctrine and then stretched its restrictive tenets because it was convenient to their pro-southern efforts.[36] Most Union separate-spherists, however, were neither recent in their aversion to the mixing of politics and religion nor particularly enamored with the southern Confederacy. Secondly, the Doctrine of the Spirituality of the Church was never a very coherent doctrine even among Presbyterians. Depending upon whom one asked, the doctrine meant anything from Presbyterianism's absolute divorce of religion and politics to a statement about the illegitimacy of church-sponsored social reform efforts.[37] Finally and most importantly, evangelicals in other traditions like Methodism and Baptistism did not, for the most part, embrace the Doctrine of the Spirituality of the Church until *after the war*.[38] So while the doctrine and the notion of separate spheres were in many ways alike, there is little reason to believe that most separate-spherists in the North were inspired by Southern Presbyterians and their fairly ambiguous dogma. Spirituality of the Church doctrinaires in Presbyterian strongholds like Central Kentucky were indeed separate-spherists; throughout the greater Union, however, most separate-spherists were not particularly concerned with the Doctrine of the Spirituality of the Church.

Some separate-sphere preachers were no doubt disloyal and found it convenient to embrace religious separatism as a means of both withholding their support for the Federal war effort and empowering the southern enemy. Many more were not, however, nor were they de facto occupants of some reclusive religious order somewhere out on the nation's ideological fringe. Separate-spherists instead endorsed of one of the nation's most prominent denominational attitudes towards wartime politics; as a religious writer in *The Circular* surmised in 1864, "the popular doctrine is, that religion and politics are two entirely distinct things; that the church and state must not touch one another."[39] Many Friends, Mennonites, Amish, Nazarenes, Moravians, Christian Unionists and, to a lesser degree, Old School Presbyterians, Catholics, and other mainstream denominationalists earnestly believed that their faith separated them from the rest of the world no matter how loudly the winds of war howled outside the church's walls.

II

A second position involved ministers who could not help but be concerned with slavery, the war, and other issues and affairs that were adjudicated first and foremost in the political arena. They were, however, convinced that their concern in a general sense must not devolve into focused, manifestly political proselytizing. Such parsons and their supporters spoke of the clear and distinct duties of the ministry. Thus, I have borrowed from them the term *separate-duty* Christians as a way of describing their sense of limited engagement with secular issues. Separate-duty clerics were far from anomalistic during the Civil War. As was observed by a Democratic newspaper editor, many throughout the age thought it wrong "to discuss the purely moral aspects of questions which are in themselves legitimate to the pulpit" if and when the minister's intent was "producing political results."[40] Controversial topics were not taboo in the pulpit, in other words, until the preacher made them so by addressing them from a political perspective. By this definition, the minister was free to indict the brutalism of the slave owner if he did so to rebuke the abuser and call him to repentance. But the minister became unduly political when he offered a broader course of action, be it one as basic as the enactment of stricter codes proscribing such abuses or as drastic as the abolition of slavery itself. To give another example, ministers like Presbyterian William B. Stewart considered it beyond the pale to pray that Lincoln would take this or that specific action, but in a general way, Stewart believed, clergymen were "under religious obligations to sustain the President" and were "bound, on all proper occasions like the present one, to put the people in mind to obey Magistrates . . . but this is not preaching politics, so called."[41]

In enunciating this mindset during the war, Presbyterian leader Thomas A. Hoyt of Kentucky spoke of the "time" and "mode" and "when" and "how" of the ministry as being different from ministerial "duties."[42] The time, mode, when, and how of an issue were all political considerations *in their specificity*. A preacher could not champion the time, place, and action by which a change for the good might transpire without implicitly suggesting that his listeners themselves participate in the event. A separate-duty preacher was free—even obliged—to exhort the faithful toward their ultimate duty as Christians ("pray for peace," for example), but to instruct them in the particulars of bringing about such a condition (i.e., "cease prisoner exchanges," "partake in truce negotiations," etc.) entered into the political arena. Hoyt considered such inevitably partisan entreaties inappropriate, but what is important in this instance is his conception of what constituted the political in the context of a religious sermon. Many in the antebellum and wartime years both above and below Mason and Dixon's Line shared beliefs akin to Hoyt's and felt, along with a commentator in *The Phalanx*, that the most useful objective of the minister was "not in prescribing a particular topic for each supplicant: it is in *quickening him* into a right state of feeling" and then "*getting him* to pray as he feels."[43]

Practically speaking, then, separate-duty clerics defined political preaching in terms of degrees. Most adherents allowed room for the introduction of political issues into the pulpit but in only the broadest and least determinative ways. Just before the war began, a writer in the Chambersburg, Pennsylvania, *German Reformed Messenger* warned his brethren against too eagerly embracing political causes and thus losing sight of the true prize to be won as Christians. "We should not plead for an entire and absolute divorce between Church and State. The principles of our holy religion will and must influence all departments of human life," he offered, but the church must not become overly willing to "dabble in politics." "After all," he concluded, "our political liberty, good as it is, and worthy of our best efforts to preserve and maintain, is only a worldly good, and slavery, whether a good or an evil as the two sections will have it, is only a worldly good or evil. Civil liberty cannot save a soul . . . and slavery does not necessarily bring salvation or condemnation."[44]

Their recognition of the need to protect their political liberties, along with an unwillingness to compromise the purity of their faith in that effort, characterized most separate-duty preachers. Thus, even when Christian ministers led parishioners toward a general understanding of their duties as citizens, it was always in the knowledge that Christ—and not the state—came first. Another editor of the *Messenger* passionately exhorted his readers, along with the rest of "the Christian portion of the nation," to "implore the Divine interposition in our complicated and darkening trials." Christians were to pray diligently for the Union and were to "esteem it a great privilege" that they were free to do so. More importantly, however, they were to put their trust in a power greater than presidents, cabinets, and armies. "Whilst it is our duty humbly and diligently to use second causes," the editor concluded, "they cannot deliver us. Our only hope is in the great first Cause, the arm that can calm the waves of passion and tell the tumultuous sea, 'Peace, be still.'"[45] Equally intent upon preserving the predominance of the church over the state were the Pennsylvania Brethren who declared "our sympathies and prayers are with and for . . . our country" and who "cheerfully accord to the 'powers that be' our cordial and sincere regards." Referencing the most commonly cited separate-duty scripture, the Brethren nevertheless avowed, "Resolved that in the injunction, 'Render to Caesar the things that are Caesar's, and to God the things that are God's,' we recognize first, our duty to God, and secondly to our country; that in our allegiance to the latter we declare our unaltered attachment to 'Constitution and the Union,' founded under God by our fathers."[46]

Father James Keogh of Pittsburgh, a rare wartime Catholic believer in separate-duty discourse, likewise hoped that the church would never be guilty of "treating worldly things, unless when they enter the sphere of spiritual duties." Empowered in Keogh's estimation to tell "the nations and their rulers their mutual rights and duties," the church was however now faced with such an instance. The war threatened the government of the United States but had not yet sealed its doom. In a lecture drawn from "those principles which are taught by Catholic theologians, and practically inculcated by the Church herself," Keogh instructed his listeners that, "As long as the government of the United States exists, to it you owe your allegiance. Nay, more, whatever you believe necessary to sustain it, that, if it comport with your condition in life, and with your other duties, you are obliged in conscience to contribute to do."[47] As was true even of smaller wartime Protestant denominations like the Lutheran, Evangelical, and German Reformed churches—denominations populated at once by evangelical revivalists and introverted pietists—the Catholic Church was sometimes home to absolute separate-spherists, theologically motivated separate-duty Christians like Keogh, and unabashedly political members at the same time.

Separate-duty ministers and lay leaders came from numerous Christian quarters during the war. Most mainstream denominations like Baptists, Methodists, and Presbyterians had conservative members and branches that sought an appropriate level of patriotism and support for the Union while simultaneously guarding against the loss of piety and the maintenance of their church's central gospel mission. Moreover, some ministers in mainstream denominations adopted separate-duty positions when that was the most that their individual situation made available to them. Methodist Reverend Silas Swallow, for instance, characterized southern Pennsylvania as a veritable "battlefield between those who stood for the preservation of the Union . . . and those who from party affiliation or political training were opposed to the war and to the freeing of the four million slaves."[48] Against the advice of his more traditional senior preacher, Swallow preached "one sermon on loyalty to the government," a sermon in which there was not one "word of partisan politics, nor of denunciation of traitors or their sympathizers, but a calm presentation of the duty of Christian men to sustain their government in so far as it harmonized with God's laws."[49] Even such mildly political sermons, and perhaps especially such mildly patriotic sermons, were beyond the pale for many in Swallow's audience that Sunday morning, for when the circuit-riding Swallow returned the next month, he found the church padlocked. Undeterred, Swallow hopped atop a stump and preached a solid, albeit apolitical, Methodist message to the largely antagonistic crowd that gathered around him.

The lion's share of northern Episcopal ministers practiced a more restrained—yet still functional—kind of separate-duty preaching. In so doing, they abandoned the prevalent conservatism of prewar Episcopalianism but remained markedly less activist than ministers of other denominations. Representative of this strain of Episcopal political sermonizing was a discourse offered early in the war by New York Episcopal cleric Francis Vinton. His separate-duty logic was simple yet powerful. The Federal government was a divine institution; submission to it "and obedience to [its] magistrates is a religious obligation." Constituent aspects of the divinely ordained government were the Constitution and the union of the states that it anchored. "To destroy this Union, therefore," the Reverend Vinton offered, "is to commit a sin, which God will righteously punish by evils which no prescience can foresee, and no wisdom can repair." Vinton concluded that, because "men are prone to forget their civil obligations; and because self will . . . prompts to sedition and rebellion," Episcopal clergy needed simply to remind parishioners of their obligations as Christian citizens; a believer's proslavery attitudes or past southern sympathies, and in truth any other viewpoints a member held, were immaterial to those obligations. "In short," Vinton concluded, the circumspect minister "inculcates allegiance and compliance. And he further bases these duties of loyalty on the ground of piety."[50]

When viewed through the analytical lens of separate-duty belief, the wartime image of even the East Baltimore Conference of the Methodist Episcopal Church looks different from what most today imagine. The East Baltimore Conference is commonly discussed in the context of wartime treachery.[51] To an extent, this is warranted. It remained a part of the Baltimore Conference of the Methodist Episcopal Church in the United States, or northern Methodism, but governed churches in a good deal of territory that was kept in the Union predominantly by force. As was the case with the greater city, the conference's clergy included a number of indubitable southern sympathizers. Indeed, one of the great historians of American Methodism later declared Methodists in wartime Baltimore "probably more disloyal than any others in the northern Church."[52] But church pulpits in the East Baltimore Conference were filled by many more patriots than traitors, and on numerous occasions the conference's leaders in assembly issued separate-duty-like expressions of support for President Lincoln and the Lincoln administration. Truth be told, the wartime minutes of the conference's denominational meetings are fairly replete with pro-Union exclamations, but because those avowals were often coupled with statements about the dangers of church politicization, historians have as a rule discredited their veracity.

Given that formal and recorded endorsements of the Union and the president were not anathema to East Baltimore Conference Methodist leaders, it seems plausible that what some conference members characterized as principle-based—what I call separate-duty—reservations about political preaching were just that. The 1862 East Baltimore Conference enacted a series of resolutions that disparaged the war as a treasonable affair that threatened to "retard the advancement of civil liberties throughout the world" and endorsed the "present wise and patriotic government administration of the Federal Government." For these resolutions to pass, the topic of political preaching and preachers needed to be addressed, for as was clear in the debate over other proposed and defeated resolutions, too many at that year's assembly had too many concerns about mixing faith and politics to pass declarations without comment on the subject. The issue was settled in a way that simultaneously did not stain the Church's evangelical banner with politics but acknowledged, from a distinctly separate-duty viewpoint, the role of the sermon in both written and spoken form. "Resolved," the last enacted resolution under the heading "National Affairs" pronounced, "In our patriotic efforts in the past or present to sustain the Government of our country, in this her time of severe trial, we are not justly liable to the charge of political teaching; and in the inculcation of loyal principles and sentiments, we recognize the pulpit and the press as legitimate instrumentalities."[53] Individual members were often even more adamantly patriotic—and adamantly separate duty—than the representative assembly. According to the recorder of events for the 1864 East Baltimore General Conference, for instance, the Reverend A. A. Reese elicited cheers when he said of President Lincoln, "there is no man since the days of the Father of his country, whom I honor more." Reese received more "immense applause and cheering" when he seconded the declaration of a loyal Methodist minister from Tennessee. Reese made clear his intent to strike down "everything but the law of God, to preach Jesus and save my country, and yet I am law-abiding; in religion, a Methodist, and in politics a Union man!"[54]

As was the case in Baltimore, upper-southern preachers with conservative denominational roots sometimes acted with open-mindedness. One of the most influential religious leaders in the border states, Presbyterian Robert Jefferson Breckinridge of Kentucky, was a renowned minister, educator, and former moderator of Old School Presbyterianism's General Assembly.[55] Like his denomination, Breckinridge was a man of contradictory elements. Ultimately remembered for his piety, during his ministerial training Breckinridge was introduced to the clergymen of the West Lexington Presbytery by a senior presbyter who warned, "Brethren, you had better be careful how you receive young Mr. Breckinridge, he will either make or break the Presbyterian Church. Before his conversion, he was considered the best dancer, the best hunter, and best stump speaker in Kentucky."[56] Once ordained, he was a self-avowed Old Schooler even though he followed New School beliefs like antislavery and pro-revivalism.[57] His antislavery views were surely complicated. From the 1830s he was an antislavery cleric who presented the institution as the sin of the nation, yet he was also a planter who owned slaves. Breckinridge supported Lincoln in 1860 and served as a delegate to the Baltimore convention that re-nominated Lincoln in 1864. His nephew, however, was 1860 Democratic presidential candidate John C. Breckinridge, and two of his sons, William and Robert Jr., sided with the Confederacy. None of these truths deterred Breckinridge from espousing separate-duty views about the war or portraying the struggle as one that threatened the direst political consequences imaginable.

In Breckinridge's estimation, the Civil War was not so much about the *restoration* of the Union as it was its *preservation*. "The more thoroughly the nation understands that it is fighting neither for vengeance nor for conquest but directly for self-preservation . . . the more it will be disposed to prosecute the war forced upon it in the manner which becomes such a people driven into such a conflict."[58] As Breckinridge asserted in a paper authored in 1862, the clergy was to educate congregants on this issue. But in his essay, Breckinridge steered clear of prescribing specific political behaviors for Presbyterians, admonishing them instead simply to "let a spirit of quietness, of mutual forbearance, and of ready obedience to authority, both civil and ecclesiastical, illustrate the loyalty, the orthodoxy, and the piety of the church."[59] Breckinridge was overwhelmingly practical in his estimation of political preaching as a means toward a justified end, that of the Union's preservation. He eschewed passion-tinged motives like revenge for more logical ones like political stability. Breckinridge represents the scores of loyal but yet manifestly separate-duty preachers from conventional denominational backgrounds who understood that the war required of them a new level of activism as clerics but who likewise hoped to honor the conservative teachings of their respective church traditions.[60]

III

Many northern clerics disagreed with the separate-sphere and separate-duty positions and instead assumed a third wartime stance on political preaching. Men such as Alfred Lee, a leader of Protestant Episcopalism in New England, and Universalist leader Richard Eddy believed that it was impossible for preachers, be they inside or outside of the pulpit, to keep political and religious concerns in separate and distinct realms. Ministerial duty, moreover, could no more be broken down and prioritized than could the benevolence of God. To these men, there was really no such thing as "political" preaching. All sermons on any topic that concerned any of God's children, they believed, were appropriately spiritual. At the war's outset, Alfred Lee instructed his fellow ministers concerning their duties:

> The Christian citizen desires to do his whole duty, both as a Christian and as a citizen. He may reasonably look for counsel to his spiritual guides and expect from the sanctuary a word in season. And his pastor should be prepared to give it. This is no time for anyone, in any station, to evade responsibility or refuse to look stern realities in the face. While our great object as Ministers of Christ is to bring sinners to repentance and inquirers to Jesus, and Christians to growth in grace, and souls to heaven, we are at the same time called to apply the principles of the Gospel to cases as they arise, and to present actual duty in the light of the word of God.[61]

The unconditional commingling of religious and political concerns and sentiments, an approach in which both sacred and secular topics were fundamental if separate components of the minister's hybrid pulpit and public purview, was believed by many to be the recipe not only for victory but also for hastening the advent of the millennial kingdom. Richard Eddy declared in 1864 that the politically mindful Christian's avowal of loyalty to his country, coupled with his bold proclamation of faith in its ultimate victory, constituted a true allegiance to God that was "nourished and strengthened by the consciousness of faith in the Divine Purpose, and of effort for its fulfillment, that the kingdoms of this world shall become the Kingdom of our Lord and his Christ."[62]

It is impossible to imagine a wartime preacher more possessed of this sep-arate-component mindset than Henry Ward Beecher. He and other Congre-gationalists lived entirely in the North (the 1860 census listed no Congregationalist houses of worship in any of the states that formed the Confederacy or in Maryland, Kentucky, Missouri, or Delaware). Most Congregationalist ministers took up the political banner of the Union.[63] Still, Beecher loomed so large in the affairs of Civil War–era America that he alone is the reason many Americans past and present associate the war-time Congregational clergy with an all-inclusive brand of political preaching. Beecher led his local flock at Brooklyn's Plymouth Church—and for that matter the larger American Congregationalist denomination—into the politi-cal arena without reservation, firm in his belief that the activist Christianity handed down to him from his famous father Lyman required nothing less. "I declare that although our American church has thought itself bound, as a church, in its individual pulpits, and in its collective forms, to speak against ten thousand vices . . . yet in respect to the great fundamental questions . . . it has deliberately asserted that it had nothing to do with them, on the ground that it was not to meddle with or touch politics." To those who claimed that such avoidance of political issues by churches and ministers was appropriate, Beecher asked, "Now, the church that does all its duty, except teaching the people how to conduct themselves rightly in the performance of this highest of duties . . . what is such a church worth?"[64]

From the pulpit and in the secular press that routinely reprinted his abolitionist sermons, Beecher unflaggingly urged total support of the war and in time embraced the violence it entailed as a holy exercise. He sent his own son and other family members into the army; members of his church, at Beecher's urging, provided pistols and other trappings of war to fellow churchmen who left their number to join the ranks of the Federal army.[65] That

his involvement with the accoutrements of death and destruction horrified
other ministers bothered Beecher not in the least. In fact, during the war
Beecher was perhaps most indefatigable in his criticisms of other ministers,
particularly those who exalted the freedoms of democracy but were unwilling
to admit the sacrifices it required of Christians. In the end, no national
religious figure took up the cause of an unabashedly politicized ministry more
than Beecher.

As often as not, Beecher preached about what was required especially
of preachers. The minister in his pulpit, Beecher surmised, was a figure of
unparalleled importance, an importance that only increased during times
of great national woe. "The pulpit is still a power," Beecher offered midway
through the war, a "growing and not a waning power; we believe that its
offices are becoming more and more sacred, and that its rule is becoming
more and more established."[66] In Beecher's estimation, the moral authority
of the minister was augmented by his courage in speaking against *all* of the
evils of the day, political or otherwise. Of such a preacher Beecher offered,
"His ground is conceded to him by mankind. They will take him in his arms,
and put him in his pulpit, and they hold him there, so long as he stands for
conscience, and fairly interprets the moral law."[67]

In Beecher's opinion, the hypocritical bawling of the critics of political
preachers was to be expected. "The power of the pulpit is confessed . . . in the
attacks that are made on it, in the avowed jealousy of its influence in times
of popular excitement," Beecher asserted, and "in the attempts to suppress
it which are inaugurated by the demagogue." Slave owners and rebellious
traitors and the northerners who offered them political succor were no doubt
especially critical of politically conscious preachers, for according to Beecher,
"tyrants dread the pulpit; the upholders of vicious customs dread the pulpit;
the friends of unhallowed power dread the pulpit."[68] Reflecting a separate-
component philosophy, Beecher not only believed it acceptable for Christian
ministers to entertain political issues in the pulpit but considered it their
obligation. "In a country where every citizen is called to make magistrates
and laws, where he must shape policies or leave wicked men to do it," Beecher
declared, "if one is bound more than another to be acquainted with public
affairs, and to enlighten men concerning them, it is the religious teacher."[69]

Beecher's views found a national audience thanks to the extensive
circulation of Congregationalist organs like Boston's *Congregationalist* and
New York City's *Congregationalist Independent*, the latter of which he edited

throughout much of the war. And secular New York papers like the *Evening Post*, the *Observer*, and the *Tribune* habitually reprinted Beecher's sermons in whole or in part; smaller newspapers throughout the North then reprinted those sermons as they had appeared in the larger papers. In short, the words of no other religious figure, and perhaps no other American with the exception of Abraham Lincoln, were read more often during the Civil War than those of Henry Ward Beecher. It is true that most Congregationalist ministers need little prompting to preach politics. Certainly the oldest and most revered Congregationalist minister alive when the war began, ninety-nine-year-old former Chaplain of the House of Representatives Daniel Waldo, was as likely to wax political from the pulpit as was Beecher.[70] But because Congregationalists had no unifying hierarchy that prescribed and monitored clerical behavior, the persuasive power of Beecher's uncensored "bully" political pulpit set the separate-component example that many Congregationalists—and many others in other denominational traditions—followed during the war.

Among that number were northern Baptists who, as much or more than even the most radical Congregationalists or Presbyterians, became known for their liberal politics and antislavery agitation during the post-schism years (1845–60). When the war came, it was typical for Baptist clergymen in the North to declare, as did those present at a convention of believers in Pennsylvania, their "profound conviction of the intimate relation . . . between the cause of human liberty and the cause of pure religion, and also set our purpose as citizens, as Christians, and as Christian ministers, to employ our whole influence in supporting the supremacy of our National Constitution against all enemies whatsoever."[71] A representative group of staunch northern Baptist preachers from New Jersey had no qualms about instructing believers concerning the religious embrace of political issues given that the Rebels were engaged in an almost unprecedented political sin against God. "The Southern Conspiracy against our Nation's life," the New Jersey clergymen surmised in 1864, "is the greatest political atrocity since Israel rebelled against Jehovah."[72] Equally vehement were most Reformed Presbyterians, who like Congregationalists were to be found almost exclusively in free states (there were a few Reformed Presbyterians in and around Baltimore and in western Virginia) by the time the Civil War arrived. Prone to antislavery sentiment and critical of the southern clergy before the war, Reformed Presbyterian preachers like New York City's Reverend J. R. W. Sloane commonly capped off political sermons with "earnest exhortation[s] to all to understand the great issue involved in the struggle and aid by every means in their power the Government in this hour of peril. All that concerned us as men, as Christians, as Reformed Presbyterians, was at stake."[73] Given such high stakes, how could any good shepherd be daunted in his "earnest exhortations" by the profanely irrelevant charge that he was practicing political preaching?

American Catholicism was characterized by conservativism (which is not to say Copperheadism) during the Civil War. As we have seen, certainly most within the wartime Catholic ranks were separate-spherists. However, a number of influential Catholic leaders belied their church's innate conservatism and enthusiastically embraced separate-component positions concerning political preaching. Bishop Michael Domenec in Pittsburgh and Archbishop John Baptist Purcell in Cincinnati, to name but two, were avidly pro-Union and said as much from their pulpits. Purcell was unique in his pronounced hatred of slavery. Reminding his parishioners of the Golden Rule, he admitted, "many people had supposed that the question of slavery could never be discussed by Catholic citizens." Archbishop Purcell was convinced otherwise. Catholics, and especially Catholic priests, must talk about slavery and the war then being waged to end the vile institution. Such issues were not different from other spiritual concerns; all worthy causes required action by the devout. "It is impossible for a religious people to consider slavery, as a moral question, without being filled with horror at its enormities," Purcell believed, adding, "Its aspect is everywhere repulsive." For those critical of the church's involvement in politics, Purcell asserted, "To talk about argument, when the question under discussion is the sale of a man's wife and children, is ridiculous. When a political or moral question comes to that, the strong arm of the injured man is the only answer it deserves."[74]

Along with individual actors, important publications like the Pittsburgh *Catholic,* the Cincinnati *Catholic Telegraph,* and the Boston *Pilot* expressed separate-component convictions. Most evident, however, in its editor's belief that church and political concerns were inseparable during times of war was Orestes Brownson's *Quarterly Review.* Not an official church organ as were most Catholic offerings of the day, Brownson's newspaper engaged in constant criticizing of the conservative Catholic leaders and their editors who refused to move beyond the dogmatic strictures of the Catholic Church and its conformist past. "All loyal men," Brownson wrote, "Protestants or Catholics, Republicans, Democrats, or Abolitionists, whether black or white, red or yellow," were friends of Brownson and his fellow Catholics at the

Review. Racist but loyal Protestants (and most in the Union were both) must have fallen in line behind Brownson when he made known his most patriotic sentiments. "Next to religion, and never separable from it, is the cause of our country, and humanity honors, next to her saints, the brave and heroic soldier. . . . He who marches to the battle-field, and pours out his life in defence of his country is the brother of him who marches to the stake of the scaffold, and gives his life for his faith."[75]

New School Presbyterian preachers often joined the separate-component ranks. While Presbyterian Reverend William Adams of New York believed that the chief role of the clergy was "to announce those truths which affect man in his highest relations—to God and immortality," he also held that true religion should pervade the whole of one's being, for "the Sabbath, the closet, the church, are not its [religion's] exclusive sphere; his business and his politics belong to it as well."[76] And, in an essay published in a leading Presbyterian journal, Reverend R. B. Thurston of Massachusetts admitted that, along with the "ministers [who] have been constrained by clear and strong convictions of duty to discuss in the pulpit subjects obviously having a political bearing" were "good men [who] have been alarmed lest they should lose sight of the gospel in their ministrations."[77] Those good men need not fret, Thurston believed, for just as the civil magistrate was God's minister to the public citizen, so was the preacher. Both took up arms, be they in the form of the sword or the Bible, under an all-encompassing "divine warrant and a sacred responsibility." In essence, there were no disjointed areas when political issues were so morally important. As to war, slavery, and loyalty, Thurston asserted: "All this is indeed political; and politics, not in the degraded sense which general wickedness has given to the term, but in a genuine and high sense, is a scriptural science, embracing a most important part of morals, and next in dignity and sacredness to theology itself. Hence to unfold in due proportion those oracles of God which should govern rulers is a part of the minister's official work, divinely appointed. . . . This may be called 'preaching politics.' Be it so. It is preaching the politics of the Bible and of Christ; and it is more than right; it is obligatory."[78]

The notion of a topically untethered clergy troubled many in the country, even during a time of war. Not a few conservative church leaders reminded their fellow Americans that Thomas Jefferson, who more than anyone else raised America's ideological wall of separation between church and state, consistently stressed the difference between a minister's right to take political stands in his private writings and conversations as opposed to his formal sermons. As historian McKinley Lundy has observed, Jefferson believed "the moment of sermonic delivery, as it is employed as a religious act, is what transforms inviolable speech, the brand enjoyed by every citizen, into a different category of communication."[79] Maligning Henry Ward Beecher's mixing of politics and religion, a Unitarian editor of Jeffersonian opinion proclaimed, "Strongly as we may feel upon matters of party politics . . . sadly as we may be disappointed in persons and policies . . . earnestly as we would express ourselves about them on other occasions, we should not feel at liberty to make the sermon or the prayer of the church the vehicles of our expression."[80] In the minds of numerous wartime northern church leaders, the idea that the holy lectern should be home to all of the varied concerns of mankind smacked of the dangerous intuitive and mystical doctrines of the late antebellum years that threatened the very legitimacy of organized religion. The criticisms aimed at politically active clergymen, in other words, ranged from measured arguments against the misguided efforts of sincere and otherwise respectable clergymen to charges of religion-threatening heresy. In the estimation of separate-component church leaders, however, all such charges, no matter whence they came, were equally specious.

Most separate-component clergymen believed that "political preaching" was a manufactured charge lacking merit, a red herring. They rather effortlessly dismissed the charge as superfluous. When called to task for political sensitivities, for instance, separate-component churchmen fought back in the manner of a group of northern Methodist editors in 1864. Accused of turning both their newspaper and their pulpits over to political preaching, the pro-Republican and liberal clerical editors of Boston's *Zion's Herald and Wesleyan Journal* pointed out the proslavery, Copperhead, anti-administration, and generally "arch-traitor" political agenda of those making the charge. At the same time, the all-encompassing denominational newspapermen insisted that their own actions were neither pro- nor anti-anything, politically speaking, but were entirely religious in derivation. Responding for all of the clerical editors of one of American Methodism's most influential papers, an unnamed clergyman wrote:

> Behold the tricks of the politician. They know that the conviction is quite general that ministers . . . ought not to meddle with politics. From this point they push their platforms and party creeds over the

bounds of their rightful empires, when justly opposed in their attempts to violate the natural, moral, and sacred rights of the people, or to frame iniquity into a law of the land, they cry out in horror, and bring against ministers and editors the charge of meddling with or preaching politics. . . . If a preacher stands his ground like a moral hero . . . he is rewarded by his opponents . . . with the title of "political preacher."[81]

And farther south, in Cincinnati, when the erudite Reverend D. Owen Davis of the Fifth Street Presbyterian Church issued a written indictment of the Cincinnati Synod for encouraging political preaching, apparently separate-component clerics noted the hypocrisy. An essayist in the *Presbyter* characterized Davies as "holding to the doctrine of total separation between the spiritual and the secular, and deeming it a sin for the Church to pronounce upon the wickedness of the present rebellion, as that is mixing politics and religion." Nevertheless, the commentator continued, Reverend Davis felt no qualms, it seemed, about going "boldly into the discussion of political matters, and distinctly enunciated his opinions upon the present issues of the country."[82]

By alleging hypocrisy on the part of their maligners, separate-component ministers not only found it easy to dismiss charges of impropriety, but also to recast the accusations in positive terms. Chicagoan and Methodist clergyman George Peck, for instance, noted that loyal Christian ministers "are severely censured by the peace men for their encouragement of the war" and subject to "an abundance of cant from politicians" accusing such clergymen of "political preaching" and of "entering the arms of politics." Ministers were to be men of peace, Peck agreed, "but some of us think that the only way to have an honorable and a Christian peace is to put down the rebellion."[83] Peck was far from alone in his belief that political preaching's practical value in helping to snuff out the rebellion earned for it a newfound acceptability.

Finally, a small number of homefront clergymen were de facto separate-component ministers even when their conservative denominational backgrounds meant that they never would have openly endorsed the wholesale mixing of preaching and politics. Such was true of an Old School Presbyterian minister and editor who noted in the conservative Old School *Danville Quarterly Review* that, "current phrases like 'pulpit politics,' 'mixing politics and religion,' and 'taking political action,'" all frequently used at the time, "present language quite indeterminate in its meaning." Whatever the application, the editor "freely admit[ted] that to bring politics, in any just acceptation of the term, into the pulpit for discussion . . . is a perversion of the functions of the ministry and the authority of the church." However, he then laid out five conditions that, if met, made political issues proper fodder for the pulpit. If the topic was: (1) addressed in the Scriptures, (2) addressed in the creeds and/or confessions of the Presbyterian Church through the ages, (3) the former focus of "frequent deliverances" occasioned by past "particular exigencies" that affected the Church, (4) addressed in the published writings of the Presbyterian Church's past "great lights," or, (5) such that the negative of the proposition is "not sustained by any clear teachings of Scriptures . . . nor by any evangelical creeds or explicit church action of former times, nor by any prominent names in the ministry," then the topic was sermon-suitable. Of course, almost any morally relevant political issue could fit within these parameters. The publishers of the Danville paper straddled the fence by reproving political preaching in article after published article but then printing an essay that, while condemning political preaching in theory, provided so many caveats that none could ever be guilty in practice.[84]

American church leaders and laypeople used the phrase "political preaching" to mean many things during the Civil War. Some, whom I have coined separate-spherists, believed anything that was not unequivocally religious—i.e., exculpated from the Bible and applied to the consideration of man's relationship with God, his biblically sanctioned earthly family, and his church as a child of God—was political and thus not suitable for ministerial discourse. This belief closely resembled the way prewar Americans defined political preaching, but with one important difference. Although antebellum Americans, especially in the North, commonly used such a simple dichotomization in defining political preaching, they just as commonly divorced the definition of political preaching from judgments about the act's legitimacy. As it was applied during the war, however, separate-spherism was an ultraconservative doctrine in which everything but the most expressly scripture-based sermons was likely to be characterized as unduly political and preachers who offered such sermons malevolent.

In the middle of the spectrum belong the separate-duty Christians. These believers held that ministers had a responsibility to exhort their flock toward a desired personal or collective state of existence but not the authority to tell them how or when to get there. This most popular wartime definition of political preaching cast the difference between the specific and the general and the difference between political and religious preaching as one and the same. At the far end of the continuum, finally, were those separate-component Christian leaders and laypeople convinced that the earthly duty of the minister was expansive and that the notion of religious and political sermons was a false dichotomy manufactured by critics with their own worldly agendas and opposing political viewpoints. And whether Universalists, Unitarians, Congregationalists, New School Presbyterians, Episcopalians, Methodists, northern Baptists, Catholics, or members of any number of other faiths, separate-component clerics reveled in what their enemies pejoratively called political preaching.

Virtually all of the wartime instances in which ministers were accused of political preaching were predicated on some version of one of these definitions. No matter the camps involved, however, at the heart of all such charges were fundamental questions about the relationship between Americans and the state. All agreed that both political participation and religiousness—including preaching as one of the most respectable manifestations of religiousness— were rights of citizenship equally safeguarded by the Constitution. But the nation's founders had distinguished between religion and the state by virtue of the First Amendment. Were wartime Americans justified in conflating what the Founders had disentangled? Or conversely, if political freedom and religiosity were equal parts of the privileges that white, male, and free people enjoyed in an ostensibly free society, how could one find fault with Christians who tempered their politics with piety, or vice-versa? Most conventional northern Christians, be they separate-sphere or separate-duty adherents, insisted that political life and religious life were distinct entities as envisioned by both denominational fathers and the Founders no matter how practical such a mingling might seem during a time of war. But separate-component adherents believed such rhetoric was cant. They did not propose that the state should orchestrate the religion of the citizenry, but rather that true religion should and must shape every endeavor of the Christian citizen. Separate-component ministers recognized the different elements of life in America— Henry Ward Beecher did not imagine himself an elected official, for example, no matter how public his persona became—but they saw no division between what Americans of the day called spheres.

The denominational diversity represented in the separate-spheres, separate-duty, and separate-component camps during the Civil War no doubt surprises many today. The leaders of many northern denominations such as the Congregationalist, Unitarian, Universalist, northern Baptist, and numerous Presbyterian churches are often assumed to have been altogether liberal in their understanding of the clergy's political obligations. The captains of other denominations such as the American Catholic, Methodist, Old School Presbyterian, Protestant Episcopal, and for perhaps more unsullied reasons, Dutch Reformed, Mennonite, Brethren, and Friends churches are depicted as avoiding political preaching without reservation. But within virtually every Christian tradition were individuals who both sought to honor the dictates of their denominational creed and live honorably in a nation beset by threats to its very existence. Multiple forces, moreover, and not just church affiliation shaped an individual's attitudes about political preaching and political preachers, no matter the denomination he or she privileged. Thus the debate over a politicized clergy, conducted within Protestant and Catholic churches first and foremost but also in the secular and religious presses, the institutions of government, in lecture halls and social clubs, in kitchens and sitting rooms, and in the fields of country hamlets and streets of tumultuous cities was never as neat and tidy as historians have assumed. Most northern church leaders supported their country, but many of them also voiced principled and theologically rooted reservations about the commingling of spiritual concerns with what they imagined were political issues—issues like slavery, secession, Federal authority, and the war itself.

6

THE CONFEDERATE MINISTRY

A CENTRAL REALITY PLAGUED the South's brief foray into nation building: the Confederacy was not original unto itself. Most in Dixie identified with their fellow southerners in a fundamentally different way than they did Americans elsewhere. But even if most in the South believed themselves a separate people by 1861, that did not make it easy for them to abandon old loyalties. Just as the colonists' declaration of sovereignty had once challenged British authority, so too did the creation of the Confederacy challenge the power and perpetuity of an existent nation. As was true of the nascent United States in 1776, the controversial—and depending upon one's perspective at the time, illegitimate—circumstances of its 1860–61 conception assured that the Confederate States of America was born into war. The difficulties of its nativity did not assure an infant's death for the Confederacy, however. Southern leaders believed the Confederacy could win the Civil War in spite of its material and economic disadvantages, and many scholars have since confirmed the reasonableness of such hopes held by the likes of Jefferson Davis and Robert E. Lee.[1] But there was little room for dissent or even ambivalence. Victory would come, southern leaders recognized, only when the majority of southerners offered their hearts and stores to the Confederate cause. As southern leaders resultantly cultivated and then solidified allegiance to the new government, no group played a more prominent role than the denominational clergy.

If one has read very much about southern preachers on the wartime homefront, it is likely they have learned of the guilt that some Confederate clerics felt over the institution of slavery and the ways in which they then hindered, in their guilt, the southern war effort.[2] This chapter offers an alternative take, one in which southern ministers—key catalytic actors in southern life both before and after the war—bolstered the war effort on the homefront much more than they impeded it.[3] Divines in Dixie, for example, played a key role in the important wartime process of Confederate identity formation.[4] And once such nationalism was produced, southern leaders relied upon clergymen to sustain and monitor Confederate allegiance and devotion on the homefront. Accordingly, Confederate clergymen, especially those once slow to join the Confederate ranks, were essential to the transformation of numerous southern Unionists into Confederates, and preachers became important arbiters of Confederate loyalty. And in all of this, there was a great deal of continuity of southern ministerial behavior before and during the Civil War.

I

Preachers carried out an important cultural function in the Old South. More than perhaps anyone else, they oversaw the cultivation of a common southern consciousness built in exaltation and defense of slavery.[5] Slavery, the source of the South's wealth and political clout and the cultural institution against and through which southerners forged their personal identities, was the South's lodestone. Religiously speaking, slavery ensured that denizens of the greater South spurned religious activism and millennialism alike, both characteristics of the antebellum North. Instead, the need to reconcile Christianity with a lucrative but exploitive system of human bondage served as the primary impetus behind a distinctly "Old Southern" gospel, and slavery's satellite issues—such as tariffs, settlers' property rights in the territories, and states' rights—found important secondary places in Old South religiousness.[6] The religious defense of slavery and validation of related key political positions solidified antebellum southern consensus. Paying homage to Benjamin Franklin, the leader of the Methodist Episcopal Church in South Carolina proclaimed five days before that state's legislature voted to secede in December 1860, "the interests of the Southern States are identical, and we must hang together or hang by ourselves."[7] Because distinctly southern concerns were foundational to the new Confederate nation formed by, for, and in southern interests, Christians who intended to "hang together" with the Palmetto State parson cared little that their devotion was invested in a political nation that was nonexistent for most of their lives. Nor did they construe as disloyal their abandonment of the United States in their certainty that the United States had abandoned them first.

Not all southern ministers were disunionists. But if not all prewar southern ministers and their congregants were rabid secessionists, most *were* ardent anti-reformists.[8] As such, they disdained the so-called progress of northern society and championed instead a racially stratifying and economically simplistic Jeffersonian agrarianism.[9] Historian James Farmer describes the typical theological anti-reformer as "engaged in an effort to understand the human condition and to fit the institutions of society to it. Whatever misgivings he may have had about Southern society, he found it increasingly preferable to the outside world, whose tendencies he read as frightening." Spurred on by these fears, Farmer adds, the southern anti-reformer articulated "the values of his region for itself and the outside world."[10] Most significantly, anti-reformers in the southern clergy defended slavery as a God-ordained and righteous institution. In so doing, they offered the South a powerful and unifying rationalization while simultaneously creating for themselves a prominent societal role as one of slavery's chief defenders. Most southerners, although heavily invested in the idea of separate church and political worlds, nevertheless abided and even grew dependent upon such clerical guardianship of slavery.[11] At the end of the day, the proslavery ideology that late-antebellum ministers proffered anchored southern consensus and provided, in time, the basis of Confederate nationalism.

The anti-reformist tradition in the southern evangelical clergy proved transformative in another way as well. In the days and weeks after Fort Sumter, anti-reformists by the droves, including many who had long feared disunion, perceived the war as an attack on southern provincialism. Unable to imagine any southern shortcoming glaring enough to force them into the opposite camp, they rose to the South's defense. And when they did, even those churchpeople most hesitant to accept the Confederate banner as their own were conditioned by decades of religious life to consider the model set by preachers who at long last "saw the (Confederate) light."

Anti-reformists and one-time anti-secessionist preachers experienced what historian Bertram Wyatt-Brown has characterized as an "abrupt transition to Confederate allegiance" that effectively "freed the new clerical loyalists from former deference to northern conservative church opinion."[12] With war, opponents of disunion in the clergy such as Protestant Episcopal Bishop James H. Otey of Tennessee and Presbyterian James Henley Thornwell of South Carolina reversed course, just two of the scores of clerics who by mid-1861 had embraced secessionism in their fears of societal discomfit and antagonistic congregations and, more than anything else, in their loyalty to rebel kindred and neighbors.[13] After all, the sense of solidarity that facilitated the secession movement in the first place was deeply rooted in the southern preacher's us-against-them rhetoric. When Tennessee Unionist Oliver P. Temple recalled the tens of thousands "of men who had no heart for secession" but "did have heart for their neighbors" and were, in that camaraderie, drawn together "in behalf of a cause which one-half of them disapproved," he attributed the trend to their "universal fellowship" as southerners. In so doing, Temple gave testament to the importance of newly Confederate preachers.[14]

Given the nature of the Confederacy's challenge—convincing Unionists that the new nation *deserved* their allegiance—the clergyman's supposed prewar history of calm conservatism and anti-disunionism bespoke the South's believed innocence in the current conflagration, and was thus particularly effectual. Their collective lesson allowed hesitant southerners to imagine and embrace the Confederacy as the predestined political embodiment of a peace-loving society consecrated to the preservation of all of the rights and privileges of white, Christian citizens. In the days, weeks, and months after secession and primarily through the power of example (for they lacked the cultural authority to force, by caveat, Unionists into the Confederate camp), preachers were vanguards in the movement of countless southerners away from Unionism and toward Confederate identity, nationalism, and loyalty.[15]

Of course, the post-Sumter religious chiefs who cultivated the image of the clergy as "living proof" of the South's prewar forbearance were, at least in a general sense, wrong. In holding anti-secession preachers and their congregations up as the prewar norm, church leaders highlighted opinions that were voiced by a minority of antebellum southern ministers, a minority moreover that was often criticized at the time for being weak and overly accommodationist. But there *were* late-antebellum southern ministerial calls for patience and conciliation—enough anyway for southern clergymen after secession to effectively hang their revisionist hats upon. Wartime ministers made much of specific acts of prewar clerical restraint, such as the one recorded in the Methodist Episcopal Church's *Christian Advocate* (Nashville) in January 1861. An unnamed cleric at that time had urged his congregants to "resist the temptation" to rebuke brethren who voted erroneously on political matters. In such resistance, the preacher added, Christians might yet ward off the hostilities that were apparently on their way and earn, through God, "deliverance out of all our troubles."[16]

Similarly, the editor of Virginia's Baptist *Religious Herald* had written in 1860 that the Almighty alone might yet "disperse the black and angry clouds of disunion," but he had also reminded churchpeople that upon them rested the responsibility of prayer. All of the faithful, the moderate Baptist told his readers, were to "ask the aid of God to quell the attacks of Southern disunionists and Northern fanatics" alike.[17] Under similarly reserved clerical leadership and as post-secession apologists in the clergy were quick to recall, even entire congregations had supposedly resisted separation as long as they could. Noting that the upcoming national election might elicit behavior inclined to foment secessionism and war, the leaders of the Arkadelphia (Arkansas) First Baptist Church had resolved in 1860 "[t]hat the church shall not be occupied hereafter by any person or persons making public speeches, lectures, or giving any kind of concerts or exhibitions."[18]

Instances of prewar restraint and levelheadedness in the southern clergy, especially away from the Upper South, had been the exception and not the rule. But when presented as the norm, such incidents allowed wartime southern preachers to cast the entire affair wholly in terms of self-defense. As the editors of the Methodist *Christian Advocate* (the same paper that just months before habitually featured positive stories about anti-secession clerics like the one featured above) representatively offered in the weeks after Sumter, the war was an attack by "trained bands and fanatic legions" upon a peaceful but separate people who had "simply determined, as equal and original partners, to withdraw formally from a governmental compact, the spirit and letter of which they [northerners] themselves have broken." In the face of such an attack, the editors offered, "There is no middle ground. He that is not for the South at this hour is against her."[19]

In the collective southern mind, no event better epitomized the North's unwarranted aggression, unjustifiable belligerence, and vile intentions—not to mention the South's innocence—than did President Lincoln's call for 75,000 troops in the days after the southern attack on Fort Sumter. Lincoln's actions did more than provide fodder for already convinced southern nationalists. By ostensibly compelling *some* southerners to make war against others, Lincoln effectively forced *all* southerners to offer a pledge of fidelity to an increasingly usurpatious Federal authority, as many southerners saw it, or to their neighbors. The majority chose the latter. Unconditional Unionist Congressman Horace Maynard of Tennessee warned that Lincoln's call for troops had loosed "a tornado of excitement that seems likely to sweep us all away." Southerners who had "heretofore been cool, firm and Union loving," Maynard observed, were now "perfectly wild" and "aroused to a phrenzy of passion" in their certainty that the President's newly expanded army would be used "to invade, overrun and subjugate the Southern states." Maynard concluded that the call for troops "has done more, and I think I speak considerately, to promote disunion, than any and all other causes combined."[20]

William Holden of North Carolina believed that, had Lincoln called for troops solely to defend Washington, he would have found widespread support among southerners. But by calling for men to subdue the Confederacy, Lincoln had "crossed the Rubicon." Lincoln's call was essentially a "proclamation of war," Holden deduced, "and as such will be resisted."[21] As straight-talking North Carolinian Josiah Cowles explained, "I was as strong a union man as any in the state up to the time" of Lincoln's call for troops; "I then saw that the South had either to submit to abject vassalage or assert her rights at the point of a sword."[22]

Many southerners required nothing more than Lincoln's call for troops to convince them to cast their lot with the Confederacy. Others no doubt *still* needed the clergy's sanction before breaking their few remaining ties to the United States. Lincoln could alienate millions of southerners, but southern preachers alone could assure their extremely religious countrymen that the South had sought peace until peace was no longer an option and thus Confederates were spotless in God's eyes. The call for troops vindicated their own conversion to secessionism and their subsequent efforts as ministers to promote Confederate nationalism even as it provided others, both in and out of the clergy, the ideal opportunity to do and act the same. As an unnamed but purportedly preeminent southern Presbyterian minister who had only recently opposed disunion offered the day after Lincoln's call, "It may seem strange to you that *I* should be in favor of disunion. But, alas! The Union *is already dissolved,* whatever Mr. Lincoln may choose to say. What was once *our* country is dismembered by the blind folly of our rulers.[23] Like William Holden and Josiah Cowles, almost all who participated in the post-Sumter rush of former Unionists to the Confederate banner were affiliated Christians. As such, they took seriously the examples set for them by denominational church leaders. In the creation of the Confederacy, leaders of the church *and* the state marched together, albeit down a primrose path.

II

In short order after Sumter, loyalty to the church and to the nation became so interchangeable that in most parts of the South to hesitate in one's support of the Confederacy was to court the reproach of the church. Historian W.

Harrison Daniel has offered that "Christian faith and patriotism" became "practically synonymous during the war. Silence or neutrality was portrayed as a crime not much short of treason, and those who were not sympathetic to the Confederacy were advised to 'go to the enemy.'"[24] David Chesebrough has seconded this assertion, arguing that during the war "all Christians, all denominations, all churches, and all clergy were called upon to support the new nation with unwavering and unquestioning loyalty."[25] At least where church members and informally affiliated Christian believers were concerned, denominational preachers became the South's chief promoters of Confederate nationalism. In their church oversight, sermons, and personal examples, ministers maintained homefront support of the Confederate war effort by enunciating the war's meaning, identifying and castigating those whose fealty to the Confederacy seemed dubious, and in both word and deed providing examples of patriotic service to the Confederacy.

Denominational leaders considered service in the Confederate ranks a religious endeavor, spoke out against anyone slow to answer their country's call, and ultimately made it the church's place to police disservice. The editors of Columbia, South Carolina's *Confederate Baptist* for example characterized desertion as "rebellion against God and against Caesar" that must result in an offending member's expulsion from the Baptist ranks," while a Virginia Baptist association "declared its opinion that deserters from the [southern] army should be arranged [sic] before the Churches of which they are members and expelled."[26] Southern families who hid sons from Confederate conscription officers were banished from church rolls, as were those who left the South for political or personal reasons, those who took oaths of allegiances to the Federal government, and church-member slaves who fled to Union lines.[27] And church leaders in the South used every resource at their disposal in their assumed regulatory role. The leaders of the Methodist Episcopal Church, South, for instance threw the weight of their considerable publishing empire behind the cause of Rebel service. Printing not only Confederate-friendly religious publications like denominational newspapers, religious tracts, pamphlets, and a pocket testament proclaimed as the first Bible entirely stereotyped in the Confederacy, but also secular offerings like the *Confederate States Almanac*, the *Confederate Primer*, and the *First Confederate Speller*, Methodists taught Confederate nationalism to southerners young and old alike.[28]

To a degree that southern political leaders could not match, preachers sustained the Confederacy by counteracting the citizenry's customary disdain for centralized authority. True enough, the Confederate government and various state governments passed multiple laws that made nonsupport of the Confederacy a crime. In August 1861, the Confederate Congress for instance passed an Alien Enemies Act that forced every male above the age of fourteen to swear an oath of allegiance or face deportation. Subsequent legislation allowed Confederate authorities to seize the property of alien enemies who remained in the South, restricted the rights of the kinfolk of declared alien enemies, and declared that all who left the Confederacy to avoid conscription lost all rights to their land and property.[29] But then as now, true allegiance and loyalty could not be mandated by the state no matter how severe its proscriptive efforts became.[30]

Fears of reprisals limited some southern Unionists in their defiance, but governmental decrees likely had little positive impact on the public's willingness to sacrifice in the name of the Confederate States. Even for southerners who identified with the new nation, political decrees did not trump primary personal responsibilities—farms that needed attention, wives that needed husbands, children that needed fathers. James Chesnut of South Carolina, in palliating the low number of South Carolinians who answered the call during a Confederate recruitment drive in early 1862, explained simply that even in the cradle of secessionism men did not eagerly enlist because the "time of the call was unpropitious to the agricultural interests," the presumed area of deployment of new enlistees was "unhealthy at that season," and they were influenced by "the desire to pursue ordinary vocations."[31] And Henry Yeatman of Tennessee was "pulled between two inclinations" but admitted that, of the two, his "first and strongest" impulse, even more than doing his part as soldier, was to stay and see to his "precious wife and little daughter."[32] No matter how representative of southern society the Confederate nation was, it was difficult for many to imagine that they were truly obliged to make painful and personal sacrifices in its name.

Enter the denominational cleric. Evangelical religion carried great clout in the South, where clergymen had for decades preached the religious sanctification of southern society. When those same spiritual leaders, in establishing loyalty to the Confederacy as the Christian duty of all southerners, struck the same chords of agrarian exceptionalism, white supremacy, and northern usurpation that they had been sounding for decades, their voices were heard and their impact was real. Not only were preachers well versed in spurring their listeners to patriotic action, but their heated jingoism was also a powerful deterrent against such behaviors as draft evasion and desertion. No doubt many on the southern homefront were kept in line by the clergy's constant reminder of the societal and spiritual consequences of breaking a supposed sacred vow to the Confederacy. Especially effective on this front were southern ministers who, in the rich tradition of the American Jeremiad, spent the war predicting God's rebuke of the collective Confederate people and the ruination of every individual offender if they continued to engage in such nationally debilitating transgressions as hoarding, refusing to pay the various state and Confederate tariffs and taxes imposed during the war, and trading with the enemy.[33]

Jeremianic clerics portrayed these and other sins of the Confederate people (including Sabbath-breaking, drunkenness, swearing, slothfulness, and even the abuse of slaves) as the bitter fruits of the South's former association with the now-profane United States. By improving upon such shortcomings and thus, in the eloquence of New Orleans Presbyterian Benjamin Palmer, bringing "back the purer days of the republic, when honest merit waited, like Cincinnatus at his plow, to be called for service," southerners identified themselves as the redeemers of American republicanism.[34] "And I do not wonder," Reverend Palmer went on to say, "that to save us from total demoralization, God has let loose upon us this political storm, in order to bring up from the depth of the nation's heart its dormant virtue."[35] But in an immediate sense, practitioners of the Confederate Jeremiad such as Palmer, Episcopal Bishop Stephen Elliott, Methodist Bishop George Foster Pierce, and Baptist Reverend Thornton Stringfellow criticized their fellow southerners with an unwavering severity in the application of what operant conditionists today call negative reinforcement.[36] Like Georgia's Baptist Reverend Henry Tucker, they reminded their fellow southerners that the chastising hand of God would be stayed and the future redeemed, complete with Confederate victory in the war, only when repentant southerners "become what we ought to be."[37]

Southern preachers likewise offered messages that emphasized the defensive nature of the South's efforts. In so doing, they interpreted the war's meaning for their worried constituents, the same war-defining role played by church leaders in the North, although Union parsons rarely privileged the notion of "defense."[38] Southern clerics defended their rebellious efforts by asserting that the South, and especially southern ministers, had not wanted war but had it thrust upon them. But in encouraging their fellow southerners, preachers did more than point the finger of blame. Confederate clerics were celebrated for their indictments of those who still espoused the ideology of pacifism. Men who had previously "differed with the preachers in politics and war," like journalist and prose writer John Beauchamp Jones, suddenly held dear "the Southern preachers who are now in arms against the invader," convinced of the clergy's leading role in a war that was "one of the providences of God, and certainly no book chronicles so much fighting as the Bible."[39]

Exemplifying self-sacrifice, scores of ministers left their homes and churches behind to serve as chaplains. As church historians Randall Balmer and John Fitzmier have said of Presbyterian preachers but as was true of southern ministers of every denominational ilk, preachers routinely "left their congregational duties" to preach "to enormous gatherings of soldiers, [attend] to the wounded and dying, and in some cases [lead] successful religious revivals."[40] Those who remained with their flocks orchestrated loyalty-boosting congregational efforts that were at the same time materially useful to southern soldiers in the field.

When church members met in worship houses to engage in behaviors as diverse as the formation of sewing circles, the harvesting of scrap metal for weapons, the collection of cotton and silk for bandages, and the constant sending up of sustaining prayers for the Confederacy, they did so under the authority if not the direct oversight of their local pastor. Church-based activities offered southern denominationalists an occasional sense of contribution and a fleeting reprieve from the sense of general helplessness that pervaded the homefront. In all of this, the southern military especially garnered the collective concern of evangelical leaders, as was the case with the Tennessee Baptist leaders who considered the Confederate States Army— made up of men in noble service to "our young and gallant nation struggling for the establishment of civil and religious freedom"—a great mission field of men who deserved the best efforts of the church.[41] Another group of Tennessee ministers concluded their patriotic declarations in 1862 by praying for godly intervention on all things Confederate but "especially for the welfare of our soldiers, both spiritually and temporally."[42]

As the war dragged on, Confederate ministers helped southern Christians process troubling events, bolstering flagging Confederate morale when affairs were at their worst. In the estimation of most on the homefront, one of the South's most hurtful blows was the death of Stonewall Jackson on May 2, 1863. Clergymen across the South offered southerners—many of whom questioned for the first time the rectitude of the Confederate cause in the wake of the death of one so virtuous—cause-affirming interpretations of the heartrending event and reassurance that the Almighty would yet reward their sufferings. Prefacing its commentary with admonishments to "Be still and know that He is God," the Confederate Presbyterian General Assembly counseled: But in the depth of our own sadness, we would speak a word of cheer to our bereaved countrymen; that in the disappointment of many of our most reasonable calculations, no less than in unexpectedly blessing us when all seemed dark and forbidding, God seems to us only the more to have charged Himself with the care and protection of this struggling Republic; and in this new chastising we recognize the token of Him whose way it is to humble those whom it is His purpose to exalt and bless."[43] Such convictions among denominational church leaders did not waver, by and large, throughout the war, as evidenced by the General Synod of the Evangelical Lutheran Church in the Confederate States of America in June 1864. Gathering in South Carolina in the days after the bloody nightmare of Cold Harbor, the synod "[r]esolved . . . [t]hat we are now more clearly than ever convinced, by the barbarity and ferocity of our enemies, that it was the right and duty of these Confederate States to secede from a union which had become intolerant and oppressive in its character."[44]

Confederate ministers similarly portrayed the war as the South's responsibility to their forebears. We have seen how Louisiana Presbyterian Reverend Benjamin Palmer and those of his ilk called their fellow southerners to greater service by depicting the war as one to rescue the republican tradition of the Founding Fathers.[45] Numerous other divines, with Presbyterian Moses D. Hoge perhaps chief among them, portrayed the slaveocratic Confederacy's war effort as a campaign to preserve liberty. He wrote in April 1861, "With my whole heart and mind I go into the secession movement. I think providence has devolved on us the preservation of constitutional liberty, which has already been trampled under the foot of a military despotism at the North." Lincoln's actions had tipped the scales, Hoge believed. "And now that we are menaced with subjugation for daring to assert the right of self-government," he continued, "I consider our contest as one which involves principles more important than those for which our fathers of the Revolution contended."[46] Echoing such sentiment were the leaders of the Sweetwater (Tennessee) Baptist Association, who surmised in memorializing one of their clergy members who had fallen in battle that the war was nothing more or less than an "invasion of a bloody and despotic and haughty foe."[47]

Importantly, after Sumter such rhetoric could be offered, for the first time, without accompanying apologetics. As Peyton Harrison Hoge wrote in his remembrance of his uncle Moses, after 1861 most "sober, Christian men" in Virginia and the South generally recognized that southern independence was no longer "a question of slavery, of secession, or of Union. It was a question of self-defence, self-government, and constitutional liberty."[48]

As is apparent in the words of both the Presbyterian General Assembly and Reverend Moses Hoge, southern ministers buttressed Confederate loyalty by reminding their countrymen of the role that divine intervention played in all things. This simple but popular clerical position was representatively stated by Presbyterian Joseph Atkinson in a sermon that later became a popular pamphlet. Atkinson observed that "the only proper view of this Revolution, is that which regards it as the child of Providence."[49] No matter what came their way, spiritual captains like Virginia Baptist Thomas Dunaway reassured Confederates, all of the "calamities and scourges which befall nations, are ordered by and under the control of an Allwise though mysterious Providence." To deny the hand of God in all things, Dunaway continued, was "to close the book of Revelation and plunge ourselves into inextricable difficulties."[50] The Confederacy must not be abandoned in thought or deed, for to do so was to admit that God had failed. Confederate preachers reminded their charges on the homefront that theirs was not to doubt, but to believe that the Confederate nation, and especially the success of its war effort, was entirely in God's hands. As Baptist Reverend J. J. D. Renfroe stated in 1863, "the Great God sits at the helm of the ship of war, to vindicate the doctrine that the battle is His."[51]

Ministers on the greater southern homefront reinforced loyalty to the Confederacy in one last but important way. Similar to the actions taken by Unionist church leaders in the North, southern denominational leaders in assembly issued numerous pronouncements of patriotism during the war. Such declarations of allegiance to the Confederate States focused chiefly on celebrating the supposed foundational tenets of the Confederacy like self-determination, proclaiming the God-ordained legitimacy of the southern cause, and establishing the righteousness of the South's effort to resist coercion. In early May 1861, a ten-point resolution offered by the Southern Baptist Convention meeting in Savannah encompassed all of these themes. Baptist leaders invoked divine intervention in the South's efforts, placed the blame for disunion and war squarely on the shoulders of the United States, endorsed the creation of the Confederate States of America, and "admire[ed] and applaud[ed] the noble course of that government up to the present time." In closing, the resolutions called upon all affiliated Baptists to pledge their fortunes and their lives to "the good work of repelling invasion."[52] The clerical leaders of a smaller association of Tennessee Baptists were less specific but equally sincere in urging members to unceasingly pray "to God for his guidance, in all matters pertaining to the interests of the Confederate States."[53] And although bemoaning the dissolution of the United States that had been forced upon them by extremists, a group of Alabama Baptists in late 1861 nevertheless declared as righteous all southern efforts to "resist northern encroachment and domination."[54]

While Unionist and Confederate church leaders alike routinely published declarations of loyalty to their respective nations, in one key respect their reasons for issuing such proclamations differed. Only northern church leaders typically included in their resolutions admonitions and directives meant to ensure the proper behavior of affiliated clergymen (lest preachers give their fellow citizens cause to doubt their fidelity). For two reasons, the need for church leaders to ensure ministerial propriety was less pronounced in the Confederacy. First, the persistent prewar and wartime presence of Unionist bodies in the Upper South, where southern ministers loyal to the United States were most likely to be found, meant that by the time the war was underway most clerics who were antagonistic toward the Confederacy had *already* separated themselves from their secessionist-leaning brethren and the churches disunionists typically called home. Thus the wartime resolutions penned by the leaders of the Southern Baptist, Methodist, Protestant Episcopal, and Presbyterian Churches (among others) were offered to members and clergymen who were in almost perfect agreement about the faithfulness they owed the Confederacy. And second, the provincial nature of the southern slaveocratic society assured that politically disputatious sermons—that *by definition* scrutinized values so culturally informative and religiously imbued as to be sacrosanct— were forcefully suppressed. Indeed, during the war numerous southern states and the Confederate government enforced some form of litmus test for clerics, and the Confederate Army, southern courts, and vigilante groups alike censored clerical dissent.[55]

There were southern men of the cloth whose convictions were so strong that they would not abandon the Union even in the face of such scrutiny.[56] Such men did not, however, come from the ranks of the Confederate clergy. Few ministers within the Protestant Episcopal Church in the Confederate

States of America, the Presbyterian Church in the Confederate States of America, or the Southern Baptist Convention, for example, were ever inclined to rock the Confederate boat. And even had they been of such a mind on some rare occasion, the short list of probable outcomes that they would have faced as ministers within Confederate traditions who challenged the loyal majority was so discouraging as to surely give them pause.

But, when situated safely within the confines of popular local and member opinion (as most were) and likewise unhindered by occupying Federal troops, Confederate ministers could unabashedly promote fidelity to their new nation in ways that Unionist preachers in the tortured border states often could not. Southern pastors rarely crafted messages meant for divided congregations but almost always preached to parishioners of one accord and with whom they were in political agreement. Consensus among members of church bodies allowed denominational ministers in the Confederacy to continue to shape and bolster Confederate nationalism and morale throughout the war. Divided congregations in the hills of East Tennessee, western North Carolina, the Shenandoah Valley of Virginia, and a few other places in the South were not unheard of, but conflicting allegiances within faith traditions in the Confederacy resulted most often in divided church conferences, synods, and counsels, and not in divided local churches. Most common even in the Upper South were circumstances like those endured by members of the Tennessee Baptist Association of Stockton Valley, an organization comprised of both Confederate and Unionist *congregations* that possessed little Christian love for one another by the time the war was over.[57]

Neither of these truths—that ministerial loyalty was a minor concern to southern denominational leaders and that local church memberships in the wartime South were generally of a common political opinion—is in any way a reflection of some mythical superiority of southern constancy, the claims of fervent postwar "Lost Causers" notwithstanding. The consensus within and between local church memberships and their leaders was but a by-product of the political, religious, and cultural hegemony achieved by the purveyors and benefactors of southern slavery. In the North and select parts of the Upper South, differences could still be construed in terms of electoral politics. Democrats and Republicans could still worship side by side because to be a Democrat was not *automatically* to be a southern sympathizer any more than to be a Republican was to be an abolitionist, although extremists in both political camps admittedly sometimes argued as much. Simply put, amid the agitation of war and the escalation of suspicions, northern church members sometimes found themselves politically at odds with fellow church members, but in the greater Confederacy such questions were more cut and dried.

Unless one belonged to an apolitical Peace Church, uncommon in the Confederacy outside of North-Central Virginia, a southerner was likely either for the Confederacy or not, likely either a Unionist or a Confederate. In most of the South by this time, political partisanship had been rendered all but non-existent because the democracy held absolute sway. Even in the extreme Upper South, moreover, where the tenacity of political pluralism at the state and local level—political Whiggery still thrived in Tennessee and North Carolina when the war began—allowed for a degree of late-antebellum political dissent, the secession and then joining of the Confederacy of mother states pushed many churchpeople into alignment. Thus all over the South by the summer of 1861, proclaiming one's political allegiances could no longer entail support of a party or particular region of the South alone. As a group of Virginia Baptists proclaimed in 1863, "Resolved: That the war which the U.S. government has forced upon us, involving as it does, our social and religious freedom, must be met with unfaltering determination and earnest cooperation of every Christian."[58] With the formation of the Confederate government, the largest part of southern churchmen and women felt compelled into allegiance to a nation, be that nation the Confederate States of America or the United States of America. Most cast their lot with the South, and no group did more to monitor and promote that allegiance than the denominational clergy.

III

The prevailing historiographical depiction of the Confederacy as a universally transformative or innovatory experience, although true in the main, is problematized by the examination of the Confederate clergy on the homefront.[59] However much they privileged a revolutionary rhetoric that effectively recast southern deists, slave owners, and secularists all in religiously sanctified terms, Confederate clergymen nevertheless operated in tried and true ways that they claimed were apolitical but were in truth anything but. If with an elevated sense of urgency, Confederate clerics essentially continued the slavery-defending and dichotomous sermonizing they had perfected before the war. By so doing, Confederate preachers allowed citizens of the new country to imagine themselves in both historically justified and sacred terms and through a religious idiom that drew on long-established practices. The story of the clergy on the Confederate homefront, then, is a story of continuity and not radical change.

Confederate Christians thought theirs was a legitimately independent nation. And likely they would, for ostensibly apolitical southern preachers had told them for years that the slave-based and provincial southern system and the free-labor and reformist northern system were representative of separate peoples and cultures. In a poem published in denominational newspapers throughout the South in the days after the Battle of Fort Sumter, Jane T. H. Cross put into words convictions held by most southerners. Her poem began, "We Hail your stripes and lessened stars / As one may hail a neighbor! / Now forward move—no fear of jars, / With nothing but free labor! / And we will mind our slaves and farm, / And never wish you any harm, / But greet you— over the River!"[60] If with perhaps a bit of bluster—at one point she wished the United States fair sailing, but in the Confederacy's wake—Cross confirmed that the formation of the Confederacy simply politicized the separateness that southerners had heard about on past Sunday mornings too numerous to count. Although the southern nation desired nothing more than to govern itself in its own best interests, Cross asserted, the United States appeared intent upon refusing it that right. If only the United States would treat its southern "neighbor" with Christian friendship, the able poetess surmised, the American flag could fly unmolested over the United States' free-labor system while the Confederate standard waved over the South's agrarian empire. Reprinted dozens of times in church newspapers throughout the burgeoning Confederacy, the popularity of her bagatelle indicates how accurately Miss Cross enunciated southerner churchgoers' attitudes. Southern Christians nodded with familiar assent when their clergymen told them of their new nation's sovereignty. For all intents and purposes, preachers had been doing as much for years.

Most southern church members embraced the Confederate nation as their own because they identified with their fellow southerners, an identification assured by the singularities of mid-century southern Protestant and Catholic life.[61] The regional ubiquity of antebellum religious primitivism (or, in the secular vernacular, anti-intellectualism) limited the likelihood that a church leader would emerge mentally prepared to challenge the South's hegemonic slave society. As was true in the North, the southern clergy was better educated and more intellectual than most in their respective societies. But as Martin Marty states, "With notoriously rare exceptions . . . tellers of the South's religious story . . . are not likely to stumble upon first-rate theological minds." There was little in the way of "high" southern culture to begin with, Marty observes, "few cultural centers" or edifying works of "religious art" that might have remedied the South's cultural antagonism toward erudition.[62] In fact, members of what might be called the southern intelligentsia (relative to everyone else in the Old South) overwhelmingly supported slavery, and the proslavery argument became "a vehicle for expression," Drew Faust has offered, "of alienation by the South's neglected intellectuals."[63] Outside of those few southern areas not entirely beholden to slavery, mainstream antebellum religious leaders evidenced little desire to challenge on purely religious grounds the slave system or the society it anchored. Churchmen who challenged the distinctly southern gospel were perceived by the majority of Old Southerners as inappropriately political. But to do otherwise, to proclaim the religious legitimacy of the southern slave republic, was ironically considered an apolitical confutation of the North's unwarranted attack against all things southern.

By the time of the Civil War, ministers who offered politically infused defenses of their society while impugning political preaching in the abstract were the southern norm. Thus few of the members of established denominations outside of the Upper South seemed to notice the inherent contradictions of an ardently Confederate clerical class. If they did, at least, they dared not say as much. Moreover, rank-and-file members of the wartime denominational clergy could have scarcely reversed course on southern nationalism even if they had wanted. Virtually every aspect of Old South religion assured that the lion's share of white Christians were in accord on the authority of the Confederacy, their class or socioeconomic status notwithstanding. Their paternalistic society was little more than the Christian brotherhood of exalted whiteness writ large. As Charles Irons has observed of Anglicans in prewar Virginia, but as was true throughout the South, church leaders—practically all of them male—accepted without question "the link between whiteness and Christianity, and between darker skin tones and savagery."[64] To dispute the Confederacy as a minister was to challenge the most dearly held tenets of a patently racist religious doctrine and the nation it propped up.

Even the nostalgia and emotionalism of the South's brand of evangelicalism bound southern ministers and their congregants together in nationalist unity.

Church hymnists for example penned songs in celebration of a monolithic South's pastoral sublimity and thus fostered a shared agrarian identity, the topographical and climactic diversity of the greater South notwithstanding.[65] According to one historian, although "most Southerners guarded their emotions with care and subordinated then to the demands of kin and community," southern evangelical preachers recognized the transformative power of such "pent-up emotions" and played upon them by conjuring up "vivid pictures of a fiery hell" and "the Devil incarnate," relying "on dreams and portents," and generally threatening individuals, families, and community members with a common fiery fate if they did not repent.[66] Although prewar southern religion privileged the individual believer over society, its leaders stressed joint experiences and the power of community. With war, free southern Christians believed that their collective well being was best ensured by the Confederate state.

The conflict became a shared political *and* religious obligation. It was a struggle, *Army and Navy Messenger* editor W. B. Wellon wrote, "for civil and religious liberty—for the right of self government, and the privilege of worshipping God according to the dictates of the conscience and the teachings of his word."[67] Consensus was quite simply the seed from which southern wartime nationalism bloomed. And to push the analogy to its extreme, wartime preachers tended the garden. They were not new to the work. In their nurturing of Confederate loyalty, and in a way discontinuity-championing historians have overlooked, Confederate preachers effectively did no more or less than they had been doing for decades.

The hegemonic accomplishment of preachers who sustained the Confederacy does not change the historical truth that upon every southern denominationalist rested the responsibility of accepting or rejecting the church's distinctly "southern" message. Southerners decided for themselves how far community cohesion went toward distancing them from previously revered allegiances and relationships. Many who supported southern slavery, for instance, fought for the Union. Troops from every southern state except South Carolina wore the Federal blue. When black and white soldiers are counted together in fact, for roughly every two southerners in the Confederate ranks there was a southerner in the Union army.[68] Thus the assumption that wartime southern Christians were *inescapably* subservient to slavery and the political machinations that slavery anchored, just like the belief that northern Christians were incapable of defying the Federal government, is incorrect.

Such oversimplifications underappreciate the sense of independence and autonomy so revered by nineteenth-century Americans, perhaps especially white Americans in the South. In the end, southern Christians were not manipulated or duped into embracing the Confederacy.

The concept of loyalty was so dear to southerners of the mid-nineteenth century that they were apt to be dedicated to something. And almost every aspect of their religious life pushed southerners toward the Confederacy. But, as both Christians and political actors, Confederates *decided* that their loyalty was best invested, along with that of their fellow southerners, in a new political nation. Individual reasons varied, and such factors as southern solidarity and the defense of their homes against perceived invaders played a part in many determinations. Undeniably, however, most became Confederates because the principles upon which that government rested, most expressly white supremacy, appealed to them far more than did those associated with the United States. Southerners were not fated to make such a decision, suddenly and for a brief moment deprived of the free will so many evangelicals of the day exalted. Compelled by a myriad of forces, most southerners nevertheless chose, in the end, to be Confederates. But they were not inescapably destined to be Confederates.

7

CONFEDERATE AND UNIONIST RELIGIOUS
LIFE UNDER THE GUN

DURING THE CIVIL WAR, ministers in the occupied South frequently found the expression of their loyalties unwelcome, often dangerous, and sometimes deadly. The presence of the Federal military, for instance, severely stifled the dulcet tones of Confederate religious leaders. In such places as Nashville, New Orleans, and countless other southern cities, towns, and country hamlets, preachers and the churchpeople they directed were resultantly forced to serve the Confederacy in imaginatively covert ways. Southern clerics defied Federal dictates even when such behavior cost them greatly. And when traditional avenues of struggle were closed off to preachers in the Confederacy, they offered their lay followers other ways to oppose occupation and maintain some sense of autonomy. It could have hardly been otherwise. The combination of aggressive Federal policy designed to squelch resistance in the South and the sacred way in which Confederates imagined their society and way of life put the Union military on a collision course with Confederate churches and church leaders from the first day of occupation.

But not every minister within Confederate borders considered himself a citizen of the new nation. Persistent Unionist clergymen could be found in several parts of the beleaguered land. While particularly common in the Upper or border South, religious leaders loyal to the United States occasionally found sanctuary of a kind in intractably Unionist enclaves deeper in Dixie as well. Wherever they were, both their religion and their politics reminded them that the United States was legitimate and sanctified, and that the Confederacy was neither. As was true in divided areas of the Union like Missouri and Kentucky, in contested areas of the Confederacy the presence of such highly loyal and religiously convinced Unionists and equally loyal and religiously convinced Confederates created tensions bound to explode into violence. And yet, in defiantly feeding their parishioners a partisan brand of ministerial care—holy manna with an agenda—Unionist preachers were essential to the sustenance of their careworn members' patriotism.

The current literature on homefront clergy in the South focuses on ministers who had the luxury of rhetorical freedom.[1] Such studies are noteworthy and bolster the argument for ministerial importance. Drew Gilpin Faust, for instance, asserts that "the authority of the clergy at least rivaled that of the new Confederate state," while Harry Stout and Christopher Grasso offer that secession and war could have never come about without the "clergy's active endorsement."[2] These fine historians' work on the clergy notwithstanding, preachers who plied their rhetorical wares in inhospitable southern environs—be they Confederates or Unionists—seldom find their way into the historiography. Indeed, only in the last two decades or so have skillful historians like David Chesebrough considered the extent to which ministers in places like Tennessee, Alabama, and elsewhere were persecuted for their loyalties or the degree to which, conversely, they persisted in their congregant-inspiring sermonizing in spite of potentially fatal consequences.[3] More such studies are needed if scholars are to better understand the role that preachers *continued* to play in the political lives of southerners away from the battlefront but nevertheless under the gun. For, no matter if they were beset by new foes in blue or old neighbors in grey, during the Civil War contrarian Confederate and Unionist ministers on the southern homefront retained their cultural and political primacy even when community, political, and military forces demanded otherwise.

I

A majority of southern denominational leaders ultimately embraced the Confederacy and exalted all that it stood for. Occupying Federal forces resultantly encountered pro-Confederate Christians dedicated to the idea of a white-supremacist and paternalistic state and who believed it their sacred duty to work toward the realization of a white man's utopia. As Methodist Reverend J. W. Tucker told his southern listeners in May 1862, "Your cause is the cause of God, the cause of Christ, of humanity. It is a conflict of truth with error—of Bible with Northern infidelity—of pure Christianity with Northern fanaticism."[4] How then could Union soldiers convince southern ministers and the congregations they influenced that no institution, not even the church, could foster resistance to the occupying Federal authority? In most cases, they couldn't.

Southern ministers fomented their society's rebelliousness toward the United States. For the most part, they were as vehement in their disdain for the Union as they were in their evident affection for the Confederacy. There was little cause to feel otherwise, for supporters of the newly established southern government did not equate loyalty to the Confederate States with disloyalty of any sort—to the United States or anyone else. They believed all obligations of fidelity to the United States ended with secession. In their own estimation as southerners supremely devoted to the Confederacy's assumed legitimate authority, preachers who resisted the power of northern troops and the government that sent them merely made the task of subjugation undertaken by a debased and illegal oppressor more difficult. Confederate clerics under occupation during the Civil War believed it right to promote among the faithful a Confederacy-affirming, religiously based defiance of Lincoln and, as any Rebel religious commentator worth his hyperbolic salt would have added, his sycophantic minions.

The hybrid social and political urge to resist Federal authority felt by Confederate ministers was augmented by their conviction that the enemy's troops were willing and eager to abuse the collective southern church after the fashion of Nero, Diocletian, and other past persecutors of the "true" faith. Time and again, for instance, soldiers apparently maltreated Confederate ministers. The Reverend R. B. C. Howell, pastor of the First Baptist Church of Nashville, was jailed for nearly two months in 1862 for refusing to swear an oath of allegiance to the United States.[5] Howell developed chronic health issues owing to the privations of prison life. After his release and return to the pulpit, he remained under military surveillance, his every sermon scrutinized by Federal authorities.[6] By Howell's estimation, during 1862 alone Union troops robbed him and other church members of over a half-million dollars' worth of property, including slaves, crops, equipment, and personal items.[7] Authorities allowed Howell to preach to his congregation from behind his own pulpit for less than two months during all of 1863, after which the congregation was forced to meet in a tiny, rented room over a grocery store. In the meantime, Union troops destroyed virtually everything within the church building, rendering it, in the words of one deacon, "so dilapidated and filthy as to be really unfit for use for any purpose whatever."[8] Given all that he and the members of his flock endured under Federal occupation, there is perhaps little wonder that Howell ultimately "marveled" that his church "escaped utter annihilation."[9]

Everywhere the Federal army went in the South, its soldiers repeated such behavior. Union troops used Rebel churches for numerous purposes while giving little thought to the destructiveness of their behavior. The First Baptist Church of Suffolk, Virginia, was "taken over by the . . . Federal army for a hospital. All the seats and pulpit were destroyed, and many window sash were carried off."[10] The Zoar Baptist Church in Virginia was first used by Federals as a troop barracks and then a stable. It was finally destroyed by Union soldiers who used wood from the structure as fuel.[11] And during the Red River Campaign, the Antioch Baptist church near Mansfield, Louisiana, burned to the ground while being used as a Federal prison.[12] Federal authorities, of course, considered commandeering the largest buildings in occupied areas, as well as silencing influential local voices of support for the enemy, matters of practicality. Collateral damage to church buildings and the indignation of church members were but unavoidable side effects. Given all this, religious historian John W. Brinsfield's recent claim that "one could trace the progress of the Union armies across Mississippi, Alabama, Tennessee, and Georgia by the desecrated and burned churches and church school buildings," though a historical overstatement, aptly represents what wartime southerners thought to be true.[13]

Not surprisingly, southern clergymen regularly attributed such behavior to more than just the exigencies of war. Confederate ministers equated the Union with evil, pure and simple. Baptist Reverend J. M. L Burnett, for instance, said of Unionist East Tennessee in July 1861, "the Devil is let loose on earth, and right here is the capital of his empire."[14] With war, Federal troops became the living embodiment of that evil in the minds of devout Confederates. The destruction of southern churches and the persecution of religious leaders during military occupation confirmed such opinions. In an 1864 article titled "Giving the Devil His Due," one infuriated clergyman for instance maligned the assumed devilish Federal habit of commandeering churches but not theaters: "the Yankees know to whom the theatre belongs, and as they are in his employment . . . they ought, of course, to let his property alone."[15]

Southern ministers' defiant attitudes, thought by their Union occupiers to be patently un-Christian, were in truth religiously sanctioned extensions of the Old South's religious indictment of virtually all things northern. Civil War–era southern preachers intermingled religion and politics to a degree not previously acknowledged historiographically. They embraced a cause dedicated to sectional autonomy, self-determination, and the defense of chattel slavery, making that amalgamated cause, and in time the political nation that symbolized it, the essential element of a unifying southern religious message.[16]

To quote Louisiana's "Fighting Bishop" Leonidas Polk, "We, of the Confederate States, are the last bulwarks of civil and religious liberty; we fight for our hearthstones and our altars; above all, we fight for a race that has been, by Divine Providence, intrusted to our most sacred keeping."[17] Accordingly, clergymen in occupied regions of the Confederacy preached that the church was the most appropriate site to challenge their Federal overlords. In fact, military occupation only enlarged the immediate threat that abolitionists, reformers, and politicians posed to southerners' godly nation, requiring of Confederate ministers still more emphasis on absolute loyalty to the cause. Most clerics were of a mind with a Methodist Episcopal clergyman and editor who proclaimed just days before the commencement of the war, "Politics forsooth! Why, brethren, if ever this country sees a question that rises above all politics, it is now here: the question of Southern independence or slavery; of freedom or subjugation. It involves our laws, homes, institutions, society, presses, churches—our present status and future history."[18]

Under occupation, scores of southern preachers remained insubordinate, endangering their freedom, safety, and lives. The Reverend Thomas H. McCallie of the Chattanooga Presbyterian Church preached regularly to Confederate soldiers and citizens alike throughout the war's early days. On September 9, 1862, Federal troops entered the city. Warned to flee lest his reputation as a Confederate bring him censure, McCallie responded, "the Lord had called me to the work in Chattanooga, that I had more right there than the Federal Army and that if the Lord wanted me there, He could take care of me, protect and sustain me." On the next Sunday, McCallie arrived at his church to find it occupied in the main by Federal soldiers who expected him to pray for Lincoln and his armies. He did not. A week later came the Battle of Chickamauga, after which McCallie's church was commandeered as a hospital. His congregation did not meet in it again until after the war was over. In the meantime, McCallie was informed by the provost marshal in July 1864 that he had been charged with treason, found guilty, and sentenced to banishment—all without trial.[19] Even when Federal forces tightened their grip and thereby rendered conventional forms of ministerial resistance like belligerent sermons and petitions to local authorities evermore dangerous, preachers in occupied regions of the Confederacy found other ways to defy the subjugation of themselves and their church mates. In so doing, they retained a degree of influence over their own fates.

Northern policy too put the Union military in conflict with Confederate churches and church leaders. From early in the war, President Lincoln embraced purely strategic rationales for occupying southern churches, as he acknowledged in 1864. "If there is no military need for the [church] building, leave it alone," Lincoln offered, "neither putting anyone in or out of it, except on finding some one preaching or practicing treason, in which case lay hands on him, just as if he were doing the same thing in any other building."[20] Focused on the president's desire to leave southern ministers unmolested save when their treasonous behavior made such lenience impossible, scholars sometimes understate the implications of the president's qualification "if there is no military need for the building."[21]

True enough, Federal policy made virtually no distinction between disloyal northern and Confederate churches. But on a practical level the consequences of Lincoln's belief that military necessity trumped sacred privilege—that church property became like every other kind of private property when a "military need" existed—were visited upon southern churches alone. These consequences corroborated southern ministers' fears that they were under attack by, as they saw it, a vile Yankee enemy. Remembering northern troops as vandals filled with a "fiendish hate," a Georgia minister reported that the Union occupiers of his Baptist church slaughtered animals in the pulpit, left the waste products of the process to stain the floor, and then desecrated graves in the church's cemetery.[22] In occupying an Episcopal Church near Bluffton, South Carolina, Union troops—purportedly with no provocation whatsoever— "totally destroyed the fine organ, smashed the window sashes, and behaved themselves generally like savages."[23] And in Clarksville, Tennessee, in late 1862, an entire congregation was held by troops under the command of A. C. Harding of the Eighty-third Illinois, who stole from the congregants numerous horses and buggies and compelled both men and women to swear an oath of allegiance or go to prison.[24]

Owing to the divided sentiments of its people, Middle Tennessee especially was the sight of widespread destruction of churches by Federal forces. In addition to listing numerous churches that were commandeered by troops for use as hospitals, barracks, and stables but spared total destruction, Methodist Church historian John Abernathy Smith records that the Methodist church of Dover, Tennessee, was burned (during the siege of Fort Donelson) as was the Palmyra Methodist Church in Montgomery County and the Triune Methodist Church in Murfreesboro. The Fountainhead Methodist Church was demolished to provide building materials for barracks, while the Hamilton

Methodist Church in Davidson County and the Mt. Zion Methodist Church in Williamson County were destroyed for unspecified reasons.[25]

Not every occupation of a southern church resulted in wanton destruction and thievery. When carried out with restraint, the short-term and tactical occupation of their churches by Federals was at least comprehensible to southern ministers, for their own armies often did the same. But if Rebel church leaders understood on some level the immediate exigencies of battle, they were not willing to compromise their politicized religious principles. Moreover, Confederate clerics were determined to defy Abraham Lincoln, whom they believed devilishly delighted in the closure of southern churches and the arrest and mistreatment of church leaders for their supposed treachery. In truth, the president preferred that his government "let the churches as such take care of themselves" when possible. It was not always possible, however. Lincoln understood—and reiterated on numerous occasions after 1862—that when an individual "in church or out of it, becomes dangerous to the public interest, he must be checked."[26] Confederates thus read ominous overtones into virtually every church-related pronouncement the president offered during the war.

Abraham Lincoln's overarching strategy, southerners believed, was to drive from their stations any preacher who refused to support the Union's war against the Confederacy and the president himself. According to one account, the pastor of Portsmouth's Trinity Episcopal Church, Reverend John H. Wingfield, was arrested in February 1864 by order of General A. E. Wild "and sentenced to three months of cleaning the streets of Norfolk and Portsmouth" for nothing more than "raising his head during the Prayer for the President of the United States."[27] A newspaperman wrote shortly thereafter:

In a late epistle of Lincoln upon ecclesiastical matters, he states that he is not capable of "running the Churches," and that he does not intend to take charge of any Church on any side. What the creature means by "running the Churches," we were at a loss for some time to comprehend. . . . Nevertheless, we think we understand the policy which is indicated in this letter. . . . The Confederate clergy are to be turned out of their pulpits, as in Norfolk and Portsmouth and, perhaps, set to work in the streets, like Rev. Mr. Wingfield, with a ball and chain, and when the President is petitioned to restore them to their sacred offices he vulgarly and cunningly replies that he can't "undertake to run the churches." He runs the southern clergy out, and runs Abolitionists in, but he can't take charge of any church on any side. His subterfuge is as vile as his language is vulgar. Need any man wonder at the brutalities of his underlings, when the prince of all blackguards sits in the Presidential chair of the United States?[28]

As all of this suggests, most cases in which occupying Federal authorities took harsh measures against ministers came as a response to what clergyman *said* rather than what they *did*.

Because Federal authorities correctly assumed that the political statements of a southern pastor represented the opinions held by his church's membership, they dealt with Confederate preachers and their church members in kind. President Lincoln characterized *preaching* treason as different but equally punishable as *practicing* treason. In Lincoln's estimation, the behavior of preachers justified arresting them when they became— often with nothing more than their words—dangers to the public interest. Acting with the tacit approval of the president, subordinates expanded upon Lincoln's position by replacing displaced clerics with unquestionably Unionists preachers and seizing the offending cleric's church. Secretary of War Edwin Stanton for instance issued multiple military orders throughout the war that placed the property of disloyal churches in the occupied South under the control of select northern denominational leaders. Most notably, in 1863 Stanton instructed commanders of the several departments (Department of the Missouri, Department of the Tennessee, etc.) to turn over the church buildings and auxiliary properties of disloyal Methodist churches under their authority to, depending upon the department, the Reverend Bishop Matthew Simpson, Edward Ames, Osmon Baker, or Edmund Janes.[29]

In time, Lincoln amended Stanton's orders to make them less malodorous to Methodists in the border states, but he did so after numerous ministers had been ousted and in a way that allowed for more than a little dragging of feet. Specifically, after Unionist Reverend John Hogan of Missouri protested Stanton's November 1863 order to place Bishop Ames in charge of rebellious churches in the western states, Lincoln urged Stanton—some three months later—to modify his order and then wrote to the affronted Hogan: "As you see within, the Secretary of War modifies his order so as to exempt Missouri from it. Kentucky was never in it; nor, as I learn from the Secretary, was it ever intended for any more than a means of rallying the Methodist people in favor of the Union, in localities where the rebellion had disorganized and scattered them. Even in that view, I fear it is liable to some abuses, but it is not quite easy to withdraw it entirely, and at once."[30]

It is clear that, although he was embarrassed by the extent to which Stanton applied the privilege, President Lincoln *had* invested in him the authority to ban preachers and close churches.[31] Would Lincoln, after all, have had the need to "learn" from Stanton his intentions had Stanton vetted his original order in the first place? And Stanton issued similar, if less remembered, wartime orders at the request of Ira Harris, the leader of the American Baptist Missionary Union and a Republican senator from New York, which allowed department commanders at their discretion to place Baptist church properties in the South at the disposal of the American Baptist Home Mission Society.[32] Unfortunately for the president, northern clergymen sometimes compounded his chagrin by coupling such occupancy with taunting that approached vindictiveness, as was true in Vicksburg after its fall in July 1863. In numerous churches throughout the city, Federal soldier F. L. Haywood boasted, clerical mercenaries made sure that "the shot-holes in the church walls are allowed to remain as a warning to future clergymen not to preach treason to their flocks." And in one particular Baptist church in Vicksburg, Haywood continued, a shell had passed through the church roof and floor and into the basement during the siege, but had not exploded. If it had, Haywood quipped, "it would have sent the house nearer heaven than those who formerly worshipped there will ever get."[33]

Commanders commonly punished congregations based on clergy behavior of two kinds: acts of verbal commission and acts of verbal omission. If the officiating minister preached against the evils of the invading Yankee horde and advised listeners to defy Federal authority and support the Confederacy, this provided a reason to shut down the reverend's church and arrest him. According to one general order from the Department of the Gulf, clerics who urged disloyal action on the part of congregants, even if the called-for action was nothing more than hoping for Confederate successes, were prohibited because they meant to "appeal to the passions or prejudices of the people or to excite hostility to the government whether in the form of prayer, exhortation, or sermon" and thus could not, "whether open or covered," be allowed.[34]

Under such a mandate Presbyterian Reverend W. H. Mitchell of Florence, Alabama was arrested and ultimately imprisoned in Illinois's Alton Penitentiary in 1862 for offering a supplication for "Jeff Davis, the success of the Confederate arms, and for the attainment of the independence of the Confederate people."[35] A Methodist preacher in Florida, the Reverend William Davies, prayed for the Confederacy one Sunday morning early in the war. The next day a detachment of Federal troops entered his church and arrested him as he taught a Bible class.[36] In Union-held New Market in East Tennessee, Presbyterian minister George F. Eagleton was threatened and whipped by Unionists and forced to flee the town. None of his neighbors offered Eagleton help for fear they too might face the wrath of the Unionists, who acted with the tacit endorsement of Federal soldiers.[37] And a Huntsville, Alabama, minister was called before Union Brigadier General Lovel Rousseau for his secessionist preaching and was ordered to desist. The minister replied, "General, this is a free country. I have always spoken boldly and fearlessly upon all subjects of religion and politics. I shall continue to do so." The next sermon the audacious minister preached, according to a Philadelphia editor, was "done in stifled whispers, himself his only auditor, and within the walls of a Federal prison-house."[38]

Specific charges were not always needed to condemn a Rebel minister. Episcopal Reverend E. R. Lippitt of Alexandria, Virginia, was arrested in the autumn of 1861 for preaching what one Federal officer vaguely titled a "secession discourse." Authorities later determined that the sermon had been written by Lippitt twelve years earlier, and the reverend was released from custody.[39] And sometimes merely the potential for rebellious sermons prompted action. As soon as William T. Sherman captured Marietta, Georgia, in 1864, the only remaining minister in town was preemptively banned from the pulpit and consigned to house arrest for little more than his general secessionist leanings.[40]

A second category of behavior that provoked a Federal response concerned ministerial acts of verbal omission. Major Generals James McPherson, Benjamin Butler, and other commanders routinely ordered ministers in the occupied Confederacy to pray for the United States, its president and armies in the field, and less often, to take an oath of allegiance to the United States. A preacher's refusal to adhere to the dictates of local military officials was considered as odious as openly praying for the success of Confederate armies and the demise of the Union. In other words, Confederate preachers felt that they were not only prohibited from espousing their true political and religious sentiments, but were also compelled to utter contemptible declarations in the church, their most holy of places. Likely the Nashville ministers taken into custody for refusing to take an oath of allegiance to the United States in 1862 believed as much. After their arrest upon the order of military governor Andrew Johnson, the Reverends Baldwin, Schone, Lawrie, Ford, and Howell were sent to the Tennessee state penitentiary.[41]

Similarly defiant was the Episcopal Reverend J. R. Stewart of Alexandria, Virginia. In early 1862, Stewart ignored local military orders to pray for the president of the United States, a prayer customary in Episcopal services.[42] On the morning of February 9, 1862, a State Department detective aware of the reverend's insolence ordered Stewart to include a prayer for Lincoln. When he ignored the scandalous interruption, members of the Eighth Illinois Cavalry entered Stewart's pulpit and, with swords drawn and "pistols to his head," took Stewart into custody.[43] And finally, General Alexander McCook's meeting with Rebel Episcopal ministers in Nashville left no doubt what actions earned arrest:

You clergymen choose to take part in this rebellion, even in your prayers—supposing, I guess, that your cloth will protect you, but in this you are mistaken. I have plenty of guard houses and jails, and it may be that shortly I should circumscribe your limits. I have reports from your church of last Sunday. I was prepared to hear it here and now, once and for all, I give you to understand, that clergymen of the Episcopal [C]hurch will be required to use their prayer books just as they are printed. You shall pray for the President of the United States or be hung. . . . We are handling you now with kit gloves. That is only an experiment. If it doesn't succeed better than it seems to be doing, we will try something else. We will try the virtue of *ropes*, which, in my opinion, should have been done from the start.[44]

The relationship between wartime Federal policy and the behavior of southern church leaders was circular. When southern clerics flaunted vaguely worded mandates by Federal military commanders, church closures and minister arrests inevitably followed. Closed churches in turn were routinely— and destructively—put to use by Federal troops, while arrests often entailed threats of physical violence and other rough treatment of respected southern ministers. As a Georgia Baptist summarized in 1864, under occupation Federal troops "refuse to let us have Bibles . . . drag our preachers from our pulpits, and send them to prison . . . deprive us of our churches, and burn them or use them as stables or store-houses. . . . [I]f they conquer us they will take away all our churches . . . and not even let us pray in our families as we wish."[45] Such seemingly callous conduct further hardened Confederate clerics' hearts and minds against everything "Yankee."

The vilification of Federal forces was made all the more complete as southerners refused to recognize or admit the reciprocal nature of wartime abuses. Although Rebel atrocities against citizens loyal to the United States were rampant in highly contested areas like Middle and East Tennessee and North Carolina, Confederate leaders routinely juxtaposed the supposedly abominable behavior of Union troops towards southern clergymen against the assumed restraint of southern soldiers. And all believed that the effrontery of their comparatively sadistic occupiers would have its recompense. Citing the egregious conduct of Federal troops, Braxton Bragg warned in late 1862 that it rested chiefly "with the Federal Government to decide hereafter the character which the contest [the war] shall assume." The continuation of such a one-sided distribution of cruelties, Bragg warned, especially "the indignities to our clergy at different periods and more recently in a southern city, steel[ed] the hearts and nerve[d] the arms of our people to the last degree of desperation. Union—social association with a people guilty of such acts—is henceforth an impossibility. Destitution, the prison—death itself—is preferable."[46]

From the pages of the *Official Record* and dozens of other period sources come tales of church leaders in the occupied Confederacy, thus inspired, openly defying their Federal overlords. Civilian resistance was not limited to authoritative acts of public insolence, however. As James Scott has shown, resistance can take many forms, including "dissimulation, false compliance, pilfering, feigned ignorance, slander, arson, sabotage, and so forth."[47] Ostensibly trivial and anonymous acts of resistance by leaders and non-leaders alike play an important role in the lives of their perpetrators. Most importantly, they serve as "testament[s] to human persistence" and thereby buoy the spirit of the subjugated even when their marginalization seems most pronounced.[48] Such was certainly true for numerous southern preachers during the Civil War. Faced with prison or banishment for open manifestations of defiance, many found crafty but important ways to express their loyalty to the Confederacy.

No doubt informed by the artful subterfuge of enslaved southerners that they had observed for decades, Confederate clerics under Federal occupation were especially adept at what Scott coined "false compliance."[49] Tennessee Methodist Parson Brownlow noted, for example, the insincerity of Rebel ministers who took "the hides off Union men by holding them up before their congregations in prayer, and pretending to pray for them," only to end up "condemning their 'reported' offences and deprecating their 'reported' treachery to their country."[50] Confederate clergymen thus routinely met the letter of the law handed down by military commanders, who dictated that ministers pray only for Union concerns. And when the preacher's words were less manifestly facetious (as when offered in the presence of prominent Federal authorities), his actions were yet understood by his fellow southerners as necessary to keep scrutiny at bay. With the wool pulled squarely over the eyes of their would-be overlords, ministers afforded themselves room to both rhetorically (if in clandestine meetings with parishioners) and materially pursue Confederate designs. According to one Federal general, such ingenuity made southern ministers "more dangerous than a company of the Rebel army" and caused them to be considered "the best recruiting officers in the South."[51]

Sometimes opportunistic southern church leaders turned the tables on Federal troops by urging their memberships to engage in pilfering, another common form of everyday resistance.[52] Members of a Methodist church in Waverly, Tennessee, for instance, pleased their pastor by stealing "a bell from a Union gunboat at Johnsonville as the result of a raid by Forrest's cavalry." Aware that the tide of war can ebb and flow, the resourceful Rebel Methodists buried the bell for the duration of the war, unearthing it and hanging it in the church's belfry only when Federal troops were no longer a concern.[53] Most often orchestrated by local preachers, such secretive but rewarding exploits sustained beleaguered churchpeople, reminding them that not all power was ceded to their occupiers.

Equally sustaining were celebrations of their distinctiveness as southern Christians. Rebellious church members in Morristown, (East) Tennessee, acting with the approval of the church's minister, took advantage of a respite from Federal attention to use their Methodist church as a locale for a slave auction and delighted in the impudence of the culturally binding affair. "Let Mrs. Harriet Beecher Stowe," a chronicler of the event cackled, "assign this incident a place in her next serial of serious tom-foolery about an imaginary Uncle Tom."[54] The same Memphis editor reported "bidding that was spirited, if not spiritual, and not one word did I hear . . . suggestive of a suspicion of impropriety in the action of those who conducted the venue." The editor rejoiced in the East Tennesseans' commitment to the southern cause and wished to "Proclaim throughout the domains of Abraham Lincoln that even here in East Tennessee, the boasted kingdom of Andrew Johnson . . . even here, a vast multitude assembled, and in a house erected to honor the God of our fathers, Africans were sold at public auction."[55] For these slave-selling Methodists in Tennessee, the physical church building constituted a key component of their resistance efforts.

Even when the physical meetinghouse was no longer open to them, Confederates found ways to maintain the bonds of their church family. When their church was occupied by Federal troops and their pastor and the largest part of their church's membership were exiled, a few members of the First Baptist Church of New Bern, North Carolina, met in private homes. In clandestine assemblies that persisted until the war's end, they replicated the role of their absent spiritual leader by taking turns overseeing meetings and welcoming members of other Christian denominations.[56] Their behavior reveals much about the influence of Rebel clerics during occupation. Confederate churchpeople followed the examples set *both* by openly defiant southern ministers, who would not relent in their pro-rebellion rhetoric, and by more furtive parsons, who offered ambiguous and innuendo-laden prayers and performed dichotomous public and private ministries. Thus influenced in their own everyday deeds of defiance and unanimity—petty acts of material vandalism, church-based endorsements of white hegemony, and clandestine religious meetings—southern churchpeople engaged in a very real kind of political action. Such daring deeds helped loyal Confederates maintain a sense of faith-based agency in the face of a powerful occupying force.

Ministerial influence likewise fortified the underappreciated resistance to Federal occupation offered by southern churchwomen. Federal authorities marveled at the degree to which female Confederates took up the mantle of opposition.[57] Members of the First Baptist Church of LaGrange, Georgia, for example, formed the "Nancy Harts," an all-female home guard organization named "in honor of the Revolutionary heroine of Georgia." Their church was never occupied by Federal troops, but in 1865 a detachment of Wilson's Raiders threatened LaGrange. The Nancy Harts surrendered only after receiving the Federals' promise that the town would not be looted.[58] And in occupied Vicksburg, a number of local ladies left their church when their imposed-upon minister began to pray for Lincoln. For this they were summarily banished from the city and all surrounding Federally held territory, but they refused to relent.[59]

Likewise inspired by clergymen including kinsmen in the ministry, southern church women sometimes acted without the accompaniment of other women. Diana Smith, according to one account a "member of the Methodist Episcopal Church" who "has always been regarded as very pious and exemplary," responded to the capture of her minster/father by disguising herself as a man and joining the Confederate Army. "Her devotion to Southern rights, in which her father so nobly engaged," her chronicler deduced, spurred her to action; in time "her trusty rifle . . . made more than one vile Yankee bite the dust."[60] Clara Judd of Winchester, Tennessee, widowed upon the 1861 death of her Episcopal clergyman husband, took to smuggling goods into Tennessee shortly after the Federal occupation began in 1862. Provost Judge John Fitch concluded that Judd was "a dangerous person to remain in these lines; that she is probably a spy as well as a smuggler," and that "cases of this kind being of frequent occurrence by females, examples should be made." Mrs. Judd was sent to the Federal prison in Alton, Illinois.[61]

It is no coincidence that these and many other primary accounts of resistance feature women, for gendered opposition was not unusual among churchwomen in occupied parts of the Confederacy. Southern church memberships of the day were overwhelmingly female, and women members moreover attended church more faithfully than did men. Women were therefore more likely even than southern men to be well versed in the pervading message preached by southern clerics, a message that sacralized the Confederacy and prodded them to resistance. Along with the loss of male church members to the military, this meant that female members often led the struggle against the worst abuses of occupation.[62] In so doing they became independent political actors capable, to borrow from Nina Silber, of "more than just endorsing their men's beliefs."[63] The wartime resistance of southern women necessitated "a new way of thinking about women's loyalty (or disloyalty)," Silber continues; what emerged—at least among Unionists—"was a view that insisted on making southern white women more accountable for their anti-Union sentiment, and to have them take personal responsibility for their 'irresponsible' views."[64] In the postwar years, female church members played a central role in establishing and perpetuating the politically powerful "Lost Cause" myth through their participation in memorial societies.[65] Clearly a link exists between the messages preached by wartime ministers, the organized and perhaps even politicized resistance efforts of wartime southern church women, and the public role women played in shaping public memory in the postwar South.[66]

James Scott warns against confining the analysis of resistance to behavior alone, pointing out that, unlike behavior, consciousness is not literally tied to the real world. Human beings can imagine and be empowered by behaviors even if those behaviors in reality never transpire. The marginalized (or in the case of southerners under occupation, *temporarily* marginalized) maintain real if not apparent control of their religion, culture, education, and media—what Antonio Gramsci labeled the ideological sectors of society—by effectively "thinking themselves free."[67] In the darkest days of occupation, when both church attendance and private gatherings of like-minded believers were denied them, Confederate southerners engaged in such tangible kinds of contemplative defiance, convinced by their faith that their cause remained both righteous and viable. The consciousnesses of southern Christians were likely shaped more by the sermons that they heard and by the published expositions on the Bible that they read, in short by the South's denominational ministers, than by anything else.

In Murfreesboro in 1862, military commanders issued edicts ordering prayer for President Lincoln; "It seems hard that we are not permitted to pray to God, when and how we want to," young Kate Carney wrote in May 1862.[68] But hope abided in Kate. At the urging of Jefferson Davis and her minister to entreat God for the "protection of our army, and the Southern Confederacy," Carney resolved that "we can pray all the more at home." In the estimation of Kate and her pro-Confederate brothers and sisters, no matter how oppressive the occupying representatives of the United States were, their power was limited and would prove temporary. "They can't deprive us of our thoughts," Kate offered, "though I have no doubt, they would, if they could. We will certainly know how to appreciate freedom," she concluded, "when we have it once more restored."[69] For some pious southerners, resistance meant denying Federals of the most precious asset they possessed—their Christian love. A Georgia woman admitted, "I used to have some Christian feeling towards Yankees, but now that they have invaded our country and killed so many of our men and desecrated so many homes, I can't believe that when Christ said 'Love your enemies,' he meant Yankees. Of course I don't want their souls to be lost, for that would be wicked, but as they are not being punished in this world, I don't see how else they are going to get their deserts."[70]

Finally, southern Christians under occupation resisted Federals by offering them their complete and utter loathing. Thus common were sentiments like those expressed late in the war by a devout Georgia woman, who upon considering the carnage and compromises that occupation wrought, declared, "If all the words of hatred in every language were lumped together into one huge epithet of detestation they could not tell how I hate Yankees."[71] When every physical avenue of opposition to occupation was closed to southern churchpeople, their resistance persisted. Such rebelliousness was no fluke, for the ministerial offerings of southern preachers had for decades included predictions of the storm to come and reminders of their Christian obligations when that storm arrived. Defiance was thus thought of by Confederates as both a duty and a blessed affliction. It matters little, in terms of the sustaining power of opposition, that such defiance occurred within the confines of southerners' own minds.

Northerners entered the Civil War convinced that the only righteous elements involved were the United States and the Constitution on which its government was based. In time, many added to that number the ruination of the immoral system of social, economic, and political control that was slavery. Believing that the southern rebellion was illegal and its prosecutors traitors, loyal Unionists in both the North and South were not willing to abide, even in the name of religious freedom, behavior that advanced the ungodly southern cause and threatened the blessed, if secular, United States. Confederates, conversely, entered the war well versed in the tenets of a unifying southern gospel that the southern clergy had long proffered, a gospel that like most everything else in the dominant southern culture by 1861 exalted whiteness and slavery, posited a difference between the North and the South and a separateness of their respective peoples, and sacralized the southern position on the key political issues of the day. The southern clergy's highly ecclesiastical conception of the state, moreover, allowed the southern laity, indeed forced the southern laity, to construe wartime attacks on their nascent political nation as attacks upon their religion.

Thankfully, in the end the North won and thus ultimately so did the notion of a sanctified and perpetual Union. However, the efforts of Confederate church leaders and, consequently, church members to defend their imagined country and express their loyalty through religion, often in ways productively covert, merit continued scholarly analysis. Such study might more fully reveal the forms and fashions of southerners' resistance and the ways in which that resistance, no matter how subdued, sustained wartime southerners' belief in their religious-political cause throughout the Civil War and, as its seminal role in the "Lost Cause" reveals, beyond. Finally, such inquiries must necessarily deal with the realities of Civil War–era southerners' politicized religious life and not perpetuate the myth that the religious and political leaders of the Old South practiced the separation of church and state as much they preached it. Alexander Stephens once criticized preachers, along with newspaper editors and unscrupulous politicians, as men who possessed more zeal than wisdom and who "by their power over the passions and prejudices of the multitude . . . precipitated the Southern people into reassumption of their independence as States, more as an escape from anticipated wrongs than from actual grievance."[72] If true, this triumvirate of powerful players gives testament to the fact that wartime southern culture was a conglomerated entity comprised of equal parts religion and politics, chronicled by partisan pundits, and watched over by church leaders who believed their burgeoning Confederacy was to be a sanctified theocratic republic.

II

Sometime late in 1863, a Cocke County, Tennessee, Unionist and Methodist Episcopal minister known to history only as "Mr. Kelley" had his ears cut off and then was clubbed to death with gun butts by Rebel partisans or "freebooters" said to be under the command of a Captain Rumbough.[73] Because he was suspected of piloting Unionist refugees and stranded Federals out of the region, Methodist Reverend Levi Carter and his son Robert were brutally murdered by partisans on September 27, 1863, near Georgetown in Meigs County, Tennessee. After their deaths, the body of young Robert was mutilated, his eyes cut from his head and delivered to the pro-Confederate mother of one of the murderers as a keepsake. When commanding Confederate Cavalry General Joseph Wheeler heard of the affair, he laughed.[74] Presbyterian minister and unapologetic Unionist John H. Aughus of Mississippi avoided a similar fate by escaping to the North. According to historian Eugene Wait, Aughus was sure a hanging awaited him if he stayed in Mississippi, for he had already been insulted, imprisoned, and while incarcerated, all but starved.[75] Such atrocities were unfortunately visited upon Unionist clergymen in contested areas of the Confederacy with some regularity.[76] Given such dire and unfortunately common outcomes, the exploits of Unionist clergy in the Confederate South comprise one of the truly heroic chapters in America's historical annals.[77]

Unionist ministers could be found throughout the war and in every Confederate state. But for many of the same reasons that pro-Confederate churchpeople in the North resided overwhelmingly in peripheral Union states such as Missouri and Kentucky, a majority of Unionist preachers in the Confederacy were found in mountainous or upper-southern areas like Middle and East Tennessee, western North Carolina, and northwestern Virginia. Unlike the plantation-privileging Deep South, the late antebellum border-state South was home to a comparative political pluralism that allowed for indictments of slavery. Such criticisms found particular grip in sermons offered to a people whose hardscrabble existences spared them the dependence upon slavery that characterized most within the Old South. And as recent studies have shown, more than just anti-slave-owner bias informed the eventual Unionism of many southerners. Kinship and family tradition often led southerners to identify with the political viewpoints of relatives rather than with the broader, hegemonic southern society.[78] In truth, then, a number of forces contributed to Unionism in the South. The appealing component elements of Americanism such as democracy, loyalty to the vision of the nation's founders, and individual independence played a leading role, as did family connections and familial strains of evangelical religion. Certainly the economic autonomy and related regional self-image that had been forged antithetically to the planter elite took at least part of the place of slavery in defining many southerners' worldviews. Until very late in the antebellum period, such elements could be safely (if not always comfortably) touted by anti-secession ministers in much of the border South without concern for a particular "southern" and slavery-exalting gospel.

Before looking at those Unionist preachers who stayed in Dixie, it must be said of course that many clerics who opposed the Confederacy were both affluent enough *and* conveniently untethered enough—that is to say, not overly constrained by personally felt commitments to parishioners—to make their way northward. Consider Pennsylvania-born George Junkin, the Presbyterian minister and head of Virginia's Washington College who opined in January 1861 that "God made this government & he will not let man destroy it." Junkin's confidence proved warranted in the long run, but his Unionism would not allow him to wait on the Lord's outcome in Virginia. In May 1861, Junkin moved to Philadelphia, never to see Dixie again.[79] But lacking the wherewithal or inclination to leave hearth, home, and fellow members of a common church body, other Unionist preachers, most notably in East Tennessee and northern Georgia, stayed in the South, often becoming constant sources of consternation to Confederate and state leaders.

No matter how divided a village, town, or region—and by extension, denominational conference or other-named group of churches—might have been, ministers and their church members in the Upper South were *usually* in political agreement. In a geographic area characterized by such highly polarized communities, however, clergymen increasingly found themselves in opposition to at least some members of their local congregations. For most of the war in the Upper South, such circumstances were visited overwhelmingly upon Unionist preachers. As historian Robert Tracy McKenzie has said of racist East Tennessee (where Unionism was, in McKenzie's words, "anything but straightforward and uncomplicated"), thanks to the efforts of local secessionist Democrats working in "the aftermath of Lincoln's election, opposition to secession became tantamount to endorsement of the 'Black Republican' agenda."[80] The same can be said for towns and villages throughout the Upper South. Before the arrival of Federal troops in such volatile areas, a minster's Unionism exposed his entire congregation to reprisals by Confederate authorities and local vigilantes, a potentiality that members of a headstrong minister's flock often recognized and acted to avoid.[81] Thus when Christian Church leader David Lipscomb wrote in his *Gospel Advocate* of a church in which the Unionist minister and deacons were troubled by some secessionist women in the church who refused to take communion when it was passed to them by Unionist hands, it was no small matter.[82] Lipscomb and other preachers understood that in such a time and place of Rebel ascendancy, the defiance of even a few shut-mouthed Rebel women could bring unwanted Confederate attention a minister's way. At best, such attention might prompt other members to reconsider their choice of ministers. At worst, it might lead to the minister's arrest and persecution.

Tennessee Baptist Reverend James Madison Pendleton, a self-described "emancipator" who nevertheless owned slaves, was unwaveringly loyal to the United States. Thus Pendleton could not bring himself even to look at the Confederate flag as it made its way up the courthouse flagpole in Murfreesboro in the summer of 1861.[83] He was in the minority, for in his estimation most of the members of his church and "almost everybody in Murfreesboro turned against the Union." But not Pendleton. Because of his devotion, he believed, his life was in danger. "There was something said about hanging me," Pendleton recorded, a threat that might have been carried out "if so many men had not been sent away to the Army."[84]

To the east in Knoxville, emotions ran so high that, when members of several churches printed posters to advertise a "Union Prayer Service" (indicating a service featuring the memberships of multiple churches), Confederate soldiers thought they were praying for the Union and shot up the posters. Even in such an environment, the Reverend Thomas William Humes of St. John's Episcopal Church refused to speak out in favor of the Confederacy and was thus ultimately driven from his pulpit and out of town.[85] Hume's fidelity was rewarded in due time, however. After Union forces under the command of General Ambrose Burnside established control of the city in 1863, Federal authorities ordered Hume's reinstatement as the church's rector, and his church was the only one allowed to have services while every other church in town became a storehouse or hospital for Union soldiers.[86] Presbyterian minister R. J. Graves of Orange County, North Carolina, alienated his Confederate members in 1862 by writing a letter pledging his support to United States authorities. For his efforts he was arrested on charges of treason to the Confederacy.[87] Likewise arrested for his resistance to secession and dismissed by the members of his church, western North Carolinian Presbyterian Reverend James Sinclair believed that not even his priestly vestments offered protection from the abuses of Rebels. After making his way safely into the Union, Sinclair forlornly offered that "I for one would not wish to be left there in the hands of those men," his former parishioners.[88]

While Unionist ministers at odds with Rebel congregants were not altogether remarkable in the Upper Confederacy, even more prevalent were Unionist parsons who were in accord with their memberships but at odds with members of the local public. The extra-church community's prescriptive power could be great. When members of predominantly Unionist congregations in the Upper South nevertheless endorsed secessionism, for example, they did so most often because they feared that their Confederate neighbors might otherwise direct the wrath of local and state officials their way.[89] Like southern Confederate ministers and Unionist ministers in the North therefore, Unionist clerics in the Confederacy endeavored to both steel the patriotism (in this case, to the United States) of the members of their flock and help them make sense of the hardships that the war visited upon them. Such efforts were fraught with difficulty.

Steven Ash, Gordon McKinney, and others who study the clash between Unionist and Confederate civilians in the Upper Confederacy have characterized that conflict as nastier than any other aspect of the larger war.[90] Even in areas home to comparatively elevated levels of southern Unionism, to be a Unionist in the South after Fort Sumter was, as John Inscoe has observed, to be "part of a self-conscious minority viewed with suspicion and hostility, a minority whose very presence threatened the new regime and its cause."[91] Before Confederate troops ever arrived, many parts of the Upper South devolved into internecine strife that pitted neighbor against neighbor and kin against kin and were, as Unionist Daniel Dulany wrote of Falls Church, Virginia, in April 1862, "totally without civil law" and prostrate before Rebel "maurauders" who "were daily destroying the country."[92] And life for southern Unionists became even harder when Confederate and home-guard troops entered the mix. Although southern Unionists actively pestered their Rebel foes by sabotaging Confederate equipment and burning key bridges, Confederate authorities responded to such defiance by initiating ever-more-restrictive martial law aimed expressly at squashing Unionism and by enacting several Alien Enemy acts that threatened the property and the freedom of Unionists.

Consequently, Unionist preachers in the South had to do all they could to sustain their parishioners but at the same time operate with clandestine caution. Ministers understood that, even after Federal troops had arrived at last to relieve Unionists, in most cases the future Federal military presence in a southern town or city was not assured. Aware of this fact, North Carolinian merchant and churchman Josiah Cowles warned his Unionist brother Calvin in 1863, "There is great trouble in store for all of us, and it is best for every one to preserve silence on the political affairs of the day. . . . I beseech you to be very careful of what you say."[93] The Federal or Confederate presence in, and control of, a given southern town was sometimes so variable that Unionist churches found it difficult to maintain alliances with other churches owing to the dangers of sending minister delegates to distant meetings, thereby exposing them to Confederate bushwhackers.[94] Regular church meetings were replaced by assemblies away from the church house proper in the interest of safety, and more that a few southern Unionist church records contained wartime passages like the one penned by the secretary of the Christian Chapel Church in Henderson County, Tennessee, who wrote, "During the great political rebellion of 1860 we continued to meet until sometime in the year 1862. Owing to the troubled condition of the country, the members thought best for their personal safety and well being to absent themselves until more favorable opportunity should offer and [there] was no regular meeting until sometime in the year 1865."[95]

Agonizingly, Unionist pastors routinely could not minister to the particular wartime needs of their congregants in meaningful ways. Public funerals for Unionists, for instance, were dangerous in the Confederacy, and thus at times southern denominationalists were deprived of the opportunity to bury their loved ones with the proper respect. Church historian Edith Hutton lamented, "Northern churches prayed openly for the cause. Their clergymen held memorial services for the dead. The Southern churches prayed openly for Confederate victory. When death came, families were comforted by their clergymen." But, Hutton concluded, for Unionist members of a Lake City, Tennessee, Baptist church, "older church members were dying, the soldiers were dying, but their families could not receive the comfort of their church."[96]

Significantly, there were Unionist ministers below the Upper South. As David Chesebrough writes, "In the lower South, the dissenting clergy were fewer in number, but they did exist; and the consequences they paid for their nonconformity were severe."[97] Presbyterian Reverend James Lyon of Mississippi, for instance, would not be silenced in his anti-Confederate sermonizing. In addition to relentlessly harassing Lyon, Confederate officials retaliated by arresting and court-martialing his son, Theodoric, and sending him to prison in Virginia.[98] Another Mississippian and Presbyterian parson named Galladet, made aware of even more draconian measures that awaited him for his Unionism, was "compelled to abandon his church and escape to the North in order to save his life."[99] Likely Galladet was not overstating the danger in which he stood. According to Presbyterian Reverend John Hill Aughey, another Mississippi minister imprisoned by Confederate officials for his loyalty to the United States, "Our property is confiscated, and our families left destitute of the necessities of life; all that they have, yea, all their living, being seized upon by the Confederates, and converted to their own use. Heavy fetters are placed upon our limbs, and daily some of us are led to the scaffold, or to death by shooting."[100] But no matter where they were in the South, Unionists preachers found novel ways to support both their careworn congregants and the Federal war effort. And in *both* the heart and the edges of the Confederacy, when discovered in their Unionist efforts, preachers often paid the ultimate price for their patriotism.

A single newspaper account of affairs in East Tennessee in 1863 reported the murders of Dutch Reformed Reverend Bowman in Washington County, previously mentioned Methodist Reverend Levi Carter and his son of Georgetown, Baptist Reverend Blair in Hamilton County (his throat cut in the presence of his family), and Presbyterian Reverend Hiram Douglas in Monroe County, all for their Unionist activities.[101] Christian Church minister Rama Dye was one of forty Unionists hanged in Texas in 1862 for supposed membership in what was in effect a secret Union League called the Peace Party and, in that membership, terrorizing Texas Confederates in numerous ways.[102] In Macon, Mississippi, when Presbyterian Reverend James Phelan was forced to resign his pastorate owing to his Unionism, his enemies were still unsatisfied. Unknown gunmen tried to kill Phelan as he strolled near his country home, but the resilient rector was only wounded. Apparently having learned of this former failure, three men returned to Phelan's home and were welcomed in by the hurt but mending minister after asking for something to eat. The men revealed their true colors by referring to the hospitable preacher as an "infernal Unionist and abolitionist" before fatally shooting him, in his own parlor, with his wife at home.[103] More heartbreaking still was the fate of an unnamed Methodist lay pastor in Knoxville, Tennessee. According to one eyewitness, the unfortunate soul, "a poor old man of sixty-five, and his son of twenty-five, were marched out at one time and hanged on the same gallows. They made that poor old man . . . sit by and see his son hang till he was dead, and then they called him a damned Linconite [sic] Union shrieker, and said, 'Come on; it is your turn next;' He sank, but they propped him up and led him to the halter, and swang both off the same gallows."[104]

Although southern Unionist preachers were violently persecuted during the war for materially aiding the invading Union Army, Unionist sentiment alone was usually enough to seal a minister's fate.[105] Confederate recruiting agent Lieutenant Colonel Sidney L. Jackman, in recording the capture and court-martial of an elderly Unionist preacher near the Arkansas-Missouri border, avowed that "no evidence of any crime whatever, was proved against him, except the fact, that he was a Union man, and that he admitted himself." However Jackman's fellow jurors, two Rebel officers who "regularly conducted such drumhead trials against avowed Yankee sympathizers," regarded such sentiment as "ample evidence . . . to justify execution." Only Jackman's pleading spared the old preacher's life.[106]

As these examples suggest, there were more than a few wartime murders of denominational ministers throughout the South, murders of and by both Confederates and Unionists. The bulk of such atrocities was carried out in the Upper South, and a majority of them featured victims who were in the Unionist clergy. Fairly representative of all such affairs was the murder of

Baptist preacher John B. Reed by men under the command of Confederate General John B. Mosby. Reed, the "supply" (occasional) preacher of the Columbia Baptist Church in Falls Church, Virginia, had opened a school for freedpeople after the enactment of the Emancipation Proclamation and served as a member of the local Unionist citizen's guard.[107] While serving in the latter capacity, Reed was captured by Mosby's men early on the morning of October 19, 1864. He was brutally murdered in a dense pinewood near Falls Church. The nature of the event is suggested by the surgeon's report, which stated, "There is no doubt concerning the murder of Mr. Reed, as the surgeon, who has made an examination of the body, states that the skull at the base of the brain is blown to atoms, and the flesh about the wound is filled with powder, as if the pistol had been placed close to the head."[108] The Confederate version of the incident, however, maintained that Reed was never taken prisoner but was shot while attempting to blow a horn of warning for his encampment as Mosby's men stealthily advanced. Some locals claimed that Mosby and his men dealt with John Reed so harshly because they mistook him for Hiram Read, a noted Union agent in the area. Falls Church historian Melvin Steadman refuted such claims, asserting, "Mosby had a good deal against J. B. Reed, including his obtaining information from wounded Confederate soldiers who were staying in the church, which was a [Federal] hospital. The information was given to the Union army."[109] Indeed, one eyewitness to the event reported that an unnamed ranger in Mosby's command asserted coldly after Reed's death, "The Baptist preacher Reed got what was coming to him."[110] Whatever the case, the brutal story of Reverend John Reed exemplifies both the many ways in which Unionist ministers in the Confederacy served the Union cause and the price they sometimes paid for the privilege.

Subjected to the authority of occupying forces or to the dictates of perceived illegitimate (local, state, and national) governments, southern preachers and the men and women to whom they ministered could not ignore the realities of the day. Even those preachers who longed to retreat into their churches and close the doors to the world outside found the war thrust upon them. But southern preachers saw the Civil War not just when they looked through their church windows outward; when they looked inward into their own hearts and downward into the faces of their congregants, the war was there as well. Like every other Christian, preachers applied their faith to their own political and secular determinations. Rebel ministers were conditioned by decades of apologetics to believe that slavery's political fruits, secession and the formation and maintenance of the Confederacy, were divinely sanctioned. They may or may not have had deep-seated qualms over the contradictions inherent in a so-called Christian slave state, but if so they almost never said as much. And, if Confederate preachers made smooth the way for the Confederacy's arrival and saw it as the denouement of the particularly southern gospel they had been proselytizing for decades, southern Unionist ministers continued throughout the war to scold those ministers who supported such a fiendish incarnation as the CSA.

Southern ministers, as individual occupants of pulpits and as component members of denominational bodies, became arbiters of their churchpeople's nationalism even when under the gun. When the Yankees came, and loyalty to their new but dear Confederate nation became perilous to express, harassed denominational clergymen ministered to their beleaguered countrymen in new and novel ways. Both directly through their admonitions and physical church leadership and indirectly through the gospel that they had effectively driven into the hearts of their flock members, southern denominational ministers counseled, mandated, and sanctified resistance and offered the church as its organizational nexus. Denied under Federal occupation the opportunity to edify southern congregants with pro-Confederate sermons, preachers helped their fellow Confederate churchmen carry by leading and/or ideologically facilitating furtive opposition to Federal dominion.

Perhaps even more undaunted were southern Unionist ministers. Confederates celebrated loyalty to a new nation devoted, for all practical purposes, to chattel slavery. But most Unionist ministers and lay members in the Confederacy had never evidenced fealty toward the Old South slaveocracy and now saw little reason to prove disloyal to their increasingly sacralized nation, the United States. The purveyors of southern white supremacy proved exceedingly effective, both before and after the Civil War, in convincing millions of Christian people that slavery and then race trumped any and all other political or cultural or even religious allegiances. But, they were not able to bring all southerners into the deluded fold. In a significant way no doubt, that failure is attributable to Unionist preachers who would not desist in their opposition to such cant. Such ministers faced persecution that was at times almost unimaginably brutal, persecution moreover that historians have only lately commenced to chronicle and understand. Unionist ministers in the Confederacy helped both their fellow southern Unionists through their spiritual leadership and Federal forces through their dangerous and dissident efforts as sustenance givers, saboteurs, informants, and pilots. Southern Unionist and Confederate preachers were alike motivated by—and dedicated to the promotion of—political loyalty. Their ideas about loyalty were chiefly informed by their religious sensibilities.

Rebel preachers believed what they believed about the Confederacy not because of some knee-jerk reaction to the election of Abraham Lincoln or the firing on Fort Sumter, but essentially because their past public and church lives had been spent believing in the biblical soundness of slavery, the cultural oneness of white southerners who lived in the shadows of slavery, and the wickedness of those who would proscribe their separate society. By contrast, southern Unionists believed in the United States, for the most part, because their past lives had been absent such preeminent reverence for the slave system.[111] Religious leaders thus had a tenacious viability in the public life of a religiously conscious but pluralistic state. That importance, moreover, is exponentially broadened when a nation and its people pass through stormy days. The degree to which preachers can and do shape the actions of adherents rendered hesitant and unsure by the apparent combustion of their worlds is perhaps a lesson best not forgotten.

8

BLACK CHURCH LEADERS AND
POLITICS IN THE CIVIL WAR

T HE AFRICAN AMERICAN clergy's antislavery efforts constituted its
most important role during the Civil War.[1] While historians have
acknowledged the centrality of black preachers in the struggle for
freedom, however, they have sometimes failed to note the nuances and
variants of wartime African American clerical leadership.[2] This stems from
the scholarly tendency to accentuate the immediate impact that emancipation
had on how black Americans imagined the political arena. In other words,
because both emancipation and military service implied a future of black
citizenship and therefore male electoral participation, acknowledgments that
post-emancipation African Americans continued to view politics in the same
expansive way that they had for decades are commonly lacking in works on
wartime black leaders. Among recent studies, only *A Nation under Our Feet*
forcefully emphasizes what author Steven Hahn called the African American
"relational and historical" conceptualization of politics that encompassed a
comparatively diverse array of "collective struggles for . . . socially meaningful
power" and continued throughout the wartime and postwar era.[3]

In neglecting wartime preachers whose efforts were socially and politically
consequential but perhaps not easily discernible in the era's formal political
arena (that is to say, in the formation of state, national, and military policy),
we have all but overlooked an entire category of wartime African American
political activism.[4] Only through such an emphasis in the literature on the
ways and degree to which wartime black clerics amassed and exercised
political clout, however, can the implications of black ministerial passivity be
completely struck from America's collective memory of the Civil War. Indeed,
although black ministers were often unique in their wartime messages and, by
necessity, the literal and emblematic platforms they mounted in their delivery,
they were often equal or superior to white ministers in the widespread
political influence they wielded within their communities of faith and the
degree to which they, as individual men of conviction, maintained their
ideological independence.[5]

African Americans during the Civil War years were political in a myriad of
ways, and the Emancipation Proclamation did not erase the collective memory

of decades of subaltern political activism. The family, the field, and now the front constituted spaces of political contestation and negotiation for African Americans just as much as did the lecture hall and lyceum. Ministers certainly understood this aspect of black life. There was no threefold categorization or consideration of ministerial duties in the African American clergy. Black clerics deemed it their job to instruct their charges on any and every issue that might somehow impede the faithful in their Christian walk, and such issues as morality, manhood, and education were part of the African American political world. In many ways, wartime parsons proffered African American improvement as a means toward political independence and viability. A small cadre of scholars has questioned the contemporary take on black-originated "racial uplift" campaigns as middle and upper-class expressions of accommodationism (or even worse, an acceptance of defeat) and exclusively a product of the post-Reconstruction age. Adding ministers to the mix of African Americans who championed self-improvement during the Civil War era expands the understood scope of African American ministerial influence and better replicates the comprehensiveness of the black church of the day.

No matter how crucial non-electoral political endeavors were to mid-century African Americans, however, universal emancipation and the expectation of enfranchisement changed the way that southern black people conceived of the *immediate* political realm. Limited no longer to informal and often unspoken negotiations with white authority over religious and familial autonomy and labor arrangements, millions of freedmen anticipated involvement in the same sanctioned political channels that characterized white political life. Dedicated to the idea of African American unity, moreover, post-emancipation northern black leaders touted a virtually limitless *collective* African American political future.[6] Both adjustments jibed with African Americans' belief in prophetic scripture, and clerics naturally steered the course into the new age. But ministers within northern and independent (from white oversight) black faith traditions—the men who unquestionably carried the standard of African American electoral politics forward—were often bitterly divided over some of the key political issues of the day, issues such as colonization and military enlistments.[7]

I

As defined by a leading authority on American racial-improvement theories, African American "uplift "efforts have always emphasized "self-help, racial solidarity, temperance, thrift, chastity, social purity, and the accumulation of wealth."[8] While there is nothing inherently deferential in any of these objectives, racial uplift is nevertheless most often discussed either in the pejorative terms of accommodationism or as a response to the ideas of scientific racism prevalent during the Gilded Age. When discussing the former, scholars customarily associate uplift with Booker T. Washington or with ostensibly autonomous, but often white-funded, black church groups (especially Baptists) in the post-Reconstruction South. In such associations, racial uplift is cast as a defeatist strategy. Left little other recourse in the wake of Reconstruction's demise, the narrative goes, Washington and other gradualists hoped against hope and the lessons of history that the cultivation of appropriate "American" values in poor and working-class African Americans would change white attitudes and public policies and allow black people to somehow earn social equality and full-fledged citizenship.[9] When considering the latter—the notion that racial uplift was a response to the racist exigencies of Victorian America—contemporary scholars make particular note of middle- and upper-class black people who hoped to differentiate themselves from the masses of poor and uneducated African Americans.[10] And no matter how they imagine its motivations, the largest part of scholars portray African American–originated racial uplift campaigns as post-Reconstruction developments.[11]

This study suggests a broader reality, one in line with the findings of those who have recently found agency within numerous nineteenth-century African American self-help campaigns (although none of these historians has focused solely on wartime ministers).[12] Certainly many strong and independent black preachers of the Civil War era advocated racial uplift, often using the very term itself.[13] And as a rule, they did not do so because they hoped black servility might appeal to white magnanimity or that African American performance and behavior might somehow earn white trust. In truth, the wartime black clergy's initiative was one almost providentially unconcerned with white thought. In their doctrines of betterment and as was true of earlier black newspaper editors and members of voluntary associations, African American preachers during the Civil War sought to prepare all of their brethren and sisters for their coming and long-prophesied day of political and societal liberation.

Such should come as no surprise, for racial uplift was an integral part of forceful church leadership in the antebellum age. As a matter of practicality, black Christians during the so-called "Era of Reform" recognized that if they were to benefit from the improvements of the age, they would have to take up the mantle for themselves. As one critic of white Christianity offered in 1848, "we have observed with regret and profound sorrow, that while American Christians have been prolific of benevolent plans to elevate and improve the condition of persons of their own complexion, they have usually excluded, as utterly unworthy of their regard and attention, the far more destitute and needy colored people of the land."[14] But while they often dealt with the immediate realities of black life in America (such as poverty, landlessness, and, of course, slavery), the prewar ministers who hoped to achieve African American improvement and betterment never lost sight of their struggle's ultimate objective, universal emancipation.[15]

The clergymen who orchestrated the National Negro Convention movement between 1830 and 1864 expressly linked racial elevation with liberty.[16] Led by Congregationalist Reverend James C. Pennington, for instance, delegates to the 1853 convention (Rochester, New York) offered not to improve black people so that all might be free but rather insisted that freedom would allow all black people to improve. "We would not lay our burdens upon other men's shoulders," the conventioneers avowed, "but we do ask, in the name of all that is just and magnanimous among men, to be freed from all the unnatural burdens and impediments with which American customs and American legislation have hindered our progress and improvement."[17] As Patrick Rael concludes, such "black jeremiads served to unite African Americans in the common cause of moral elevation" while simultaneously linking them, in their rhetorical efforts on behalf of black people everywhere, to a broader diasporic community.[18] Owing to the collectivistic nature of African-descendant Christianity in the Atlantic realm and the multinational organizational model of African Methodist Episcopalism, many African American ministers before the Civil War looked to carry the gospel of betterment into "the Western Isles, and then to the great continent of Africa."[19]

And yet an earlier generation of historians found it difficult to imagine that advocates of racial uplift within the antebellum black clergy were anything other than accommodationist "Uncle Toms."[20] No doubt due in part to the historiographical influence such scholars wielded, more recent writers have cast wartime ministerial proponents of racial uplift in a similarly disparaging light. Although Edward Wheeler is unique in his evenhanded consideration of postwar uplift theory as a mixed bag, he limits the importance and effectiveness of African American advocates of racial uplift *during the war itself* by positing that only after Union victory in 1865 "was there even the slightest chance that the hope for uplift could be translated into reality."[21] In his masterful examination of black Methodism after emancipation, Reginald Hildebrand similarly questions the impact of wartime uplift efforts. Chronicling a post-emancipation and late-wartime "Gospel of evangelical morality" in which black church leaders in the South "admonished African Americans to value honesty, sobriety, hard work, and family life," the author nevertheless characterizes that gospel as essentially "conventional and conservative" and hence accommodationist. As preached by Methodists in New Orleans and elsewhere, the pre-Reconstruction ministers in Hildebrand's account were to inculcate "industry, economy and frugality" as a component part of a message designed to promote "peace and order, by urging upon the emancipated a cheerful obedience to law, and a patient waiting for those civil rights to which they aspire."[22]

As these examples suggest, black-originated arguments for racial improvement during the war are often cast as accommodationist alternatives to, and not a means of bringing about, immediate black empowerment. More likely, however, is that African American preachers who cultivated uplift during the war thought it part and parcel of immediate and collective political progress. They were uninterested in justifying African Americans' access to the rights of citizenship. Instead, they hoped to prepare their charges to make the most of those rights when they soon arrived, aware that the fruits of emancipation might spoil on the vine if they as a people were not ready to exercise the "full enjoyment of those privileges of full citizenship, which . . . are indispensable to that elevation and prosperity of our people."[23] Those indispensible elements were twofold: preachers and politicians alike agreed that African Americans would thrive in the postwar period through the vote and access to land ownership in America. Preparing their people to make the most of both, African American church leaders stressed the uplifting forces of moral improvement and education.

In their efforts to vouchsafe the present and future for all African Americans, wartime church leaders equated morality with dedication to the greater cause of freedom. They believed such attributes might soon prove indispensible. By as early as 1864, Republican leaders had begun to uncouple emancipation and victory in the hopes of appealing to racist northern voters. Secretary of State William Seward, for instance, argued that the legalities and illegalities of emancipation were not germane to the quest for victory, but that with the war's close the issue of slavery would "pass over . . . to the courts of law."[24] The implications of such equivocations seemed dire, and church leaders feared that African Americans might yet have to endure a great deal of discrimination and oppression. In addition to appealing for the obvious necessities of collective success like a decent wage in the North and a "fair share" of land for freedmen and women in the South, therefore, the preachers who presided over the "colored men's convention" that met in Boston's Twelfth Baptist Church in October 1864 called for African Americans to cultivate black unity even as they nurtured in themselves a "sound morality."[25] Such personally steeling and culturally fusing moral improvement would no doubt prove determinative if the predictions of an AME minister identified as "Junius" came true. Anticipating the persistence of white supremacy in America and no doubt expressing the fear of many, Junius observed late in the war that the "signs of the times point clearly to another revolution in this country; and every soldier should bear in mind that he may yet be called on to lead an army, in defence of his manhood, on this continent. Soldiers, be ready for any movement! Look well to your muskets, and keep your powder dry."[26]

Black church leaders believed that the roads to both progress and self-defense were paved with African American virtue. They exalted the merits of honesty, sobriety, hard work, familial dedication, and above all, morality as a collective means to a politically participatory end. Bemoaning a decline in the number of African American Christians who taught morality at home, for example, "Golden Rule"–espousing Congregationalist Reverend Samuel Harrison (wartime chaplain of the famous Fifty-fourth Massachusetts) reminded African Americans, "If we as American citizens would have a prosperous government, and one to hand down to future generations, we must 'do justly between man and man, love mercy, and walk humbly before God.'"[27] The probity of black soldiers in the field was similarly of great concern to church leaders. The black religious press routinely printed reports from chaplains attached to African American regiments, and common were reports like the one published in the *Anglo-African* in 1863. Penned by Chaplain John N. Mars, the report boasted that, of the 1,500 men he attended to on a daily basis as their spiritual guide, Mars had not seen a single soldier drunk (or even imbibing) and had heard very little in the way of profanity.[28]

Such wartime attention to morality and moral improvement was typically anything but integrationist or assimilationist. Throughout the war, for instance, the outspoken African Methodist Episcopal Rev. Lewis W. Woodson advocated black separatism and toward that end called upon black people to engage in a transformative "moral revolution."[29] Reminding whites in the North and South of their own ethical shortcomings, an anonymous African American advocate of uplift urged whites in the North and South alike to let black people attend to would-be freedmen. "Mind your business," he demanded, "and let them mind theirs. . . . [W]hen you, our white fellow countrymen, have attempted to do anything for us, it has generally been to deprive us of some right, power or privilege which you yourselves would die before you would submit to have taken from you."[30] And more than a few church leaders believed in the amended "evangelical goodness" message proffered by lay minister, former fugitive slave, and abolitionist writer W. Wells Brown (famous for historicizing the regal ancestry of African Americans). Wells did not plead for political integration based on black equality. Instead, he urged *all* African Americans to demand *all* of the rights of citizenship as members of a morally superior race. That supremacy, in turn, rendered African Americans more self-sacrificing, brave, patriotic, and intuitively intelligent than depraved whites. Wells remembered years later that during and after the war "the colored men had the advantage of being honest and sincere in what they undertook, and labored industriously for the good of the country."[31]

In the name of political practicality plus the elemental Christian command to "do right," wartime ministers sought to improve African American morality and virtue on several fronts.[32] Black church leaders during the war instructed their listeners and readers on temperance, the evils of tobacco, the proper (and domestic) place of Christian women, and Sunday schools.[33] Purity was the byword, and vice the foil of African American progress. Numerous ministers in the North and South feared that slavery had disoriented the moral compass of freedpeople. AME Bishop Henry McNeal Turner for example observed that drunkenness had left black men in Smithville, North Carolina, all but incapacitated in the war's last days, a result of the lack of attention to the slave's moral conscience.[34] Thievery and sexual promiscuity were believed to have been particularly enabled, and even inculcated, by enslavement. Most clerics agreed with African American Baptist minister Edward M. Brawley, who lamented that the slaves' "ancestors had been stolen; he himself was stolen; his civil liberty was stolen," and slaves were "not taught the sacredness of married life." Therefore if "the two great vices charged against the Negro race are theft and adultery," Brawley asserted, they were the result of "the long training slavery gave. Indeed, slavery was largely a training ground in moral evil."[35]

As to thievery, ministers were aware of the many meanings the act had long held for numerous black people. Ubiquitous in the Old South, theft was both an understood form of resistance and an understandable means of familial and personal survival for enslaved African Americans (in the free North, black churchpeople were largely untarnished by any such association).[36] The task now for many ministers, and for that matter, Freedmen's Bureau agents, as they imagined it was to enhance the freedman's understandably deficient appreciation of the autonomy of labor and the sanctity of its product, personal property. African American ministers were confident that freedmen and women could make that transition and that their past vices and former degradation were a product of experience and environment rather than any inborn slavishness.[37] Conversely, other morally minded clerics were confident that African Americans knew full well the virtues of labor but were hesitant to believe those who would preside over their employment. The African Methodist Episcopal, Presbyterian, and Baptist ministers who addressed the black and white citizens of Richmond two months after Appomattox argued that African Americans were not morally deficient or lazy, as many whites claimed, but merely poor and distrustful. Because "the colored man knows that freedom means freedom to labor and to enjoy its fruits," if he then "is not to be found laboring for these late owners, it is because he cannot trust them." The remedy to labor gridlock was clear to all freedmen, the ministers believed: "If the planters want his labor (and they do), fair wages and fair treatment will not fail to secure it." But because moral improvement through the autonomy and self-determination of employment was crucial, African American men could not sit by as their dehumanizing poverty waxed. "Be up and active," the ministers concluded, "and everywhere let associations be formed having for their object the agitation, discussion, and enforcement of your claims of equality before the law."[38]

The meaning of marriage too now changed for millions of African Americans. Emancipation's promise of self-ownership and the related benefit of spousal choice rendered marriage and family life more political than ever before. Preachers understood this and took it upon themselves to set down the terms of African American marriage in the post-emancipation age, aware that opponents of black equality made much of the perceived immorality of nontraditional unions and quasi-marriages. Therefore, church leaders in both the North and the South grew more interested in sexual propriety, often expelling unmarried male and female members who engaged in inappropriate trysts with members of the opposite sex.[39]

And Federal authorities privileged the notion of male-dominated households in the post-emancipation South.[40] African American preachers shared this patriarchal vision of family life not only because it was ordained in the scriptures, but because it was thought essential to the maintenance of structurally sound black families, the protection of African American women, and the empowerment of African American manhood.[41] Just as Freedmen's Bureau agents instructed freedmen to "keep their wives in subjection," black church leaders affirmed that within black families the "'ruling power' is unquestionably invested in the husband." When black men and women seemed slow to put the tenets of male familial supremacy into practice, African American clerics attributed such reticence to the memory of enslavement, when "our ladies were not always at our own disposal." In stressing that times had changed and that African American men could now expect to reign supreme in their marriages, ministers fueled the fast-developing belief among freedmen that, in the words of Amy Dru Stanley, "the right to have a wife at their own disposal [w]as a bequest of emancipation. . . . [I]n stating exclusive claim to her, they declared themselves slaves no more."[42] Marriage therefore was an empowering proposition for freedmen, one thought fundamental to moral improvement and thus racial uplift. As the arbiters of such unions, African American clerics grew evermore central to black political and social life.

The ministerial desire to formalize slave marriages was not about morality alone, of course. White politicians—often patently racist figures like Andrew Johnson—conceded a degree of authority to black parsons in exchange for their oversight of marriages and other social institutions. In a way that history suggests must have been insincere, Johnson greeted a contingency of ministers with a pledge to see "the temporal and eternal interest of the black race . . . advanced to the fullest extent" before soliciting their assistance in remedying the shameful fact that in the South "four millions of people" still lived in "open and notorious concubinage."[43] Such white utilization of black ministers was of course convenient and varied in form during the war, as when the New York Merchant's Relief Committee asked black ministers to orchestrate relief claims or President Lincoln played cat-and-mouse with Washington's African American clergy to test the waters on colonization in the summer of 1862.[44] But the moral authority attendant in such roles, no matter how those roles came to pass, expanded the African American preacher's ability to successfully promote uplift as a means toward a politically beneficial end.

Perhaps nothing represents the wartime African American clergy's commitment to moral improvement more than its emphasis on manhood. As was evident in their delineation of gendered marriage roles, black ministers recognized the emasculating natures of southern slavery and northern marginalization and dedicated themselves to fostering African American male confidence and self-actualization.[45] If perhaps paternalistic, manhood rhetoric as a hedge against the degradation of African American men was by and large not misogynistic during the prewar and wartime years, and indeed was often championed as a step toward protecting black womanhood.[46] But it was also considered infinitely necessary during the war, and church leaders like AME Bishop W. J. Gaines considered "rehabilitating" African American manhood the black church's primary task."[47] Important elements of racial uplift like moral betterment and education, it was believed, could only be accomplished when African American men believed *themselves* to be fully capable. Otherwise, as AME Bishop Daniel Payne observed, the African American man's confidence waned and he internalized a misplaced sense of inferiority that confirmed in his own mind "the oft-repeated assertions of his enemies, that he really is incapable of self-government and self-support."[48]

Manhood meant many things for African Americans during the era. First and foremost, manhood meant bold participation in the battle for freedom. According to historian Dudley T. Cornish, many Americans initially believed that "a slave was not a man," but when afforded the opportunity the "Negro soldier proved that the slave could become a man."[49] The Civil War was, after all, an age when even so-called friends of African Americans questioned their full humanity. A white army chaplain who preferred serving black regiments considered slavery the "sum of all villanies" and admired African American patriotism nevertheless understood the rampant "anti-negro sentiment in the army." "It is useless . . . to throw a false halo of romance about the negro," he wrote. "If we attempt to apply the rule of New England morality to the negroes, who are as much heathen as are the natives of the Sandwich Islands, of course they will be found wanting. . . . [T]he freedmen are not angels, they are not even civilized men."[50] Most black ministers knew that negative assessments of African American capacity were not only wrong but hypocritical. As white Marylander James Gooding admitted, his fellow southerners argued that "the negro cannot learn or reason, and yet laws must be made against teaching him to read." Similarly, Gooding added incredulously, "some argue that the negro is inferior to the whites . . . incapable of civilization and progress. And yet they boast of the improvement that negroes undergo in a state of slavery."[51]

Convinced of the potential of black soldiers, many (but not all) ministers enthusiastically pointed men toward the ranks, confident that service would allow African American men from the North and South to prove to the world, friend and foe alike perhaps, what they had always known and long proclaimed about themselves and their male congregants: they were men and had been created by God as men. "The time is now at hand," a pair of AME reverends identified as "S.H." and "J.C." observed in March 1863, "when the colored man shall be able to prove his indomitable capacity . . . as was formerly shown in the Revolution."[52] And certainly black soldiers did not disappoint. AME Reverend John Randolph offered proudly in 1864 that "the heroic deeds of colored men on the battle field, will so far remove our difficulties, as to enable us to show to the world that we are deserving the rights and titles of citizens—a people worthy to be free—worthy to be respected."[53] And so it did, at least to some. After the Battle of Petersburg, veterans from Hancock's Corps—unquestionably among the best soldiers in the Army of the Potomac— sounded the praises of their brave fellow soldiers and treated them with dignity and respect. "A few more fights like that," one officer observed, "and our Colored boys will have established their manhood if not their Brotherhood to the satisfaction of even the most prejudiced."[54]

More important than what black military service said to whites, however, was what it meant for African Americans themselves. Of course the individual soldier was empowered by service. "This was the biggest thing that ever happened in my life," a slave-turned-soldier remembered, "I felt like a man with a uniform on and a gun in my hand."[55] But as Jacqueline Bacon reminds us, in the nineteenth century "the language of morality and self-improvement that fostered community solidarity was often combined with masculine terms that suggested that individual masculine behavior [like soldiering] had an impact on *all* African Americans."[56] Certainly ministers, the effectual intelligentsia of the African American community, knew of mid-nineteenth-century American historian John Lothrop Motley's ideas on the transformative nature of participation in a common military defense. "We might . . . refer to that period in Greek history when the Hellenic race rose as one man to repel the Persian invasion," Motley theorized, "or to the Crusades . . . the Lutheran Reformation . . . and French Revolution, with its madness, but its devotion also. Such enthusiasms uplift whole races into higher regions."[57] Preachers and other black leaders held up soldiers as examples of black manhood for all to see, and black soldiers welcomed the responsibility. "I have been in sublimity,"

Joseph E. Williams of the Thirteenth U.S.C.T. (United States Colored Troops) wrote from Johnsonville, Tennessee, because he and his brothers-in-arms had thus far so nobly borne "the pressing weight of the great future of my beloved race, particularly that class who have emerged from the condition of chattels, to a sense of true manhood."[58] It was this intraracial value more than anything else that made military service so edifying for African Americans during the Civil War.

Naturally manhood rhetoric touched upon other issues like marital authority, self-respect, intellectual growth, and moral character. But no matter the issue at hand, African American manhood rhetoricians looked for manifestations of what moral improvement meant *to and for black people* intrinsically. Manhood was linked to morality, in other words, not because African American men feared the judgment of whites but because in all of their doings they felt the weight of their obligation to their own people.[59] Wartime free black men took upon their backs a huge but welcome burden, a responsibility that they recognized had to be theirs. In their public interactions, marriages, businesses, places of employment, and especially soldierly ranks, they felt compelled to be morally circumspect, confident that their accomplishments would make obvious that the subjugation of African Americans was depraved and unnatural.[60] And again while such discourse encompassed several areas of endeavor between 1861 and 1865, in the wartime context nothing bespoke their manhood more than did African Americans' bravery, daring, and proficiency as soldiers. Black ministers played a leading role in facilitating African American service in the war and thereby added to the causes of African American manhood, moral improvement, and ultimately, racial uplift.

Wartime racial uplift rested upon twin towers. Moral improvement in all its facets was important to the fight in the opinion of black church leaders, but no more so than education. Freedmen and women instinctively knew that their own personal education would be integral to their collective improvement as a people, else their former masters would not have tried so diligently to restrict it. "I'm going to school now to try to learn something," a young freedman said in Georgia in 1865, "which I hope will enable me to be of some use to my race."[61] Ministers like Presbyterian leader (and future South Carolina state treasurer) Francis Cardoza certainly recognized that self-help was limited in its potential if black people, especially those in the South, were not taught the prerequisite skills of learning. His was an "abiding faith in the efficacy of education," a faith—really *the* faith—from which his hopes for African American uplift sprang.[62] And he was not alone in his ideas about education and uplift. One of the original directors of Wilberforce University in Ohio, African Methodist Episcopal Rev. Lewis Woodson was so dedicated to establishing black churches and church schools without the help or benevolence of whites that some have labeled him the father of Black Nationalism.[63] Connecticut Congregationalist minister and political activist Amos G. Beman championed education as the most important antecedent of uplift. Convinced of "the efficacy of Christianity and moral reform," Beman instructed church members to "be ambitious and hardworking, temperate and virtuous," and "to avoid debt and illicit relationships."

But dedicated to other elements of collective racial growth though he was, Beman urged African Americans first, foremost, and "above all, while seeking learning for themselves, to endure any sacrifice for the proper upbringing and education of the children." When Beman's words were directed at whites, he continued to sound the praises of uplift through education. Although speaking during the antebellum debate over re-enfranchising African Americans in Connecticut, his words capture perfectly the attitude of moral uplifters of the war era, and his argument was repeated by wartime emulators. "You have an interest then whether you feel it or not, in our welfare; in our being intelligent, virtuous, and good citizens," Beman reminded. "We cannot be ignorant, vicious and degraded without an injury to yourselves."[64]

As with moral improvement, scholars who have considered early post-emancipation efforts to educate freedmen and freedwomen have often looked through white eyes.[65] If not warranted, such is perhaps understandable. Freedmen's Bureau directors preferred white teachers initially, and thus white teachers greatly outnumbered black teachers during the war. Not until 1869 did African American teachers make up a majority of the more than three thousand freedmen's teachers in the South.[66] But African American church leaders took up their people's own education to a far greater extent than most historians suggest. In the South, African Americans placed education at the top of their political objectives. As a contributor to the *Friend's Review* recorded in March 1865, seventy minister-led residents of Savannah "took immediate steps for their improvement" upon Federal occupation of that city. They formed a society "to look after their own interests" and in short order hired ten African American teachers, contributed nearly "one thousand dollars in 'greenbacks'" to the school-forming effort, and with General John White

Geary's blessing, took possession of an old slave market (wonderful irony that) for use as a school building. "The whole movement," the reporter concluded, "is characterized as one of intelligent, self-sacrificing endeavor for self-support and self-respecting independence."[67]

Similarly, the minister-rich State Convention of the Colored Men of Tennessee that met in August 1865 (and was thus one of the earliest Freedmen's Conventions) called boldly for educational opportunities, setting a precedent eagerly followed by other African American conventioneers throughout the South.[68] And many well-educated black ministers who traveled South after emancipation offered themselves up as both models for matriculating freedmen and living refutations of the racist aspersions of local whites. Born in South Carolina but educated in New Hampshire, AME Reverend James Lynch for instance avowed in 1865, "I hope the reporters will take me down as saying 'dis' 'dat' 'de oder,' and the 'deformities of de constitution.' I know more syntax than them all put together. They ridiculed me because my skin was darker than theirs. It won't pay! It won't pay!"[69]

The desire for educational self-sufficiency was not unique to freedmen and church leaders in the South. Eager to instill in his readers a needed appreciation for intraracial education, an African American commentator in a California paper bemoaned the tendency of black people to doubt the intelligence and insight of their own community's political and educational leaders. "We must learn to respect leadership among us," he chided, "we must learn to respect men in their legitimate and proper callings [and] in their professions." Such veneration, the author hoped, would effectively end the aggravating local habit of placing their money in the hands of white men instead of funding more black schools and churches themselves.[70] The unnamed proponent of African American self-help would have no doubt revered Methodist Reverend Charles Avery, even though Avery was white. Committed to facilitating black self-help, Avery entered the ministry after making a fortune in a number of industries, including iron, copper, and pharmaceuticals. He was unique, therefore, in his ability to merge spiritual leadership with financial support of the educational wings of the African Methodist Episcopal and AME Zion Churches.[71] Among other donations, while living Avery gave $150,000 to the American Missionary Association to educate black children and $25,000 to fund fifty scholarships for African Americans at Oberlin College.[72] When he died, Avery left "$800,000 in his will to various black societies and to schools that were educating young black people." The financial security his benevolence assured for African American churches in Pittsburgh and Allegheny City afforded those churches an opportunity to lead wartime black self-education efforts in the Lower North.[73]

Like Charles Avery, wartime African American church leaders understood that black people as a rule were more earnestly devoted to African American education than were whites and sought to procure black teachers whenever and wherever possible. African American missionaries in the post-emancipation South wanted "colored teachers sent down among them," for according to AME Zion Bishop Joseph Jackson Clinton, "the white teachers did not go the right way to work." Education as an autonomous means of uplift was expressly endorsed by Clinton. "We are more fully convinced than ever," the bishop told a New York audience, "that one of the main remedies for the evils South whether they be educational, agricultural or social, is the idea . . . that the colored people should be made, as far as possible, their own uplifters—the aid to be given to be that . . . which will enable the colored man the soonest possible to help himself."[74] Among AME ministers, such talk was not idle. In 1863 alone the AME Church and its ministers founded ten colleges that proved vital to black education in the South and Midwest for decades to come.[75] Thus early post-emancipation advocates of black uplift through education did not depend on the Freedmen's Bureau or white religious and benevolent groups exclusively. African Americans preachers during the Civil War looked to their own denominational memberships for support as well. Every successful African American–originated educational endeavor, in turn, demonstrated the black clergy's commitment to the uplift of their race.

African American–initiated racial uplift was not original to the post-Reconstruction age and was not simply the accommodationist fallback position of increasingly put-upon black church and business leaders. Nor was it, in its inception, an attempt by middle- and upper-class African Americans to distance themselves from their less fortunate countrymen and, in that distance, to find room to avoid the worst abuses of scientific racism. Scholars must reexamine the earlier roots and Civil War–era expressions of racial uplift and grant its proto-nationalist purveyors the respect they deserve. With its dual themes of moral improvement and education, wartime uplift rhetoric opened one path for black preachers to lead African Americans into a new political age even as they as clergymen grew, through that leadership, their own political and social importance. In all of this, black and white preachers filled similar roles. White clerics were not engaged in campaigns of ethical improvement and basic schooling, it is true, but like African American clerics they attended to the moral and educational issues that most affected their flocks. By turns reminding parishioners that their side was morally in the right (whatever "their side" happened to be) and wondering if setbacks were reckonings for their own moral shortcomings, they explained the war and framed its events in useful and educational ways. Morally concerned and educationally integral, black and white preachers during the Civil War were more comparable than they perhaps recognized.

II

Just as white preachers battled over the propriety of political preachers and, relatedly, the merits of slavery, scope of Federal authority, and nature (either holy or hellacious) of the war, African American clerics were at times at odds over what *they considered* the controversial political issues of the day. Chief among those issues of contestation were colonization and military enlistments.[76] However, for three reasons few have noted the level of disagreement that existed within the ranks of wartime African American ministers over these political issues. First, the trend in the scholarly literature on religion and the Civil War *in general* has been to underplay differences of opinion within common groups, ministers included.[77] Second, historians have mistaken black Christianity's historical emphasis on the *collective*, in matters both of faith and of politics, with *consensus*, assuming that African American preachers who hoped to arrive at a common day of freedom must have agreed upon every issue along the way.[78] And last, the nature of archival material on black preachers of the war years seems to suggest accord. Much of the available evidence consists of memoirs penned decades after the war, when disputes were usually settled and often forgotten. Moreover, the church-based collection of materials on black clerics lends itself to considerations of ministers within a single African American faith tradition, which in turn limits the likelihood that disagreements, although they surely occurred, were diligently recorded.[79] But thanks to the wartime existence and subsequent archival preservation, copying, and now digitizing of a number of religious and secular newspapers and the rediscovery over the years of primary documents by scholars working on the war, at last fissures within the wartime African American clergy can be seen.[80]

Highlighting these differences connects with a small group of scholars who have challenged old ideas about the uniformity of African American thought during the nineteenth century. In his examination of antebellum slave neighborhoods, for instance, Anthony Kaye refutes the notion that chattel slavery was characterized by overarching communities that built hegemony. Instead, he shows that southern African Americans in fact varied in social practices, outlooks, and attitudes when separated by as little as a few miles of fields, roads, and buildings.[81] And Patrick Rael convincingly argues that treatments of African Americans in the prewar North have likewise overused the "community-studies/culturalist paradigm." In truth, Rael establishes, antebellum blacks were far too complicated and diversely opinionated to be reduced to one-dimensional labels.[82] Rael's work underscores historian Rita Roberts's belief that "the reductionistic categories that have dichotomized or grouped antebellum northern blacks in earlier studies are unsustainable."[83]

Postwar African Americans too have been the subject of recent reconsideration, and scholars have found important signs of intraracial difference. William A. Blair for instance details the varying ways southern black people thought about political issues like commemoration and their betrayal by the Republican Party. In so doing, he shows that a single and unvariegated African American community never really existed in the postwar age.[84] In his assessment of racial uplift during the post-Reconstruction era, moreover, David Blight chronicles ministerial divisions and "stern disagreements" over such topics as emigration and accommodationism.[85] These and other studies have left space, however, for a consideration of *wartime* African Americans, and especially preachers. For like white ministers, African American spiritual leaders differed on important issues between 1861 and 1865, just as they had during the antebellum and postwar years.

Any discussion of African American ministerial leadership on the patently political issues of the day must necessarily privilege northern-centered and independent black denominations, particularly the African Methodist Episcopal Church.[86] Aside from its famed agitation for immediate and complete emancipation, the mid-nineteenth-century AME Church's most distinguishing characteristic was its insistence on independence and separation from whites. After emancipation, this prompted AME clerics in the North and South to proffer a "Gospel of Freedom" that advocated immediate separation of former slaves from whites, especially their former owners.[87] Moreover, the AME Church was an international organization with churches in Africa and throughout the Atlantic realm. Because African Americans believed so fully in biblical prophecies of an ascendant African-descendant race, during the prewar years many saw the pan-nationalist AME Church as "unquestionable evidence" and a "harbinger" of the soon-transpiring day of black redemption when "princes shall come out of Egypt" and "Ethiopia shall . . . stretch forth her hands unto God."[88] Between 1830 and 1860 membership in the AME Church grew by an astounding 400 percent while membership in many other black denominations declined.[89]

According to one historian, during the antebellum era there was "a veritable hurricane of spiritual restlessness and rebellion" that benefited African Methodist Episcopalism and other northern church groups that "sought to exercise their powers of leadership and control their own affairs."[90] Even under the burden of slavery, African Americans learned of the AME Church. Long after becoming a renowned AME minister, for instance, Andrew Brown remembered that as a self-professed "poor bare-footed and bare-headed man" in Georgia,

I saw the A.M.E. Church in 1844 as bright as I see her tonight. I then prayed that I might outlive the surrounding circumstances, and see in reality as I then saw it in my mind. . . . [W]hile in the woods upon my knees, God showed me this church. The day was dark, but, thank God, we waited on and on. God's horse was tied to the iron stake. For a longtime he failed to prance in Georgia and South Carolina. The day the first fire was made at Sumter, I saw the Gospel Horse begin to paw. He continued to paw until he finally broke loose and came tearing through Georgia. The colored man mounted him and intends to ride him.[91]

It is true that pre-emancipation and immediate post-emancipation southern black people both enslaved and free were most likely to be affiliated with the Methodist Episcopal Church South, the Baptist Church, the Presbyterian Church, or the Catholic Church. And certainly clergymen in these traditions ministered to their congregants on the non-electoral and unsanctioned political issues that dominated their lives, issues like family and morality and the virtues of racial betterment. But black Christians within these denominations, at least in the South, were almost always under ultimate white authority if not direct oversight, and the ability of their parsons to speak openly on issues like freedom, rebellion, and black unity had long been arrested.[92]

To say the least, black people resented such monitoring. In short order after emancipation, therefore, AME missionaries not only won the hearts and minds of many freedmen and women, but they won their denominational memberships as well. Because of the African Methodist Episcopal Church's history of abolitionism, its identification with African American and African-descendant unity, and its hierarchical and centralized structure that facilitated a constancy of message, wartime AME preachers became the understood delineators and disseminators of black political opinion—for black Americans everywhere—when the issue at hand concerned collective African American rights and obligations within the body politic.[93]

But while guiding African Americans on state-related political issues like colonization and military enlistments, AME preachers often disagreed in the particulars of such leadership. Prior to the issuance of the Emancipation Proclamation in September 1862, perhaps no issue was more persistently divisive than colonization. African Americans had been debating the merits of a mass African American movement to Liberia or South America for more than four decades when the war started. Mark E. Neely notes that many of the nation's most prominent African American families, including that of Frederick Douglass, were sometimes torn over the issue.[94] But as Kate Masur has shown, the wartime issue of government-supported black colonization was divisive to an extent seldom recognized by scholars today.[95] The initiation of hostilities did little to bring about consensus on the matter, and black clerics continued to display real venom in its deliberation. For instance, editor and AME Zion minister Thomas Hamilton called Joshua Leavitt a "pervert" when the abolitionist cleric supposedly "converted" (or, "perverted") from abolitionism to "the hell-born creed of the expatriation of freed colored men from the soil and homes which they have earned by their sufferings and their toil."[96]

AME clerics advocated a mass movement of African Americans to Liberia, Haiti, or South America for several reasons. Many were convinced that black people in America would never reach their full potential under the limiting thumb of white prejudice. In 1861 and 1862, Bishop Alexander Crummell represented this viewpoint, even though he recognized that most black Americans were not of the same opinion.[97] "We therefore say to our colored brethren in America," Crummell wrote in 1862, "emigrate anywhere, and everywhere, until you find some country where you can be a free and a great people."[98] Others were motivated by the AME Church's characteristic pan-nationalism. An unnamed editorialist in the *Christian Recorder* argued that

American slavery had actually been a part of God's plan for the exaltation of
Africa:

> In the strange workings of Divine Providence this *race* in has been
> brought to this land, and put under a tutelage for a great future, and
> that Africa, its home, may become the recipient of blessings, the
> foundation and preparation for which were made in this country. The
> bondage of the Israelites in Egypt was not an accident, but a divinely
> ordered procedure, which had a striking bearing upon the character
> of the Jew and shaped his whole after history. It was a work of
> preparation, and it was not done in a short time. . . . American slavery,
> like this Egyptian bondage, will have its results on the future of Africa.
> In saying this, of course no reader will suppose that there is in the
> thought a justification of slavery . . . [but] it is impossible to discuss the
> future of the black people in this country immediately being brought
> into contact with the future of Africa.[99]

And, some felt an obligation to existing colonies of expatriated African
Americans already in Africa and elsewhere. Liberia and other settlements
needed "more emigrants from America to keep the Colonies from degenerating
and to enable them to extend their influence over the interior," one African
American columnist wrote. "Thus far," he continued, "the jealousy of all that
favored the rise of the negro race, has kept down much of the sympathy that
would otherwise have been expressed for the Colonization movement."[100]
Lastly, reflecting the strong independent streak possessed by so many AME
clerics, a few ministers championed colonization because they did not want
to be told they couldn't emigrate. "*We are going just where we please,*" Henry
McNeal Turner wrote in December 1862, "going to church, going to stay here,
going away, going to Africa, Hayti, Central America, England, France . . . and
then we are going to the jails, gallows, penitentiary, whipping-post, to the
grave, heaven and hell. But we do not intend to be sent to either place unless
we choose."[101]

Following President Lincoln's controversial meeting with a committee of
five leading Washington ministers to discuss a possible plan of government-
assisted colonization in August 1862, a few AME ministers seemed taken
by the president's argument and believed he meant black people well. In a
letter penned before the Emancipation Proclamation, a Rhode Island minister

writing to the AME's *Christian Recorder* declared his certainty that "the President has no wish to harm us by this colonization scheme." And perhaps African Americans should jump at the Lincoln plan, the writer added, for "instead of giving us $5,000 and sending us to Central America, he could send us to the battlefield. This is my birthplace, and I dislike to leave it, but for the precious boon of freedom, I will dare even death. Such are the kind of men that are going to found a colony."[102] Even after emancipation the issue was not settled among all within the AME clergy. Bishop Crummell believed emancipation and colonization were not mutually exclusive; one historian has noted that in late 1862 and 1863, "at the very moment when many black Americans perceived that the tide of American race relations was turning, Crummell stubbornly forged ahead and obstinately renewed his commitment to colonization."[103] And in arguing for immediate emigration to Liberia, AME Reverend Dr. Martin H. Freeman of Pennsylvania's Avery College publicly stated in September 1863, "Mere emancipation is not . . . the only good for which the black man sighs," nor was it enough that blacks in America "should pass from a state of servitude to the individual, to one of bondage to society."[104]

These dissenting ministerial ideas about wartime colonization are seldom historiographically remembered, and in truth were minority views. Most AME preachers shared the opinion voiced by (AME Zion lay minister) Frederick Douglass in 1862, when he fretted that the emigrationist talk of a few black church leaders might wrongfully suggest a lack of accord on the part of African Americans.[105] And not a few AME ministers believed quite simply that emigrationism was but a pie-in-the-sky plan that distracted African Americans from reality. "Some people talk of emigration for the black race," Reverend John W. Hood of New Bern, North Carolina, noted in 1865, "some of expatriation, and some of colonization. I regard this as all nonsense. We have been living together for a hundred years or more; and we have got to live together still; and the best way is to harmonize our feelings as much as possible, and to treat all men respectfully."[106] But no matter why an AME cleric argued for or against colonization during the war, it must be noted *that they argued.*

AME ministers also saw to the recruitment of African American soldiers. Roughly 180,000 African Americans served in the Federal armies during the Civil War, while 18,000 served in the United States Navy (of those nearly 200,000, over 20 percent—more than 40,000—lost their lives, most from disease). African American soldiers were essential to Union victory. According to Joseph Glatthaar, black troops came into the army "when the Union needed them most" and "helped to make the difference between victory and stalemate or defeat."[107] AME ministers acted as de facto recruiting agents, spurring their members to enlist and their congregants at home to support Union soldiers in the field. One preacher remembered with only a bit of bluster that during the war he "put more men in the field, made more speeches, and organized more Union Leagues . . . than any other man" in his state.[108]

Common after January 1863 were meetings like the one reported in an Ohio newspaper. At a revival in Baltimore, black ministers one after the other stepped into the pulpit in an effort to whip the males in their audience into an enlistment frenzy. "This protracted meeting will continue," the reporter predicted, "during the present week, and it is believed the colored people of Baltimore will enlist a full brigade; and, if so, we predict it will be a brigade equal if not superior, to any colored brigade ever known on this continent."[109] Another account from Indiana provides insight into the methodology at work at such meetings. At an AME church in Indianapolis, a "war meeting" was convened under the direction of AME "Reverend W. Bailey" and "Reverend Mr. Broyles." The meeting was "set off" by Sergeant Miller, who presented the "reasons that colored men should enlist in Western regiments." Several speakers spoke in order, until finally came "Sergeant Stains, who spoke of several wounds he had received in battle, adding that he was yet willing to do and to die for his country. The roll was presented for volunteers; several signed, whilst the audience sang 'Rally, Boys, Rally!' Dr. Boyd (white) made a few remarks, encouraging the enlistment of colored soldiers, and reciting their chivalric and daring deeds at Port Hudson, Morris Island, and other points, during the war."[110] In their ability to inspire African American patriotism and participation in the war effort, black ministers gained a degree of political importance in America that even President Lincoln and his cohorts would have been foolish to overlook.[111]

And yet, acclaimed studies of black soldiers during the Civil War have neglected the role of African American preachers in recruiting and maintaining African American enlistments. Dudley Taylor Cornish's seminal *The Sable Arm*, for instance, makes no reference to preachers, while James McPherson's excellent *The Negro's Civil War* includes only a few references to articles in the *Christian Recorder*.[112] So too have more recent studies overlooked the value of African American preachers as recruiting agents, with the notable exception of Edwin Redkey's essay on the wartime service of Henry McNeal

Turner in *Black Soldiers in Blue*.[113] Simply stated, black ministers were the unquestioned political leaders of their communities and routinely used their pulpits to steer young men into the military after 1862. That wartime participation, however, was not conducted without debate among AME ministers.

Ministers believed that African American service in the military would aid in their efforts to foster black manhood. Moreover, even before black soldiers were welcome in the Federal ranks, AME clerics understood that the Civil War was a war to end slavery.[114] For these reasons they urged all African Americans, both enslaved and free, to avail themselves of any opportunity to serve in the Union military. A minister in the AME's *Christian Recorder* urged black people to fight manly for victory as they had always fought boldly for freedom, for they were now one and the same. "The hostility between slavery and freedom is not new," the unnamed parson wrote in 1861, and "a careful examination will detect it in our history, from the war of Independence to the present year."[115] Another minister proclaimed the absolute dedication of African Americans to both the cause and to future generations of African Americans. "There is no duty which the crisis may bring upon order-loving citizens," the AME minister advised, "who desire to transmit the priceless blessing of a good government to their posterity, from which we would shrink."[116]

Later in the year, an African American clerical commentator supported participation in the war effort no matter the black man's status. Again arguing for the enlistment of southern freedmen, he stated unequivocally that "it is sheer justice that slaves and escaped fugitives should aid" in the war's successful prosecution.[117] Ministers reminded the president, moreover, that freedpeople not only wanted but *expected* to fight under the Union banner. Afraid that Lincoln, in an effort to court border-state slave owners, might abandon his commitment to making soldiers of freedmen, a delegation made up mostly of New York ministers warned the president in 1864, "You are sure of the enmity of the masters—make sure of the friendship of the slaves; for depend on it, your Government cannot afford the enmity of both."[118]

Indeed the pages of African American religious journals, newspapers, and conference minutes suggest that AME preachers and lay members overwhelmingly supported service in the Union armies. But as was the case with colonization, there was a palpable degree of dissent in the ranks over the issue of black enlistment and recruitment that has never been fully acknowledged. If there were multiple reasons ministers advocated enlistment, however, one overwhelming motivation prompted AME clergymen to defy majority opinion and counsel non-service. Almost all who advised against enlistment referenced the discrimination that existed in the military or the Lincoln administration as the reason African American men should not seek military service. "The same cruel prejudices which exclude us from the halls of science," one AME cleric wrote, "also repels us from the militia and the standing army. Therefore to offer ourselves for military service now, *is to abandon all self-respect, and invite insult.*"[119] Calls for an African American boycott of the Union military effort based upon white mistreatment persisted well beyond the war's chaotic opening days. Not only did AME Bishop Jabez P. Campbell impugn President Lincoln's motives in prosecuting the war—Lincoln held "no quarrel whatever with the south, upon the slavery question," Campbell wrote—he also advised African Americans to celebrate their inability to serve as soldiers and to ignore the president's declared day of humiliation, prayer, and fasting.[120] Neither the Federal government's decision to recruit African Americans into the military nor the Emancipation Proclamation rendered Campbell mute.

Even after the Federal draft was expanded to include African Americans in 1863, some AME pundits believed that the conditions visited upon black soldiers warranted continued resistance to service. Many bemoaned the army's discriminatory compensation policies. Noting the ongoing solicitation of black men by Federal recruiting agents, a contributor to the *Christian Recorder* in early 1864 observed that African Americans were "not so willing to enlist as they were before." Although thousands of black men had enrolled with the promise of equal pay and then served gallantly at Milliken's Bend and Port Hudson and elsewhere, he continued, they had received inferior wages. "The question now is," the author rhetorically asked in conclusion, "has Congress allowed the colored soldier the same pay as the white? Has the colored soldier received it? Has the compact, now sealed in the blood of Africa's sons, been kept?"[121] The answer was of course no, at least until Congress passed an act equalizing the pay of all soldiers no matter their race in June 1864.[122] But that measure was predictably slow in its implementation. Thus another columnist later that year scolded "our Government, in order to succeed, [to] do justice to all men. . . . Colored men are being drafted and sent to the war. To-day, while we write, there are two colored men in New Jersey, who have been drafted, looking for substitutes, and say, that they would not mind going if they knew that they were to be treated like men."[123]

Colonization and soldier's rights were not the only political issues on the minds of wartime AME preachers. When Congress passed a bill abolishing slavery in the District of Columbia on April 11, 1862, for instance, AME leader Alexander Payne parlayed his national prominence into a meeting with President Lincoln, Illinois Congressman Elihu Washburn, and General Carl Schurz in an effort to ensure the president's endorsement of the bill. Payne reminded Lincoln of his farewell message in Springfield, when the president-elect had "begged the citizens of the republic to pray for you," and assured the president that "from that moment we, the colored citizens of the republic, have been praying" incessantly.[124] And AME lay minster and attorney (and onetime Oberlin theology student) John Mercer Langston, the inaugural president of the National Equal Rights League in 1864, worked tirelessly against discriminatory laws in northern states and for the "free and untrammeled use of the ballot" by black men.[125] But while AME ministers engaged in numerous wartime areas of formal politics, in no other enterprise did they cultivate their own political clout more than when they parsed out the meaning and merits of colonization and orchestrated the enlistments of African Americans. In those roles, they equaled and perhaps exceeded the intracommunity influence of white parsons.

Wartime and post-emancipation ministers of mainstream African American denominations did not abandon their own thoughts and proclivities and become uncritical cheerleaders for the Union. Rather, most continued to act as opinionated and autonomously minded men of faith.[126] And black preachers who championed racial uplift during the Civil War did not do so as an accommodation to or a compromise with racist whites. Nor were they gradualists, convinced that making concessions to the limitations of today might better allow them to realize the promises of (a distant) tomorrow. Racial uplifters in the wartime church were instead promoters of African American dignity and independence, men engaged in an unflagging effort to edify the *individual* while maximizing African American *collective* political influence and potential.

Likewise, while the preachers who set the tone for black people's wartime engagements in formal and state politics—in most instances, leaders of the African Methodist Episcopal Church—agreed upon most things, at times they clashed over vital issues like colonization and military service. The power of religious belief during the Civil War, then, was manifested not only in the beliefs of millions of white and black Americans about the holy principles of Union and freedom and democracy, but in the simple consistency with which black men of the cloth refused to allow anything to deprive them of their voices or their most earnest convictions. Their consistency proves moreover that political influence was not the provenance of white ministers alone—not some product of an amalgamated set of superior educational, intellectual, and spiritual traits. On the contrary, black clergymen of the war and immediate postwar years were every bit the equals of white church leaders in their political abilities, their political significance, and yes, their political differences as well.

EPILOGUE

HE END OF THE Civil War did not bring an end to all of the rhetorical battles between church members of common denominations or between preachers and their parishioners. Even those traditions that achieved a comparably amicable division, as was true of Episcopalianism, did not realize postwar reunion painlessly. Protestant Episcopals, overwhelmingly Democratic in the prewar North and South, split along sectional lines in 1862. Southern Episcopals maintained that separation had been thrust upon them, brought about by no malevolent act of their own but by the secession of the states wherein their dioceses sat. As the war neared its close and denominational reconciliation became increasingly feasible, their northern countrymen generally conceded the point. For instance, when one leader of northern Episcopalianism opined that secession was contemptible and that "all concerned in the attempt bore their share of the awful cost," he was quick to add (upon church reunification in 1865) that none bore that cost "with a better grace or more patient dignity" than those southern members who out of necessity had formed the short-lived Protestant Episcopal Church in the Confederate states.[1] And yet, according to a respected historian of Episcopalianism in America, Episcopal reconciliation proved tenuous at best in the early postwar months, its orchestrators constantly challenged by "grave difficulties" between southern and northern members born in the "sore temper on the one hand, and the triumphant one on the other."[2]

So too Lutheranism, long assumed to have emerged from the war virtually unscathed, experienced postwar troubles.[3] Lutheranism staved off separation until 1862, when southern Lutheran congregations severed their ties with the Lutheran General Synod and established a separate body in the Confederacy. Like Episcopals, southern Lutherans maintained that their actions were but a concession to the difficulties of maintaining a joint body. Not surprisingly, most Lutherans in the immediate postwar North were conciliatory as well; the prewar Lutheran hierarchy in its entirety was conservative on most issues, did not indict slavery, and in no way championed political preachers before the war. But beginning immediately after the war, church leaders instigated numerous reconciliatory efforts in the North and South that met with retort and counter-retort and bore little real fruit. Although never prone to the vitriol exhibited by the members of other larger denominationalists, Lutherans did not achieve formal national unity until 1918.[4] And if largely likeminded members of national denominations experienced postwar bitterness, imagine the difficulties faced by the leaders of long-alienated traditions like Methodism and Baptistism.

As was true before the war, the leaders of America's foremost Protestant churches found it difficult to put their differences aside. For example, while white Methodist Episcopal South leaders disagreed about the implications of bidding their African American members farewell—hundreds of thousands left their ranks for ascendant independent traditions like African Methodist Episcopalism—almost all of them felt real animosity toward the black and white northern Methodists who effected their departure. Moreover, Methodists in the old and new Baltimore conferences famously engaged in bitter feuds over such issues as church property and national affiliation.[5] Farther down in Dixie, the Methodist Episcopal Church's missionary efforts, to say nothing of the privileges of authority over "Rebel" churches in the South that the Federal government granted "Yankee" Methodist missionaries and agents of the Baptist-led American Home Mission Society after the war, often resulted in vicious quarrels between churchmen.[6]

Very often, attempts at reunification spawned even more schisms. The Louisville, Kentucky, Presbyterian ministers who in 1866 refused to sacrifice their vote in the General Assembly (pending an investigation into their assumed Copperheadism by a committee of fellow, i.e., northern, ministers) predictably then balked at the dissolution of their existing Louisville Presbytery and the establishment of a new presbytery "to be called by the same name, occupy the same territory, and have care of the same churches" but to be led by a new cadre of ministers who repudiated all past rebellious behavior. Ultimately, the 1866 imbroglio led to the formal division of the Presbyterian Church in Kentucky and Missouri, something the war itself had not done in these two Union states.[7] As Methodist historian Edmund Hammond offered in 1935, in the immediate postwar climate "it would have been ideal if some far-visioned ecclesiastical genius could have arisen with . . . a proposal for reconciliation," but because "the wounds of the time were deep," they would be long in healing. Indeed, Hammond offered, given the immediate postwar differences that separated churchman from churchman and made reconciliation unlikely, "one might as well expect men to sprout wings."[8]

Even churchmen and women in faith traditions unencumbered by the dictates of denominational hierarchies sometimes maintained their animosity toward each other. In East Tennessee, the Unionist Baptist Reverend P. H. Hopkins gave a poignant blueprint for healing, asking members in the association's once-Rebel churches, "You have yielded, Brethren, to the temporal authorities and will you not for the sake of Fellowship with Brethren you once professed to love make some concessions or will you yield to men because overpowered and refuse to do that which would in all human probability advance the cause of Christ on earth?" Former secessionists, Hopkins advised, should further confess, "We are sorry that we did not act in a way that would have tended to maintain peace and prevent war." But the onus of healing did not rest on former Rebels alone. "Do not require from your erring Brother," Hopkins advised Unionists churches and their members within the association, "more than Christ has required. The Rebellion has been put down by the strong arm of the government. It exists no longer. Our government has forgive[n] them and shall not the professed followers of Christ be as merciful as our earthly rulers or shall it be said by the world See, See, those that once professed to love one another biting and devouring one another like wolves."[9] Although one cannot state with certainty how Hopkins's eloquent pleadings were received, it is likely that Baptists in his region remained at odds. For had they acted otherwise, they would have been out of character for Baptists in the tortured region; virtually all of the Southern Baptist associations and voluntary conferences that met in 1865 and 1866 opted to maintain their separation from their northern or recently Unionist brethren.[10]

More than anyone else, in these denominational battles during the weeks, months, and early years after Appomattox, preachers staked out the positions of the various camps. Thus while it was true that the immediate postwar climate was in many ways not conducive to the cultivation of ministerial influence, because these arguments often mirrored still unresolved political differences of opinion, ministers were all but compelled into the postwar political fray. Politics still mattered, and weary congregants looked to peacetime parsons for answers to all kinds of political questions just as they had during the war—no matter if they admitted as much or not. The political preacher was rendered much less important during Reconstruction than was true before and during the war and would be further reduced in relevance in the post-Reconstruction age, but he still had a role to play in the bitter politics of division that many American Christians engaged in during and after 1865. Historians must begin to integrate this sub-story of Reconstruction into the greater narrative. As Paul Buck has observed, during Reconstruction "churches remained sectional bodies, an antagonistic element in the integration of national life."[11] And yet, no historian since Buck has properly imagined the dampening impact that such divisions had on national reconciliation or the degree to which such entanglements allowed ministers to maintain, if for but a little while longer, a distinct political profile.

The Civil War's impact upon the American clergy of course did not end with the demise of Reconstruction. By the 1880s, most Americans had abandoned their once-common dream of a Christian state led, if not ruled outright, by the denominational clergy.[12] It is impossible to overstate the significance of that abandonment, and one can only speculate about the theocratic turn America's democratic experiment might have taken had the growing prestige and influence of preachers, especially in the North, not been checked. Most Americans entered the post-Reconstruction age unwilling to allow ministers to call the shots, convinced that clerics had made political matters worse rather than better in the prewar years and had then done little to redeem their image during Reconstruction. But more than just the fear of a politically powerful clergy prompted northerners to reassess the place of the minister.

The minister's distinctiveness diminished during the 1870s, 1880s, and 1890s in part because the larger church became worldlier throughout the age. Virtually all northern postwar religious developments were predicated on the secularization of the church and its agents and the sacralization of the market. True though it was that northern society in its entirety drifted toward secularization, other professional sorts actually *benefited* from the standardization of society; only ministers *lost* cultural authority by becoming more like everyone else.[13] For example, even though northern churches played a key role in establishing scientific professionalism and patriarchal service as the religious responsibility of middle and upper-class Americans, in the process the preacher himself became increasingly extraneous. By the close of the century, northern clergymen had been replaced in importance by George Fredrickson's famous "ethical economists." Financiers, politicians, business leaders, and academics hammered out the tenets and ideologies of the Social

Gospel. Ministers embraced most of the movement's principles, but they were not determinative in their formation. Industrial Christianity and the Social Gospel established beyond doubt that the prewar and wartime role of the collective clergy as the caretaker of northern public values, ethics, and morals had been an impermanent one.[14]

The minister's role in the post-Reconstruction South was different from that of his northern equivalent. In the immediate postwar decades, southern preachers remained essential to southern morale and "Redemptive" political turns in their rhetorical efforts to salvage the Confederate cause. As Gaines M. Foster and others have established, many postwar southerners wanted desperately to believe that their cause had been just and that God would yet validate them.[15] Preachers facilitated such ideas, reminding southerners that their military defeat and all of its attendant sufferings were instructive and tempering and that their "Cause," as such, had never been discredited. Granted, numerous societal forces played a role in the de facto reclamation of the Confederacy (with women's benevolent and memorial societies perhaps chief among them), but only preachers of the gospel could "legitimately" argue the religious righteousness and biblical rationale of the Lost Cause.[16]

Through this function, preachers remained much more politically integral in the postwar South than was true in the North. Aware that their power of influence stemmed from their identification as arbiters of virtue, moreover, postwar southern preachers steered clear of the internecine feuds between former Confederate military and political figures over who and what caused the war and southern defeat. Instead, between the end of the war and roughly 1880 southern ministers consistently sounded but one note (with only occasional variations on the theme), that of the holy nature of the South's campaign for self-determination.[17] As Charles Regan Wilson succinctly declares of the southern preachers who refused to entertain thoughts of southern culpability and who rhetorically transformed the South's military defeat into a religious victory, "eventually, their view triumphed throughout the South."[18]

Even the emerging "New South" creed in the 1890s and later did not altogether divorce southern preachers from political sway. Most importantly, during the period the so-called "people's" churches took up the defense of the new elite. As Fredrick Bode has stated, "Southern white Protestantism . . . became one of the mechanisms of the ruling–class hegemony."[19] White church leaders, especially those in the Baptist and Methodist traditions, in the 1890s and onward sympathized with business and political leaders, for pecuniary reasons no doubt. But they found the supremacist rhetoric of southern political demagoguery effective in forging white *religious* allegiances, allegiances moreover that crossed lines of class and education and thus expanded their sphere of influence. In tendering religious justification for Jim Crow's ascension to his ungodly southern throne, southern clerics effectively reprised their pre–Civil War role as the defender of slavery and all things white and thereby assured their centrality in New Southern life. And again, that such centrality was linked expressly to ideas of race and not modernity was of preeminent importance. It mattered little if a cleric longed for the (idealized) agrarianism of the Old South or the increasingly industrialized Dixie that many southern leaders now sought. He was equally free do either as long as he spoke in the culturally unifying (for whites, anyway) language of ideological conservativism—or in essence, white supremacy.[20]

However, while "New Southern" preachers maintained a pronounced political profile when compared to their northern post-Reconstruction brethren, too much should not be made of it. As was true during their clerical validation of slavery and their perpetuation of the Lost Cause myth, by the end of the century the evangelical southern clergy had been essentially co-opted by the political and economic benefactors of Jim Crow and the perhaps not-so-new "New" South. Thus while it is easy to discern the political *role* that post-Reconstruction southern clerics played, it is much more difficult to assess their real political *influence* per se.

More than white clerics in the North or South, African American preachers maintained their political primacy throughout Reconstruction and the post-Reconstruction age. This was due to two key factors. First, the postwar African American church itself continued to serve as a nexus of political organization and education for African Americans throughout the rest of the century and into the next. Preachers, as overseers of the local church, could therefore not help but become political organizers, supremely determinative figures within the community who identified issues of concern and plotted out courses of activism and resistance. Second, black church leaders, particularly those within traditionally activist denominations like African Methodist Episcopalism, for the most part ignored both the secular attacks against religion (the ubiquitous scientific criticism, for example) and the interdenominational quarrels over biblical literalness that distracted white clerics of the day. Thus they were free to focus on the political issues that were of most concern to their charges.

It is certainly true that African American clerics in both the North and South directed the church's constant expansion into *every* facet of their parishioners' lives, be it in their leadership of many denominational colleges throughout the South or their participation in multidenominational organizations like the YMCA in the North. But more than anything else, black church leaders shepherded their flock through the hills and valleys of post-Reconstruction politics. For instance, forceful preachers sometimes led their congregations in campaigns to oust perceived political quislings from their ranks, often to the point of excommunicating those who did not share the political ideas of the preacher or the majority of members.[21] As the promise of Reconstruction faded and the scope of collective black political participation contracted, preachers grew evermore dedicated to procuring African American rights and defending their social and political equality. Although they often disagreed on how best to do that—some proto-nationalists within the AME Church counseled emigration to Liberia or elsewhere for instance, while other churchmen sounded the praises of populism and other forms of biracial political engagement—African American preachers were at the forefront of every collective political movement undertaken by black people in the late-nineteenth century and, indeed, into and throughout the twentieth century as well.[22]

Before the Civil War, many African American preachers in the North and South were political in often non-formal ways. After the war and throughout the remainder of the century, black clerics habitually added novel political questions (the endorsement of socialism, for instance) to their collection of non-sanctioned and—at long last—sanctioned political concerns and attendant techniques.[23] But no matter how they were political, from start to finish most nineteenth-century black preachers were always political. Similarly, white clerics in the New South in essence replicated their prewar selves. Among the most respected defenders of the slaveocracy, preachers loomed large in Old South life. But in that defense, most ministers were also at the service of slavery—or more specifically, at the service of the elite who presided over the infernal institution. Thus, even as postwar clerics resounded their voices on the southern political stage, they returned to their autonomy-denying habit of singing a cultural tune called by someone else, be it the prewar planter elite or the post-Reconstruction South's political and economic bosses. Simply stated, the war was not fundamentally transformative—*at least in terms of the significance of the political influence they wielded within their communities*—for African American and white southern preachers.

Only northern clerics can be rightfully placed within an analytical framework of change. Certainly scholars love to assess the years between 1861 and 1865 in terms of continuity and discontinuity, commonly portraying the Civil War as the watershed event in America's national existence. It was, the narrative holds, a catastrophic yet necessary conflagration that rendered everything that followed somehow different from everything that had transpired before. In virtually no other instance is that discontinuity-privileging hypothesis more believable than with the white denominational ministry in the North. Throughout the first half of the nineteenth century, the northern clergy evolved into a prestigious and influential force. The preacher's prominence grew exponentially, moreover, in just the last two prewar decades, as evangelical denominationalism especially tightened its grip on the hearts and minds of the American people. But the power of the white cleric was irrevocably arrested by the war. And as the postwar years mounted and the North grew increasingly secularized, with each passing day the denominational cleric became more and more like everyone else and less and less politically important. True enough, from time to time in late-nineteenth and twentieth-century America individual denominationalists amassed and exercised real political sway. But the likes of Billy Sunday, Father Charles Coughlin, Aimee Semple McPherson, Martin Luther King Jr., Jerry Falwell, and Billy Graham notwithstanding, since the Civil War the expansive influence of the collective American clergy has never been the same.

NOTES

1. The terms "denominational Christianity" and "denomination" are used in this study to refer to both any recognized branch of Christianity (Roman Catholic, Eastern Orthodox, Oriental Orthodox, Anglican, Protestant, etc.) and any of the distinct subgroups of Protestantism that do not maintain a common and unifying theology or recognize a common earthly leader or hierarchy of authority. The main categories of consideration are Protestant groups of various organizational scopes and Catholic groups divided into organizational units (diocese, archdiocese, etc.).

2. E. Brooks Holifield, "The Penurious Preacher? Nineteenth–Century Clerical Wealth: North and South," *Journal of the American Academy of Religion* 58, no. 1 (Spring 1990): 17–36, 17.

3. Mark A. Noll, *The Civil War as a Theological Crisis* (Chapel Hill: University of North Carolina Press, 2006), 28.

4. *The War of the Rebellion: A Compilation of the Official Records of the Union and Confederate Armies, Prepared Under the Direction of the Secretary of War, By Bvt. Lieut. Col. Robert N. Scott, Third U.S. Artillery and Pursuant to Act of Congress Approved June 16, 1880* (Washington, DC: Government Printing Office, 1880). Abbreviated hereafter as *Official Records*.

5. Jean Baker, *Affairs of Party: The Political Culture of Northern Democrats in the Mid-Nineteenth Century* (Ithaca, NY: Cornell University Press, 1983); see also Paula Baker, "The Mid-Life Crisis of the New Political History," *Journal of American History* 86, no. 1 (June 1999): 158–66, 158. It is important, however, to guard against the "new political" history's tendency toward reductionism (that is, ignoring such forces as morality and nationalism in the behavior of individual actors and instead assigning too much determinative weight to ethnocultural concerns). On this matter, see Eric Foner, *Politics and Ideology in the Age of the Civil War* (New York: Oxford University Press, 1980).

6. Steven Hahn, *A Nation under Our Feet: Black Political Struggles in the Rural South from Slavery to the Great Migration* (Cambridge, MA: Harvard University Press, 2003); Tera Hunter, *To 'Joy My Freedom: Southern Black Women's Lives and Labors after the Civil War* (Cambridge, MA: Harvard University Press, 1998).

7. Mitchell Snay, "Civil War Religion—Needs and Opportunities," *Civil War History* 49, no. 4 (December 2003): 388–94, 387. More attention has been paid to the antebellum period and the role that religious leaders played in bringing on the war. See Richard Carwardine, *Evangelicals and Politics in Antebellum America* (New Haven, CT: Yale University Press, 1993); Dan McKanan, *Identifying the Image of God: Radical Christians and Nonviolent Power in the Antebellum United States* (New York: Oxford University Press, 2002); John McKivigan, *The War Against Proslavery Religion: Abolitionism and the Northern Churches, 1830–1865* (Ithaca, NY: Cornell University Press, 1985); Edward R. Crowther, *Southern Evangelicals and the Coming of the Civil War* (Lewistown,

NY: Edwin Mellen Press, 2000); Mitchell Snay, *Gospel of Disunion: Religion and Separatism in the Antebellum South* (Chapel Hill: University of North Carolina Press, 1997); C. C. Goen, *Broken Churches, Broken Nation: Denominational Schisms and the Coming of the Civil War* (Macon, GA: Mercer University Press, 1985); Paul Conkin, *The Uneasy Center: Reformed Christianity in Antebellum America* (Chapel Hill: University of North Carolina Press, 1995); and Bertram Wyatt-Brown, *Yankee Saints and Southern Sinners* (Baton Rouge: Louisiana State University Press, 1985).

8. Most studies of wartime parsons have examined their interactions with soldiers. See for example Steven E. Woodworth, *While God Is Marching On: The Religious World of the Civil War Soldiers* (Lawrence: University Press of Kansas, 2003); John Wesley Brinsfield et al., *Faith in the Fight: Civil War Chaplains* (Mechanicsburg, PA: Stackpole Books, 2003); Warren B. Armstrong, *For Courageous Fighting and Confident Dying: Union Chaplains in the Civil War* (Lawrence: University Press of Kansas, 1998); Phillip Thomas Tucker, *The Confederacy's Fighting Chaplain: Father John B. Bannon* (Tuscaloosa: University of Alabama Press, 1992). The role played by ministers in the formation and abandonment of Confederate ideology has been examined in detail as well. Leonard Allen and Richard Hughes reference a nationalistic orthodoxy that united denizens of the Confederacy and was rooted in a primitive religiousness that tied slavery to the southern way of life. Drew Gilpin Faust posits not only that religion was the linchpin of Confederate nationalism, but that religious leaders in the Confederacy were as powerful as political leaders and that southerners believed their effort was ordained by God. And Eugene Genovese argues that southerners, many of whom felt an unspoken guilt over slavery before the war, lost faith in the righteousness of their cause and commitment to the war in the face of repeated battlefield defeats. The southern religious voices heard in this study speak most expressly in support of Faust's argument. See Leonard Allen and Richard Hughes, *Illusions of Innocence: Protestant Primitivism in America, 1630–1875* (Chicago: University of Chicago Press, 1988); Drew Gilpin Faust, *The Creation of Confederate Nationalism: Ideology and Identity in the Civil War South* (Baton Rouge: Louisiana State University Press, 1988); Eugene Genovese, *A Consuming Fire: The Fall of the Confederacy in the Mind of the White Christian South* (Athens: University of Georgia Press 1999). See also Richard Beringer et al., *Why the South Lost the Civil War* (Athens: University of Georgia Press 1986), in which the authors largely blame religion for the Confederate defeat. Most scholars consider the minister's role in sustaining nationalism in the wartime North. Harry Stout's *Upon the Altar of the Nation: A Moral History of the United States* (New York: Oxford University Press, 2006) and Sydney Ahlstrom's classic *A Religious History of the American People* (New Haven, CT: Yale University Press, 1974) portray northern ministers almost exclusively as pro-war Lincolnites.

1. PREACHERS, SLAVERY, AND ANTEBELLUM POLITICS

1. For more on the sectional divisiveness of slavery among religionists, see Charles Reagan Wilson, "Religion and the American Civil War in Comparative Perspective," in Randall Miller et al., eds., *Religion and the American Civil War* (New York: Oxford University Press, 1998), 385–407; John R. McKivigan and Mitchell Snay, eds., *Religion and the Antebellum Debate over Slavery* (Athens: University of Georgia Press, 1998); Snay, *Gospel of Disunion;* Goen, *Broken Churches, Broken Nation.*

2. Snay, *Gospel of Disunion,* 4–5. For more on the antebellum proslavery message of

southern clerics, see Elizabeth Fox-Genovese and Eugene D. Genovese, "The Divine Sanction of Social Order: Religious Foundations of the Southern Slaveholders' World View," *Journal of the American Academy of Religion* 55 (Summer 1987): 211–34. A consideration of the subject from a denominational perspective is presented in Lewis M. Purifoy, "The Southern Methodist Church and the Proslavery Argument," *Journal of Southern History* 32 (August 1966): 325–41.

3. Drew Gilpin Faust, ed., *The Ideology of Slavery: Proslavery Thought in the Antebellum South, 1830–1860* (Baton Rouge: Louisiana State University Press, 1981), particularly Thornton Stringfellow, "A Brief Examination of Scripture Testimony on the Institution of Slavery," 136–67.

4. For more on the disunion of the era, see Elizabeth E. Varon, *Disunion: The Coming of the American Civil War, 1789–1859* (Chapel Hill: University of North Carolina Press, 2008), and William H. Freehling, *The Road to Disunion: Secessionists Triumphant, 1854–1861* (New York: Oxford University Press, 2007).

5. Michael F. Holt, *The Political Crisis of the 1850s* (New York: W. W. Norton, and Co., 1978). Holt famously argues that slavery polarized political camps, burdening the Second Party System of Whigs and Democrats to the point of collapse, and that in the void left by that collapse sectional issues took on ideological dimensions that proved politically insurmountable and brought about the Civil War. Importantly, Holt does not contend that slavery alone destroyed the Second Party System.

6. "The Two Master Passions—The Religious and Political," *The Phalanx: Organ of the Doctrine of Association* 1, no. 16 (August 10, 1844): 231–33, 232, 233. The Doctrine of Association was a Christian communitarian movement based upon the (very much modified) teachings of the French philosopher Charles Fourier. Historian Anne Rose, who has written about those who endorsed such a complementary but separate relationship between religion and politics during the period, offers that Victorian northerners preferred a clearly defined political realm when addressing the challenges of life "not simply because government addressed the secular issues they so keenly pursued but because the political process better retained its authority in the midst of competition and compromise (*Victorian America and the Civil War* [Cambridge, MA: Harvard University Press, 1992], 66).

7. Harry S. Stout, *The New England Soul: Preaching and Religious Culture in Colonial New England* (New York: Oxford University Press, 1986); Jonathan D. Sassi, *A Republic of Righteousness: The Public Christianity of the Post-Revolutionary New England Clergy* (New York: Oxford University Press, 2001); Patricia U. Bonomi, *Under the Cope of Heaven: Religion, Society, and Politics in Colonial America* (New York: Oxford University Press, 1986).

8. A notable exception to this presidential trend was Thomas Jefferson. And, while the tradition of presidentially declared days of prayer was as old as the political nation, so was the tendency of clergymen to respond to such calls in a politically partisan way. See Charles Ellis Dickson, "Jeremiads in the New American Republic: The Case of National Fasts in the John Adams Administration," *New England Quarterly Review* 60, no. 2 (June 1987): 187–207.

9. Richard B. Latner and Peter Levine, "Perspectives on Antebellum Pietistic Politics," in *Reviews in American History* 4, no. 1 (March 1976): 15–24.

10. Gerald Gamm and Robert D. Putnam, "The Growth of Voluntary Associations in America, 1840–1940," *Journal of Interdisciplinary History* 29, no. 4 (Spring 1999): 511–57, 520. Not all voluntary associations were religiously concerned, as was true of militias, fire companies,

and sporting groups, for instance. See also Carwardine, *Evangelicals and Politics in Antebellum America;* William A. Clebsch, *From Sacred and Profane: The Role of Religion in American History* (New York: Harper and Row, 1968); McKanan, *Identifying the Image of God.*

11. The politicization of temperance is addressed deftly by J. Christopher Soper in *Evangelical Christianity in the United States and Great Britain: Religious Beliefs, Political Choices* (New York: New York University Press, 1994); Leo P. Hirrel discusses ministers and Sabbatarianism in *Children of Wrath: New School Calvinism and Antebellum Reform* (Lexington: University Press of Kentucky, 1998), 82–83.

12. Steven Mintz, *Moralists and Modernizers: America's Pre–Civil War Reformers* (Baltimore: Johns Hopkins University Press, 1995).

13. Many of these differences, in fact, had been present in the controversies that resulted in the 1810 division of American Presbyterianism and the establishment of the Cumberland Presbyterian Church. See Walter L. Lingle and John W. Kuykendall, *Presbyterians: Their History and Beliefs* (Louisville, KY: Westminster John Knox Press, 1978), 73.

14. Goen, *Broken Churches, Broken Nation,* 68–69; It warrants noting that a number of Old Schoolers in the North were personally opposed to slavery, but very few were in favor of any church action against it, and fewer still supported abolitionism. See Conkin, *The Uneasy Center,* 264.

15. *Journal and Luminary* (Cincinnati), January 15, 1837. All emphasis in the original.

16. John T. Tigert, *A Constitutional History of American Episcopal Methodism* (Nashville: Publishing House of the Methodist Episcopal Church, South, 1894); Goen, *Broken Churches, Broken Nation,* 87.

17. Donald G. Mathews, *Slavery and Methodism: A Chapter in American Morality, 1780–1845* (Princeton, NJ: Princeton University Press, 1965); David Edwin Harwell Jr. et al., *Unto a Good Land: A History of the American People,* vol. 1: *To 1900* (Grand Rapids, MI: William B. Eerdmans, 2005), 464–65.

18. Samuel S. Hill, *One Name but Several Faces: Variety in Popular Christian Denominations in Southern History* (Athens: University of Georgia Press, 1996), 18.

19. See esp. Charles S. Sydnor, *The Development of Southern Sectionalism, 1819–1848* (Baton Rouge: Louisiana State University Press, 1934).

20. Allan Nevins, *Ordeal of the Union,* vol. 2: *A House Dividing, 1852–1857* (New York: Collier Books, 1947); see also Goen, *Broken Churches, Broken Nation,* 103–6.

21. Goen, *Broken Churches, Broken Nation,* 87.

22. John Patrick Daly, *When Slavery Became Freedom: Evangelicalism, Proslavery, and the Causes of the Civil War* (Lexington: University Press of Kentucky, 2002), 76.

23. Ibid., 76–78.

24. Debby Applegate, *The Most Famous Man in America: The Biography of Henry Ward Beecher* (New York: Random House, 2006), 234.

25. Lawrence J. Friedman, "Confidence and Pertinacity in Evangelical Abolitionism: Lewis Tappan's Circle," *American Quarterly* 31, no. 1 (Spring 1979): 81–106, 99; Walter M. Merrill, *Against Wind and Tide: A Biography of William Lloyd Garrison* (Cambridge, MA: Harvard University Press, 1963), 152.

26. Friedman, "Confidence and Pertinacity in Evangelical Abolitionism," 98.

27. "Political Thanksgiving Sermon," *Emancipator and Republican,* November 11, 1847.

28. "Preaching on Peace," *Advocate of Peace* (Boston), vol. 7, no. 1 (January–February 1847): 4.

29. Friedman, "Confidence and Pertinacity in Evangelical Abolitionism," 98.

30. Eric Foner, *Free Soil, Free Labor, Free Men: The Ideology of the Republican Party Before the Civil War* (New York: Oxford University Press, 1970), 78, 78–79; Daniel Walker Howe, *What Hath God Wrought: The Transformation of America, 1815–1848* (New York: Oxford University Press, 2007), 652.

31. The Liberty Party's national candidate in 1840, abolitionist James G. Birney, received but .03 percent of the popular vote (or, about 7,053 votes out of 2,412,698 cast), even though there were roughly 250,000 members of abolitionist societies. In the 1844 contest for the White House, Birney again represented the Liberty Party, and received 62,200 votes nationally (or, 2.3 percent of the vote) (Donald J. Green, *Third Party Matters: Politics, Presidents, and Third Parties in American History* [Santa Barbara, CA: Praeger/ABC-CLIO, 2010], 10, 12). In 1847 and 1848, most members of the Liberty Party found their way into the Free Soil Movement, although New Yorker Gerrit Smith would run again as a Liberty Party candidate. In 1852 for instance, Smith received 72 votes nationally, compared to 156,667 votes, or 4.9 percent, cast for Free Soil candidate John P. Hale (Omar Hamid Ali, *In the Balance of Power: Independent Black Politics and Third-Party Movements in the United States* [Athens: Ohio University Press, 2008], 49).

32. Josiah Phillips Quincy, *Memoir of Rev. R. C. Waterston* (Cambridge, MA: John Wilson and Son/University Press, 1893), 13.

33. "Political Thanksgiving Sermon."

34. *Presbyterian Armory,* vol. 3 (1847–1848): 32; *Evangelical Repository,* vol. 3 (April 1847): 545, in Ted C. Hinckley, "Anti-Catholicism during the Mexican War," *Pacific Historical Review* 31, no. 2 (May 1962): 121–37, 133, 134.

35. *Oberlin Evangelist,* April 22, 1847.

36. Samuel Joseph May and Thomas James Mumford, *Memoir of Samuel Joseph May* (Boston: Roberts Brothers, 1873), 244.

37. Ibid.

38. See Bertram Wyatt-Brown, *Lewis Tappan and the Evangelical War Against Slavery* (Baton Rouge: Louisiana State University Press, 1997).

39. Come-outer groups emerged from many Protestant faith traditions in the antebellum period, including the Methodist Episcopal, Presbyterian (specifically, Free Presbyterian) and Baptist (American Baptist Free Mission Society) churches. See John R. McKivigan, "The Antislavery 'Comeouter' Sects: A Neglected Dimension of the Abolitionist Movement," in *Civil War History* 26, no. 2 (June, 1980): 142–254.

40. Applegate, *The Most Famous Man in America,* 234.

41. *Presbyterian Covenanter* (Kentucky), July 1846, in Hinckley, "Anti-Catholicism during the Mexican War," 124.

42. Clayton Sumner Ellsworth, "The American Churches and the Mexican War," *American Historical Review* 45, no. 2 (January 1940): 301–26, 320.

43. Hinckley, "Anti-Catholicism during the Mexican War," 132.

44. Ibid., 131.

45. Noll, *The Civil War as a Theological Crisis,* 130.

46. Ibid.; Margaret Lavinia Anderson, "The Limits of Secularization: On the Problem of the Catholic Revival in Nineteenth-Century Germany," *Historical Journal* 38 (1995): 647–70.

47. In my consideration of the northern clergy's response to the events of 1850, I differ with a generation of historians who held that northern preachers remained overwhelmingly silent in response to the Fugitive Slave Act. See Allan Nevins, *Ordeal of the Union* vol. 1: *Fruits of Manifest Destiny, 1847–1852* (New York: Collier Books, 1947), 383, 400; I side instead with those who posit that clerical opposition to the Fugitive Slave Act was much greater than clerical support of the laws. See Russell Nye, *Fettered Freedom: Civil Liberties and the Slavery Controversy* (East Lansing: Michigan State College Press, 1963), 266; Ralph A. Keller, "Methodist Newspapers and the Fugitive Slave Law: A New Perspective for the Slavery Crisis in the North," *Church History* 43, no. 3 (September 1974): 319–39, 332.

48. Laura L. Mitchell, "Matters of Justice Between Man and Man," in McKivigan and Snay, eds., *Religion and the Antebellum Debate over Slavery*, 134–65.

49. Moses Stuart, *Conscience and the Constitution, With Remarks on the Recent Speech of the Honorable Daniel Webster In the Senate of the United on the Subject of Slavery* (Boston: Crocker and Brewster, 1850). Although celebrated almost immediately as a proslavery standard, Stuart's pamphlet was in fact an exposition on the biblical shortcomings of immediatism and a defense of the Fugitive Slave Act, but one in which Stuart ultimately argued that biblical principles were antithetical to slavery (Eugene D. Genovese, "Religion in the Collapse of the American Union," in Miller et al., eds., *Religion and the American Civil War*, 74–88, 83).

50. Applegate, *The Most Famous Man in America*, 247. Founded by the Tappan brothers, by the time of the Civil War the *Journal of Commerce* would be one of a number of New York papers suspended for its incendiary and secessionist rhetoric (Jennifer L. Weber, *Copperheads: The Rise and Fall of Lincoln's Opponents in the North* [New York: Oxford University Press, 2006], 36).

51. Such preachers commonly referenced the biblical story of the runaway slave Onesimus, whom the Apostle Paul returned but with words of admonition for his master, urging him to grant Onesimus his freedom.

52. "Clerical Politicians," *Daily National Intelligencer* (Washington, DC), July 14, 1851.

53. See William Warren Sweet, "Some Religious Aspects of the Kansas Struggle," *Journal of Religion* 7, no. 5–6 (October 1927), 578–95.

54. Qtd. in Sweet, "Some Religious Aspects of the Kansas Struggle," 582.

55. Qtd. in Hugh Davis, "Leonard Bacon, the Congregational Church, and Slavery, 1845–1861," in McKivigan and Snay, eds., *Religion and the Antebellum Debate over Slavery*, 221–45, 235.

56. "Press and Post," *Boston Press and Post*, June 16, 1856.

57. Ibid.

58. Deborah Bingham Van Broekhoven, "'Suffering With Slaveholders: The Limits of Francis Wayland's Antislavery Witness," in McKivigan and Snay, eds., *Religion and the Antebellum Debate over Slavery*, 196–220.

59. *The Ladies Repository: A Monthly Periodical Devoted to Literature and Religion* (Cincinnati: L. Swormstedt and A. Poe, 1854), vol. 19: 332.

60. Archibald M. Howe, "Tribute to Dr. Joseph Henry Allen," in *Transactions: Publications of the Colonial Society of Massachusetts, 1897, 1898* (Boston: Published by the Society, 1902), 310–15, 311.

61. "For the Patriot. Political Preachers," *New Hampshire Patriot and State Gazette* 8, no. 378 (August 16, 1854): 2.

62. "Press and Post."

63. Anonymous, "Pulpit Politicians" (Gettysburg, PA) *Republican Compiler*, March 19, 1855 (originally printed in the *Annapolis Republican*).

64. Ibid.

65. Sweet, "Some Religious Aspects of the Kansas Struggle," 583–84. In his diatribe, Douglas estimated the petitioning preachers' number at "perhaps three thousand," maligned them with the moniker "political preachers," and suggested that the offending clerics should be "required to confine themselves to their vocation, instead of neglecting their flocks, and bringing our holy religion into disrepute by violating its sacred principles" in their political activism (*Congressional Globe*, 33rd Congress, 1st Session, 618 [1854]).

66. The Christian response to the Fugitive Slave Act is expertly considered in Richard Carwardine's *Evangelicals and Politics in Antebellum America*.

67. See Conkin, *The Uneasy Center*, 253–60.

68. Although the American Party was in severe decline nationally by the close of the 1850s, its rhetoric proved a powerful draw to former northern Whigs in 1854 and 1855. See Tyler Anbinder, *Nativism and Slavery: The Northern Know Nothings and the Politics of the 1850s* (New York: Oxford University Press, 1992), 95.

69. Anbinder, *Nativism and Slavery*, 49.

70. Lou Baldwin, "Pious Prejudice: Catholicism and the American Press over Three Centuries," in Robert P. Lockwood, ed., *Anti-Catholicism in American Culture* (Huntingdon, IN: Our Sunday Visitor, 2000), 55–87, 61–62. See also the *Boston Mercantile Journal*, August 8, 1834.

71. Louis Dow Scisco, *Political Nativism in New York State* (New York: Columbia University Press, 1901), 243–46.

72. Anbinder, *Nativism and Slavery*, 50–51.

73. Alexander K. McClure, *Old Time Notes on Pennsylvania* (Philadelphia: John C. Winston Co., 1905), vol. 1: 240; see also Anbinder, *Nativism and Slavery*, 49–50.

74. John R. Mulkern, *The Know-Nothing Party in Massachusetts: The Rise and Fall of a People's Movement* (Boston: Northeastern University Press, 1990), 118–22; William E. Gienapp, *The Origins of the Republican Party, 1852–1856* (New York: Oxford University Press, 1987), 179–87.

75. Roger L. Ransom, *Conflict and Compromise: The Political Economy of Slavery, Emancipation, and the American Civil War* (New York: Cambridge University Press, 1989), 123. The 1853 bill to organize Kansas, authored by Stephen A. Douglas and first reported to the House of Representatives on February 8, 1853, was passed in the House but defeated twice in the Senate, "primarily," Allan Nevins argued in 1947, "for lack of time" (*Ordeal of the Union* 2: 89).

76. Anbinder, *Nativism and Slavery*, 48. Northern Whigs in Congress voted unanimously against the Kansas-Nebraska Act, and antislavery Whigs—including Abraham Lincoln—initially hoped to funnel northern resistance to the act through the Whig Party, fueling a Whig resurgence. Free-soilers and antislavery Democrats, however, either joined the Know-Nothings or formed anti-Kansas-Nebraska coalitions under such names as the Fusion, Independent, People's, and in time, Republican parties.

77. Bruce C. Levine, *Half Slave and Half Free: The Roots of the Civil War* (1992; rev. ed., New York: Hill and Wang, 2005), 200, 203.

78. Anbinder, *Nativism and Slavery*, 50.

79. Both qtd. in Levine, *Half Slave and Half Free*, 203.

80. Ray Allen Billington, *The Protestant Crusade, 1800–1860* (New York: Macmillan and Co., 1938), 425. The quote is taken from a northern Know-Nothing resolution of the day.

81. Jay P. Dolan, *The Irish Americans: A History* (New York: Bloomsbury Press, 2010), 98.

82. William James Cooper and Tome E. Terrill, *The American South: A History* (New York: Rowan and Littlefield Publishers, 2009), vol. 1: 337.

83. Anbinder, *Nativism and Slavery,* 47–48, 49–51.

84. On such traditional recalcitrance (relative to social activism) within established denominations, see John R. McKivigan and Mitchell Snay," Religion and the Problem of Slavery in Antebellum America," in McKivigan and Snay, eds., *Religion and the Antebellum Debate over Slavery,* 1–32, 10–11. For insight into the social conservatism of a major northern city's Protestant establishment, see Kathryn Long's description of New York City in *The Revival of 1857–1858: Interpreting an American Religious Awakening* (New York: Oxford University Press, 1998), 100–109.

85. On Jefferson as the southern beau ideal, see Harry S. Stout and Christopher Grasso, "Civil War, Religion, and Communications: The Case of Richmond," in Miller et al., eds., *Religion and the American Civil War,* 313–59; 325. See also Robert E. Shalhope, "Thomas Jefferson's Republicanism and Antebellum Southern Thought," *Journal of Southern History* 42, no. 4 (November 1976), 529–56.

86. Stout, *Upon the Altar of the Nation,* 10.

87. Concerning Jefferson, see Isaac Kramnick and Laurence Moore, *The Godless Constitution: A Moral Defense of the Secular State* (New York: W. W. Norton and Co., 1996); Paul Harvey, "Yankee Faith and Southern Redemption: White Baptist Ministers from 1850–1890," in Miller et al., eds., *Religion and the American Civil War,* 167–86, 167. See also David B. Chesebrough, *Clergy Dissent in the Old South, 1830–1865* (Carbondale: Southern Illinois University Press, 1996). Chesebrough notes that many southern preachers who initially and sincerely resisted the politicization of their pulpits ultimately recognized the slavery/secession crisis as "a religious and moral one, which demanded a response by religious and moral leaders" (19).

88. Faust, *The Ideology of Slavery,* 4; see also J. Mills Thornton, *Politics and Power in a Slave Society: Alabama, 1800–1860* (Baton Rouge: Louisiana State University Press, 1981). Thornton posited that slavery and the white equality it facilitated were the key components of Jacksonian democracy. With southern independence from white political slavery thus theorized as a concomitant of black slavery, secession became to southerners an exercise in Jacksonian ideology. In many ways, Thornton was influenced by George Fredrickson's concept of a southern "Herrenvolk Democracy." See George M. Fredrickson, *The Black Image in the White Mind: The Debate on Afro-American Character and Destiny, 1817–1914* (New York: Harper and Row, 1971).

89. For more on the post U.S.-Mexican War years as a time of exaggerated politicized religiousness, see Timothy L. Smith, "Historic Waves of Religious Interest in America," *Annals of the American Academy of Political and Social Science* 332 (November 1960): 9–19. Smith believed that the 1850s constituted one of four historic decades (the others being the 1790s, the years between 1895 and 1905, and the 1950s) during which American Christianity "made major adjustments of thought and practice to cope with new social conditions" (9).

90. Henry D. Bascom, "Patriotism, As Connected With the Nature and Claims of Civil Government," *Quarterly Review of the Methodist Church, South* 1 (1848): 37–52. In Ellsworth, "The American Churches and the Mexican War," 301–26, 305.

91. For editorials expressing this belief, see the *Western Baptist Review* 1 (1846): 361–67; *Nashville Baptist,* May 30, 1846. Referenced in Edward R. Crowther, "Religion Has Something . . . to Do with Politics: Southern Evangelicals and the North, 1845–1860," in McKivigan and Snay, eds., *Religion and the Antebellum Debate over Slavery,* 317–42.

92. Ross Phares, *Bible in Pocket, Gun in Hand: The Story of Frontier Religion* (Lincoln: University of Nebraska Press, 1964), 69.

93. Crowther, "Religion Has Something . . . to Do with Politics," 330.

94. Ibid., 330–31.

95. *Southern Christian Advocate* (Charleston, SC), April 5, 1850. There were numerous local newspapers titled *Christian Advocate* and affiliated with Methodism. Many are available on microfilm at the United Methodist Archives Center at Drew University in Madison, New Jersey.

96. *Christian Advocate* (Nashville), November 1, 1850.

97. *New Orleans Christian Advocate,* September 1, 1855.

98. *Christian Advocate* (Nashville), September 18, 1856.

99. Ibid., October 22, 1857.

100. *Southern Baptist* (Charleston, SC), May 10, December 6, 1854; May 6, 1856. See Crowther, "Religion Has Something . . . to Do with Politics," 331.

101. Thomas H. Long, "Preaching in the South," in Samuel S. Hill et al., *Encyclopedia of Religion in the South* (Macon, GA: Mercer University Press, 2005), 603–11, 604.

102. Ibid.

103. See esp. Steven Hahn, *The Political Worlds of Slavery and Freedom* (Cambridge, MA: Harvard University Press, 2009), 10–14. Hahn notes that, while "freedom for African Americans was highly contingent" and found only in "discrete geopolitical zones," slaveholders wielded enormous and growing power through control of the Federal government, presidency, judiciary, diplomatic corps, and the nation's economic purse strings (13).

104. Richard B. Drake, *A History of Appalachia* (Lexington: University Press of Kentucky, 2001), 87. See also John Inscoe, *Mountain Masters, Slavery, and the Sectional Crisis in Western North Carolina* (Knoxville: University of Tennessee Press, 1989).

105. Emmert F. Bittinger, "Virginia Anabaptists and the Civil War," *Mennonite Family History* 18, no. 1 (January 1999): 4–8.

106. Noble J. Talbert, "Daniel Worth: Tar Heel Abolitionist," *North Carolina Historical Review* 39 (Summer 1962): 284–404, 290, rpt. in Carl N. Degler, *The Other South: Southern Dissenters in the Nineteenth Century* (New York: Harper Torchbooks, 1974), 89.

107. Robert Tracy McKenzie, *Lincolnites and Rebels: A Divided Town in the American Civil War* (New York: Oxford University Press, 2006), 12–13. Brownlow was by no means against slavery, and believed that slavery afforded African Americans an opportunity to achieve their highest state of development. He was, however, a vehement critic of slave owners and the planter elite, considering them both the enemy of the southern yeomanry and, potentially, disunionists.

108. James McPherson, *Ordeal by Fire: The Civil War and Reconstruction* (New York: McGraw-Hill, 1982), 35.

109. Eugene D. Genovese, "The Dulcet Tones of Christian Disputation in the Democratic Up-Country," in *Southern Culture* 8 (Winter 2002): 56–68.

110. South Carolinian Andrew Butler, who along with kinsman and fellow South Carolinian

Preston Brooks and political foe Charles Sumner of Massachusetts would in time feature in the most controversial turn of events in the Senate's history, captured for instance the stance assumed by southern political leaders in 1855 when he asserted that "when the clergy quit the province assigned them" and instead took up "going about as agitators," they divested themselves of "all the respect that I can give them." Qtd. in Sweet, "Some Religious Aspects of the Kansas Struggle," 584.

111. Moncure Daniel Conway, *Autobiography of Moncure Daniel Conway* (Boston and New York: Houghton, Mifflin, and Co.; Riverside Press, 1905), vol. 1: 188.

112. Ibid., 190.

113. Ibid., 242.

114. *American Missionary Magazine* 2 (October 1858): 257, in Clifton H. Johnson, "Abolitionist Missionary Activities in North Carolina," in John R. McKivigan, ed., *History of the American Abolitionist Movement: A Bibliography of Scholarly Articles* (New York: Garland Press, 1999), 209–35, 221.

115. Copied in the *Liberator,* June 15, 1860, and rpt. in John Spencer Bassett, *Anti-Slavery Leaders of North Carolina* (Baltimore: Johns Hopkins Press Science, 1898), 15, 24–27.

116. Chesebrough, *Clergy Dissent in the Old South,* 33, 35–36.

117. James Marten, *Texas Divided: Loyalty and Dissent in the Lone Star State, 1856–1874* (Lexington: University Press of Kentucky, 1990), 8.

118. As David Chesebrough reminds us, "By the end of the decade those who criticized and dissented from the stance of the dominant southern culture and society had to a large degree been weeded out. Nonconforming voices were few in number and difficult to hear" (*Clergy Dissent in the Old South,* 48–49).

2. THE POWER AND PLACE OF THE WARTIME NORTHERN MINISTRY

1. Democratic politicians were similarly scrutinized, but given the temporal nature of elected office, politicians should not be considered a distinct professional class in nineteenth-century America. The ranks from which most northern politicians came—doctors, lawyers, teachers, and businessmen—were virtually never discussed as a collective entity in the way that was true of the denominational ministry. Of course, homefront groups defined by ethnicity and/or religion *were* sometimes maligned as a class, as was manifested in the anti-Catholic and anti-immigrant ranting in which much of the popular press engaged.

2. Historians who limit American denominationalism's influence to the physical confines of the church often deny clergymen their full place in antebellum and wartime northern society. See, for example, R. Laurence Moore, *Selling God: American Religion in the Marketplace of Culture* (New York: Oxford University Press, 1994). See also George Fredrickson, "The Coming of the Lord: The Northern Protestant Clergy and the Civil War," in Miller et al., eds., *Religion and the American Civil War,* 110–30. Frederickson posits that wartime ministers "failed to perceive . . . that their new role actually undermined their search for professional autonomy and cultural authority" by casting them as "agents of a political cause that they had sanctified in their sermons." Preachers themselves blurred the lines between the "sacred and the profane," Frederickson concludes, and in the process diminished their own separate value as arbiters of all things expressly religious ("The Coming of the Lord," 123).

3. More than 350,000 people joined Protestant churches during the Great Revival of 1857–58 alone (Kathryn Long, "The Power of Interpretation: The Revival of 1857–58 and the Historiography of Revivalism in America," *Religion and American Culture* 4, no. 1 [Winter 1994]: 77–105, 87).

4. Noll, *The Civil War as a Theological Crisis*, 28; Ahlstrom, *A Religious History of the American People*, 673; Steven Woodworth succinctly states that, "On the eve of the Civil War, Christianity suffused American society and culture" (*While God Is Marching On*, 26). See also Jon Butler, *Awash in a Sea of Faith: Christianizing the American People* (Cambridge, MA: Harvard University Press, 1992), 283. Butler contends that denominational growth in the four major Protestant denominations—Baptists, Congregationalists, Methodists, and Presbyterians—*as an aggregate number* and as a percentage of the population remained stable or increased between 1820 and 1860 in spite of the (unprecedented and largely immigration-dependent) population growth witnessed during the period.

5. Noll, *The Civil War as Theological Crisis*, 13.

6. According to Richard Carwardine, by the mid-1850s organized evangelical Christianity, encompassing not only members but also the millions of Americans who were not official enrollees but were in "close sympathy" with the tenets of one church or another, American denominationalism constituted a formidable subculture within American society (*Evangelicals and Politics in Antebellum America*, 44).

7. *Statistics of the United States (Including Mortality, Property, & c.) in 1860; Compiled From the Original Returns and Being the Final Exhibit of the Eighth Census, Under the Direction of the Secretary of the Interior* (Washington, DC: Government Printing Office, 1866).

8. Michael Williams, *American Catholics in the War [National Catholic War Council, 1917–1921]* (New York: MacMillan Co., 1921), 51. Unlike Protestant membership numbers, in which one member represented three other church people, this number is representative of all identifiable Catholics then in the country (the bulk of whom were foreign born).

9. *Statistics of the United States . . . Eighth Census*. Although this number accommodated the enumeration of most denominationalists, census takers grouped numerous denominations together under common traditions. For instance, only four categories of Presbyterians were listed (Presbyterian, Cumberland Presbyterian, Presbyterian Reformed, and Presbyterian United); the numbers suggest that smaller denominational groupings of Presbyterians were included in the first generic category. Only one category was available for those identified as Episcopalians and Methodists, for example, even though within those traditions there was denominational diversity. A catchall category, titled "minor sects churches," also appeared on the 1860 census, but because only two churches were identified as such in the entire country and because census takers in all but two of the thirty-four states and two territories entered "N/A" or its equivalent under that category, that number is woefully understated.

10. For more on this ratio, see Richard Hofstadter, *Anti-Intellectualism in American Life* (New York: Vintage Books, 1963). Also see Roger Finke and Rodney Stark, "Turning Pews Into People: Estimating 19th Century Church Membership," *Journal for the Scientific Study of Religion* 25, no. 2 (June 1986): 180–92.

11. Woodworth, *While God Is Marching On*, 26. Using the one-for-three rule for Protestants, this means that by the war's onset more than 22 million Americans were identifiably denominational Protestants or Catholics.

12. Richard Carwardine, "Methodists, Politics, and the Coming of the American Civil War," *Church History* 69, no. 3 (September 2000): 578–609, 586.

13. Miller et al., *Unto a Good Land* 1: 509.

14. Catherine Clinton, "Abraham Lincoln: The Family that Made Him, the Family He Made," in Eric Foner, ed., *Our Lincoln: New Perspectives On Lincoln and His World* (New York: W.W. Norton, 2008), 249–66, 252.

15. Frederick Abbott Norwood, *The Story of American Methodism: A History of the United Methodists and Their Relations* (New York: Abingdon Press, 1974), 239–40.

16. For more on American mysticism, see Leigh Eric Schmidt, *Restless Souls: The Making of American Spirituality* (San Francisco: Harper San Francisco, 2005), particularly "The Mystic Club," 25–62.

17. Goen, *Broken Churches, Broken Nation,* 47.

18. Nathan O. Hatch, "The Puzzle of American Methodism," *Church History* 63, no. 2 (June 1994), 175–89, 180. Methodists' gains in higher education notwithstanding, Mark Noll— referencing such examples as Presbyterian Princeton and Congregationalist Yale—argues that "American higher education continued to be conducted as primarily a Presbyterian or Congregational enterprise until the late nineteenth century" ("American Religion, 1809–1865," in *Lincoln's America,* Joseph R. Fornieri and Sara Vaughn Gabbard, eds. [Carbondale: Southern Illinois University Press, 2008], 72–93; 79).

19. There were other Methodist papers in circulation in addition to the five official organs, but they were locally owned and their editors were not appointed or approved by the General Conference of the church. The five official publications of the MEC North in 1850 were the *Christian Advocate* (New York, with a circulation of 30,000), the *Western Christian Advocate* (Cincinnati, 18,000), the *Northern Christian Advocate* (Auburn, N.Y., 13,000), *Zion's Herald* (Boston, 8,000), and the *Pittsburgh Christian Advocate* (7,000) (Keller, "Methodist Newspapers and the Fugitive Slave Law," 319–39, 319, 320).

20. Unnamed editor, *The Presbyterian* (1854), qtd. in Chester F. Dunham, *The Attitude of the Northern Clergy Toward the South, 1860–1865* (Toledo, OH: Gray Co., 1942), 8; Goen, *Broken Churches, Broken Nation,* 36–37. There were over 300 denominational newspapers in publication in America by the time of the Civil War.

21. Hatch, "The Puzzle of American Methodism," 181.

22. Michael S. Hamilton, "We're in the Money: How Did Evangelicals Get So Wealthy, and What Has It Done to Us?" *Christianity Today,* June 12, 2000, 36–43, 36.

23. Anbinder, *Nativism and Slavery,* 3; John Bodnar, *The Transplanted: A History of Immigrants in Urban America* (Bloomington: Indiana University Press, 1987), 217.

24. Indeed, because of both immigration and large second-generation American families, by the end of the nineteenth century the Catholic Church was the largest distinct denomination in the United States, and 18 percent of all Americans were Catholic (William D. Prendergast, *The Catholic Voter in American Politics* [Washington. DC: Georgetown University Press, 1999], 3). Irish immigrants tended to stay in northern port cities, especially New York and Boston, while German immigrants more often traveled to (what were then considered) western cities like Cincinnati and Milwaukee. In the earlier decades of the nineteenth century, both Irish and German immigrants had been predominantly Protestant, but by the 1850s roughly 90 percent

of Irish immigrants and a majority of German immigrants were Catholic (Anbinder, *Nativism and Slavery*, 7, 8; James M. Berquist, "German Americans," in *Multiculturalism in the United States: A Comparative Guide to Acculturation and Ethnicity*, ed. John D. Buenker and Lorman A. Ratner [Westport, CT: Greenwood Press, 2005], 149–72, 153). For more on why late-antebellum European immigration so shaped northern life but was of relatively little importance in the South, see Joseph P. Ferrie, *Yankeys Now: Immigrants in the Antebellum United States, 1840–1860* (New York: Oxford University Press, 1999).

25. Frank Lambert, *Religion in American Politics: A Short History* (Princeton, NJ: Princeton University Press, 2008), 66–67.

26. Orestes A. Brownson, *The American Republic: Its Constitution, Tendencies, and Destiny* (1865; Wilmington, DE: ISI Books, 2003), 239. See also Lambert, *Religion in American Politics*, 67. Brownson is referencing the Catholic believer's familiarity with divided government, as is the case in every facet of Catholic life from the threefold division of the ministry (Episcopate, Presbyterate, and Diaconate) to the categories of church organization (Dioceses, Archdioceses, Ecclesiastical Provinces, etc.). Moreover, as with federalism there is within the Catholic Church an order of precedence of the various offices and ministries, indicative of the supremacy/subservience of various offices in the church.

27. William Warren Sweet, *The Story of Religion in America* (1930; New York: Harper Brothers, 1950), 223; Ahlstrom, *A Religious History of the American People*, 365.

28. Millennialism, a belief in the coming earthly reign of Christ, was the dominant theme of mid-nineteenth-century Christianity. Northerners were usually post-millennialists who believed that the gradual defeat of evil and perfection of humanity would trigger Christ's return (post-millennialism thus explains the northern reformist ethos of the age). Many northerners imagined the war as a means of eradicating impediments to the establishment of Christ's new order. A minority of northerners and southerners were pre-millennialists who believed apocalyptic destruction—a purification through fire—must precede the new Christly kingdom. Because of its "New England" origins, many southern Christians rejected millennialist thought in all of its forms but believed the southern slave society was unsurpassed in its Christian sublimity, and thus any sacrifice offered in its defense was warranted.

29. See particularly Roger Finke and Rodney Stark, *The Churching of America, 1776–2006: Winners and Losers in Our Religious Economy* (Piscataway, NJ: Rutgers University Press, 2005), 55–116. Arminianism, based broadly upon the teachings of Dutch Reformed theologian Jacobus Arminius, differs most distinctly from Calvinism in its emphasis on free will. Where Calvinism holds that the "elect" (recipients of salvation) were appointed by God before the foundation of the world, Arminianism offers that Christ's atonement was made for all people but that each man and woman can either reject or accept salvation.

30. Hatch, "The Puzzle of American Methodism," 180. Historian Marianne Perciaccante defines formalists as those denominationalists preeminently concerned with moral order, while antiformalists were concerned with spiritual fervor. Formalists, by which she means Presbyterians and Congregationalists primarily, resisted revivalism but supported more structured societal reform efforts, while antiformalists, mainly Baptists and Methodists in Perciaccante's study, fomented evangelical and revivalist zeal in the interest of the righteousness of individual members and then, in time and by natural extension, the community (*Calling Down*

Fire: Charles Grandison Finney and Revivalism in Jefferson County, New York, 1800–1840 [Albany: State University of New York Press, 2003]).

31. "Abraham Lincoln to General Conference of Methodist Episcopal Church, May 18, 1864," in Roy P. Basler, ed., *The Collected Works of Abraham Lincoln* (Piscataway, NJ: Rutgers University Press, 1953), vol. 6: 351.

32. See Carwardine, "Methodists, Politics, and the Coming of the Civil War," 586.

33. Wendell Phillips, "The Lesson of the Hour," in *Disunion: Two Discourses at Music Hall, on January 20th, and February 17th, 1861* (Boston: Robert F. Wallcut, 1861), 3.

34. Henry Ward Beecher, "Preaching Christ," in *Sermons by Henry Ward Beecher, Plymouth Church, Brooklyn* (New York: Harper and Brothers, 1868), vol. 2: 167–88, 182.

35. Wilson, *The Presbyterian Historical Almanac, and Annual Remembrancer of the Church for 1862,* vol. 4: 78. Emphasis in the original.

36. Rev. Joseph Horner, A.M., "Christianity and the War Power," in *Methodist Quarterly Review, 1865,* ed. D. D. Whedon (New York: Carlton and Porter, 1865), 165–86, 185.

37. In a religious sense, of course, the Christian emphasis on salvation as the preeminent concern in a person's life meant that ministers who had for decades pleaded for the souls of men and women could not become any more important than they had always been.

38. After hearing "a political sermon" about slavery and the role its purveyors played in bringing about the war, for example, Browning concluded the lecture a sound one but one "not fit for the pulpit or the Sabbath." From "Sunday, June 28, 1863," in Theodore Calvin Pease and James G. Randall, eds., *The Diary of Orville Hickman Browning,* vol. 1: *1850–1864* (Springfield: Illinois State Historical Library, 1925), 635.

39. "Sunday, June 12, 1864," in Pease and Randall, eds., *The Diary of Orville Hickman Browning,* 672.

40. "Letter to George Funkhouser from Cyrus Mortimer Hanby, February 18, 1862," Funkhouser Family Papers, 1551-2-1: 2, 3, and 9.

41. "Sunday, August 4, 1861," *Diary of Sarah Preston Everett Hale, 1796–1866,* American Women's Diaries Series (New England), Microfilm D285, Reel 974, M15.

42. For more on millennialist thought during the American Civil War, see James H. Moorhead, *American Apocalypse: Yankee Protestants and the Civil War, 1860–1869* (New Haven, CT: Yale University Press, 1978).)

43. "Sunday, July 28, 1861," *Diary of Caroline Barrett (Mrs. Francis Adams) White,* American Antiquarian Society, replicated in American Women's Diaries Series (New England), Microfilm D239, Reel 17.

44. "Thanksgiving Sermon, By Rev. Samuel J. Niccolls," *Franklin* (Chambersburg, PA) *Repository,* December 23, 1863.

45. On the commonality of wartime sermon topics, see David B. Chesebrough, *God Ordained This War: Sermons on the Sectional Crisis, 1830–1865* (Columbia: University of South Carolina Press, 1991).

46. Father Joseph Fransioli, *Patriotism, a Christian Virtue. A Sermon Preached by the Rev. Joseph Fransioli, at St. Peter's (Catholic) Church, Brooklyn, July 26th, 1863* (New York: Loyal Publication Society, 1863); Reverend Thomas Brainerd, *Patriotism Aiding Piety: A Sermon, Preached in the Third Presbyterian Church, Philadelphia, On the 30th of April, 1863, the Day Appointed by the President of the United States for Humiliation, Fasting and Prayer* (Philadelphia: W. F. Geddes, 1863).

47. Samuel Spear, "National Gratitude," in *National Preacher* 39, no. 1, Whole No. 949 (January 1865): 1–16, 5.

48. Samuel Dunham, *Retrospect of a Happy Ministry* (Binghamton, NY: Vail-Ballou Co., 1914), 25.

49. "Monday, August 25, 1862," *Diary of George A. Funkhouser*, Funkhouser Family Papers.

50. Edward K. Spann, "Union Green: The Irish Community and the Civil War," in *The New York Irish*, ed. Ronald H. Bayor and Timothy J. Meagher (Baltimore: Johns Hopkins University Press, 1996), 193–209.

51. Kevin Kenney, *Making Sense of the Molly Maguires* (New York: Oxford University Press, 1998), 88; *Official Records*, ser. 1, vol. 19, pt. 2: 500.

52. Richard Carwardine, "Abraham Lincoln, the Presidency, and the Mobilization of Union Sentiment," in *The American Civil War: Explorations and Reconsiderations*, ed. Susan-Mary Grant and Brian Holden Reid (New York: Longman Press, 2000), 68–97, 87–88.

53. Richard Carwardine, "Whatever Shall Appear to Be God's Will, I Will Do: The Chicago Initiative and Lincoln's Proclamation," in *Lincoln's Proclamation: Emancipation Reconsidered*, ed. William A. Blair and Karen Fisher Younger (Chapel Hill: University of North Carolina Press, 2009), 75–101, 96.

54. Ibid., 94.

3. PARTISANSHIP AND POTENTIAL DAMAGE

1. Antiwar ministers from pacifistic faith traditions were not, as a general statement, maligned in the wartime North. Without exception moreover, suspected disloyal ministers belonged to either the "separatist spheres" (chiefly) or the "separate duty" (to a lesser degree) classes of preachers. I can find no example of a wartime northern clergyman who believed the church was to be unabashedly political (or, a "separate component" minister) and at the same time preached a pro-southern or anti-Union gospel.

2. In Diana Hochstedt Butler, *Standing against the Whirlwind: Evangelical Episcopalians in Nineteenth-Century America* (New York: Oxford University Press, 1995), 157. See also Stephen P. Budney, *William Jay: Abolitionist and Anticolonialist* (Westport, CT: Greenwood Publishing, 2005).

3. Robert Livingston Stanton, *The Church and the Rebellion Against the Government of the United States; and the Agency of the Church, North and South, in Relation Thereto.* (New York: Derby and Miller, 1864), 207.

4. Most who have focused on domestic dissent in the North and the ways in which that dissent was identified and policed have largely ignored the clergy. Most recently in 2006's otherwise excellent *Copperheads*, for instance, Jenifer Weber offers no consideration of ministers as agents of treason—or voices of opposition for that matter—whatsoever.

5. "A Short Sermon upon a Recent Text," *Harper's Weekly*, February 20, 1864 (114).

6. Bryon C. Andreasen, "Lincoln's Religious Critics: Copperhead Christian Reactions to the President and the War," *Politics and Culture of the Civil War Era: Essays in Honor of Robert W. Johannsen*, ed. Daniel McDonough and Kenneth W. Noe (Selinsgrove, PA: Susquehanna University Press, 2006) 199–219, 203.

7. The central role of the denominational press is explored elsewhere in this study.

8. *Philadelphia Press,* August 28, 1861.

9. "The Church and the Rebellion," *Franklin Repository* (Chambersburg, PA), November 18, 1863.

10. "The New Church Creed," *The Dakotian* (Yankton, SD), May 10, 1864.

11. "Why Do Ministers of the Gospel Meddle With Politics?" *Beaver Argus* (Beaver Falls, PA), November 16, 1864.

12. "The Cost of War, Political Preaching," *Harper's Weekly,* December 20, 1862.

13. *The Agitator* (Wellsboro, PA), May 1, 1861.

14. "Religion and the War," *Philadelphia Press,* November 29, 1861.

15. Andreasen, "Lincoln's Religious Critics," 211, 210.

16. "Religion and Politics," *Atlantic Democrat* (Egg Harbor City, NJ), September 9, 1863.

17. "Another Great Work to Do," *Weekly Patriot and Union* (Harrisburg, PA), February 2, 1863.

18. "Political Priests," *Cincinnati Inquirer,* January 24, 1863.

19. "Political Preachers," *Republican Compiler* (Gettysburg, PA), August 25, 1862.

20. "The Episcopal and Catholic Clergy against Abolitionism," *New York Herald,* October 8, 1861.

21. "The Clergy and Conscription," *Democratic Watchman* (Bellefonte, PA), April 3, 1863.

22. "The Church and the War," *Erie Observer,* December 1, 1864.

23. "A Lesson on Political Preachers and Political Preaching," *Newark Advocate,* January 1, 1864; originally in the *Ohio Eagle.* At issue in this instance were the actions of a preacher in Central Ohio who preached a political message against slavery, in response to which his Democratic-majority church membership (of Rushcreek Presbyterian Church) passed resolutions against political preaching. Other area Presbyterians, led by members of the Muskingum Presbyterian Church, demanded a retraction of the resolutions and had the offending members deposed. The deposed Democratic members from Rushcreek then took steps to rid themselves of their current obligations to denominational authority and establish their own church, effectively rending asunder their old church.

24. "Political Church Papers," *Rome Sentinel,* October 4, 1864.

25. "Desecration of the Pulpit," *Valley Spirit* (Chambersburg, PA), November 16, 1864. Emphasis in the original.

26. Ibid., July 13, 1864.

27. "Abolition Preaching—Its Ultimate Result," *Democratic Watchman* (Bellefonte, PA), January 15, 1864.

28. "Political Parsons," *Johnstown* (PA) *Democrat,* November 7, 1864.

29. See, for instance, Frank L. Klement, *Dark Lanterns: Secret Political Societies, Conspiracies, and Treason Trials in the Civil War* (Baton Rouge: Louisiana State University Press, 1984). Klement, in the words of James McPherson, dismissed supposed northern traitorous conspiracies "as mostly figments of Republican propaganda, but a close reading of this book reveals a considerable core of truth to them in Klement's own evidence" (McPherson, *The Battle Cry of Freedom: The Civil War Era* [New York: Oxford University Press, 1988], 782).

30. When Brough defeated Clement Vallandigham in an Ohio gubernatorial election in 1863, President Lincoln famously wired Brough, "Glory to God in the Highest. Ohio has saved the Union." In Eric L. McKitrick, *Andrew Johnson and Reconstruction* (New York: Oxford University Press, 1988), 45.

31. See Gerard N. Magliocca, *Andrew Jackson and the Constitution: The Rise and Fall of Generational Regimes* (Lawrence: University of Kansas Press, 2007). See also Larry D. Kramer, *The People Themselves: Popular Constitutionalism and Judicial Review* (New York: Oxford University Press, 2005; Christian G. Fitz, *American Sovereigns: The People and America's Constitutional Tradition Before the Civil War* (New York: Cambridge University Press, 2008).

32. James Etienne Viator, "The Fourth Amendment in the Nineteenth Century," in *The Bill of Rights: Original Meaning and Current Understanding* (Charlottesville: University of Virginia Press, 1991), 172–83, 172, 173.

33. Donald L. Drakeman, *Church-State Constitutional Issues: Making Sense of the Establishment Clause* (Westport, CT: Greenwood Press, 1991), 85.

34. The constitutional consideration of treason appears in Article Three, Section Three, of the U.S. Constitution.

35. Joseph Wheelan, *Jefferson's Vendetta: The Pursuit of Aaron Burr and the Judiciary* (New York: Carroll and Graf, 2005), 234.

36. In his 1848 American usage dictionary, for instance, Noah Webster defined treason in Great Britain by kind (high treason and petit treason, one against the king or state and the other a breach of fidelity against an individual agent or actor), but in discussing American treason, simply reiterated the vagaries of the Constitution in writing, "Treason against the United States consists in levying war against them, or in adhering to their enemies, giving them aid or comfort" (*An American Dictionary of the English Language* [New York: Harper and Brothers, 1848], 1046).

37. United States District Court D., Massachusetts. *Charge to Grand Jury-Treason, Case No. 18, 274, District Court D. Massachusetts, March, 1863* (2 Sprague 292, 30 F. Cas. 1042, F. Cas. No. 18274, 1863 U. S. District LEXIS 10 D. Mass 1863), 1044.

38. Ibid., 1043.

39. Ibid., 1044.

40. Stanton, *The Church and the Rebellion against the Government*, 207.

41. For example, as commander of the Department of the Ohio headquartered in Cincinnati, General Ambrose Burnside declared, "The habit of declaring sympathy for the enemy will not be allowed in this department. Persons committing such offenses will be at once arrested with a view of being tried or sent beyond our lines into the lines of their friends. It must be understood that treason, expressed or implied, will not be tolerated in this department" ("General Order No. 38," *Official Records*, ser. 1, vol. 23, pt. 2: 23).

42. "Catholic Loyalty to the Union" (Cincinnati) *Catholic Telegraph and Advocate*, May 11, 1861. Emphasis in the original.

43. "Treason in the Pulpit," *Wisconsin State Register*, October 12, 1861. No charges were brought against Stearns by authorities as a result of the sermon.

44. Edward J. Stearns, A.M., *The Sword of the Lord: A Sermon, Preached in the House of Prayer, Newark, New Jersey, on Thursday, September 26, 1861, Being the National Fast Day* (Baltimore: James S. Waters, 1861), iv.

45. "Disloyal Preachers," *Scioto* (Chillicothe, OH) *Gazette*, January 12, 1864. Originally in the *Philadelphia Press*.

46. Ibid.

47. Stanton, *The Church and the Rebellion Against the Government*, 209; *Atlantic Democrat and Cape May County Register* (Egg Harbor City, NJ), November 21, 1863; "Episcopal," *Banner*

of the Covenant (Philadelphia), April 5, 1862; Bryon C. Andreasen, "Civil War Church Trials: Repressing Dissent on the Northern Home Front," in Paul A. Cimballa and Randall M. Miller, eds., *An Uncommon Time: The Civil War and the Northern Home Front* (New York: Fordham University Press, 2002), 214–42, 220.

48. W. W. Orwig, *Journal of the General Conference of the Evangelical Association, Held at Buffalo, N.Y. 1863* (Cleveland, OH: Book Establishment of the Evangelical Association, 1863), 7. Such dirges are ubiquitous in the Evangelical Association's General Conference minutes from throughout the war.

49. Ibid., 63.

50. "Select Poetry," *The Agitator* (Wellsboro, PA), October 19, 1864. As evidence of the poem's wide circulation, it appeared in newspapers as far west as Arkansas. *Unconditional Union* (Little Rock, AR), March 18, 1864.

51. Mary Gyla McDowell Collection, Archives of the Pennsylvania State University, Special Collections/Pattee/C9/E/03.04.01, 02, 03, 04, 05, and 06, and C9/03.05.01: Box 1, File 23, "Colonel Daniel Leasure, Commanding, to Wife, 10-17-1863."

52. "James Stewart to Mother, February 1, 1863," U.S. Army Military History Institute, Carlisle Barracks, Pennsylvania, rpt. in Timothy J. Orr, "A Viler Enemy in Our Rear: Pennsylvania Soldiers Confront the North's Anti-War Movement," in *The View from the Ground: Experiences of Civil War Soldiers,* ed. Aaron Sheehan-Dean (Lexington: University Press of Kentucky, 2007), 171–98, 179.

53. J.H. misspelled William Swan Plumer's last name as "Plummer." The accused preacher in Alexandria was a Reverend Bitting ("A Philadelphian Minister in Trouble," *Philadelphia Press,* July 21). William Swan Plumer was among the leading Old School Presbyterians in the nation and had presided over the originative Old School General Assembly in 1838. Conscribed by the directors of the Western Theological Seminary over which he was president to prove his patriotism by praying for Union successes, Plumer refused and was dismissed (Edward J. Blum, *Reforging the White Republic: Race Religion, and American Nationalism, 1865–1898* [Baton Rouge, LA, 2005], 138, 139; *The Presbyter,* October 16, 1862; James Oscar Farmer Jr., *The Metaphysical Confederacy: James Henley Thornwell and the Synthesis of Southern Values* [Macon, GA: Mercer University Press, 1986], 273).

54. "A Traitor Clergyman Arrested," *Boston Investigator,* October 9, 1861, originally in *New York Sunday Mercury;* "A Droll Copperhead Plot," *Harper's Weekly,* November 14, 1863, 723.

55. "A Droll Copperhead Plot," *Harper's Weekly,* November 14, 1863, 723. See also William H. Knauss, *The Story of Camp Chase: A History of the Prison and Its Cemetery, Together With Other Cemeteries Where Confederate Prisoners Are Buried, Etc.* (Nashville: Publishing House of the Methodist Episcopal Church, South, Smith and Lamar, Agents, 1906), 137–39.

56. "A Traitor Clergyman Arrested," *Boston Investigator,* October 9, 1863, originally in *New York Sunday Mercury.*

4. THE ASSAULT ON DISLOYALTY IN THE NORTHERN MINISTRY

1. For example, in his standard-setting work on northern dissent, *The Limits of Dissent: Clement Vallandigham and the Civil War* (1970; New York: Fordham University Press, 1998),

Frank L. Klement makes mention of Copperhead cleric Sabin Hough's ties with Vallandigham but otherwise considers the ministry as opponents of Vallandigham only, rather than as sources of dissent or opposition themselves.

2. In his definitive work on political arrests during the war, Mark E. Neely Jr. includes several instances of preacher arrests and prescriptions, but examines them within the context of governmental (federal and state) action (*The Fate of Liberty: Abraham Lincoln and Civil Liberties* [New York: Oxford University Press, 1992], 28, 39, 127, 202).

3. Stout, *Upon the Altar of the Nation*, xvii. See especially Moorhead, *American Apocalypse: Yankee Protestants and the Civil War, 1860–1869*. In this excellent analysis of northern clerical behavior, Moorhead correctly underscores the religious overtones that the war carried for most northerners but does not consider ministerial opposition in any real way.

4. Jon Butler, "Religion and the American Revolution," in Jon Butler et al., eds., *Religion in American Life: A Short History* (New York: Oxford University Press, 2003), 132–53, 132, 133; Noll, "American Religion, 1809–1865," 77.

5. Noll, "American Religion, 1809–1865," 77.

6. The term "comparatively slight" (church attendances) juxtaposes attendance during this period against attendance in both the middle of the eighteenth century, when the Great Awakening helped swell the memberships of America's churches, and the ever-increasing attendance and membership rates of the antebellum decades to come.

7. Adam Smith, *An Inquiry into the Nature and Causes of the Wealth of Nations* (London: T. Nelson and Sons, 1776), 330. See also Finke and Stark, *The Churching of America*, 54.

8. See particularly William Gribbin, *The Churches Militant: The War of 1812 and American Religion* (New Haven, CT: Yale University Press, 1973).

9. Elijah Parish, *A Protest against the War* (Newburyport, 1812), 14, qtd. in William Gribbin, "The Covenant Transformed: The Jeremiad Tradition and the War of 1812." *Church History* 40, no. 3 (September 1970), 297–305, 300.

10. Gribbin, "The Covenant Transformed," 301.

11. Jeremiah Evarts, *An Oration Delivered in Charleston, Mass., on the Fourth of July, 1812, In Commemoration of American Independence* (Charlestown, 1812), 26; Nathaniel Thayer, "A Sermon Delivered August 20, 1812 . . ." (Worcester, 1812), 15. Both rpt. in Gribbin, "The Covenant Transformed," 301.

12. Lawrence Delbert Cress, "Cool and Serious Reflection: Federalist Attitudes Toward War in 1812," *Journal of the Early Republic* 7, no. 2 (Summer 1987), 123–45, 139.

13. Ibid., 144.

14. An exception to northern society's laissez-faire attitude toward the clergy was the persecution of a number of New England (mostly) Congregationalist and Episcopal clerics during the 1810s and 1820s for their perceived association with the Federalists' Hartford Convention and related would-be secession movement.

15. In 1776, Congregationalism entailed more than 20 percent of all American church members and Episcopalianism 15.7 percent; by 1850, those percentages had plummeted to 4 percent and 3.5 percent, respectively. And although the number of people in these two denominations roughly tripled during the period as a result of the exponential growth of denominationalism in America, their real growth did not come close to keeping pace with

either the general population's growth or the growth of Presbyterianism, the third major eighteenth-century denomination to suffer a decline in percentage of all adherents because of the ascendency of Baptists, Methodists, and Catholics in the first half of the nineteenth century (Presbyterianism shrank from 19 percent to 11.6 percent of all adherents during the same period, but its growth kept pace with population growth) (Finke and Stark, *The Churching of America,* 55–57).

16. McPherson, *Ordeal by Fire,* 294. See also James G. Randall, *Constitutional Problems under Lincoln* (Urbana: University of Illinois Press, 1951).

17. Oaths of clerical allegiance were not unheard of in America before the Civil War. Methodist clergymen, in the wake of John Wesley's famous Toryism during the Revolution, were for instance compelled by patriots to offer loyalty statements. But largely owing to the backlash against Jacobin excesses in the French Revolution, which included classing clergymen as civil servants and demanding published declarations of their loyalty, the idea of preventive prescription (i.e., forcing clerics to swear allegiance to the nation as a matter of course and *not* in response to their perceived disloyalty) had long been discredited in the United States. See Conkin, *The Uneasy Center,* 76; Simon Schama, *Citizens: A Chronicle of the French Revolution* (New York: Alfred A. Knopf, 1989). On a state level, Presbyterian Reverend Samuel Worcester and Baptist Reverend Elijah Butler had been sentenced in 1831 to four years imprisonment and hard labor for refusing to sign an oath of allegiance to the state of Georgia, a violation of that state's anti-Cherokee laws. They served sixteen months of their sentences before being released (Robert J. Conley, *A Cherokee Encyclopedia* [Albuquerque: University of New Mexico Press, 2007], 265).

18. The best-focused work on loyalty oaths during the Civil War remains Harold Melvin Hyman, *Era of the Oath: Northern Loyalty Tests during the Civil War and Reconstruction* (Philadelphia: University of Pennsylvania Press, 1954). There were numerous problems of enforcement of Federal loyalty oaths, owing to the fact that officers entrusted with their enforcement often exhibited "elastic" standards of loyalty and disloyalty, that President Lincoln transferred the maintenance of internal security from State and to the War Department in 1862, and that "at no time did Congress or the President specify what oath was proper for political prisoners. As a result of this lack of definition the forms of oaths varied widely at various times and places. Government officials drew up oaths to meet the needs of the moment" (Hyman, *Era of the Oath,* 14, 34).

19. Hyman, *Era of the Oath,* 15, 21–32.

20. *Official Records,* ser. 1, vol. 22, pt. 1 (S#32): 869.

21. Joseph A. Ranney, *In the Wake of Slavery: Civil War, Civil Rights, and the Reconstruction of Southern Law* (Westport, CT: Praeger Publishers, 2006), 36.

22. *True Presbyterian* (Louisville), February 26, 1863.

23. In a groundbreaking study of "political" arrests made under the direction of William H. Seward, Mark Neely Jr. reveals that the border states witnessed 40.5 percent of so-called arbitrary arrests of citizens; 26.2 percent of arrests were of citizens of seceded and Confederate states; and 6.2 percent of arrests were made in slave-holding Washington, D.C. Thus slaveholding/border states accounted for three-fourths of all arrests, a trend that continued throughout the war until military occupation rendered an increasing percentage of arrestees from southern states. The percentages of clergymen arrested for disloyalty reflect percentages evident in the

greater population. See Mark E. Neely Jr., "The Lincoln Administration and Arbitrary Arrests: A Reconsideration." *Journal of the Abraham Lincoln Association* 5 (1983): 6–25, 13–14. Neely offers that at least 14,401 civilians were arrested by the Lincoln administration during the war (8). *The American Annual Cyclopedia and Register of Important Events of the Year 1865*, however, published immediately after the war, offered that 38,000 citizens in the North had been thus arrested. Most today put that number at between 10,000 and 15,000. See Neely, *The Fate of Liberty*, 113. See also Stone, "Civil Liberties in Wartime," 215–51, 222.

24. *Official Records*, ser. 2, vol. 4 (S#117): 62.

25. Ibid., vol. 2 (S#115): 319.

26. Richard H. Collins, *History of Kentucky, By the Late Lewis Collins, Revised, Enlarged Fourfold, and Brought Down to the Year 1874, By His Son Richard H. Collins* (1874; Covington, KY: Collins and Co., 1882), 111.

27. *Official Records*, ser. 2, vol. 34, pt. 4 (S#64): 249.

28. "Kentucky Treason," *Daily Cleveland* (Ohio) *Herald*, May 3, 1863.

29. *Official Records*, ser. 1, vol. 34, pt. 2 (S#62): 311. Lincoln in time had this order amended so that it applied only to rebellious areas.

30. Daniel W. Stowell, *Rebuilding Zion: The Religious Reconstruction of the South, 1863–1877* (New York: Oxford University Press, 1998), 30. The radically abolitionist American Baptist Free Mission Society protested; they instead favored giving ownership of confiscated churches to local African American Baptists (197). In the first four months of 1864, the ABHMS alone seized some forty southern churches. According to Stowell, Lincoln did pressure Stanton to restrict the execution of such orders to "states in rebellion, giving border state evangelicals some relief, and by early 1865 Lincoln had begun the process of restoring southern churches' property to them" (31). But Lincoln did not rescind the majority of such orders, nor did he act in any immediate sense to limit their impact in border areas. See also Edward McPherson, *The Political History of the United States of America during the Great Rebellion* (Washington, DC: James G. Chapman, 1882), 521–22.

31. *Official Records*, ser. 1, vol. 32, pt. 2 (S#71): 590.

32. McPherson, *The Political History of the United States of America during the Great Rebellion*, 524.

33. Neely, *The Fate of Liberty*, 127.

34. This is because ministers—or anyone else, for that matter—in border-state areas under military occupation or with a pronounced military presence were generally denied opportunities to print oppositional newspapers, hold dissenting political rallies, or otherwise engage in behaviors that were not patently Unionist and, in the case of the clergy, ecumenical in nature.

35. Joseph George Jr., "Philadelphia's Catholic Herald: The Civil War Years," in *Pennsylvania Magazine of History and Biography* (April 1979): 196–221, 203; Arthur Preuss, *The Fortnightly Review* (St. Louis: A. Preuss, 1917), vol. 24: 259.

36. "Rail Riding in Wales, Mass.," *Chambersburg* (Pennsylvania) *Valley Spirit*, June 1, 1861; "New England News Items. Hampden County," *Springfield Republican*, June 14, 1862. Miller's denomination or church affiliation is unknown.

37. "Demetrius," *Portland* (Maine) *Daily Advertiser*, June 6, 1863.

38. "Campbellite" refers to a Christian denomination descended from the so-called

Restoration Movement and closely affiliated with Churches of Christ and Christian Churches. "The Case of Reverend Judson D. Benedict," *New York Times*, September 26, 1862; "The Case of Reverend Judson D. Benedict, Imprisoned for Alleged Seditious Speech," *New York Times*, September 18, 1862. See also Judge N. K. Hall, *Opinion of Judge N. K. Hall of the United States District Court for the Northern District of New York on Habeas Corpus in the Case of Rev. Judson D. Benjamin* (Buffalo, NY: Joseph Warren and Co., 1862); John A. Marshall, *American Bastille: A History of the Illegal Arrests and Imprisonment of American Citizens During the Late Civil War* (Philadelphia: Thomas W. Hartley, 1871), 312–15; Alice M. Paynter, *Henry Martyn Paynter: A Memoir* (Chicago: Fleming H. Revell Co., 1895), 75–86. On Lincoln's willingness to approve harsh policies by implication if not declaration, see Mark. E. Neely Jr., "'Unbeknownst' to Lincoln: A Note On Radical Pacification in Missouri during the Civil War," *Civil War History* 44, no. 3 (September 1998): 212–16. Neely shows that Lincoln approved even the most extreme elements of General Order No. 11, and that "the president had let the generals know he would justify radical measures under the rubric of 'military necessity' if questions arose, but he did not want to be known as the author of the plans" (216).

39. Lincoln, "To Samuel R. Curtis, January 2, 1863," in Basler, ed., *Collected Works of Abraham Lincoln* 6: 33–34.

40. Lincoln, "Letter to Erasmus Corning and Others, June 12, 1863," in Basler, ed., *Collected Works of Abraham Lincoln* 6: 261–69.

41. "Charles P. McIlvaine to Abraham Lincoln, Friday, March 4, 1864," Abraham Lincoln Papers, Library of Congress, ser. 1, "General Correspondence 1833–1916" (reel 70). McIlvaine, two-time chaplain of the Senate, university president, noted author, and Episcopal bishop of Ohio, had been picked by Lincoln at the war's outset to serve as an emissary to England. McIlvaine's chief task in that role was to influence British lawmakers against entering the war on the Confederate side. Emphasis in the original.

42. Richard Carwardine, *Lincoln: A Life of Purpose and Power* (New York: Alfred A. Knopf, 2006), 270.

43. There is a rich literature on Lincoln and civil religion. Among the best studies are Robert N. Bellah, *The Broken Covenant: American Civil Religion in Time of Trial* (New York: Seabury Press, 1975); Glen R. Thurow, *Abraham Lincoln and American Political Religion* (Albany: State University of New York, 1976); Frank J. Williams and William D. Pederson, eds., *Abraham Lincoln, Contemporary: An American Legacy* (Campbell, CA: Savas Woodbury Publishers, 1996); Lucas E. Morel, *Lincoln's Sacred Effort: Defining Religion's Role in American Self-Government* (Lanham, MD: Lexington Books, 2000); and Hans L. Trefousse, "Nationalism as a Civil Religion in the Thought of Abraham Lincoln, Carl Schurz, and Otto von Bismarck," in Elisabeth Glaser and Herman Wellenreuther, eds., *Bridging the Atlantic: The Question of American Exceptionalism in Perspective* (Cambridge, MA: Cambridge University Press, 2002), 103–16.

44. "Questions for the Church Again," *True Presbyterian*, August 14, 1862. Emphasis in the original.

45. "Letter from Father Washburn," *Zion's Herald and Wesleyan Journal* (Boston), September 16, 1863.

46. "Personal," *Lowell* (Massachusetts) *Daily Citizen and News*, May 3, 1861.

47. "Political Preaching," *Christian Inquirer*, February 7, 1863.

48. "New York Conference of the Methodist Episcopal Church," *The Independent . . . Devoted to the Consideration of Politics, Social and Economic Tendencies, History, Literature, and the Arts* (New York), May 7, 1863.

49. See particularly Todd M. Brenneman, "Religion," in *The Encyclopedia of Slave Resistance and Rebellion*, ed. Jumius P. Rodriguez (Westport, CT: Greenwood Publishing Group, 2007), 412–26, 423.

50. "Crisp Letter from Rev. Peter Cartwright," *Chicago Tribune*, July 1, 1861.

51. "Lincolnism in a Kentucky Pulpit," *Camden* (South Carolina) *Confederate*, November 15, 1861.

52. "Commencement at Middletown," *Zion's Herald and Wesleyan Journal*, August 3, 1864.

53. "New York Conference of the Methodist Episcopal Church," *The Independent . . . Devoted to the Consideration of Politics, Social and Economic Tendencies, History, Literature, and the Arts*, May 7, 1863.

54. "New York East Conference," *Zion's Herald and Wesleyan Journal*, April 13, 1863.

55. Andreasen, "Civil War Church Trials," 221.

56. "William C. Blundell File (1864)," Illinois Annual Conference Trial Records, Archives of the United Methodist Church Illinois Great Rivers Annual Conference, Bloomington, Illinois. Rpt. in Andreasen, "Civil War Church Trials," 223.

57. Andreasen, "Civil War Church Trials," 235.

58. Stanton, *The Church and the Rebellion against the Government*, 208. See also "William Rollinson Whittingham" in *The National Cyclopedia of American Biography, Being the History of the United States* (New York: James T. White and Co., 1896), vol. 6: 223–24.

59. Andreasen, "Civil War Church Trials," 237.

60. Charles William Heathcote, A.M., *The Lutheran Church and the Civil War* (New York: Fleming H. Revell Co., 1919), 82–83.

61. Stanton, *The Church and the Rebellion against the Government*, 246.

62. Throughout the war the Old School General Assembly was inconsistent concerning clerical speech. The Gardiner Spring Resolutions of the 1861 Assembly notwithstanding, the 1863 General Assembly (Peoria, Illinois) passed loyalist resolutions but voted down, by a significant majority, a motion to raise the American flag over the church edifice in which the assembly met. The General Assembly became more activist in 1864 and for the first time equated slavery with sin. In a resolution supported by a majority of the attending clergymen, the 1864 assembly (Newark, New Jersey) declared, "the General Assembly does hereby devoutly express its gratitude to Almighty God for having overruled the wickedness and calamities of the rebellion, so as to work out the deliverance of our country from the evil and guilt of slavery, as the root of bitterness from which has sprung rebellion, war, and bloodshed." By the May 1865 meeting in Pittsburgh, the General Assembly was no longer under the influence of Princetonian conservatism, and a vindictive spirit toward southern clerical rebels and northern sympathizers was apparent. See James M. Wilson, *The Presbyterian Historical Almanac, and Annual Remembrancer of the Church for 1864 (Old School)* (Philadelphia: Joseph M. Wilson, 1864), vol. 6: 45, 78–79; James M. Wilson, *The Presbyterian Historical Almanac, and Annual Remembrancer of the Church for 1865 (Old School)*, vol. 7: 49–50.

63. James M. Wilson, *The Presbyterian Historical Almanac, and Annual Remembrancer of the*

Church for 1862 (Old School) (Philadelphia: Joseph M. Wilson, 1862), vol. 4: 78. All emphasis in the original.

64. *Minutes of the Sixty-Ninth General Assembly of the Presbyterian Church in the United States of America (Old School), A.D. 1863* (New York: Presbyterian Publishing Committee, 1863), vol. 13: 245.

65. Orwig, *Journal of the General Conference of the Evangelical Association, Held at Buffalo, N.Y. 1863,* 60.

66. For insight into events at general conferences from throughout the war, see especially Raymond W. Albrights, *A History of the Evangelical Church* (Harrisburg, PA: Evangelical Press, 1956). See also J. D. Shortess, A. D. Gramley, and W. E. Peffley, *History of the Central Conference of the Evangelical Church* (Harrisburg, PA: Evangelical Press, 1940).

67. *Minutes of the General Assembly of the Presbyterian Church in the United States of America (New School): With an Appendix, A.D. 1865* (New York: Presbyterian Publication Committee, 1865), vol. 14: 20.

68. "The Lutheran General Synod. Patriotic Resolutions," *Northampton County Journal* (Easton, PA), May 14, 1862.

69. M. L. Stover, "Our General Synod," (Gettysburg, PA) *Evangelical Quarterly Review* 53 (October 1862): 97.

70. "Session Three, June 12, 1861," *Minutes of the Lebanon Conference (Lutheran), East Pennsylvania Synod, 1856–1867,* MG 3m.37, Pennsylvania State Archives, Harrisburg. Emphasis in the original.

71. Ibid.

72. That the directive may have been aimed at the membership as well is likely; many Southern Pennsylvania Lutherans, largely of German descent, were Democrats. While the loyalty of most Germans and German Americans would become clear as the war progressed, denominational leaders might have had their doubts in June 1861.

73. "Maine Unitarian Convention," *Christian Inquirer,* August 1, 1863.

74. Although denominations varied in the degree of Unionist rhetoric they included in such offerings, a brief foray into the wartime minutes of various denominational governing bodies reveals that there was virtually no mainstream faith tradition that failed to issue a loyalty resolution of some sort and that even the pietistic and pacifistic denominations that resisted service commonly offered such resolutions as well.

75. Thomas Curtis, "Is Christianity Any Guide for Human Duty?" *Boston Investigator,* June 5, 1861.

76. Dr. Thomas L. Nichols, *Forty Years of American Life* (London: John Maxwell and Co., 1864), vol. 2: 91.

77. "The Recent Insult Offered by the *New York Times* to the American Catholics," *New York Herald,* May 27, 1861.

78. "New York Conference of the Methodist Episcopal Church," *The Independent . . . Devoted to the Consideration of Politics, Social and Economic Tendencies, History, Literature, and the Arts* (New York), May 7, 1863.

79. A.R.A., "Conditions of National Safety and Peril," *Universalist Quarterly and General Review,* October 1863.

80. Goen, *Broken Churches, Broken Nation,* 117.

81. Reverend Jacob MacMurray, *Civil War Letters: Rev. Jacob S. MacMurray,* Archives of the Pennsylvania State University, Special Collections Call # NO3. 02.

82. "The Draft and the Clergy," *Philadelphia Inquirer,* July 25, 1863.

83. "The Bible and Bullets," *Johnstown* (PA) *Democrat,* April 1, 1863. A reprint of a story that originally ran in the notoriously Copperhead *Chicago Times,* the piece erroneously refers to the Republican preacher as "Cropp." Copp was ultimately brought up on charges before the Northern Indiana Conference of the Methodist Episcopal Church for his maligning of the Methodist church members Dr. Lemmon and Methodist Elder Winans. See "The Riot at Calumet, Indiana— Arrest of the Murderer—Infernal Conduct of an Abolition Preacher," *The Crisis* (Columbus, OH), March 3, 1863; *Valparaiso* (IN) *Republican,* March 12, 1863; Reverend Eugene D. Daniels, *A Twentieth-Century History and Biographical Record of Laporte County, Indiana* (Chicago: Lewis Publishing Co., 1904), 269; "The Riot at Calumet, Indiana—Arrest of the Murderer—Infernal Conduct of an Abolition Preacher," *The Crisis* (Columbus, OH), March 3, 1863.

84. See, as a representative "Copperhead" article, "Civilization in the Free and 'Slave' States," *The Old Guard* 2, no. 5 (May 1864).

85. "Personal," *New York Times,* August 4, 1862.

86. C. C. Burr, "Mr. C. C. Burr Not a Sympathizer with Secession—A Note from That Gentleman," *New York Times,* August 5, 1862.

87. "A Midnight Speech by Vallandigham, He is Serenaded at the New York Hotel by Capt. Rynders, Ben. Wood, James McMasters, and a Host of Democrats," *New York Times,* December 13, 1862.

88. Commenting on the wartime tolerance of disloyalty in New York City, for instance, R. L. Stanton observed, "The congregating of disloyal clergymen who have been exiled from New Orleans and other Southern cities . . . in the city of New York, for example—the head-quarters of rebel sympathizers—affords greater facilities for aiding the rebellion than they would have had if they were back in the Crescent City, under the watchful eye of military police" (*The Church and the Rebellion Against the Government,* 212).

89. John T. Reily, *History and Directory of the Boroughs of Gettysburg, Oxford, Littlestown, York Springs, Berwick, and East Berlin, Adams County, PA.; With Historical Collections* (Gettysburg, PA: J. E. Wible, 1880), 21.

90. Samuel H. Ranck et al., *Franklin and Marshall College Obituary Record* (Lancaster, PA: Franklin and Marshall College Alumni Association, 1901), no. 5, vol. 2, pt. 1: 75; Reily, *History and Directory of the Boroughs of Gettysburg, Oxford, Littlestown, York Springs, Berwick, and East Berlin, Adams County, PA.,* 21; *Directory of Trinity Reformed Church Cor. High and Stratton Streets Gettysburg, Pa. In Honor of the Fifth Anniversary of the Pastorate of the Rev. Paul Reid Pontius Minister* (Gettysburg, PA: Trinity Reformed Church, 1921), 30.

91. *Directory of Trinity Reformed Church Cor. High and Stratton Streets Gettysburg, Pa.,* 33.

92. "Gettysburg's 'Rebel Church,'" *Blue and the Gray Magazine* 5, no. 4 (1988): 23–24, 24.

93. *Trinity Reformed Church Minute Book, 1833–1891,* transcribed by Ms. Sarah Fuss (Gettysburg, PA: Adams County Historical Society, n.d.), 63–64.

94. L. L. Crounse, "The Treatment of the Union Soldiers by the People of Gettysburgh," *New York Times,* July 24, 1863. For more on the after-battle behavior of Gettysburg's residents, see

George Sheldon, *When the Smoke Cleared at Gettysburg: The Tragic Aftermath of the Bloodiest Battle of the Civil War* (Nashville: Cumberland House Publishing, 2003). An excellent treatment of the behavior of Gettysburg's citizens before, during, and after the battle is presented in Jim Weeks, *Gettysburg: Memory, Market, and an American Shrine* (Princeton, NJ: Princeton University Press, 2003).

95. In churches within the German Reformed tradition, Consistory Panels were the congregation's governing body of elected elders and deacons (making the body similar to the Session in the Presbyterian tradition, for instance). Thus a Joint Consistory Panel was comprised of elected officials from more than one affiliated church.

96. *Trinity Reformed Church Minute Book*, 62.

97. Ibid., 65. Hoke qualified his claim that Bucher fraternized with Rebel officers; he was quoted in the Consistory Minutes as admitting such a claim "may have been a mistake." Moreover, Hoke's charge that Bucher prevented a Unionist Reverend Phillips from occupying the church's pulpit was contradicted, the Panel concluded, in a letter from Phillips himself (63).

98. *Directory of Trinity Reformed Church Cor. High and Stratton Streets Gettysburg, Pa.*, 33. The quote is from the Minutes of the Joint Consistory Meeting as they were rpt. in the 1921 text.

99. *Trinity Reformed Church Minute Book*, 62.

100. Moses McClean, H. J. Stahle, J. C. Weed et al., "To His Excellency Horatio Seymour, Gettysburg, PA Aug. 18th 1864," Records of the Adjutant General, New York State Archives, Albany. In a novel maneuver, Miller recruited a select number of the town's leading Democrats, some of whom were members of his church, to write to Democratic Governor of New York Horatio Seymour and ask the governor to make Miller a chaplain of a New York regiment.

101. George M. Marsden, *The Soul of the American University: From Protestant Establishment to Established Nonbelief* (Oxford: University Press of Mississippi, 1994), 136; David Lavender, *California: Land of New Beginnings* (Lincoln: University of Nebraska Press, 1987), 247; His stance against vigilantism won for Scott the respect and friendship of William T. Sherman, a friendship that would last until Scott's death. See Merrill Drury, *William Anderson Scott: No Ordinary Man* (Glendale, CA: H. Clark Co., 1967), 194, 288.

102. Rev. William A. Scott, D.D., *Esther; The Hebrew-Persian Queen* (San Francisco, CA: H. H. Bancroft and Co., 1859), 150.

103. Drury, *William Anderson Scott*, 238.

104. The Scotts owned, among other slaves, a "mammy" named Mila, a stable keeper named Albert, and a house servant named Hannah (Drury, *William Anderson Scott*, 121; Larry E. Tise, *Proslavery: A History of the Defense of Slavery in America, 1701–1840* [Athens: University of Georgia Press, 1987], 366; *African Repository, and Colonial Journal*, January 1849, 7; John C. Pinheiro, "Religion Without Restriction: Anti-Catholicism, All Mexico, and the Treaty of Guadalupe Hidalgo," *Journal of the Early Republic* 23, no. 1 [Spring 2003]: 69–96, 96).

105. These sentiments were expressed by Scott in a private letter to his wife. Drury, *William Anderson Scott*, 122.

106. The reason public sentiment turned against Scott so quickly was that many believed he was indeed mixing politics and preaching but doing so in an inappropriately neutral way by praying for "all presidents and rulers and all officers of the Army and Navy" (G. H. Tinkham, *California Men and Events; Time 1769–1890* [Stockton, CA: Record Publishing Co., 1915], 196, rpt.

in John B. Astles, "Rev. Dr. W. A. Scott, A Southern Sympathizer," *California Historical Society Quarterly* 27, no. 2 [1900]: 149–56, 151).

107. Drury, *William Anderson Scott*, 238.

108. Astles, "Rev. Dr. W. A. Scott, A Southern Sympathizer," 151.

109. The Doctrine of the Spirituality of the Church, its origins chiefly in antebellum Southern Presbyterianism, was predicated on the belief that the church should offer no opinion or play no role in the affairs of this world and should instead dedicate all of its efforts to the salvation of souls.

110. "A Disloyal Clergyman at the Gridiron," *New Haven* (CT) *Daily Palladium*, June 13, 1865.

111. "Intestine Troubles of a Religious Society. Sharp Correspondence Concerning a Trustee's Opinion of His Ministers," *New York Times*, July 11, 1865.

112. Ibid.

113. Nevertheless, the level of tolerance for political dissent exhibited on the northern homefront was extraordinary given that the Civil War was, after all, a rebellion of citizens. See especially Geoffrey R. Stone, "Civil Liberties in Wartime," *Journal of Supreme Court History* 28, no. 3 (2003): 215–51.

5. WHAT THE PREACHERS THOUGHT

1. Historian Frank Klement for instance identifies the undermining efforts of Copperhead Catholic church leaders in the Union, while Bryon Andreasen skillfully does the same for their Protestant equivalents. See Frank L. Klement, "Copperheads as Catholics during the Civil War," *Catholic Historical Review* 80, no. 1 (January 1994): 36–57; Andreasen, "Lincoln's Religious Critics." For an earlier example of such works, see Ralph E. Morrow, "Methodists and 'Butternuts' in the Old Northwest," *Journal of the Illinois State Historical Society* 49 (Spring 1956): 34–47. During the war, virtually all northerners were familiar with the fictional character Petroleum V. Nasby. Invented by Ohio editor David Ross Locke, Nasby was presented as the stereotypical Copperhead minister—hypocritical, ignorant (he was a notoriously bad speller), corrupt, deceitful—and was especially enjoyed by President Lincoln. See also such non-religiously focused works as Wood Gray, *The Hidden Civil War: The Story of the Copperheads* (New York: Viking Press, 1942), 79, and Frank L. Klement, *Lincoln's Critics: The Copperheads of the North* (Shippensburg, PA: White Mane Books, 1999), 32.

2. Most of the important works on religion and the Civil War make use of this dichotomy. See Stout, *Upon the Altar of the Nation;* Genovese, "Religion in the Collapse of the American Union." A notable exception of late has been the emerging literature on Peace Church–affiliated participants in the war. See for example James Lehman and Steven Nolt, *Mennonites, Amish, and the American Civil War* (Baltimore: Johns Hopkins University Press, 2007). By showing the ways in which some Peace Church members, who "seldom thought they had to choose between peace principles and political goals," engaged in the war, authors like Lehman and Nolte add to our understanding that religion—even mainstream religion— was not compromised during the war but remained largely "an independent variable in the interpretation of human choices that shaped the 1860s rather than a secondary measure of something else" (7).

3. Lee Benson and later ethnoculturalists posited that religious affiliation (not belief, per se)

was politically determinative in the nineteenth century; Episcopalians and Congregationalists were Whigs, members of liturgical denominations and Irish Catholics were Democrats, etc. (*The Concept of Jacksonian Democracy: New York as a Test Case* [Princeton, NJ: Princeton University Press, 1961]). While I admire the new political history's sensitivity to group affiliation and the power of consensus, I am less enamored with its ethnoculturalism (that essentially casts religious groups as little more than political parties and individual members as partisans unconcerned with specific issues). For a primer on the dangers of too closely associating nineteenth-century denominations with political parties, see Latner and Levine, "Perspectives on Antebellum Pietistic Politics," 15–24.

4. *Minutes of the General Assembly of the Presbyterian Church in the Confederate States of America with an Appendix, A.D. 1862* (Augusta, GA: Steam Power Press Chronicle and Sentinel, 1862), vol. 2: 5.

5. As is clear by the inclusion of Peace Church adherents like Mennonites and mainstream denominationalists in the same category, the separate-spheres camp as here defined included those who stressed that not only was the church to be free from political considerations, but the individual was as well—in *all* his various walks. Thus in their non-church or outside-of-the-church lives, separate-spherists *could or could not be political.*

6. John Van Buren Flack, *Life History of J. V. B. Flack, D.D.* (Excelsior Springs, MO: Christian Union Herald, 1912), 43. Cited in Bryon C. Andreasen, "Prescribed Preachers, New Churches: Civil Wars in the Illinois Protestant Churches during the Civil War," *Civil War History* 44, no. 3 (September 1988): 194–211, 196.

7. Andreasen, "Prescribed Preachers, New Churches," 196.

8. Ibid., 209. As Andreasen makes clear, "New Church" members and ministers' aversion to political preaching was also accompanied in almost every case by pro-southern and pro-slavery sentiments.

9. "The Christian Union," *Zion's Herald and Wesleyan Journal* (Boston), July 6, 1864.

10. H. K. Carroll, LL.D., *The Religious Forces of the United States, Enumerated, Classified, and Described on the Basis of the Government Census of 1890; With an Introduction on the Condition and Character of American Christianity* (New York: Christian Literature Co., 1893), 99, 100.

11. Dickson, "Jeremiads in the New American Republic," 187–207, 198.

12. "A Caution to Friends," *Friend's Intelligencer,* September 10, 1864; 21, 27, rpt. from "A Caution to Friends," *Friends Miscellany, Being a Collection of Essays and Fragments, Biographical, Religious, Epistolary, Narrative, and Historical,* ed. John and Isaac Comly (Philadelphia: J. Richards, 1839), vol. 12: 197–204.

13. "The Early Christians on War," *Herald of Truth, Devoted to the Interests of the Denomination of Christians Known as the "Mennonites"* 1, no. 4 (April 1864).

14. James M. Wilson, *The Presbyterian Historical Almanac, and Annual Remembrancer of the Church for 1863 (Old School)* (Philadelphia: Joseph M. Wilson, 1863), vol. 5: 126, 127.

15. Ibid., 128.

16. Noah Hunt Schenck, *Christian Moderation: The Word in Season, to the Church and the Country. A Sermon, Preached in Emmanuel Church, Baltimore, on the Evening of Whitsunday, May 19, 1861,* 2nd ed. (Baltimore: Entz and Bash, 1861), 14, 16, 17, 15, 15–16.

17. Milton, "Clergymen as Clergymen, In the Political Arena," *The Liberator,* December 26, 1862. Italics in the original.

18. "Political Preaching," *American Monthly* 65, no.1 (January 1865): 85–89, 85.

19. "Politics or Religion—Which?" *Universalist Quarterly* 2 (January 1865): 114–21, 114.

20. *The Presbyter* (Cincinnati), March 16, 1864.

21. "Religious Intelligence," *The Constitution* (Middletown, CT), November 2, 1864.

22. "Tired of Hearing About the War," Macon (GA) *Weekly Telegraph*, February 21, 1863.

23. "Political Preaching Cured," *Deseret News*, November 11, 1862 (originally in the *Hartford* [CT] *Times*).

24. "His Holiness Pope Pius IX to President Davis . . . Given at Rome, at St. Peters, the 3d day of December, 1863, in the eighteenth year of our Pontificate," in *Record of the American Catholic Historical Society at Philadelphia* (Philadelphia: American Catholic Historical Society, 1903), 269–71, 269, 270.

25. Nichols, *Forty Years of American Life* 2: 91. Archbishop Hughes both acted as an informal American emissary to Europe, at Lincoln's request, and helped, through his sermons and other priestly efforts, in the recruitment of New York City's Irish population.

26. "Pastoral Letter of the Third Provincial Council of Cincinnati," *New York Freeman's Journal and Catholic Register* (Cooperstown), May 18, 1861. Although few Catholic leaders of the war years championed the moderate mix of politics and preaching, some, most notably Cincinnati's Archbishop Purcell and Pittsburgh's Michael Domenec, embraced a thoroughly Unionist ideology during the war.

27. F.E.T., *The Kenrick-Frenaye Correspondence: Letters Chiefly of Francis Patrick Kenrick and Marc Anthony Frenaye, Selected from the Cathedral Archives, Philadelphia* (Philadelphia: Archdiocese of Philadelphia, 1920), 457.

28. Finbar Kenneally, O.F.M., ed., *United States Documents in the Propaganda Fide Archives, A Calendar* (Washington, DC: Academy of American Franciscan History, 1971), ser. 1, vol. 3: 24, 47.

29. "His Holiness Pope Pius IX to Archbishop Hughes, of New York . . . Dated Rome, at St. Peters, October 18, 1862 in the seventeenth year of our Pontificate," in *Record of the American Catholic Historical Society at Philadelphia* (Philadelphia: American Catholic Historical Society, 1903), 264–66; 265–66.

30. George, "Philadelphia's Catholic Herald: The Civil War Years," 196–221, 203.

31. J. Thomas Scharf, *History of Maryland from the Earliest Period to the Present Day* (Baltimore: John B. Piet, 1879), vol. 3: 664.

32. "Peace Men in Maryland Legislature," *Catholic Mirror* (Baltimore), January 25, 1862.

33. Arthur Preuss, *Fortnightly Review* (St. Louis, MO: A. Preuss, 1917), vol. 24: 259.

34. Rpt. in Edward A. Pollard, *Observations in the North: Eight Months in Prison and On Parole* (Richmond, VA: E. W. Ayres, 1865), 89.

35. Joseph George Jr. makes the case that descriptions of the *Catholic Herald* as a Copperhead rag overstate the case, and that "the paper was basically moderate in its opposition to Lincoln's Administration and in its support of the Democratic Party" ("Philadelphia's Catholic Herald: The Civil War Years," 196–221; 196).

36. Farmer, *The Metaphysical Confederacy*, 256, 260; Jack P. Maddex, "From Theocracy to Spirituality: The Southern Presbyterian Reversal on Church and State," *Journal of Presbyterian History* 54 (1977): 438–57, 449.

37. Maddex, "From Theocracy to Spirituality," 447; Farmer, *The Metaphysical Confederacy*, 57. See also Preston D. Graham, *A Kingdom Not of This World: Stuart Robinson's Struggle to Distinguish*

the Sacred from the Secular during the Civil War (Macon, GA: Mercer University Press, 2002), 103.

38. Joe L. Coker, *Liquor in the Land of the Lost Cause: Southern White Evangelicals and the Prohibition Movement* (Lexington: University Press of Kentucky, 2007), 89–92.

39. "Unfeigned Faith," *The Circular: Devoted to the Sovereignty of Christ* (Oneida, NY), January 14, 1864.

40. *Democratic Watchman* (Bellefonte, PA), August 30, 1867.

41. Reverend William B. Stewart, *The Nation's Sins and the Nation's Duty. A Sermon, Preached in the First Presbyterian Church, Pottstown, Pennsylvania, on National Fast Day, April 30, 1863* (Philadelphia: William S. and Alfred Martien, 1863), 11.

42. Stanton, *The Church and the Rebellion against the Government*, 214.

43. "The Two Master Passions—The Religious and Political," 231. Italics in the original.

44. "The Church and the Crisis," *German Reformed Messenger*, March 6, 1861.

45. "Day of Fasting and Prayer," *German Reformed Messenger*, August 28, 1861.

46. Paul E. Holdcraft, "Highlights from the Conference Minutes, 1862," in *History of the Pennsylvania Conference of the Church of the United Brethren in Christ* (Fayetteville, PA: Craft Press, Inc., 1939), 69. The commentator was referencing Matthew 22:21.

47. Rev. James Keogh, D.D. *Catholic Principles of Civil Government, A Lecture by Rev. James Keogh, D.D., of Pittsburg, PA* (Cincinnati: Catholic Telegraph Print, 1862), 1, 17, 19.

48. Rev. Silas Comfort Swallow, D.D., *III Score and X, or Selections, Collections, Recollections of Seventy Busy Years* (Harrisburg, PA: United Evangelical Publishing House, 1914), 50.

49. Ibid.

50. Francis Vinton, D.D., *The Christian Idea of Civil Government: A Sermon Preached in Trinity Church, New York, on the Occasion of the Prov. Bishop's Pastoral Letter* (New York: George F. Nesbitt and Co., 1861), 4, 11.

51. After the schisms of the 1840s, the Baltimore Conference remained under the auspices of the Methodist Episcopal Church in the United States (or, MEC North) and pledged as a conference to avoid discussions about slavery. The conference grew so large under this plan that, in 1857, it was divided and the "auxiliary" East Baltimore Conference was created. In 1860, the General Conference passed a resolution that condemned slavery, and two Baltimore conferences, one loyal to the Northern embodiment of the ME Church and based in Maryland and one sympathetic to the ME Church South and based in Northern Virginia, took shape—both with the same name. The East Baltimore Conference remained ostensibly loyal to the ME Church in the United States (North). See Charles F. Irons, *The Origins of Proslavery Christianity: White and Black Evangelicals in Colonial and Antebellum Virginia* (Chapel Hill: University of North Carolina Press, 2008), 228–29, 318. Both sides—even those proslavery Methodists in the Maryland and, especially, the Virginia-based branches—were overwhelmingly Unionist after secession.

52. Charles Baumer Swaney, *Episcopal Methodism and Slavery, With Sidelights on Ecclesiastical Politics* (1926; New York: Negro Universities Press, 1969), 307. The conference was by resolution affiliated with the northern church but was not formally under its authority.

53. *The Fifth Annual Register of the East Baltimore Conference of the Methodist Episcopal Church Held in Monument Street Church, Baltimore, MD. March 3–14, 1862* (Baltimore: James Young, 1862), 31–32.

54. *The Seventh Annual Register of the East Baltimore Conference of the Methodist Episcopal*

Church Held in Altoona, PA., March 25, 1864. Published by the Secretaries (Altoona, PA: McCrum and Dern, 1864), 16.

55. For more on R. J. Breckinridge, see particularly James C. Klotter, *The Breckinridges of Kentucky, 1760–1981* (Lexington: University Press of Kentucky, 1986).

56. Robert Stuart Sanders, *Sketch of Mount Horeb Presbyterian Church, 1827–1952* (n.p., n.d.), 18. Original held by Presbyterian Church in America Historical Center, 12330 Conway Road, St. Louis, MO.

57. Breckinridge was Old School for numerous reasons. Chief among them was his belief that New Schoolers compromised the authority of the ruling hierarchy through their utilization of voluntary organizations and weakened the ministry through their relaxed standards for ordination.

58. "Rev. Dr. Breckinridge Rebuking Treason," *Bangor Daily Whig and Courier*, June 29, 1861.

59. Wilson, *The Presbyterian Historical Almanac, and Annual Remembrancer of the Church for 1863 (Old School)*, vol. 5: 117.

60. As one nineteenth-century commentator said of Breckinridge, "Previous to the civil war he had been inclined to conservatism, though disposed to deprecate slavery: but when the war came he was from the first intensely loyal." In John Fiske and James Grant Wilson, eds., *Appleton's Cyclopedia of American Biography* (New York: D. Appleton and Co., 1888), vol. 1: 365.

61. Alfred Lee, *The Christian Citizen's Duty in the Present Crisis. A Discourse Delivered in St. Andrew's Church, Wilmington, Del. On Sunday, April 21st, 1861* (Wilmington, DE: Henry Eckel, Printer, 1861), 5–6.

62. Rev. Richard Eddy, *The Necessity for Religion in Politics. A Sermon Preached to the United Congregations of Universalists, in Philadelphia, in the Second Church, Thanksgiving Morning, November 26, 1863* (Philadelphia: King and Baird, 1863), 20.

63. *Statistics of the United States . . . Eighth Census.*

64. Henry Ward Beecher, "Guilt of the Church and Ministry," *The Liberator* 32, no. 18 (May 2, 1862).

65. *Black River Herald* (Boonville, NY), May 10, 1861.

66. Henry Ward Beecher, "Altar, Pulpit, and Platform," *Christian Examiner* (New York), vol. 73, no. 2 (September 1863): 242–57; 254.

67. Ibid., 247.

68. Ibid., 255.

69. Henry Ward Beecher, "Preaching Christ," in *Sermons by Henry Ward Beecher, Plymouth Church, Brooklyn* 2: 167–88, 182.

70. See "A Venerable Clergyman," *New York Evening Post*, July 17, 1861.

71. H. B. Ashmead, "Voice of 40,000 Baptists of Pennsylvania, at a Stated Meeting," *Christianity Versus Treason and Slavery: Religion Rebuking Sedition* (Philadelphia: H. B. Ashmead, 1864), 8.

72. "The Baptists of West New Jersey and the Union," *The Liberator*, September 30, 1864.

73. "The Third Reformed Presbyterian Church," *New York Times*, September 27, 1861. The General Synod of the Reformed Church in America, to which Sloane belonged, was then the largest separate reformed Presbyterian denomination in the country.

74. *American Catholic Telegraph* (Cincinnati), June 10, 1863.

75. *Brownson's Quarterly Review,* Third New York Series (New York: D. and J. Sadler and Co., 1862), vol. 3: 49, 115.

76. Rev. William Adams, D.D., "Politics and the Pulpit," *American Presbyterian and Theological Review (New School)* 1, no. 1 (January 1863): 122–44, 122, 123. Adams was one of the group that founded the most important New School institution in America, New York's Union Theological Seminary, in 1836.

77. Rev. R. B. Thurston, "The Relations of the Pulpit to the State," *American Presbyterian and Theological Review (New School),* New Series, no. 7 (July 1864): 371–90, 371.

78. Ibid., 378.

79. McKinley S. Lundy Jr., "Thomas Jefferson and Political Preaching: Two Case Studies of Free Religious Expression in the American Pulpit," master's thesis, Vanderbilt University, 2005, 52–53. See also "Thomas Jefferson to Peter H. Wendover" (March 15, 1815, unsent) in Adrienne Koch and William Peden, eds., *The Life and Selected Writings of Thomas Jefferson* (New York: Modern Library, 1972), 279.

80. "Treatment of Henry Ward Beecher, and Political Preaching," *Monthly Religious Magazine* (October 1866), 36.

81. "Religious—Not Political," *Zion's Herald and Wesleyan Journal* (Boston), February 17, 1864.

82. *The Presbyter,* October 23, 1862.

83. Reverend George Peck, "A Compromise Rejected," *Christian Advocate and Journal* (Chicago), November 3, 1864.

84. "Politics and the Church," *Danville Quarterly Review* 2, no. 4 (December 1862): 611–39, 613.

6. THE CONFEDERATE MINISTRY

1. For more on contingency and the chances of Southern victory, see especially McPherson, *The Battle Cry of Freedom,* 857–58.

2. This argument is prominent in such works as Richard Beringer, Herman Hattaway, Archer Jones, and William N. Still Jr., *The Elements of Confederate Defeat: Nationalism, War Aims, and Religion* (Athens: University of Georgia Press, 1988); Paul D. Escott, *After Secession: Jefferson Davis and the Failure of Confederate Nationalism* (Baton Rouge: Louisiana State University Press, 1992); and Armstead L. Robinson, *Bitter Fruits of Bondage: The Demise of Slavery and the Collapse of the Confederacy, 1861–1865* (Charlottesville: University of Virginia Press, 2005). Essentially, most such works contend that a latent guilt over slavery dampened the commitment of southern clerics to the Confederate nation and cause. I put little stock in the "guilt over slavery" thesis as it pertained to the wartime southern church, and find such arguments overly speculative. For more on this controversial but intriguing thesis, see particularly Gaines M. Foster, "Guilt over Slavery: A Historiographical Analysis," *Journal of Southern History* 56, no. 4 (November 1990): 665–94; Charles G. Sellers Jr., "The Travail of Slavery," in Charles G. Sellers Jr., ed., *The Southerner as American* (Chapel Hill: University of North Carolina Press, 1960), 40–71; Genovese, *A Consuming Fire.*

3. Those who study the Civil War with any vigor have likely read of the ways in which preachers shaped the "separate people" consciousness of late prewar southerners, encouraged

secession, maintained the Christianity-fueled morale of southern armies, and assisted in the reestablishment of white dominion in the postwar South. Representative of works detailing how religious leaders helped shape a common late-antebellum southern identity is Snay, *Gospel of Disunion;* helped bring about secession, Goen, *Broken Churches, Broken Nation;* Crowther, *Southern Evangelicals and the Coming of the Civil War;* Faust, *The Ideology of Slavery;* bolstered morale in the field, James W. Silver, *Confederate Morale and Church Propaganda* (Tuscaloosa, AL: Confederate Publishing, 1957); and helped the South return to its white/hegemonic ways, Blum, *Reforging the White Republic.*

4. The southern cleric's role in Confederate identity formation is understudied, although studies of how political worldviews, historical ideals, and an attacking enemy compelled southerners to side with the Confederacy are far from uncommon. See for instance John G. Barrett, *The Civil War in North Carolina* (Chapel Hill: University of North Carolina Press, 2005); Aaron Sheehan-Dean and Aaron Charles, "Everyman's War: Confederate Enlistment in Civil War Virginia," *Civil War History* 50, no. 1 (March 2004), 5–26.

5. Thanks to historians like Charles Regan Wilson, Christine Leigh Heyrman, and Edward R. Crowther, most students of southern history know the elements of that unifying religious message. See Wilson, *Baptized in Blood: The Religion of the Lost Cause, 1865–1920* (1980; Athens: University of Georgia Press, 2009); Heyrman, *Southern Cross: The Beginnings of the Bible Belt* (Chapel Hill: University of North Carolina Press, 1997); Crowther, *Southern Evangelicals and the Coming of the Civil War.*

6. Thus, as Dianne Bunch has written, in the late prewar South, "church-going became a Christian and civic responsibility used to stabilize all Southern social institutions" ("Guilt," in Hill et al., *Encyclopedia of Religion in the South,* 362–64, 363).

7. Franklin quipped, upon signing the Declaration of Independence, "Now we must all hang together, or most assuredly we will hang separately" (Franklin, rpt. in David C. King, *American Heritage, American Voices: Colonies and Revolution* [New York: John Wiley, 2003], 96–97). Charles Elliott, *South-Western Methodism: A History of the M.E. Church in the South-West, from 1844 to 1864. Comprising the Martyrdom of Bewley and Others; Persecutions of the M. E. Church, and Its Reorganization, etc.* (Cincinnati: Poe and Hitchcock, 1868), 229.

8. To this point, Drew Gilpin Faust asserts, "Emphasizing the need for individual moral uplift rather than widespread social change, southern reformers strove to avoid the dangerous 'isms'—feminism, socialism, abolitionism—that had emerged from northern efforts at social betterment. As a result, the proliferation of reform movements that spread through the rest of nineteenth-century America did not take as firm a hold in the South" (*The Creation of Confederate Nationalism,* 29–30). See also Bertram Wyatt Brown, "The Antimission Movement in the Jacksonian South: A Study in Regional Folk Culture," *Journal of Southern History* 36 (November 1970): 501–29.

9. Even southern Whigs were antireformists. According to Enrico Dal Lago, Whigs supported agricultural reform and improvements in transportation and technology but only when reconciled with the slave system and the veneration of southern life. James Oakes, moreover, points out that Whiggery in the South maintained white supremacy by attempting to *reconcile* industry and agriculture, defending "economic development among whites while insisting that agricultural labor be maintained as the special preserve for blacks" (Dal Lago, *Agrarian Elites:*

American Slaveholders and Southern Italian Landowners, 1815–1861 [Baton Rouge: Louisiana State University Press, 2005], 221); Oakes, "From Republicanism to Liberalism: Ideological Change and the Crisis of the Old South," *American Quarterly* 37 (Fall 1985): 551–71, 563. See also John Ashworth, *Slavery, Capitalism, and Politics in the Antebellum Republic,* vol. 2: *The Coming of the Civil War* (New York: Cambridge University Press, 2007).

10. Farmer, *The Metaphysical Confederacy,* 40.

11. Ibid.

12. Bertram Wyatt-Brown, "Church, Honor, and Secession," in Miller et al., eds., *Religion and the American Civil War,* 89–109; 103.

13. Ibid. See also James Henley Thornwell, D.D., *Our Danger and Our Duty* (Columbia, SC: Southern Guardian Steam-Power Press, 1862). See also Kurt O. Berends, "Confederate Sacrifice and the 'Redemption' of the South," in *Religion in the American South: Protestants and Others in History and Culture,* ed. Beth Barton Schweiger and Donald G. Mathews (Chapel Hill: University of North Carolina Press, 2004), 94–124, 105. Berends notes that "Clergy who waffled on secession up to the onset of the war made similar [pro-Confederate] statements throughout the war. With secession settled, most Christians vigorously channeled their energies into supporting the new nation, and they subsumed their loyalty to the church into their loyalty to their new nation."

14. Oliver P. Temple, *Notable Men of Tennessee from 1833 to 1875, Their Times and Their Contemporaries* (New York: Cosmopolitan Press, 1912), 243, rpt. in Daniel W. Crofts, *Reluctant Confederates* (Chapel Hill: University of North Carolina Press, 1989), 345.

15. Farmer, *The Metaphysical Confederacy,* 40.

16. "A Word for the Times," (Nashville) *Christian Advocate,* January 31, 1861.

17. *Religious Herald* (Richmond, VA) August 9, 1860.

18. Ray Grande, *An Enlarged Tent: Arkadelphia First Baptist Church, 1851–2001* (n.p., n.d.), 11, Southern Baptist Historical Library and Archives, Nashville.

19. "Civil War—Our Duty," (Nashville) *Christian Advocate,* April 25, 1861.

20. "Horace Maynard to Edward Bates, April 18, 1861," *General Records of the Department of Justice,* RG 60, National Archives, rpt. in Crofts, *Reluctant Confederates,* 334.

21. *North Carolina Semi-Weekly Standard,* April 20, 1861, rpt. in Crofts, *Reluctant Confederates,* 335.

22. "Josiah Cowles to Calvin J. Cowles, June 3, 1861, Calvin J. Cowles Papers, North Carolina Division of Archives and History, qtd. in John Inscoe, "Slavery, Sectionalism, and Secession in Western North Carolina," Ph.D. diss., University of North Carolina at Chapel Hill, 1985, 261, and rpt. in Crofts, *Reluctant Confederates,* 335.

23. Peyton Harrison Hoge, *Moses Drury Hoge: Life and Letters* (Richmond, VA: Presbyterian Committee of Publication, 1899), 143. Writing more than three decades after the fact, Hoge offered by way of footnote that "the name would add greatly to the strength of the letter, but is withheld for obvious reasons" (144). All emphasis in the original.

24. W. Harrison Daniel, "The Southern Baptists in the Confederacy," *Civil War History* (December 1960): 389–401, 394.

25. Chesebrough, *Clergy Dissent in the Old South,* 50.

26. "Church Treatment of Deserters," *Confederate Baptist,* November 9, 1864.

27. "Minute Book of the Mt. Hermon (Virginia) Baptist Church, March 6, April 30, 1864; "Minute Book of the Lebanon (Virginia) Baptist Church, November 26, 1864; *Virginia Baptists Minutes, 1862*, 44; "Minutes of the Rappahannock Baptist Association, October 1864," 334. All rpt. in W. Harrison Daniel, "Virginia Baptists, 1861–1865," *Virginia Magazine of History and Biography* (January 1964), 94–114; 100.

28. John Abernathy Smith, *Cross and Flame: Two Centuries of United Methodism in Middle Tennessee* (Nashville: Commission on Archives and History of the Tennessee Conference, 1984), 142–43.

29. Frank Moore, ed., *The Rebellion Record: A Diary of American Events* (New York: G. P. Putnam, 1862), vol. 2: 492.

30. Arch Frederic Blakey, *General John H. Winder, C.S.A.* (Gainesville: University Press of Florida, 1990), 52; William Blair, *Virginia's Private War: Feeding Body and Soul in the Confederacy, 1861–1865* (New York: Oxford University Press, 1998), 46; Jan Ellen Lewis, "Defining the Nation: 1790 to 1898," in Daniel Farber, ed., *Security v. Liberty: Conflicts between Civil Liberties and National Security in American History* (New York: Russell Sage Foundation, 2008), 117–64, 161.

31. James Chesnut Jr. "Report of the Chief of the Department of the Military of South Carolina to His Excellency, Governor Pickens, 1862," Charles Ramsdell Microfilm Collection, Center for American History (University of Texas at Austin), microfilm reel no. 786.47. Rpt. in Mark A. Weitz, *More Damning than Slaughter: Desertion in the Confederate Army* (Lincoln: University of Nebraska Press, 2005), 40.

32. Weitz, *More Damning than Slaughter*, 57.

33. Among the best concise treatments of the southern Jeremiad are Faust, *The Creation of Confederate Nationalism*, 29–33; Stout and Grasso, "Civil War, Religion, and Communications"; Ellis Merton Coulter, "Money, Bonds, and Taxes," in *The Confederate States of America, 1861–1865* (Baton Rouge: Louisiana State University Press, 1950), 149–82. Taxes were routinely collected either in cash or in kind, as with the collection of farm stuffs. According to Coulter, such laws were "undoubtedly widely evaded," and "the states paralleled the Confederacy rather closely in their tax policies and thereby aggravated the general situation," 180, 182.

34. Benjamin Morgan Palmer, *National Responsibility Before God: A Discourse, Delivered on the Day of Fasting, Humiliation, and Prayer, Appointed by the President of the Confederate States of America, June 13, 1861* (New Orleans: Price-Current Steam Book and Job Print Office, 1861); Faust, *The Creation of Confederate Nationalism*, 30–31.

35. Palmer, *National Responsibility Before God.*

36. Elliott was in fact the presiding bishop of the Protestant Episcopal Church in the Confederate States of America; "negative reinforcement" is a term coined by B. F. Skinner in his theory of operant conditioning to describe the process in which a response or behavior is strengthened or encouraged by removing or avoiding a negative outcome or aversive stimulus (William O' Donohue and Kyle E. Ferguson, *The Psychology of B. F. Skinner* [Thousand Oaks, CA: Sage Publications Ltd., 2001], 73–100).

37. Henry Holcombe Tucker, *God in the War: A Sermon Delivered Before the Legislature of Georgia, In the Capitol at Milledgeville, on Friday, November 15, 1861, Being a Day Set Apart for Fasting, Humiliation, and Prayer, by His Excellency the President of the Confederate States* (Milledgeville, GA: Boughton, Nisbet, and Barnes, 1861). See also Faust, *The Creation of Confederate Nationalism*, 30.

38. Societal and cultural unity is, of course, altogether different from societal and cultural consensus. For example, most in America today consider themselves patriots, and yet a great number of conflicting political, religious, and cultural attitudes divide the populace. Confederates were in accord societally and culturally, else they wouldn't have been Confederates, but the South's political and religious leaders understood that to achieve their independence they needed to be of a like mind about the war as well.

39. John Beauchamp Jones, "May 24, 1861; Diary of John Beauchamp Jones, May, 1861," *A Rebel War Clerk's Diary at the Confederate States Capital* (Philadelphia: J.B. Lippincott and Co., 1866), vol. 1: 392.

40. Randall Balmer and John Fitzmier, *The Presbyterians* (Westport, CT: Greenwood Publishing Group, 1993), 71. It should, however, be noted that there was a general shortage of military chaplains during the war.

41. *Minutes of the Holston Association of Baptists Held With Union Church, Washington County, Tennessee, August 9th and 10th, 1861* (Jonesborough, TN: Wm. A. Sparks and Co., 1861), 13, Southern Baptist Historical Library and Archives, Nashville.

42. "Twenty-fourth Annual Meeting of the East Tennessee Association of United Baptists Held at Concord Church, Greene County, September 1862," *Tennessee Baptists Association, East Tennessee Baptist 1841–1955*, Publication Number 836, Addenda Positive, Southern Baptist Historical Library and Archives, Nashville.

43. *Minutes of the General Assembly of the Presbyterian Church in the Confederate States of America, 1863* (Columbia, SC: Steam Power Press, 1863), 153. See also Daniel W. Stowell, "Stonewall Jackson and the Providence of God," in Miller et al., eds., *Religion and the American Civil War*, 187–207, 192.

44. "Position of the Lutherans," *Confederate Baptist,* June 8, 1864. See also E. Clifford Nelson, *The Lutherans in North America* (Minneapolis: Fortress Press, 1980), 210–52, for more about the Lutheran Church in the Confederacy.

45. Palmer, *National Responsibility Before God*; Faust, *The Creation of Confederate Nationalism*, 30–31.

46. Qtd. in Henry Alexander White, *Southern Presbyterian Leaders* (New York: Neale Publishing Co., 1911), 430–31.

47. "Sweetwater Association of United Baptists, 1862 Meeting at Christianburg Church, Monroe County, September 1862," *Tennessee Baptists Association Sweetwater 1830–1870*, Publication Number 836, Addenda Positive. Southern Baptist Historical Library and Archives, Nashville.

48. Hoge, *Moses Drury Hoge,* 145. See also Wyatt-Brown, "Church, Honor, and Secession," 103.

49. Joseph M. Atkinson, *God, The Giver of Victory and Peace: A Thanksgiving Sermon, Delivered in the Presbyterian Church, September 18, 1862* (Raleigh, NC: unpublished, 1862; Confederate Imprints Microfilm Series 4123), 11.

50. Thomas S. Dunaway, *A Sermon Delivered by Elder Thomas S. Dunaway, of Lancaster County, Virginia, Before Coen Baptist Church* (Richmond, VA: unpublished, 1864; Confederate Imprints Microfilm Series 413802), 3–4

51. J. J. D. Renfroe, *"The Battle Is God's": A Sermon Preached Before Wilcox's Brigade* (Richmond, VA: unpublished, 1863; Confederate Imprints Microfilm Series 4186), 7. See also Jason Phillips,

Diehard Rebels: The Confederate Culture of Invincibility (Athens: University of Georgia Press, 2007), 15–16.

52. "Baptists and the Civil War: Southern Baptist Convention Approves Confederacy," *Baptist Features* (Nashville: Baptist Press News Service of the Southern Baptist Convention, 1962), 3.

53. "24th Annual Meeting of the East Tennessee Association of United Baptists Held at Concord Church, Greene County, September 1862," *Tennessee Baptists Association, East Tennessee Baptist 1841–1955*, Publication Number 836, Addenda Positive. Southern Baptist Historical Library and Archives, Nashville.

54. Frederick Abbott Norwood, *The Story of American Methodism: A History of the United Methodists and Their Relations* (New York: Abingdon Press, 1974), 45.

55. Chesebrough, *Clergy Dissent in the Old South,* 50.

56. Mark Neely has argued that such southern campaigns threatened more dire consequences for dissenters than was true of comparable efforts in the North. Mark E. Neely Jr., *Southern Rights: Political Prisoners and the Myth of Confederate Constitutionalism* (Charlottesville: University of Virginia Press, 1999).

57. "For the Brethren from P. H. Hopkins, October 25, 1865," *Tennessee Baptist Association, Stockton Valley, 1805–1960*, Publication no. 836 Positive, Southern Baptist Historical Library and Archives, Nashville.

58. *Meeting of July 6, 1863, Minute Book, Elon Baptist Church, Dover Association, 1857–1866*, rpt. in Willard E. Wight, "The Churches and the Confederate Cause," *Civil War History* 6 (December 1960): 361–73, 361.

59. More than any other scholar, Emory B. Thomas is synonymous with this thesis. See his *The Confederacy as a Revolutionary Experience* (Englewood Cliffs, NJ: Prentice-Hall, 1971), and the more recent *The Confederate Nation, 1861–1865* (New York: Harper and Row, 1979). The Confederacy as a revolutionary event is an accurate description in most every *other* respect (that is to say, other than with the ministry).

60. Jane T. H. Cross, "Over the River" (April 1861), *War Poetry of the South*, ed. William Gilmore Simms (New York: Richardson and Co., 1867), 126–27. The poem ran as early as April 25, 1861, in southern denominational newspapers like the Methodist (Nashville) *Christian Advocate*.

61. Pope Pius IX virtually acknowledged Jefferson Davis as a sovereign leader, and eleven of the twelve bishops who presided over Catholic sees in what would become the Confederacy supported secession (Aloysius F. Plaisance, "The Catholic Church and the Confederacy," *American Benedictine Review* 15 [June 1964]: 159–67, 160). See also Benjamin J. Blied, *Catholics and the Civil War* (Milwaukee, WI: Benjamin J. Blied, 1945), 71.

62. Martin E. Marty, "Foreword," in Donald G. Mathews, *Religion in the Old South* (Chicago: University of Chicago Press, 1977), x.

63. Faust, *The Ideology of Slavery,* 7. This argument is more fully articulated in Drew Gilpin Faust, "A Southern Stewardship: The Intellectual and the Proslavery Argument," *American Quarterly* 31 (1979): 63–80.

64. Irons, *The Origins of Proslavery Christianity,* 33.

65. See esp. E. Lawrence Abel, *Singing the New Nation: How Music Shaped the Confederacy* (Mechanicsburg, PA: Stackpole Books, 2000).

66. Randy J. Sparks, "Religion in the Pre–Civil War South," in John B. Boles, ed., *A Companion to the American South* (Malen, MA: Blackwell Publishers, 2002), 156–75, 165–66. See also Heyrman, *Southern Cross*.

67. W. B. Wellon, "Our Paper," *Army and Navy Messenger*, December 15, 1864. Rpt. in Berends, "Confederate Sacrifice and the 'Redemption' of the South," 105.

68. For more, see William W. Freehling, *The South Versus the South: How Anti-Confederate Southerners Shaped the Civil War* (New York: Oxford University Press, 2002).

7. CONFEDERATE AND UNIONIST RELIGIOUS LIFE UNDER THE GUN

1. Most works on southern wartime ministers are not homefront studies, but rather works that assess their contributions as chaplains or evangelicals to soldiers. The bulk of works on southern preachers at home focuses their contributions to the secessionist movement before the war or their role in formulating the "Lost Cause" mythology of the postwar age. See Snay, *Gospel of Disunion*; Goen, *Broken Churches, Broken Nation*; Conkin, *The Uneasy Center*; Wyatt-Brown, *Yankee Saints and Southern Sinners*; Woodworth, *While God Is Marching On*; and Stowell, *Rebuilding Zion*.

2. Faust, *The Creation of Confederate Nationalism*, 22; Stout and Grasso, "Civil War, Religion, and Communications," 318.

3. The best such work is Chesebrough's *Clergy Dissent in the Old South*; For a work on dissent that deals with ministers in much less detail, see Stephen V. Ash, *When The Yankees Came: Conflict and Chaos in the Occupied South, 1861–1865* (Chapel Hill: University of North Carolina Press, 1995).

4. J. W. Tucker, "God's Presence in War," May 16, 1862, qtd. in Ronald Glenn Lee, "Exploded Graces: Providence and the Confederate Israel in Evangelical Southern Sermons, 1861–1865," M.A. thesis, Rice University, 1990, 63; rpt. in Berends, "Confederate Sacrifice and the 'Redemption' of the South," 105.

5. Lynn E. May Jr., *The First Baptist Church of Nashville, Tennessee, 1820–1970* (Nashville: First Baptist Church, 1970), 97–98.

6. Ibid., 98.

7. Ibid., 96.

8. Unnamed deacon qtd. in Reuben Herring, *Valleys, Plateaus, Peaks: A 170-Year History of First Baptist Church, Nashville, Tennessee* (Nashville: First Baptist Church, 1990), 16. The church was made available to congregants for even less (only a few days) of 1864.

9. May, *The First Baptist Church of Nashville, Tennessee*, 98.

10. Minute Book of the First Baptist Church, Suffolk (undated), rpt. in Daniel, "Virginia Baptists, 1861–1865," 94–114, 112.

11. Minute Book, Zoar Baptist Church, 88, rpt. in Daniel, "Virginia Baptists, 1861–1865," 94–114, 112.

12. Floy Finis Schochler, "Louisiana Baptists and the War for Southern Independence," master's thesis, Louisiana State University, 1958, 38, Southern Baptist Historical Library and Archives, Nashville.

13. John Wesley Brinsfield, *The Spirit Divided: Memoirs of Civil War Chaplains: The Confederacy* (Macon, GA: Mercer University Press, 2006), 225

14. J. M. L. Burnett, "Dear Brother Cody" (July 18, 1861), in *A Collection of Thirty-Eight Letters Written or Received by the Reverend J. M. L. Burnett and The Reverend Edmund Cody*, ed. Edmund Cody Burnett (Morristown, TN: Toomey Desk-top Publishers, Ltd., 1992), Southern Baptist Historical Library and Archives, Nashville.

15. "Giving the Devil His Due," *Confederate Baptist*, August 24, 1864.

16. See esp. Faust, *The Creation of Confederate Nationalism*.

17. "Reverend Traitors," *Daily Cleveland* (Ohio) *Herald*, July 12, 1861.

18. "Dabbling in Politics, "The (Nashville) *Christian Advocate*, May 9, 1861.

19. "Memoirs of Thomas Hooke McCallie (1901–1912)," McCallie Family Papers, McCallie School, Chattanooga, TN. Qtd. in Stowell, *Rebuilding Zion*, 17. McCallie was in the end spared extradition and allowed after some time to preach within his own home.

20. The order related to a church in Memphis, Tennessee, and was issued on May 13, 1864 (Franklin Steiner, *The Religious Beliefs of Our Presidents: From Washington to F.D.R.* [New York: Prometheus Books, 1995], 143).

21. For example, see Morel, *Lincoln's Sacred Effort*, 105–6.

22. Lila Copeland and R. A. Rainer, *History of McDonough* (Georgia) *Baptist Church, 1825–1965* (n.p., n.d.), 31; Southern Baptist Historical Library and Archives, Nashville.

23. "Civilized Warfare," *Confederate Baptist*, October 15, 1862.

24. *Official Records*, ser. 1, vol. 17: 731.

25. Smith, *Cross and Flame*, 146–47.

26. "Abraham Lincoln to Samuel R. Curtis, January 2, 1863," in Basler, ed., *Collected Works of Abraham Lincoln* 6: 33–34; see also Louis S. Gerteis, *Civil War St. Louis* (Lawrence: University Press of Kansas, 2001), 185.

27. Dr. Robert Brooke Albertson, *Images of Portsmouth, Virginia* (Charleston, SC: Aracadia Publishing, 2002), 24.

28. "Running the Churches," *Richmond Daily Dispatch*, March 11, 1864.

29. *Official Records*, ser. 1, vol. 34: 311. See also Robert D. Clark, "Bishop Matthew Simpson and the Emancipation Proclamation," *Mississippi Valley Historical Review* 35, no. 2 (September 1948): 263–71.

30. Lincoln, "Endorsement to John Hogan, February 13, 1864," in Basler, ed. *Collected Works of Abraham Lincoln* 7: 182–83. The letter is quoted in its entirety.

31. As to Lincoln's embarrassment, the commonly cited letter is his to Stanton penned on February 11, 1864: "In January 1863, the Provost-Marshal at St. Louis, having taken the control of a certain church from one set of men and given it to another, I wrote Gen. Curtis on the subject, as follows: 'the U.S. Government must not, as by this order, undertake to run the churches. When an individual, in a church or out of it, becomes dangerous to the public interest, he must be checked; but the churches, as such, must take care of themselves. It will not do for the U.S. to appoint trustees, Supervisors, or other agents for the churches.' Some trouble remaining in this same case, I, on the 22nd. of Dec. 1863, in a letter to Mr. O. D. Filley, repeated the above language; and, among other things, added 'I have never interfered, nor thought of interfering as to who shall or shall not preach in any church; nor have I knowingly, or believingly, tolerated anyone else to so interfere by my authority. If anyone is so interfering by color of my authority, I would like to have it specifically made known to me. . . . I will not have control of any church on

any side.' After having made these declarations in good faith, and in writing, you can conceive of my embarrassment at now having brought to me what purports to be a formal order of the War Department, bearing date November 30th. 1863, giving Bishop Ames control and possession of all the Methodist churches in certain Southern Military Departments, whose pastors have not been appointed by a loyal Bishop or Bishops, and ordering the Military to aid him against any resistance which may he made to his taking such possession and control. What is to be done about it? Yours truly A. Lincoln" ("To Edwin M. Stanton, February 11, 1864," in Basler, ed., *Collected Works of Abraham Lincoln* 7: 179–80).

32. "Baptists and the Civil War," 22; Rebel Presbyterian churches were likewise confiscated and placed under the direction of Unionists church leaders. See Norwood, *The Story of American Methodism,* 244. Lincoln's willingness to approve harsh policies by implication rather than declaration has been established by the likes of Mark. E. Neely Jr. In "'Unbeknownst' to Lincoln," Neely shows that Lincoln approved the most extreme elements of General Order No. 11 in Missouri and then let his generals "know he would justify radical measures under the rubric of 'military necessity' if questions arose, but he did not want to be known as the author of the plans" (216).

33. F. L. Haywood, "Our Army Correspondence, Camp of the 1st Minnesota Battery, Vicksburg, Miss., Jan. 6, 1864," *Vermont Phoenix* (Brattleboro), February 5, 1864.

34. *Official Records,* ser. 1, vol. 15: 624.

35. "Traitor Clergyman Arrested," *Daily Cleveland Herald,* August 13, 1862; Henry M. Painter, *Brief Narrative of Incidents in the War in Missouri, and of the Personal Experience of One Who Has Suffered* (Boston: Press of the Daily Courier, 1863), 9.

36. "A Methodist Preacher Imprisoned," *Daily South Carolinian* (Columbia), July 20, 1861.

37. Noel C. Fisher, *War at Every Door: Partisan Politics and Guerrilla Violence in East Tennessee* (Chapel Hill: University of North Carolina Press, 1997), 84.

38. "Anecdotes of Gen. Rousseau," *Philadelphia Inquirer,* August 8, 1862. See also Moore, ed., *The Rebellion Record,* 56.

39. "Preaching Treason," Lowell (MA) *Daily Citizen and News,* August 14, 1861.

40. Ash, *When The Yankees Came,* 57.

41. "Governor Johnson's Dealings with Disloyal Clergymen," *Vermont Chronicle* (Bellows Falls), July 8, 1862. The names "Schone" and "Lawrie" used in this article are erroneous and were in fact "Sehone" and "Saurie"; the Reverends Baldwin, Sehone, and Saurie were Methodists, while Ford and Howell were Baptists. By order of General Henry Halleck, the ministers were eventually exchanged for captured Federal troops ("Baptists and the Civil War," 16).

42. *Official Records,* ser. 2, vol. 2: 218. Stuart's ongoing omission of the prayer was reported to the government by Brigadier General W. R. Montgomery (William H. Rehnquist, *All the Laws but One: Civil Liberties in Wartime* [New York: Alfred A. Knopf, 1998], 47–48).

43. Joseph Blount Cheshire, D.D., Bishop of North Carolina, *The Church in the Confederate States: A History of the Protestant Episcopal Church in the Confederate States* (New York: Longmans, Green, and Co., 1912), 172–73; *Official Records,* ser. 2, vol. 2: 218. It is difficult to quantify the number of southern ministers who were arrested for refusing to pray for Lincoln and the Union, but my research suggests that such incidents numbered in the hundreds.

44. "Vulgar Insolence," *Christian Observer and Presbyterian Witness* (Richmond, VA), May 1, 1862. Emphasis in the original.

45. Thomas Conn Bryan, *Confederate Georgia* (Athens: University Press of Georgia, 1953), 240, rpt. in Brinsfield, *The Spirit Divided: The Confederacy*, 224–25.

46. *Official Records*, ser. 2, vol. 5: 2, 3.

47. James C. Scott, *Weapons of the Weak: Everyday Forms of Peasant Resistance* (New Haven, CT: Yale University Press, 1985), 29. The analogy between the peasantry and churchmen and women in the wartime South is not a perfect one, for white southerners were once accustomed to wielding power, unlike peasants, and southerners' obscure forms of resistance were sometimes surprisingly organized, which differs from the peasant resistance Scott chronicles. That said, the bulk of behaviors characterized by Scott as covert forms of everyday peasant resistance can be likewise attributed to pro-Confederate churchmen and women in the occupied South. Moreover, Scott argues in *Domination and the Arts of Resistance: The Hidden Transcript of Subordinate Groups* (New Haven, CT: Yale University Press, 1990) that all subordinate groups resist in ways similar to peasants.

48. Scott, *Weapons of the Weak*, 33.

49. Ibid., 29.

50. W. G. Brownlow, *Sketches of the Rise, Progress, and Decline of Secession; With a Narrative of Personal Adventures Among the Rebels* (Philadelphia: George W. Childs, 1862), 141.

51. Herman Will, "War and Peace in the Methodist Tradition," in *Freedom under Grace: Papers Presented to the Methodist History Symposium, Baker University, October 30, 31, November 1, 1984* (Baldwin, KS: Baker University, 1985), 105–38, 110.

52. Scott, *Weapons of the Weak*, 29.

53. Smith, *Cross and Flame*, 146.

54. "East Tennessee Correspondence," (Memphis) *Daily Avalanche*, April 25, 1862.

55. Ibid.

56. Edna Avery Cook, *In the Beginning—Baptists: The History of the First Baptist Church, New Bern, North Carolina, 1809–1984* (n.p., n.d.), 49, Southern Baptist Historical Library and Archives, Nashville.

57. Among the best works on southern female resistance to Federal military occupation, including the shocked Federal response to such resistance, is undoubtedly Jacqueline Glass Campbell's *When Sherman Marched North from the Sea: Resistance on the Confederate Home Front* (Chapel Hill: University of North Carolina Press, 2003). See also Elizabeth Leonard, *All the Daring of the Soldier: Women of the Civil War Armies* (New York: W. W. Norton, 1999); Nina Silber, *Gender and the Sectional Conflict* (Chapel Hill: University of North Carolina Press, 2008); LeeAnn Whites, "The Civil War as a Crisis in Gender," in *Divided Houses: Gender and the Civil War*, ed. Catherine Clinton and Nina Silber (New York: Oxford University Press, 1992); Drew Gilpin Faust has offered much on southern women during the war but has placed most of her emphasis on and drawn most of her conclusions from the actions of the elite. Moreover, the totality of Faust's work suggests that southern women hampered, and did not help, the southern war effort. See esp. Drew Gilpin Faust, *Mothers of Invention: Women of the Slaveholding South in the American Civil War* (Chapel Hill: University of North Carolina Press, 1996); Drew Gilpin Faust, "Altars of Sacrifice: Confederate Women and the Narratives of War," in *Divided Houses*, ed. Clinton and Silber, 171–99; An important recent collection on the leadership role of women in southern resistance efforts, although largely devoid of religious considerations, is LeeAnn Whites

and Alecia P. Long, eds., *Occupied Women: Gender, Military Occupation, and the American Civil War* (Baton Rouge: Louisiana State University Press, 2009).

58. Grady Fowler, *One Hundred Fifty Years of History, First Baptist Church, LaGrange, Georgia, 1828–1978* (n.p., n.d.), 36, 37, Southern Baptist Historical Library and Archives, Nashville.

59. *Official Records*, ser. 2, vol. 6: 776.

60. Frank Moore, *The Civil War in Song and Story, 1860–1865* (New York: P. F. Collier, 1889), 223, 224.

61. *Official Records*, ser. 2, vol. 5: 620–21. Judd was arrested carrying quinine, morphine, nitrate of silver, and other items used in the treatment of wounded southern soldiers.

62. The male presence at numerous southern churches during the war was often so slight that churches amended their attendance-taking procedures. Some took to recording the names of male members who were actually there, as opposed to the prewar custom of recording the names of members, male and female, who were absent. See "1862" in Elmer Oris Parker, *A History of Jones Creek Baptist Church, Long County, Georgia, 1810–1985: 175 Years of Dedication* (Ludowici, GA: The Church, 1985).

63. Silber, *Gender and the Sectional Conflict*, 61.

64. Ibid.

65. See esp. William A. Blair, *Cities of the Dead: Contesting the Memory of the Civil War in the South, 1865–1914* (Chapel Hill: University of North Carolina Press, 2004). See also Caroline E. Janney, *Burying the Dead but Not the Past: Ladies' Memorial Associations and the Lost Cause* (Chapel Hill: University of North Carolina Press, 2007).

66. Silber hints at such a link by noting how southern women's soldier's aid societies—most of which were church-based or at least church-affiliated—evolved into memoralization groups after the war (*Gender and the Sectional Conflict*, 72).

67. Scott, *Weapons of the Weak*, 38–39, 39. See also Antonio Gramsci, *Selections from the Prison Notebooks* (London: Lawrence and Wishart, 1971). Unlike Scott, Gramsci did not believe that the everyday resistance of peasants proved that they had not consented to dominance.

68. *Diary of Kate S. Carney*, May 16, 1862, 368, Southern Historical Collection, University of North Carolina, Chapel Hill, and replicated in the American Women's Diaries Series (Southern Women), Microfilm A246, Reel 19.

69. Ibid., 362.

70. Eliza Frances Andrews, *The Wartime Journal of a Georgia Girl* (New York: D. Appleton and Co., 1908), 149.

71. Qtd. in James Ford Rhodes, *History of the Civil War, 1861–1865* (New York: Macmillan Co., 1917), 391.

72. Alexander Stephens, *Recollections of Alexander H. Stephens: His Diary Kept When a Prisoner at Fort Warren, Boston Harbour, 1865: Giving Incidents and Reflections of His Prison Life and Some Letters and Reminiscences*, ed. Myrta Lockett Avary (New York: Doubleday, 1910), 326. Southern denominational newspapers found ways to continue publication during the war, adding to the negative image of Federal troops. Columbia, South Carolina's *Confederate Baptist*, for example, routinely featured stories like "Death of a Confederate Minister," in which a venerated old Rebel minister died after months of tyrannical abuse by Yankees, and his family was immediately evicted so that the Federals might commandeer their home ("Death of a Confederate Minister," *Confederate Baptist*, April 20, 1864).

73. *Official Records*, ser. 1, vol. 32: 29.

74. John W. Cook, ed., *History of the Rebellion in Bradley County, in East Tennessee* (Indianapolis: Downey and Brouse, 1866), 245, 245–56.

75. Eugene M. Wait, *The Opening of the Civil War* (Commack, NJ: Nova Science Publishing, 1999), 15.

76. Certainly all Unionists in the South, and not just preachers, were potential targets of Confederate attacks. However, ministers were especially victimized. Referencing Tennessee, but as was true throughout the Upper South, Steven V. Ash notes that "the ideological implications of the defection of the unionists, especially of those who were among the heartland's leaders, most deeply disturbed the mass of Middle Tennesseans and provoked their extreme reaction" (*Middle Tennessee Society Transformed, 1860–1870: War and Peace in the Upper South*, 2nd ed. [1988; Knoxville: University of Tennessee Press, 2006], 78–79); Ministers were routinely the most prominent leaders within southern communities. Thus David Chesebrough has said, "If the clergy and the churches played such leading roles in the sectional strife, it is little wonder that dissident clergy were looked upon, on both sides of the Mason-Dixon Line, as the ultimate traitors and thus became the recipients of harsh reprisals" (*Clergy Dissent in the Old South*, 94).

77. Unionist ministers in Confederate-held regions of the Union were likewise persecuted. See, for instance, Reverend W. M. Leftwich, *Martyrdom in Missouri: A History of Religious Proscription, the Seizure of Churches, and the Persecution of Ministers of the Gospel, in the State of Missouri During the Late Civil War and Under the "Test Oath" of the New Constitution* (St. Louis, MO: S. W. Book and Publishing Co., 1870), vol. 1.

78. A rich literature has taken shape in recent years addressing the role of kinship in the· South, and especially in the formation of Unionist ideas. For a representative work, see Victoria E. Bynum, *The Long Shadow of the Civil War: Southern Dissent and Its Legacies* (Chapel Hill: University of North Carolina Press, 2010).

79. "George Junkin to Francis McFarland, January 19, 1861," Francis McFarland Papers, Mss 053, Leyburn Library, Washington and Lee University, Lexington, Virginia. Washington College is now Washington and Lee University.

80. Robert Tracy McKenzie, "Contesting Secession: Parson Brownlow and the Rhetoric of Proslavery Unionism, 1860–1861," *Civil War History* 48, no. 4 (December 2002): 294–312, 301, 301–2.

81. Unionist preachers at odds with their members found themselves not only subject to harassment from within the church but, without the protective shield of a loyal church following, vulnerable to extra-church attacks as well. Conversely, when Federal control was firmly established in areas of the Upper South, Unionists could prove just as repressive and vindictive toward Confederate church people and ministers. See, for example, Fisher, *War at Every Door*, 84–86; Ash, *When The Yankees Came*, 57, 173.

82. Peggy Scott Holley, "Pro-Union Sentiment Among Restorationists Within the Confederacy," *Restoration Quarterly* 40, no. 2 (1998): 81–89, 83. See also David Lipscomb, "Appointment of Officers," *Gospel Advocate*, January 18, 1877.

83. Homer Pittard, *Pillar and Ground* (Murfreesboro, TN: First Baptist Church, 1968), 52, 54.

84. James M. Pendleton, *Reminiscences of a Long Life* (Louisville, KY: Press Baptist Book Concern, 1891), 122; Homer Pittard, *Pillar and Ground* (Murfreesboro, TN: First Baptist Church, Murfreesboro, Tennessee, 1968), 54.

85. Nancy J. Siler, *The First Baptist Church of Knoxville, Tennessee, 1843–1993: Proud Past . . . Dedicated Present . . . Looking to the Future* (Knoxville, TN: First Baptist Church, 1992), 18.

86. Ibid., 18. See also Lucile Deadrick, *The Heart of the Valley: A History of Knoxville, Tennessee* (Knoxville: East Tennessee Historical Society, 1976), 40.

87. W. Harrison Daniel, *Southern Protestantism in the Confederacy* (Bedford, VA: Print Shop, 1989), 43; Chesebrough, *Clergy Dissent in the Old South*, 66.

88. Chesebrough, *Clergy Dissent in the Old South*, 66.

89. Edith Wilson Hutton, *A Promise of Good Things: Longfield Baptist Church, 1831–1981* [Lake City, TN] (Oak Ridge, TN: Adroit, Inc., 1982), 109.

90. See, for example, Ash, *When The Yankees Came;* John C. Inscoe and Gordon B. McKinney, *The Heart of Confederate Appalachia: Western North Carolina in the Civil War* (Chapel Hill: University of North Carolina Press, 2000).

91. John Inscoe, "Introduction," in *Enemies of the Country: New Perspectives on Unionists in the Civil War South,* ed. John C. Inscoe and Robert C. Kenzer (Athens: University of Georgia Press, 2001), 1–17, 2.

92. Betty-Jo Dawkins, *A History of the Church: Columbia Baptist Church, Falls Creek, Virginia, 1856–1981* (Falls Church, VA: Columbia Baptist Church, n.d.), 15.

93. "Josiah J. Cowles to Calvin Cowles, September 12, 1863," Cowles Papers, North Carolina Department of Archives and History, rpt. in Inscoe and McKinney, *The Heart of Confederate Appalachia*, 98.

94. See Hutton, *A Promise of Good Things*, 120.

95. "Christian Chapel Church (Henderson County, TN)," unpublished, rpt. in Holley, "Pro-Union Sentiment Among Restorationists Within the Confederacy," 81–89, 83.

96. Hutton, *A Promise of Good Things*, 120. Through the issuance of licenses and permits and often contingent upon oaths of allegiances, Federal authorities likewise often limited to Unionists the privilege of performing such public ceremonies as weddings and funerals. See Ash, *Middle Tennessee Society Transformed*, 101.

97. Chesebrough, *Clergy Dissent in the Old South*, 66.

98. M. Shannon Mallard, "'I Had No Comfort to Give the People': Opposition to the Confederacy in Civil War Mississippi." *North and South: The Official Magazine of the Civil War Society* 6, no. 4 (May 2003): 78–86, cited in Sally Jenkins and John Stauffer, *The State of Jones* (New York: Doubleday, 2009), 78.

99. Chesebrough, *Clergy Dissent in the Old South*, 67.

100. John H. Aughey, Benjamin Clarke, and John Robinson, "Letter to Hon. William H. Seward, Central Military Prison, Tupelo, Ittawamba Co., Mississippi, July 11th, 1862," in Rev. John H. Aughey, *The Iron Furnace: Or, Slavery and Secession. By Rev. John H. Aughey, A Refugee from Mississippi* (Philadelphia: William S. and Alfred Martin, 1863), 136–39, 137.

101. "Rebel Barbarities in East Tennessee," *Daily Cleveland* (Ohio) *Herald*, November 24, 1863.

102. Richard B. McCaslin, *Tainted Breeze: The Great Hanging at Gainesville, Texas, 1862* (Baton Rouge: Louisiana State University Press, 1994), 87, 117; Holley, "Pro-Union Sentiment Among Restorationists Within the Confederacy," 81–89, 87. There was at least one other minister among the 150 or so Unionists arrested, but he was not hanged.

103. Chesebrough, *Clergy Dissent in the Old South*, 79.

104. Jon L. Wakelyn, *Southern Unionist Pamphlets and the Civil War* (Columbia: University of Missouri Press, 1999), 116.

105. W. Harrison Daniel, "Protestant Clergy and Union Sentiment in the Confederacy," *Tennessee Historical Quarterly* 23 (September 1964): 284–90.

106. "Sidney L. Jackman Memoirs," #45–46, Arkansas History Collection, Manuscript Collection no. 613, University of Arkansas at Fayetteville, rpt. in Robert R. Mackey, *The Uncivil War: Irregular Warfare in the Upper South, 1861–1865* (Norman: University of Oklahoma Press, 2004), 42–43.

107. Victorian Society at Falls Church, *Images of America: Victorian Falls Church* (Mt. Pleasant, SC: Arcadia Publishing, 2007), 31.

108. *Official Records*, ser. 3, vol. 40, pt. 2: 415.

109. Qtd. in Walter E. Bass, *A History of the Pastors: Columbia Baptist Church, Falls Creek, Virginia, 1856–1981* (Falls Church, VA: Columbia Baptist Church, n.d.), 328, 327.

110. Victorian Society at Falls Church, *Images of America*, 31.

111. The element of contingency must never be ignored, and southern Confederate ministers even in the heart of the slave South could have recognized the evils of slavery and the folly of secession. See esp. Chesebrough, *Clergy Dissent in the Old South.*

8. BLACK CHURCH LEADERS AND POLITICS IN THE CIVIL WAR

1. See, for example, James H. Cone, *Black Theology and Black Power* (Maryknoll, NY: 1997); and Charles V. Hamilton, *The Black Preacher in America* (New York: Morrow, 1972). Most who have written on religion or ministerial behavior during the Civil War years have looked at either black or white preachers, but not both.

2. For an important recent work on black ministers and the antebellum freedom struggle, see Richard S. Newman, *Freedom's Prophet: Bishop Richard Allen, the AME Church, and the Black Founding Fathers* (New York: New York University Press, 2008). See also Benjamin Quarles, *Black Abolitionists* (New York: Da Capo Press, 1991); Gayraud S. Wilmore, *Black Religion and Black Radicalism: An Interpretation of the Religious History of Afro-American People* (Maryknoll, NY: Orbis Book, 1998).

3. Hahn, *A Nation under Our Feet*, 3; Others have recognized the ongoing role that family and labor autonomy played in the lives of post-emancipation African Americans but have not made that role the lynchpin of their efforts. See for example Aaron Sheehan-Dean's well-done "A Fearful Lesson: The Legacy of the American Civil War," in *Struggle for a Vast Freedom*, ed. Sheehan-Dean (Oxford, UK: Osprey Publishing, 2006), 237–53, 238–39.

4. An earlier generation of scholars not only implied the passivity of black ministers during the Civil War but openly argued as much. See William H. Becker, "The Black Church: Manhood and Mission," in Timothy E. Fulop and Albert J. Raboteau, eds., *African-American Religion: Interpretive Essays in History and Culture* (New York: Routledge, 1997), 177–210. Becker identifies E. Franklin Frazier and Benjamin Mays as progenitors of this "classic" interpretation that presents black ministers as passive. See E. Franklin Frazier, *The Negro Church in America* (New York: Schocken Books, 1965); and Melville J. Herskovits, *The Myth of the Negro Past* (Boston: Beacon Press, 1958).

5. Although no longer the norm, past historians who examined the ways in which black and white clerics of the period were comparable routinely did so without acknowledging black ministerial initiative in any real way. Joel Williamson, for example, argued that black preachers were like white preachers, if in form and fashion only, because "the most distinctive trait of the black man's religion was its emulation of the white ideal" (*After Slavery: The Negro in South Carolina during Reconstruction, 1861–1877* [Chapel Hill: University of North Carolina Press, 1965], 201). The real story is not one of emulation but of cultural diffusion. As John Boles has correctly observed, the impact of white values and practices was more apparent in black religious services than in any other aspect of post-emancipation African American cultural life, but such does not mean that African Americans copied or imitated white Christians per se or that white religion was not similarly informed by black practices (*Black Southerners, 1619–1869* [Lexington: University Press of Kentucky, 1984], esp. 165). For more on the wartime differences between black and white ministers, see Stowell, *Rebuilding Zion*, 68; Leon Litwack, *North of Slavery: The Negro in the Free States, 1790–1960* (Chicago: University of Chicago Press, 1961), esp. 187–213, "The Church and the Negro"; David E. Swift, *Black Prophets of Justice: Activist Clergy Before the Civil War* (Baton Rouge: Louisiana State University Press, 1989); and Wilmore, *Black Religion and Black Radicalism*.

6. See Stephen Tuck, *We Ain't What We Ought to Be: The Black Freedom Struggle from Emancipation to Obama* (Cambridge, MA: Harvard University Press, 2010), esp. 11–36, "The Freedom War 1861–1865."

7. The AME Zion Church was first among mainstream black traditions to ordain women, in 1894. The AME Church did not ordain women until the twentieth century, although numerous resolutions were proposed and rejected within and by the church between 1844 and the twentieth century, and Bishop Henry McNeal Turner ordained a female deacon in 1885, only to see her ordination overturned by the General Conference in 1888. See Rev. Sandra E. H. Smith Blair, *Her-Story of Women in Ministry African Methodism*, August 7, 2007 ("Women in Ministry, African Methodist Episcopal Church, Second Episcopal District," www.sedwim.org).

8. Kevin Kelly Gaines, *Uplifting the Black Race: Black Leadership, Politics, and Culture in the Twentieth Century* (Chapel Hill: University of North Carolina Press, 1997), 2.

9. See William H. Brackney, *Baptists in North America: An Historical Perspective* (Malden, MA: Blackwell Publishing, 2006), 185–91; Albert A. Avant Jr., *The Social Teachings of the Progressive National Baptist Convention, Inc., Since 1961: A Critical Analysis of the Least, the Lost, and the Left-Out* (New York: Routledge, 2003); Wilbur C. Rich, *African American Perspectives on Political Science* (Philadelphia: Temple University Press, 2007), 154; David H. Jackson, *Booker T. Washington and the Struggle Against White Supremacy: The Southern Educational Tours, 1908–1912* (New York: Palgrave Macmillan, 2008).

10. For a solid treatment of the subject that casts racial uplift as a response to scientific racism, see Jacqueline M. Moore, *Booker T. Washington, W. E. B. DuBois, and the Struggle for Racial Uplift* (Wilmington: Delaware Scholarly Resources, 2003).

11. Anne-Elizabeth Murdy, *Teach the Nation: Pedagogies of Racial Uplift in U.S. Women's Writing of the 1890s* (New York: Routledge, 2003); Marlon Bryan Ross, *Manning the Race: Reforming Black Men in the Jim Crow Era* (New York: New York University Press, 2004). Scholarly considerations of white-sponsored black improvement efforts are warranted as well. For white members of

liberal church groups in antebellum America, the claim that black people were inferior but improvable carried a mandate to work toward their betterment but did not suggest the reformers' own limitations. See *Minutes of the Adjourned Session of the Twentieth Biennial American Convention for Promoting the Abolition of Slavery and Improving the Condition of the African Race, Held at Baltimore, Nov. 1828*, in Jacqueline Bacon, *Freedom's Journal: The First African American Newspaper* (Lanham, MD: Rowman and Littlefield, 2007), 102. The opinion of black potential most often heard in the white South was clearly (if disturbingly) enunciated by Thomas Jefferson. For Jefferson's views on the supposed mental and physical inferiority of black people as a fact of nature, see his *Notes on the State of Virginia* (Richmond, VA: J. W. Randolph, 1853), 138–42.

12. Jacqueline Bacon and Frankie Hutton, for example, highlight the ways in which the late-antebellum free-black press promoted temperance, education, and debt avoidance in the hopes of empowering African Americans (Bacon, *Freedom's Journal*, 99–120; Frankie Hutton, *The Early Black Press in America, 1827 to 1860* [Westport, CT: Greenwood Publishing Group, 1993]). Craig Wilder argues that prewar African Americans' Afro-centric rhetoric challenged the societal conflation of virtue and whiteness and therefore demonstrated a connection with a "West African legacy" of morality even as it facilitated social work within the antebellum black community (*In the Company of Black Men: The African Influence on African American Culture in New York City* [New York: New York University Press, 2001], 88). For more on pan-African identification, see Patrick Rael, *Black Identity and Black Protest in the Antebellum North* (Chapel Hill: University of North Carolina Press, 2002), 14–15. Samuel Roberts shows that virtue and its pursuits allowed antebellum African Americans to "maintain a credible identity despite racist attempts to trivialize, demean, and deny the full humanity of black people" (*In the Path of Virtue: The African American Moral Tradition* [Cleveland, OH: Pilgrim Press, 1999], 118). Finally, Leslie Alexander details the ways in which African Americans in antebellum New York City struggled to reconcile their increasingly African identity (achieved via mutual relief, religious, and political associations that were infused with African cultural traditions and values) with moral improvement campaigns and the desire to be fully "American" (*African or American: Black Identity and Political Activism in New York City, 1784–1861* [Urbana: University of Illinois Press, 2008]).

13. On the prewar and wartime development of uplift terminology, see James Brewer Stewart, *Abolitionist Politics and the Coming of the Civil War* (Amherst: University of Massachusetts Press, 2008), 20–21, 39–40, 48, 74–77, 175, 194, 214–15. The term "uplift" was not always expressed as a formal theory during the prewar and wartime eras, as when a prewar African American leader advocated the establishment of newspapers "able to counsel and uplift the African Race generally" (*Frederick Douglass' Paper*, May 13, 1853) or an early postwar commentator lauded "the efforts philanthropists and others are making to educate and uplift the Freedmen" ("Concert Hall," *Christian Recorder*, March 3, 1866). During the Civil War, ministers used the terms "uplift," "improvement," "progress," "self-help," and "elevation" interchangeably.

14. "First Annual Report of the General Agent of the Board of National Popular Education, With the Constitution of the Board," *North Star*, March 10, 1848. The *North Star* was renamed *Frederick Douglass' Paper* after merging with the *Liberty Party Paper* in 1851; it was renamed again in 1858, becoming *Douglass' Monthly*, and would remain thus until it ceased publication in 1863.

15. Gaines, *Uplifting the Black Race*, 22–23.

16. See Howard Holman, ed., *Minutes of the Proceedings of the National Negro Conventions, 1830–1864* (New York: Arno Press, 1969).

17. Clifton H. Johnson, "The Negro Convention Movement before the Civil War," *The Crisis* 77, no. 10 (December 1970): 397–99, 398–99.

18. Rael, *Black Identity and Black Protest*, 175, 14–15.

19. *Christian Recorder*, April 9, 1864.

20. Rael, *Black Identity and Black Protest*, 283. Kenneth Stamp famously reduced slave preachers who counseled virtue, piety, and general self-betterment but eschewed messages of rebellion and resistance to quislings interested in doing the white man's bidding (*The Peculiar Institution: Slavery in the Ante-Bellum South* [New York: Knopf, 1956]). Ronny Turner indicted southern free and slave ministers alike, writing that in the prewar South the black pastor was routinely little more than "a pawn controlled by the whims of white slaveowners" ("The Black Minister: Uncle Tom or Abolitionist," *Phylon* 34, no. 1 [Spring 1973]: 86–95; 86).

21. "On the one hand," Wheeler writes, "uplift meant accommodation and surrender" to white hegemony, but "on the other, uplift was a denial of what white society meant by accommodation, for it spoke of a possibility to move beyond the limits prescribed by the dominant society" (Edward L. Wheeler, *Uplifting the Race: The Black Minister in the New South, 1865–1902* [Lanham, MD: University Press of America, 1986], xvii, xiii).

22. Reginald F. Hildebrand, *The Times Were Strange and Stirring: Methodist Preachers and the Crisis of Emancipation* (Durham, NC: Duke University Press, 1995), 101. Hildebrand quotes from the *Annual Report of the Missionary Society of the Methodist Episcopal Church: Forty-Seventh, 1865*, 138.

23. Colored Citizens of Norfolk, *Equal Suffrage. Address from the Colored Citizens of Norfolk, Va., to the People of the United States. Also an Account of the Agitation Among the Colored People of Virginia for Equal Rights. With an Appendix Concerning the Rights of the Colored Witnesses Before the State Courts* (New Bedford, MA: E. Anthony and Sons, 1865).

24. Qtd. in Tuck, *We Ain't What We Ought to Be*, 32.

25. Ibid.

26. *Christian Recorder*, March 25, 1865.

27. Reverend Samuel Harrison, *Shall a Nation Be Born at Once? A Centennial Sermon Delivered in the Chapel of the Methodist Episcopal Church, July 2, 1876* (Pittsfield, MA: Chickering and Axtell, Steam Book and Job Printers, 1876), 24–25, African American Pamphlet Collection, Library of Congress.

28. *The Anglo-African*, August 15, 1863. See also Patricia L. Richard, *Busy Hands: Images of the Family in the Northern Civil War Effort* (New York: Fordham University Press, 2003), 82 n. 29.

29. Gayle T. Tate, "Free Black Resistance in the Antebellum Era, 1830 to 1860," *Journal of Black Studies* 28, no. 6 (July 1998): 764–82, 772.

30. "What Shall Be Done with the Slaves if Emancipated," *Friends Review: A Religious, Literary and Miscellaneous Journal*, February 1, 1862.

31. W. Wells Brown, *The Rising Son; or, The Antecedent and Advancement of the Colored Race* (Boston: A. G. Brown and Co., 1873), 414.

32. For an insightful discussion of the postwar black church as a nexus of political activism, see especially William Montgomery, *Under Their Own Vine and Fig Tree: The African-American Church in the South, 1865–1900* (Baton Rouge: Louisiana State University Press, 1993).

33. For but a few examples, see the *Christian Recorder,* "Woman's Work," August 24, 1861; "Tobacco," November 1, 1861; "The Genesee Annual Conference," September 27, 1862; "Notice: Public Temperance Meeting Will Be Held Every Wednesday, at 7 1/2 o'clock, In the Mission School-House, St. Mary's St. Below 7th, For the Elevation of the Colored Population, and the Promotion of this Good Work," November 12, 1864.

34. *Christian Recorder,* March 4, 1865; Montgomery, *Under Their Own Vine and Fig Tree,* 287.

35. Rev. Edward MacKnight Brawley, "Is the Young Negro an Improvement, Morally, on His Father?" in Daniel Wallace Culp, ed., *Twentieth Century Negro Literature* (Naperville, IL: J. L. Nichols and Co., 1902), 254–56, 255.

36. Ira Berlin, *Cultivation and Culture: Labor and the Shaping of Slave Life in the Americas* (Charlottesville: University of Virginia Press, 1993); Jeff Forret, *Race Relations at the Margins: Slaves and Poor Whites in the Antebellum Southern Countryside* (Baton Rouge: Louisiana State University Press, 2006).

37. James T. Campbell, *Songs of Zion: The African Methodist Episcopal Church in the United States and Africa* (Chapel Hill: University of North Carolina Press, 1998), 55.

38. *Address by a Committee of Norfolk Blacks, June 26, 1865,* rpt. in C. Peter Ripley et al., eds., *The Black Abolitionist Papers,* vol. 5: *The United States, 1859–1865* (Chapel Hill: University of North Carolina Press, 1985), 334–49, 341. All but one of the eight members was a preacher, and Presbyterian legend H. Highland Garnet was an "honorary member" of the committee.

39. Noralee Frankel, *Freedom's Women: Black Women in Civil War Era Mississippi* (Bloomington: Indiana University Press, 1999), 85. This of course did not happen where church officials were absent. Freedmen's Bureau agents bemoaned the absence of religious officials in a given area and the corresponding high numbers of "took-up" unions (or concubinage, as most white soldiers in the South would have then named such relationships), 92.

40. See Frankel, *Freedom's Women;* Amy Dru Stanley, *From Bondage to Contract: Wage Labor, Marriage, and the Market in the Age of Slave Emancipation* (New York: Cambridge University Press, 1998); Stephanie McCurry, "War, Gender, and Emancipation," in *Lincoln's Proclamation,* ed. Blair and Younger ,120–50.

41. "Matrimonial Happiness," *Christian Recorder,* July 9, 1864; Rebekah L. Miles, *The Bonds of Freedom: Feminist Theology and Christian Realism* (New York: Oxford University Press, 2001), 47. See Ephesians 5:23–32 for the scripture most often cited by advocates of male household authority.

42. "Matrimonial Happiness," *Christian Recorder,* July 9, 1864; Stanley, *From Bondage to Contract,* 49.

43. "The President and the Members of the National Theological Institute For Colored Ministers," *Daily National Intelligencer* (Washington, DC), May 13, 1865. Organized by the Baptist Rev. Edmund Turney earlier in 1865, the National Theological Institute for Colored Ministers (headquartered in Washington, DC) was dedicated to the task of training and educating southern-born ministers and freedmen.

44. Louis B. Gates Jr., ed., *Lincoln on Race and Slavery* (Princeton, NJ: Princeton University Press, 2009), 235; Ripley, *The Black Abolitionist Papers* 5: 155.

45. This "Gospel of Manhood" was particularly associated with African Methodist Episcopalism and the much smaller African Methodist Episcopal Zionism, Northern traditions

synonymous with black independence and black nationalism. James T. Campbell writes that during the Civil War the AME Church had a "virtual obsession with racial manhood" (*Songs of Zion,* 51).

46. Such despairingly sexist views, characteristic of twentieth-century black religious and nationalist leaders like Malcolm X ("Since the time of Adam and Eve in the Garden, woman has led men into evil and the one she was created to serve became her slave"), Maulana Ron Karenga ("What makes a woman appealing is femininity, and she can't be feminine without being submissive"), and Imiri Baraka (LeRoi Jones; black women must be taught "submitting to [their] natural roles"), to name but a few, were largely absent in religiously connected manhood rhetoric before the end of Reconstruction. See Demetrius K. William, *An End to This Strife: The Politics of Gender in African American Churches* (Minneapolis: Fortress Press, 2004), 121, 119–22; "Appeal to the Colored People of State of Pennsylvania," *Christian Recorder,* December 24, 1864.

47. Campbell, *Songs of Zion,* 51. See also Bishop W. J. Gaines, D.D., *The Negro and the White Man* (Philadelphia: A.M.E. Publishing House, 1897), 24, 26–28, 163–66.

48. Bishop Daniel A. Payne, *A History of the A.M.E. Church,* vol. 1: *1816–1856* (Nashville: A.M.E. Sunday School Union, 1891), 9–10.

49. Dudley Taylor Cornish, *The Sable Arm: Black Troops in the Union Army, 1861–1865* (Lawrence: University of Kansas Press, 1956), 291. See especially "even the slave becomes a man," 261–91; Daniel P. Black, *Dismantling Black Manhood: An Historical and Literary Analysis of the Legacy of Slavery* (New York: Routledge, 1997), 137–74.

50. "The Work to be Done," *The Liberator,* April 3, 1863.

51. "Capacity of the Negro," *Christian Advocate and Journal,* July 18, 1861.

52. "The Colored Race in America. By New Contributors," *Christian Recorder,* March 14, 1863.

53. "The Capabilities of Our Race," *Christian Recorder,* May 21, 1864.

54. Qtd. in Joseph T. Glatthaar, "Black Glory: The African American Role in Union Victory," Michael Perman, ed., *Major Problems in the Civil War and Reconstruction* (New York: Houghton Mifflin, 1998), 307–8.

55. Qtd. in Glatthaar, "Black Glory," 305.

56. Bacon, *Freedom's Journal,* 129.

57. "Art. V.—The War" (Unitarian) *Christian Examiner* 71, no. 1 (July 1861): 95–116, 112.

58. "Mr. Editor," *Christian Examiner,* July 16, 1864.

59. Ibid.

60. See Wilder, *In the Company of Black Men,* 94.

61. Qtd. in Leon Litwack, *Been in the Storm So Long: The Aftermath of Slavery* (New York: Vintage Books, 1980), 485.

62. Qtd. in Edward F. Sweat, "Francis L. Cardoza—Profile of Integrity in Reconstruction Politics," *Journal of Negro History* 46, no. 4 (October 1961), 217–32, 219.

63. See for instance Floyd Miller, "The Father of Black Nationalism: Another Contender," in *Civil War History* 17, no. 4 (December 1971): 310–19.

64. Robert A. Warner, "Amos Gerry Beman—1812–1874, A Memoir on a Forgotten Leader," *Journal of Negro History* 22, no. 2 (April 1937): 200–220; 214, 210. Beman predicted the wartime opinion of New England educators. "Let the benign influence of Christian Education . . . diffuse

among both races the intelligence which shall uplift the one and meliorate the disposition of the other," a white Massachusetts educator wrote in 1864, "and a new order of civil and social life will be inaugurated" ("The Educational Future of Our Southern States," *Massachusetts Teacher and Journal of Home and School Education*, September 1861).

65. See Jessica Enoch, *Refiguring Rhetorical Education: Women Teaching African American, Native American, and Chicano/a Students, 1865–1911* (Carbondale: Southern Illinois University Press, 2008).

66. Paul Alan Cimbala, *The Freedmen's Bureau: Reconstructing the American South after the Civil War* (Malabar, FL: Krieger, 2005), 83; Foner, *Reconstruction*, 66.

67. "Looking After Themselves," *Friends Review; a Religious, Literary and Miscellaneous Journal*, March 4, 1865.

68. Philip S. Foner and George E. Walker, eds., *Proceedings of the Black National and State Conventions, 1865–1900* (Philadelphia: Temple University Press, 1986), 115–29.

69. "State Convention of the Colored Men of Tennessee, Nashville, August 7, 1865." In Foner and Walker, eds., *Proceedings of the Black National and State Conventions, 1865–1900*, 120.

70. "Pertinent Colored News," *Daily Evening Bulletin* (San Francisco), February 7, 1862.

71. Laurence C. Glasco, ed., *The WPA History of the Negro in Pittsburgh* (Pittsburgh: University of Pittsburgh Press, 2004), 232.

72. Ellen N. Lawson and Marlene Merrill, "The Antebellum 'Talented Thousandth': Black College Students at Oberlin Before the Civil War," in *Journal of Negro Education* 52, no. 2 (Spring 1983), 142–55, 150.

73. William J. Switala, *The Underground Railroad in Pennsylvania* (Mechanicsburg, PA: Stackpole Books, 2001), 86.

74. "The Freedmen of the South: A Colored Bishop's Experience Among the Freedmen— Account of a Tour Through the South—The Condition of the Freedmen," *New York Times*, September 1, 1865.

75. They were Allen in South Carolina, Campbell in Mississippi, Edward Waters in Florida, Kittrell in North Carolina, Lampton (later merged with Campbell) in Louisiana, Morris Brown in Georgia, Payne in Alabama, Shorter in Arkansas, and Western in Kansas (Richard W. Wright, *The Encyclopedia of the African Methodist Episcopal Church* [Philadelphia: Book Concern of the AME Church, 1947], 12).

76. Among African Americans there was little distinction made between political and appropriately religious preaching, slavery was of course an absolute evil, the Federal government was considered justified in anything it did to defeat the Rebels and end slavery, and the war was a prophesied event that would lead African Americans as a people into a new age of liberty and freedom. Although any number of books might be cited to establish how African Americans perceived the war and its key issues, see particularly John Hope Franklin and Alfred A. Moss, *From Slavery to Freedom: A History of African Americans* (New York: Knopf, 1994).

77. Stout, *Upon the Altar of the Nation*, xvii.

78. For more on the collectivity of black faith, see Mary Pattillo-McCoy, "Church Culture as a Strategy of Action in the Black Community," *American Sociology Review* 63, no. 6 (December 1998): 764–84.

79. See, for instance, Campbell, *Songs of Zion*; and Hildebrand, *The Times Were Strange and*

Stirring. The same is far less true of white clerics of the age because so many more of their secular contemporaries were literate and thus recorded the actions, words, and sermons of ministers. Moreover, white preachers were much more likely to appear in the secular press, especially as they became embroiled in political issues like abolitionism and secession.

80. The AME's *Christian Recorder* was foremost among such papers. Other important wartime papers include the *Anglo-African Magazine* (New York, 1859–65), *Douglass' Monthly* (Rochester, 1858–63), *Mirror of the Times* (San Francisco, 1857–62), and the *Weekly Anglo-African* (New York, 1859–61).

81. Anthony E. Kaye, *Joining Places: Slave Neighborhoods in the Old South* (Chapel Hill: University of North Carolina Press, 2007).

82. Rael, *Black Identity and Black Protest,* 8, 283.

83. Rita Roberts, "Book Review: Black Identity and Black Protest in the Antebellum North," *Journal of Southern History* 69, no. 4 (March 2003): 902–3, 902.

84. Blair, *Cities of the Dead.*

85. David W. Blight, *Race and Reunion: The Civil War in American Memory* (Cambridge, MA: Harvard University Press, 2001), 324.

86. By 1861 there were some 500,000 free black men and women in the United States, just under half in the free states and just over half in slave states. With more than four million Americans enslaved, that meant that free African Americans represented about 9 percent of all black Americans and 2 percent of all Americans (*Statistics of the United States . . . Eighth Census*). This chapter's discussion of the AME Church includes members of the related African Methodist Episcopal Zion Church as well, and it should be assumed that any characteristic of the AME clergy is applicable to AMEZ preachers. The differences between the AME and AMEZ churches of the period in terms of theology and politics were minute. The differences in memberships before the Civil War were pronounced. There were only 4,600 AMEZ members in all of America when the Civil War began, and just over 100 AMEZ preachers (there were over 50,000 members of the AME Church). See Charles Eric Lincoln, *The Black Church in the African-American Experience* (Durham, NC: Duke University Press, 1990), 58; and Campbell, *Songs of Zion,* 32.

87. Hildebrand, *The Times Were Strange and Stirring,* 33.

88. James W. Hood, *One Hundred Years of the African Methodist Episcopal Zion Church* (New York: A.M.E. Zion Book Concern, 1895), 55; Wilmore, *Black Religion and Black Radicalism,* 167. For more on the nationalism and pan-Africanism of the AME Church, see Dennis C. Dickerson, *A Liberated Past: Explorations in AME Church History* (Nashville: AMEC Sunday School Union, 2003).

89. Clarence E. Walker, *A Rock in a Weary Land: The African Methodist Episcopal Church during the Civil War and Reconstruction* (Baton Rouge: Louisiana State University Press, 1982). On the difficulties experienced by other groups, see Finke and Stark, *The Churching of America,* 156–234; For an example of a more focused look at the trend, see Gardiner H. Shattuck, *Episcopalians and Race: Civil War to Civil Rights* (Lexington: University Press of Kentucky, 2003).

90. Wilmore, *Black Religion and Black Radicalism,* 125.

91. John Wesley Gaines, *African Methodism in the South; or Twenty-Five Years of Freedom* (Atlanta: Franklin Publishing House, 1890), 18.

92. See Ira Berlin, *Slaves without Masters: The Free Negro in the Antebellum South* (New York: New Press, 1974); Donald Lee Grant, *The Way It Was in the South: The Black Experience in Georgia* (Athens: University of Georgia Press, 2001), 268–69.

93. Frederick C. Harris, *Something Within: Religion in African-American Political Activism* (New York: Oxford University Press, 1999); Michael Dawson, *Behind the Mule: Race and Class in African-American Politics* (Princeton, NJ: Princeton University Press, 1994), 99–100; Kwando Mbiassi Kinshasa, *African American Chronology: Chronologies of the American Mosaic* (Westport, CT: Greenwood Pres, 2006), 41; Walker, *A Rock in a Weary Land*; Pattillo-McCoy, "Church Culture as a Strategy of Action in the Black Community"; Grant, *The Way It Was in the South*.

94. Mark E. Neely, "Colonization," in *Lincoln's Proclamation*, ed. Blair and Younger, 45–74, 53.

95. Kate Masur, "The African American Delegation to Abraham Lincoln: A Reappraisal," *Civil War History* 56, no. 2 (June 2010): 117–44, 119.

96. "Rev. Joshua Leavitt D.D.—A Pervert," *Weekly Anglo-African*, April 12, 1862.

97. Wilson Jeremiah Moses, *Alexander Crummell: A Study of Civilization and Discontent* (New York: Oxford University Press, 1989) 143–45.

98. Ibid., 144.

99. "The Future of the Colored Race in America," *Christian Recorder*, September 13, 1862. Emphasis in the original.

100. "Africa and Africans," *The African Repository, Published Monthly by the American Colonization Society* (Washington: William H. Moore, Printer), January 1862.

101. "Washington Correspondence," *Christian Recorder*, December 6, 1862, rpt. in Masur, "The African American Delegation," 28. Emphasis in the original.

102. *Christian Recorder*, November 8, 1862.

103. Moses, *Alexander Crummell*, 145.

104. *The African Repository* 39 (1863): 322. See also "The Future of the Negro Population," in *De Bow's Review Devoted to the Restoration of the Southern States* (Nashville) (1866): 59–67 63.

105. "Colored Men Petitioning to Be Colonized," *Douglass' Monthly*, May 1862, 642, rpt. in Masur, "The African American Delegation," 8. As noted earlier, the newspaper edited by Douglass was called, by turns, the *North Star* (1847–51), *Frederick Douglass' Paper* (1851–58), and *Douglass' Monthly* (1858–63).

106. The Reverend John W. Hood (AME Zion), "Gentlemen of the Convention," October 3, 1865, in Sidney Andrews, *The South since the War* (1866; rpt. Baton Rouge: Louisiana State University Press, 2004), 58–59.

107. Glatthaar, "Black Glory," 308, 310.

108. Robert F. Cason, "The Loyal League in Georgia," in *Georgia Historical Quarterly* 20 (June 1936): 137, rpt. in James Alex Baggett, *The Scalawags: Southern Dissenters in the Civil War and Reconstruction* (Baton Rouge: Louisiana State University Press, 2003), 170.

109. "The Way Negro Troops are Raised in Maryland," *Ripley* (Ohio) *Bee*, March 17, 1864.

110. "Indianapolis Correspondence," *Christian Recorder*, December 12, 1863.

111. Lincoln understood that Protestantism "did more than any other single force to mobilize support for the war," and thus knew also that black ministers were integral to black recruitment. See Carwardine, *Lincoln*, 281.

112. Cornish, *The Sable Arm;* James M. McPherson, *The Negro's Civil War: How American Blacks Felt and Acted during the War for the Union* (New York: Balantine Books, 1965).

113. See Glatthaar, "Black Glory"; Hondon B. Hargrove, *Black Union Soldiers in the Civil War* (Jefferson, NC: McFarland Press, 2003); Noah Andre Trudeau, *Like Men of War: Black Troops in the Civil War* (Edison, NJ: Castle Books, 1998); Edwin S. Redkey, "Henry McNeal Turner: Black Chaplain in the Union Army," in John David Smith, ed., *Black Soldiers in Blue: African American Troops in the Civil War Era* (Chapel Hill: University of North Carolina Press, 2002), 336–60.

114. The debate was philosophical of course until the passage on July 17, 1862, of the Second Confiscation and Militia Act.

115. *Christian Recorder,* July 27, 1861.

116. Ibid., April 27, 1861.

117. Ibid., September 14, 1861.

118. Herbert Aptheker, *A Documentary History of the Negro People in the United States* (New York: Citadel Press, 1951), vol. 1: 525.

119. *Christian Recorder,* April 27, 1861. Emphasis in the original.

120. Ibid., October 12, 1861. Campbell's letter is discussed in detail in Walker's *A Rock in a Weary Land,* 33–35.

121. "Colored Soldiers and the Government," *Christian Recorder,* February 27, 1864.

122. Ira Berlin et al., *Freedom's Soldiers: The Black Military Experience in the Civil War* (Cambridge, U.K.: Cambridge University Press, 1998), 30.

123. "The President's Call for Five Hundred Thousand More Troops," *Christian Recorder,* July 23, 1864.

124. Bishop Daniel Alexander Payne, *Recollections of Seventy Years . . .* (Nashville: Publishing House of the A.M.E. Sunday School Union, 1888), 147.

125. David Stephen Heidler et al., *Encyclopedia of the American Civil War: A Political, Social, and Military History* (New York: W. W. Norton and Co., 2000), 1144–45. The National Equal Rights League was one of the earliest national civil rights organizations dedicated to securing full and complete African American equality before the law and protecting the citizenship of all Americans at the federal level. See Nikki Marie Taylor, *Frontiers of Freedom: Cincinnati's Black Community, 1802–1869* (Athens: Ohio University Press, 2005), 184.

126. Messianic groups are those founded by charismatic individuals revered by their followers as messiahs who will *personally* lead African Americans to deliverance. Thaumaturgic religions stress rituals as holy entities in and of themselves (rather than being symbolic actions) and combine elements of spiritualism and mysticism with Protestantism or Catholicism. For instance, in some forms of Voodoo-influenced spiritualism, the ritualistic burning of candles itself is thought to *obtain* an ultimate salvation (after a cycle of incarnations) and not merely represent that salvation.

EPILOGUE

1. Samuel David McConnell, *History of the Episcopal Church from the Planting of the Colonies to the End of the Civil War* (New York: J. J. Little and Co., 1891), 373.

2. Ibid., 375.

3. Julia Huston Nguyen, "Churches," in Lisa Tendrich Frank, ed., *Women in the American Civil War* (Santa Barbara, CA: ABC-CLIO, 2008), 168–70, 170.

4. In November 1918, the United Lutheran Church in America was created by the merging of the constituent synods of the old General Synod, the General Council, and the United Synod in the South (Heathcote, *The Lutheran Church and the Civil War*, 10, 127–49).

5. "Methodists," in *The American Annual Cyclopaedia and Register of Important Events of the Year 1866, Embracing Political, Civil, Military, and Social Affairs; Public Documents; Biography, Statistics, Commerce, Finance, Literature, Science, Agriculture, and Mechanical Industry* (New York: D. Appleton and Co., 1873), vol. 1: 488–92. In 1846, members of the Baltimore Conference cast their lot with the Methodist Episcopal Church of the United States (the northern church). In 1860 the General Conference condemned slavery as sin. A majority then left the church and formed an independent conference but declared itself, although formally independent, still an integral part of the Methodist Episcopal Church (North). A minority refused to leave the parent denomination in the name of independence and simply reformed their Annual Conference, keeping (and now sharing) the name "Baltimore Conference." In 1866, the larger and newer conference joined the Methodist Episcopal Church South. Beginning in 1866, Baltimore Methodists representing the ME Church South and the ME Church in the United States (North) sued each other over property rights and the ownership of numerous churches. See Board of World's Fair Managers, *Maryland: Its Resources, Industries, and Institutions* (Baltimore: Sun Job Printing Office, 1893), 399; Charles Z. Lincoln, *The Civil Law and the Church* (New York: Abingdon Press, 1916), 362–63; Irons, *The Origins of Proslavery Christianity*, 228–29, 318.

6. Paul H. Buck, *The Road to Reunion, 1865–1900* (1937; New York: Vintage Books, 1962), 67.

7. "Presbyterians," in *The American Annual Cyclopaedia and Register of Important Events of the Year 1866*, 621–25, 621, 622.

8. Edmund J. Hammond, *The Methodist Episcopal Church in Georgia* (1935; Gretna, LA: Firebird Press, 2000), 103, 104.

9. "For the Brethren from P. H. Hopkins, October 25, 1865," emphasis in the original.

10. Buck, *The Road to Reunion, 1865–1900*, 67. See also *The American Annual Cyclopaedia and Register of Important Events of the Year 1865, Embracing Political, Civil, Military, and Social Affairs; Public Documents; Biography, Statistics, Commerce, Finance, Literature, Science, Agriculture, and Mechanical Industry* (New York: D. Appleton and Co., 1873), vol. 1: 106, 553, 706; *The American Annual Cyclopaedia . . . 1866*, 490–91.

11. Buck, *The Road to Reunion, 1865–1900*, 69.

12. Fredrickson, "The Coming of the Lord," 110–30, 126.

13. Richard Hofstadter, *The Age of Reform: From Bryan to FDR* (New York: Vintage Books, 1955), 150.

14. Fredrickson, "The Coming of the Lord," 126.

15. See Gaines M. Foster, *Ghosts of the Confederacy: Defeat, the Lost Cause, and the Emergence of the New South, 1865–1913* (New York: Oxford University Press, 1985).

16. Gaines Foster blazed this historiographical trail by emphasizing the role that the United Daughters of the Confederacy played in proffering a "New Southern" middle-class propriety that venerated the old order even as it stressed economic progress, education, and ultimately, reconciliation. Works by others who have subsequently toiled in this field include Karen L.

Cox, *Dixie's Daughters: The United Daughters of the Confederacy and the Preservation of Confederate Culture* (Gainesville: University Press of Florida, 2001); Sarah E. Gardner, *Blood and Irony: Southern White Women's Narratives of the Civil War, 1861–1937* (Chapel Hill: University of North Carolina Press, 2004); Janney, *Burying the Dead but Not the Past.*

17. Wilson, *Baptized in Blood,* 37–38.

18. Ibid., 38.

19. Frederick A. Bode, *Protestantism and the New South* (Charlottesville: University of Virginia Press, 1975), 7. See also David Edwin Harrell Jr., "Religious Pluralism: Catholics, Jews, and Sectarians," in Charles Regan Wilson, ed., *Religion in the South* (Oxford: University Press of Mississippi, 2009), 59–82, 79.

20. Harrell, "Religious Pluralism," 79.

21. John Giggie, "'Disband Him from the Church': African Americans and the Spiritual Politics of Disenfranchisement in Post-Reconstruction Arkansas," *Arkansas Historical Quarterly* 60, no. 3 (Autumn 2001): 245–64, 245.

22. For discussions of clerical emigrationists, see Hildebrand, *The Times Were Strange and Stirring,* 101–19, 121; Montgomery, *Under Their Own Vine and Fig Tree,* 339; William Seraile, *Fire in His Heart: Bishop Benjamin Tucker Tanner and the A.M.E. Church* (Knoxville: University of Tennessee Press, 1998), 137–38. The scholarship dealing with the AME Church and emigrationism is rich. See particularly Angell, *Bishop Henry McNeal Turner;* Hildebrand, *The Times Were Strange and Stirring;* Montgomery, *Under Their Own Vine and Fig Tree;* Moses, *Alexander Crummell;* and Seraile, *Fire in His Heart.* Benjamin Tanner, long-time editor of the AME Church's *Christian Recorder,* was perhaps the single most ardent opponent of emigrationism. As to black populism, see Gregg Cantrell, "Dark Tactics: Black Politics in the 1887 Texas Prohibition Campaign," *Journal of African American Studies* 25 (April 1991): 85–93, rpt. in Donald G. Nieman, *African-American Life in the Post-Emancipation South, 1861–1900* (Hamden, CT: Garland Press, 1993); Gregg Cantrell and D. Scott Barton, "Texas Populists and the Failure of Biracial Politics," *Journal of Southern History* 55 (November 1989): 659–92, cited in Anthony J. Adam et al., *Black Populism in the United States: An Annotated Bibliography* (Westport, CT: Greenwood Publishing Group, 2004), 89.

23. Robert H. Craig, *Religion and Radical Politics: An Alternative Christian Tradition in the United States* (Philadelphia: Temple University Press, 1992), particularly "African-American Christianity and Socialism," 114–29.

INDEX

Flack, John Van Buren, 95–96

Foner, Eric, 14

Ford, Rev., 151, 242n41

formalists, 215n30

Forman, Rev. A. P., 97–98

Forney, John W., 55

Foster, Gaines M., 198, 257n16

Fourier, Charles, 205n6

Franklin, Benjamin, 123, 235n7

Fransioli, Father Joseph, 40

Frazier, E. Franklin, 247n4

Fredrickson, George, 197, 210n88, 212n2

Free Presbyterians, 207n39

Free Soil Movement, 207n31

Freedmen and women. *See* African Americans

Freedmen's Bureau, 175, 176, 180, 182, 251n39

Freedmen's Conventions, 181

Freeman, Rev. Dr. Martin H., 188

Freeman's Journal, 69, 103, 231n35

Friedman, Lawrence, 13

Friends. *See* Quakers (Society of Friends)

Fugitive Slave Act, 8, 17–18, 24–26, 63, 89, 208n47, 208n49

Funkhouser, George A., 40

Gaines, Bishop W. J., 177

Galladet, Parson, 163

Gardiner Spring Resolutions, 78, 225n62

Garnet, H. Highland, 251n38

Garrison, William Lloyd, 13

Geary, John White, 180–81

Genovese, Eugene, 204n8

George, Joseph, Jr., 231n35

German immigrants and German Americans, 21, 35, 214–15n24, 226n72

German Reformed Church, 86–88, 106, 107, 228n95

Germond, Rev. Phillip, 80–81

Glatthaar, Joseph, 189

Goen, C. C., 34

Gooding, James, 177

Gramsci, Antonio, 156

Grasso, Christopher, 142

Graves, James R., 29

Graves, R. J., 161

Great Awakening, 221n6

Great Revival of 1857–58, 213n3

Gregory, Edgar, 58

Gribbin, William, 62

Hahn, Steven, 6, 168, 211n103

Hale, John P., 207n31

Hale, Sarah Preston Everett, 39

Halleck, Henry, 242n41

Hamilton, Michael, 35

Hamilton, Thomas, 186

Hammond, Edmund, 195–96

Hanby, Cyrus Mortimer, 39

Harding, A. C., 146

Harper's Weekly, 45, 47, 58

Harris, Ira, 149

Harrison, Rev. Samuel, 173

Hartford Convention, 52, 221n14

Hatch, Nathan, 37

Haywood, F. L., 149

Helper, Hinton Rowan, 30

Heyrman, Christine Leigh, 235n5

Hildebrand, Reginald, 172

Hodge, Rev. Charles, 89

Hogan, , Rev. John, 148

Hoge, Moses D., 132–33, 236n23

Hoge, Peyton Harrison, 133

Hoke, John, 86, 87, 228n97

Holden, William, 127

Holt, Michael F., 9–10, 205n5

Hood, Rev. John W., 188

Hopkins, Rev. P. H., 196

Hopson, Rev. W. H., 67

Horner, Rev. Joseph, 38

Hough, Sabin, 58–59, 69, 221n1

Howell, Rev. R. B. C., 143, 151, 242n41

Hoyt, Rev. Thomas A., 66–67, 105

Hughes, Archbishop John J., 41, 80, 102, 231n25

Hughes, John J., 77, 101

Logan, John, 51

Long, Alecia P., 244n57

Lost Cause, 92, 135, 155, 157, 198, 199

Lothrop, Samuel K., 39

loyalty oaths: for Confederate ministers
swearing allegiance to United States, 65,
143, 150–51; during French Revolution,
222n17; issuance of licenses and permits
contingent upon, 246n96; Lincoln on, 71;
problems with enforcement of, 222n18;
for wartime northern ministers, 65–66,
70, 71

loyalty resolutions, 78–81, 134

Lundy, McKinley, 117

Lutherans: and disloyal ministers, 77, 79, 88;
loyalty resolution by, 79–80; reunification
of, in early twentieth century, 194–95;
and separate-duties position, 107; United
Lutheran Church in America, 257n4

Lutherans (in Confederate States), 132,
194–95

Lyell, Charles, 34

Lynch, Rev. James, 181

Lyon, Rev. James, 163

Lyon, Theodoric, 163

MacMurray, Rev. Jacob, 83

Madison, James, 63

Malcolm X, 252n46

Mars, Chaplain John, 173

Marty, Martin, 138

Masur, Kate, 186

May, Rev. Samuel, 15–16, 25

Maynard, Horace, 126–27

Mays, Benjamin, 247n4

McCallie, Rev. Thomas H., 145, 241n19

McClure, Alexander, 22

McCook, Alexander, 151

McCuen, Oliver H., 56

McEuen, Rev. Oliver H., 76–77

McIlvaine, Charles P., 71, 224n41

McKenzie, Robert Tracy, 160

McKinney, Gordon, 161

McKinney, Rev. Solomon, 30

McMaster, James, 69, 103

McPherson, James, 28, 150, 189, 218n29

Mennonites, 28, 97, 104, 121, 230n5

Messianic groups, 256n126

Methodist Episcopal Church: Baltimore
Conference of, 195, 232n51, 257n5;
charter of, 12; come-outer groups in,
207n39; denominational publications
of, 34; and disloyal ministers, 73–77; and
draft exemption for ministers, 83; East
Baltimore Conference, 108–10, 232n51;
and separate-duties position, 108–10; and
slavery debate, 12, 257n5; and split along
sectional lines in antebellum period, 12

Methodist Episcopal Church South: African
American members of, 185, 195; and
Confederate nationalism, 128, 145; publications of, 128; and resistance to Federal
occupation, 153–54; and secession, 123,
125; and Unionist ministers, 158

Methodists: antiformalist tradition of, 37; and
antislavery rhetoric of southern minister,
30; colleges and universities founded by,
34, 35; conflicts among, after Civil War,
195; criticisms of political preaching by,
26–27; denominational growth of, 213n4,
222n15; and disloyal church leaders, 84;
and disloyal ministers, 56, 67, 68, 74–77,
78–81, 109; diversity among, regarding
political preaching, 121; and education
of African Americans, 181; and Kansas-
Nebraska Act, 18, 19; lay ministers of, 37;
loyalty resolution by, 78–81; material and
political prosperity of, 35; and political
preaching by wartime northern ministers,
39; publications of, 34–35, 214n19; and
racial uplift, 172; as revivalists, 215n30;
and separate-components position,
117–18, 120; and separate-duties position,
107–10; and separate-spheres position,